SHAKESPEAREAN CHARACTERIZATION

SHAKESPEAREAN CHARACTERIZATION

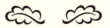

A Guide for Actors and Students

Leslie O'Dell

Greenwood Press
Westport, Connecticut • London

Library of Congress Cataloging-in-Publication Data

O'Dell, Leslie.
  Shakespearean characterization: a guide for actors and students / by Leslie O'Dell.
    p. cm.
  Includes bibliographical references and index.
  ISBN 0–313–31144–7 (alk. paper)
    1. Shakespeare, William, 1564–1616–Dramatic production. 2. Shakespeare, William,
  1564–1616–Characters. 3. Acting. I. Title.
  PR3091.O44 2002
  792.9'5–dc21   2001016106

British Library Cataloguing in Publication Data is available.

Library of Congress Catalog Card Number: 2001016106
ISBN: 0–313–31144–7

First published in 2002

Greenwood Press, 88 Post Road West, Westport, CT 06881
An imprint of Greenwood Publishing Group, Inc.
www.greenwood.com

Printed in the United States of America

The paper used in this book complies with the
Permanent Paper Standard issued by the National
Information Standards Organization (Z39.48–1984).

10 9 8 7 6 5 4 3 2 1

Contents

Preface

AN ACTOR'S GUIDE TO SHAKESPEARE'S CHARACTERS

In developing my strategies for exploring Shakespeare's characters with actors and students, I have taken insights gleaned from scholarly examinations of these topics and tested them in rehearsal halls, tutorials, and classrooms. My goal, throughout this process, has been to find a way of endowing a modern actor with the tools necessary to bridge the gap between the conventions of Shakespeare's theatre and the acting strategies which dominate our theatre practice today. Because of my interest in Shakespeare's language, I have grounded all of my strategies in the words on the page, in the hopes that my insights will result in vigorous, thrilling performances that are beautifully spoken as well as emotionally rich.

BIBLIOGRAPHY

The works listed at the end of this book represent those writers whose ideas have most influenced my approach in the classroom and rehearsal hall and that I recommend to the modern actor. For a more extensive exploration of the riches to be found in libraries, I refer the reader to *Shakespearean Scholarship* and *Shakespearean Language*, companion books to this.

CITATIONS

I often quote from Shakespeare's plays and note the act, scene, and number of the first line in parentheses immediately following the quotation; I have used the line numbers found in *The Riverside Shakespeare*, edited by G. Blakemore Evans. I include the title of the play if that has not yet been indicated. For convenience, I have used a shortened version of many of the play titles, as follows:

12th Night	Twelfth Night
1HIV	The first part of Henry IV
2HIV	The second part of Henry IV
1HVI	The first part of Henry VI
2HVI	The second part of Henry VI
3HVI	The third part of Henry VI
A&C	Antony and Cleopatra
All's Well	All's Well That Ends Well
AYLI	As You Like It
Dream	A Midsummer Night's Dream
Errors	The Comedy of Errors
HV	Henry V
HVIII	Henry VIII
JC	Julius Caesar
John	King John
Lear	King Lear
LLL	Love's Labour's Lost
Measure	Measure for Measure
Merchant	The Merchant of Venice
Much Ado	Much Ado about Nothing
R&J	Romeo and Juliet
RII	Richard the Second
RIII	Richard the Third
Shrew	The Taming of the Shrew
T&C	Troilus and Cressida
Timon	Timon of Athens
Titus	Titus Andronicus
Two Gents	The Two Gentlemen of Verona
Wives	The Merry Wives of Windsor
WT	The Winter's Tale

I have also used the character names as they appear in *The Riverside Shakespeare* so that, for example, the heroine of *Cymbeline* is Imogen, not Innogen, and the man who eventually becomes King Henry IV is known as Bolingbroke, not Bollingbrook or Bullingbrooke.

I have assumed a familiarity with Shakespeare's plays, and so have explained the context of the quotations only if that is significant to what I am discussing. It is very difficult to avoid interpretation in these discussions; I cannot help but envision the scene in performance, the product of innumerable decisions every one of which can only be right for that one performance (imaginary or remembered), and none of which should be viewed as any more or less correct or valid than the decisions you might make in your productions.

QUOTATIONS

Although I have made use of *The Riverside Shakespeare* for line numbers, I have reproduced the quotations from Shakespeare based upon the 1623 folio edition, with some modifications. I have modernized most spellings, for ease of reading aloud. I have also, on occasion, adjusted the punctuation when it might completely mislead the modern reader. When the First Folio is clearly incorrect, or when I wish to quote lines only found in a quarto edition, I have made use of whichever alternative text is best regarded by experts in early modern printing practices.

There are a few significant differences, therefore, between the quotations in this book and those found in most editions of Shakespeare's plays. Close comparison between modern practices and those of Shakespeare's contemporaries reveal the following patterns:

- The early texts use far more capitalized words, usually nouns which we consider general and which they make proper, with some adjectives, and fewer verbs also so modified.

- The early texts use commas to mark places for the actor to breathe. Modern editors regularly modify these in accordance with rules of grammar.

- The early texts use other punctuation marks quite differently than we do today. Modern editors regularly "normalize" these, privileging grammar and correct usage over an evocation of the flow of ideas in spoken communication.

- The early texts seldom made a clear differentiation between the plural and the possessive, another grammatical "error" corrected by modern editors. Unfortunately, this requires them to choose between one of the two following interpretations of Ophelia's famous line, as in *The Riverside Shakespeare* where it appears as: "The courtier's, soldier's, scholar's, eye, tongue, sword" [*Hamlet* 3.1.151], when the folio reads: "The Courtiers, Soldiers, Scholars: Eye, tongue, sword," leaving it open whether the eye, tongue, and sword in question belong to one or all courtiers, soldiers, and scholars.

- The early texts create compound words, or present as two separate words some common compound words, such as "myself" or "tomorrow."

- The early texts sometimes break up the lines of poetry differently than is customary in modern texts. In extreme cases, they present as prose entire passages which are reproduced as poetry by modern editors. In *Romeo and Juliet*, the Nurse's long meander down memory lane, in which a toddling Juliet gets a bump on her forehead, appears as prose in all three early editions. Mercutio's famous evocation of Queen Mab appears as poetry only in the first (1603) quarto; the second (1604) quarto and the First Folio both present this as prose.

Because I have recreated the choices made by the first editors, the quotations in this book might strike the modern reader as unexpected or even incorrect.

CAPITALIZATIONS

The First Folio presents no coherent pattern of making proper nouns of various objects and concepts, tempting modern editors to conclude that the practice was influenced as much by the availability of upper and lower case letters in the typesetter's box as it was by anything in the original manuscript. By including the First Folio capitals in this book, I have made it possible for you to judge for yourself, and glean what information you wish from these markers.

In making a comparison between modern punctuation and that found in the early texts, I have observed that modern editors quite often add an exclamation mark to reflect the strong emotion clearly expressed in the situation, when the first editor loaded on the capital letters and used a humble period. Consider, for example, that most famous of lines, "A horse! a horse! my kingdom for a horse!" [*RIII* 5.4.7] which in the First Folio appears as, "A Horse, a Horse, my Kingdom for a Horse." The four capital letters in that line evoke, for me, the shouting of a desperate man, a tidy equivalent to the three exclamation marks in the modern version.

Another speech from this play reminds us of the effect of linking individual and specific words to universal concepts. Here is the Duchess of York, mother of the title character, describing his childhood:

> No by the holy Rood, thou know'st it well,
> Thou camest on earth, to make the earth my Hell.
> A grievous burthen was thy Birth to me,
> Tetchy and wayward was thy Infancy.
> Thy School-days frightful, desp'rate, wild, and furious,
> Thy prime of Manhood, daring, bold, and venturous:
> Thy Age confirmed, proud, subtle, sly, and bloody,
> More mild, but yet more harmful; Kind in hatred:
> What comfortable hour canst thou name,
> That ever graced me with thy company? [*RIII* 4.4.166]

The capitalization in this speech transforms her memories into another "seven ages of man" speech, marking for us the universality of the stages of Richard's life, from his birth and infancy, through school days, to manhood and finally maturity, marked by the word "Age." When Jaques has a go at the same idea, his version makes use of similar capitalizations, describing "the Infant, /

Mewling, and puking in the Nurses arms: / Then, the whining School-boy with his Satchel / And shining morning face, creeping like snail / Unwillingly to school" [*AYLI* 2.7.142].

FIRST FOLIO ERRORS

Using the first texts can open up all sorts of fascinating possibilities for the modern actor that arise from a more direct encounter with the irregularities that modern editors customarily remove from the plays. Here, for example, is a wonderful hiccup that appears at the end of an exchange between the young Duke of York and his uncle Richard:

Richard: What, would you have my Weapon, little Lord?

York: I would that I might thank you, as, as, you call me.

Richard: How?

York: Little. [*RIII* 3.1.122]

Modern editors, in an effort to clean up what they have assumed is an error made by the compositor of this particular page, remove the delicate little stutter, so that York is given no opportunity to telegraph his glee at the approaching punch line. I am more inclined to admire Shakespeare for his intuition about juvenile joke-tellers, and honour the "as, as," in performance.

Not all errors are so attractive. Here is the mess that the compositor has made of Romeo's final speech:

> For fear of that, I still will stay with thee,
> And never from this Palace of dim night
> *Depart again: come lie thou in my arms,*
> *Here's to thy health, where ere thou tumblest in.*
> *O true Apothecary!*
> *Thy drugs are quick. Thus with a kiss I die.*
> Depart again; here, here will I remain,
> With Worms that are thy Chambermaids: O here
> Will I set up my everlasting rest:
> And shake the yoke of inauspicious stars
> From this world-wearied flesh: Eyes look your last:
> Arms take your last embrace: And lips, O you
> The doors of breath, seal with a righteous kiss
> A dateless bargain to engrossing death:
> Come bitter conduct, come unsavory guide,
> Thou desperate Pilot, now at once run on
> The dashing Rocks, thy Sea-sick weary Bark:
> Here's to my Love. O true Apothecary:
> Thy drugs are quicke. Thus with a kisse I die. [5.3.106]

The same mess appears in the 1604 quarto, clearly the copy from which this was being set. The italicized section is customarily deleted in modern editions. However, I can't help but wonder if the two endings represent two different versions of the speech. Maybe the actors quickly discovered that the shorter version was more effective, and the compositors erred in printing out the shorter as well as the longer version.

Much scholarly effort has been expended on comparing the different early texts, in those cases where we have more than one option, and there is something to be said for the theory that Shakespeare's original version was quite a bit longer than the one actually performed. In this, he would be like most playwrights of my acquaintance, whose manuscripts bear the mark of a helpful editing process instigated by the first performers. It's fascinating to find evidence of the original as well as the amended version, one after the other, thanks to an error in the printing process: almost as good as getting our hands on a copy of the manuscript with Burbage's notes in the margins.

THE SIGNIFICANCE OF THE SELF

We are so accustomed to the modern compound pronouns that we are blind to the very special insights available whenever a character speaks of her individual selfhood. When Polonius advised Laertes, "This above all; to thine own self be true" [*Hamlet* 1.3.78], we hear only the maxim, not the originality of the thought. At a time when the individual was judged to be less worthy of primary loyalty than one's god, and one's liege lord, such loyalty to self was almost heresy.

Returning to *Richard III*, we find an exchange that loses much of its rhetorical power if given a modern spin on selfhood. Lady Anne is spitting out her hatred for the murderer of her husband and father-in-law, a man who is at this moment trying to win her love:

Anne: Vouchsafe (defused infection of man)
           Of these known evils, but to give me leave
           By circumstance, to curse thy cursed *Self*.

Richard: Fairer than tongue can name thee, let me have
           Some patient leisure to excuse my *self*.

Anne: Fouler than heart can think thee,
           Thou canst make no excuse current,
           But to hang thy *self*.

Richard: By such despair, I should accuse my *self*.

Anne: And by despairing shalt thou stand excused,
           For doing worthy Vengeance on thy *self*,
           That didst unworthy slaughter upon others. [1.2.78]

By highlighting the separate word "self," we can see the antithesis between the individual and all of his enemies presented in Anne's last lines. We are also reminded of the immense significance of cursing one's own soul to eternal damnation, the sin of despair, that Anne is wishing upon Richard.

LONG SPELLINGS

Anyone who has looked at a reproduction of the First Folio can testify to the difficulty it presents the modern reader, when even a familiar passage looks like this:

> But *ſoft*, what light through yonder window breaks?
> It is the East, and *Iuliet* is the Sunne,
> Ari*ſe* faire Sun and kill the enuious Moone,
> Who is already *ſicke* and pale with griefe,
> That thou her Maid art far more faire than *ſeh*. [*R&J* 2.2.2]

Because I place such importance on sight-reading Shakespeare aloud, I have adopted modern spellings for all of the quotations in this book. However, in doing so I have sacrificed an important set of clues contained in the old manuscripts, where patterns of spelling seem to have had significance for the delivery of the lines by actors in the theatre.

If we look at Romeo's words as he spies Juliet up on her balcony, we notice that he refers to the sun twice, but that when the word appears at the end of the second line it is spelled "Sunne," though in the very next line "Sun" is the spelling. Are we to believe from this that the typesetter could spell a simple word correctly and incorrectly, side by side? Are we to imagine that the typesetter voluntarily took the time to place into the frame two additional tiny lead letters for no particular reason? Common sense suggests otherwise. Although it is difficult to base an entire interpretation of a passage upon what might be the Elizabethan equivalent of a typo, something in the pattern of longer and shorter spellings suggests a heightened significance in direct proportion to the length of the word on the page.

If we think back to the days of hand-copied manuscripts, for example the spiritual texts so lovingly copied by monks in the great medieval monastery libraries, we can see this connection in the setting up of the words on the page. The eye is naturally drawn towards the most important words like "soul" or "grace" by the copyist, who elongates the pen strokes and embellishes with curves and curls. Meanwhile, purely functional words are squeezed in and starkly drawn, perhaps even reduced to a shorthand whereby "your" becomes "yr."

It is possible that the copyists and typesetters who worked on the plays made use of a similar system of subtle emphasis, taking advantage of the fluctuation in accepted spelling to write or typeset "Sunne" and then "Sun" followed by "Moone" to suggest the relative intensity of the three words. We cannot know if, in doing this, they reproduced what appeared in Shakespeare's original manuscript, but we can acknowledge that the copyists and typesetters would have been influenced by the manner in which such words were spoken by the actors of the day.

HE OR SHE

In my writing I customarily use the word "actor" to refer to men and women; any reader alert to the nuances of language will note that I scatter male and female pronouns in connection with this noun randomly throughout the text. If I'm discussing Cleopatra or Romeo I will be more likely to have imagined a woman playing the first and a man the second, though historically the reverse has been true: the "squeaking Cleopatra" of Shakespeare's own theatre stands in memory beside Sarah Bernhard and Charlotte Cushman, two among many actresses renown for their portraits of Shakespeare's male protagonists. When appropriate, as in the sentence before this, I will use the term "actress" to make a point about the sex of the performer under discussion.

ACKNOWLEDGMENTS

I could not have completed *Shakespearean Characterization* without the support and encouragement of my academic and theatre colleagues. In particular, I owe an immense debt of gratitude to the Stratford Shakespearean Festival in Stratford, Ontario, where I have had the privilege of working with those very artists whose enthusiasms, insights, and hard work have inspired this book. Above all, it is the support of my family that has allowed me to undertake this project, and it is to my daughter Sarah Hynes that I dedicate this book.

❧ 1 ❧
Bringing Shakespeare to the Modern Stage

Either our History shall with full mouth
Speak freely of our Acts, or else our grave
Like Turkish mute, shall have a tongueless mouth.
                                              Henry [*HV* 1.2.230]

The task of a modern actor, when cast in a play by William Shakespeare, is to breathe the air of our world into the otherwise silent page markings from the past. In undertaking this activity, the actor is burdened with a daunting task of bridging a four-hundred-year gap; the actor is also ideally positioned to locate opportunities for a leap fuelled by identification and empathy. What is needed, more than anything else, is the capacity to bypass those changes in external attributes that make the characters and situations so foreign, which is something that actors have always found easy. Perhaps this is possible because, as the romantic bardolaters would have it, Shakespeare in his genius has recorded eternal human experiences that transcend the limitations of any given time or place. Alternatively, as another group of equally admiring theorists suggest, the plays contain the raw material required for each successive generation and community to superimpose onto the vibrant stage picture a contemporary framework, to tease out of the rich fabric of the plays a contemporary message.

An actor need not be concerned with this debate. An actor has to accomplish what scholars and critics strive to explain: the enduring success of these plays in the contemporary theatre.

Scientists tell us that the water in the earth's ecosystem is the same molecular substance, with no additions or subtractions, since our particular rock first turned blue as it circled our sun. Is it possible that the theatrical heart of these plays is similarly recycled, refreshed by each encounter between actor and text? I have seen actors and students fight their way through the dense language, the archaic worldview, the unfamiliar stage conventions, and suddenly find themselves deeply engaged by something that strikes them as a compelling truth of such profundity that not only the hard work, but also the worldwide adulation suddenly seems justified. Until that moment, a good number of them felt as if they *should* like Shakespeare, that something was wrong with them for finding the plays tedious. Others were working in blind faith, having sensed that the pure underground river was there somewhere, and willing to be re-freshed by the surface water readily available, if tainted with overuse. As the fresh spring water emerges out of the rock face of these intimidating, mono-lithic plays, we can be forgiven, I think, for concluding that only Shakespeare's genius could bury such human truths as would survive time and the distortions that fame engenders.

The acting strategies that I present in this book have been developed in my years of divining. I am on a lifelong quest for instruments that will allow modern actors to mine into the underground rivers of my metaphor, in order to bring Shakespeare's plays alive in the modern theatre, and also in order to put to a very special test the unique acting sensibilities of our time and culture.

In order to accomplish the combined task of making four-hundred-year-old plays live again while showcasing the greatest potential of contemporary ap-proaches to acting, actors are required to mediate between theatrical conventions of Shakespeare's time and ours, and this can only be accomplished if the actor is able to find ways of modifying both sets of conventions so that there is sufficient correspondence for the actor's talent to flow into the play, and for the play to draw out of the actor that very talent.

This is not an easy task for a contemporary actor. First of all, the acting might be almost entirely intuitive. The absence of intellectualization is by no means a weakness in an actor. Many would argue, and I would not disagree, that excessive analysis and self-scrutiny will more likely destroy than enhance a natural aptitude for acting. This attitude is reflected in the training most actors receive, which is enriched by classes in movement, stage fighting, and mask work, rather than a course on the psychology of acting. If an actor is trained in a single approach, for example the North American Method or some other variation of Konstantin Stanislavsky's theories, it is unlikely that the training has included a course that is purely theoretical, much less one that places Stanislavsky's ideas against the theories of other acting teachers within the context of psychological theory of human behavior.

The modern young actor usually stumbles by chance upon a correspon-dence between what has been mastered in acting school and what can be found in Shakespeare's plays. These discoveries are often made under the guidance of teacher-directors working in the contemporary Shakespeare industry; they can also be made in rehearsal halls with actors who are a little or a lot further ahead in a personal journey towards successful mediation between Shake-speare's theatre and ours. If it were not for this enduring apprenticeship sys-tem, and the willingness of theatrical producers and the general public to accept the "hit and miss" process that advances Shakespearean production usually at a snail's pace and occasionally by great leaps, we would have no way of know-ing that these plays can be performed brilliantly, and can summon forth a brilliant performance.

But in the rough-and-tumble pressure of rehearsal and performance, there is seldom time to contemplate, much less record, the strategies that are suc-cessful and the guiding principals that seem to be at work when a strategy is successful. And since the actor has not been trained to theorize about acting, it is not surprising that even the most successful Shakespearean actors rarely have an explanation for how they do what they do.

The second reason that an actor is not well positioned to theorize about the mediation between Shakespeare's theatrical conventions and ours is that most actors today have only the vaguest understanding of what those conventions might have been, and how they actually worked in Shakespeare's theatre. Everyone knows the obvious facts: there were no women actors, the audience was on three sides and three levels in an outdoor performance space, the plays were either prose or blank verse, which is unrhymed iambic pentameter. Any more detailed exploration of theatre history is a full-time scholarly activity; actors have made their commitment to the development of their craft.

There are many teachers and directors, and many actors, who have become amateur theatre historians, and bring to contemporary rehearsal halls countless insights that can only occur when a skilled and working theatre professional encounters the historical facts unearthed and then contemplated by academics. These individuals have pointed the way towards all that is contained in this book. They are joined by academics who have participated as observers or participants in the rehearsal process and have allowed the real-world consid-erations of the modern actor to shape their analysis of what scholarship has revealed. My function in the process is to report what I have observed and read in a manner that brings together the contributions of the two groups.

One of the reasons I wanted to record some of the acting strategies that appear in this book is something that I have observed repeatedly in rehearsals and performances. There is something about acting Shakespeare that seems to diminish a significant percentage of young actors. It's as if all that they bring to their work on contemporary plays becomes muted, restricted, and unfo-cused as they begin to comprehend the task facing them in playing a Shake-spearean role. Part of this is, I suspect, the overwhelming weight of theatrical tradition that makes it impossible to discover how this role in this particular production, at this time in your life, connects with you. But part of this is also the disorientation that sets in when all of the acting strategies that have become so familiar as to be not only effective and efficient but also "natural," suddenly have no bearing on the job to be done.

The simple truth is that contemporary approaches to the portrait of emotion, of character, and of relationships do not match up with Shakespeare's story-telling strategies, which emerged in and are shaped by the conventions of his theatre. So when a modern actor superimposes our style of acting on these plays, dislocation is the only possible outcome. Similarly, if the actor throws out all that works in our theatre today, the performance will be dislocated from its audience, with equally disastrous results.

Because we want neither boring museum pieces acting in the "correct" historical style, nor embarrassing modern productions wherein actors are cut off from the very energies that they are able to bring so vividly to their work, we have to find a way to help young actors negotiate the difference so that they enter the first rehearsal ready to mediate between Shakespeare's theatre and ours, to illuminate these wonderful plays, and to strengthen and reveal the unique contribution each brings to their profession.

AN ACTOR'S INSIGHTS

A modern actor's intuitions are the single most valuable research tool available to our understanding of Shakespeare's plays. In the absence of the discovery of hitherto unsuspected plays, letters, diaries, or theatrical artifacts, scholars have no other primary evidence with which to engage, save the insights afforded actors in the process of rehearsing and performing.

Every Shakespeare production I have worked on has afforded examples of such insights on a regular basis. Every production has also provided countless examples of the unsuitability of modern acting strategies for the playing of Shakespeare. I can only marvel at the paradox: those very skills and sensibilities that generate the insights can prove the greatest barriers to the modern actor achieving success in a classical role.

I believe that there is an unbroken connection between what actors did in Shakespeare's theatre and what they do in ours. I also believe that the conventions of theatrical performance have altered as much as the English language has evolved in the four hundred years between the first performance of these plays and the ones I work on today.

Somehow, an actor intuits her way into an expression of a shared experience that transforms the artificial storytelling strategies of the theatre into a highly energized event onto which individual members of the audience can ascribe meanings of such significance that an emotional event occurs that simultaneously transcends and reinforces the mechanics of the conventions. Whether it is a boy actor allowing an audience to believe in Juliet's love for Romeo, or a modern actress allowing a modern audience to believe that she not only thinks, but also means the words she is saying to that sexy and passionate young man, the tension between opportunities for disbelief (e.g., he's a boy; no one talks like that) and conventions (e.g., he's doing the gestures just right; she's saying the words with suitable poetic vigour) result more often than not in that very thing that, by rights, should never occur. I would argue that it is not the acting strategy in and of itself that achieves the impossible: it is not the mimicry of Elizabethan femininity for the boy actor or the correct application of emotional memory for the modern actress, but rather something that happens in spite of the acting strategies, and yet that can only be set in place through the interaction of acting strategies and theatrical conventions.

These vague speculations are all that I can offer about that "something that happens," and so I will turn my attention to the setting in place of the possibility of that something happening, which I believe occurs in the moments of interaction between acting strategy and theatrical convention.

When the writer of the playscript and the company of thespians preparing the first production are working together in a well-established theatrical tradition, the interaction of convention and strategy are almost invisible. Later, some admiring participant or observer might seek to codify all of this into a system of instruction for the training of actors; this is in essence the source of what we today call Method acting.

THE DEAD HAND OF TRADITION

Many of us have started in a new job, filled with enthusiasm and plans for exploration, expansion, revision, alteration, and thinking we had been hired for just this "fresh blood," only to be met by an unceasing litany of, "Oh, but we don't do it that way here," and "Why don't we just keep doing it the way we've always done," and "Our customers won't like it if we change too much too quickly," and so forth.

Imagine then the overwhelming weight of tradition that rests upon the creative spirit of a production company taking on Shakespeare. It's almost easier for those who adopt a "radical" approach, because their agenda is to rebel: if anyone has ever staged the moment like that before, then that staging is forbidden. If it's new, it's good. If it's old, it's dusty. Much of what occurs in such productions provides Shakespearean scholars with fuel for mockery; even the most sympathetic are likely to say, as I once overheard, "It was a lively production, great fun and I loved it. Too bad it was so *wrong*." Is it any wonder that the rebels simply turn their backs on the historical evidence and stride out in whatever direction they can find, if only to get away from the voices crying out, "wrong"?

A more severe burden is placed upon companies that attempt to "do justice" to Shakespeare (though why the rebels are viewed as not doing justice is a mystery), while still offering audiences lively theatre, and keeping their artists from succumbing to creative atrophy. "Correct, but dull" is, for theatres, a far more deadly response than "lively, but wrong."

Historical information turns out to be useful when debating with traditionalists. Is someone upset because the design calls for modern dress? It is clear that Shakespeare's company dressed in the fashions of his time whether they were playing Athenian lovers or Antony and Cleopatra. Is someone upset because a chunk of the play has been axed? It is clear that Shakespeare and his company regularly edited and reworked his plays, for any of a variety of reasons, and that no one ever thought of there being a single, correct, full version of the play.

There is so much to suggest that Shakespeare played fast and loose with whatever came to hand, be it sources, conventions, or the language itself, that I cannot help but believe that he'd feel more at home in the rebel Shakespeare theatre companies than with those that purport to be correct. Is it correct to be boring? Is it correct to be untheatrical? Is it correct to appeal only to scholars and not to the general public? In Shakespeare's day there was "correct, but dull" academic theatre. He worked in the wild and crazy "upstart" theatres across the river. "Correct," for him, might well be anything that rebels, that challenges, that adapts and manipulates in whatever way necessary to fill the theatres, please the patrons, and pay the bills.

LAZINESS

The most distressing aspect of the modern rebel productions is that a certain laziness can easily set in. This reminds me of those moments in the rehearsal process when everyone assembled runs aground. There is a moment in the play that does not seem to be solvable. If the play is a new one, or the playwright not particularly respected, the obvious conclusion is that the play is flawed at this point, and the obvious solution is rewriting, editing, revising, and otherwise serving as "play doctor." If the combined theatrical sense of those in the room has expended itself upon the problem, and the modest theatrical sense of the writer has not offered a solution, then clearly the superior experience and skill can save the day. We all know, though, that laziness is at work when, in the absence of a playwright, the production company simply reworks the play until the staging solutions are obvious. It's just easier to justify this laziness if the playwright can be deemed incompetent.

But Shakespeare was not an inexperienced playwright. He was, in fact, an experienced actor and producer of plays, being a shareholder in a profitable popular theatre company. He wrote his major roles for some undeniably great actors, as well as for less talented and/or junior members of the company who needed all the help they could get. Therefore, when we struggle with some aspect of his plays, it is probably because the crafty staging solutions he had in mind are simply not visible to us at this remove. Even if they were, they might not work for a modern audience that does not share the older conventions.

ANTI-METHOD

The limits of Stanislavsky's approach to acting, particularly as it manifested itself in the system developed by his American disciples, which is commonly referred to as "the Method," have been apparent for years. The dangers of self-indulgence, excessive attention to the internal at the expense of elemental performance skills, and the hypernaturalistic focus of the acting strategies are nowhere more apparent than when Method-trained actors attempt to perform Shakespeare. This is not to denounce the important contribution made by psychologically based acting theories. However, unless the actor has been trained in or has performed extensively in alternative, antirealist theatrical styles, but instead relies entirely upon the motivation- and emotional memory-seeking rehearsal process, unsupported by any hard-won versatility in physical or vocal expressiveness, that actor is quite simply unequipped for the demands of any pre- or postnaturalist playwright.

ROMANCE

When counselling young performers in the choice of audition monologues, we inevitably come to consider the great romantic speeches of the young lovers. Shakespeare's reputation is built in large part upon his ability to create beautiful poetry for lovers to say to or about each other, but the ability to play such scenes seems to be remarkably rare these days. And so I say, particularly to the young men, "If you can play true romance, then you must do this speech, because your auditors will be thrilled to find a young man who can play such roles."

Now, at the risk of offending my young male readers, I'm going to make a few terrible generalizations. Of course there are many exceptions, and of course there are women who fall into the same trap. That said, here is my analysis of the phenomenon I have observed.

It is almost impossible for us to believe in true love as a compelling, enduring, and fully energized human event. We are much more comfortable with a character like Benedick, who quips, "When I said I would die a bachelor, I did not think I should live till I were married" [*Much Ado* 2.3.242], even as he declares himself passionately in love with Beatrice. Later, these two tiptoe around their mutual attraction:

Benedick: I do love nothing in the world so well as you, is not that strange?

Beatrice: As strange as the thing I know not, it were as possible for me to say, I loved nothing so well as you, but believe me not, and yet I lie not, I confess nothing, nor I deny nothing. [4.1.267]

This makes sense to us, but while we can admire Romeo and Juliet, and acknowledge that the words they say are indications of a great a passionate love, when it comes time to playing lines like the following, a problem emerges.

Two of the fairest stars in all the Heaven,
Having some business do entreat her eyes,

To twinkle in their Spheres till they return.
What if her eyes were there, they in her head,
The brightness of her cheek would shame those stars,
As day-light doth a Lamp, her eyes in heaven,
Would through the airy Region stream so bright,
That Birds would sing, and think it were not night. [2.2.15]

The source of the problem is that, quite simply, we do not believe in true love, except as something to be portrayed in fantasy, romance, or fairy tale. We all remember falling in love like this, but we also all remember falling out of love, as Romeo so clearly does when he first sees Juliet and spouts another bit of pure romance:

O she doth teach the Torches to burn bright:
It seems she hangs upon the cheek of night,
Like a rich Jewel in an Ethiopes ear:
Beauty too rich for use, for earth too dear:
So shows a Snowy Dove trooping with Crows,
As yonder Lady o'er her fellows shows;
The measure done, I'll watch her place of stand,
And touching hers, make blessed my rude hand.
Did my heart love till now, forswear it sight,
For I never saw true Beauty till this night. [1.5.44]

For a young fellow who came to the party hoping for a glimpse of Rosalind, Romeo has exchanged one object for another in the blink of an eye, just as Benvolio predicted when he encouraged Romeo to crash the Capulet's party: "Go thither and with unattainted eye, / Compare her face with some that I shall show, / And I will make thee think thy Swan a Crow" [1.2.85]. All of this is apparent to those of us watching the lovers, but it cannot influence Romeo's opinion of the absolute truth of what he says about and to Juliet. It is so difficult to give him this attribute without taking away any maturity or common sense that he might otherwise have. The result is a Romeo who moons around the stage, sighing and moaning and then offing himself in a remarkable bit of shortsightedness. This of course carves the guts out of the tragedy.

What if Romeo, and the other young lovers of Shakespeare, are in fact intelligent, aware, alert, and entirely sensible individuals, and what if the experience of falling in love *increases* rather than diminishes their adult attributes? Let us have a look at one such lover, who is experiencing an admittedly remarkable sequence of events, and see what Shakespeare has given us to work with. The speaker is Sebastian, twin brother of Viola who has adopted his style of dress and manner of walking and talking in her disguise as Cesario. At this point in *Twelfth Night*, Viola has fallen in love with the boy Cesario, and Sebastian has arrived in town, so when Viola encounters Sebastian, she treats him as she would Cesario. They disappear from sight, and during the interim we can only conclude, from what follows, that Sebastian responds warmly to Viola's affections in a way Cesario/Viola never could, and that he finds himself giving and receiving an intense and profound love in the most confusing of situations. Here is what he has to say:

> This is the air, that is the glorious Sun,
> This pearl she gave me, I do feel't, and see't,
> And though 'tis wonder that enwraps me thus,
> Yet 'tis not madness. Where's Antonio then,
> I could not find him at the Elephant,
> Yet there he was, and there I found this credit,
> That he did range the town to seek me out,
> His counsel now might do me golden service,
> For though my soul disputes well with my sense,
> That this may be some error, but no madness,
> Yet doth this accident and flood of Fortune,
> So far exceed all instance, all discourse,
> That I am ready to distrust mine eyes,
> And wrangle with my reason that persuades me
> To any other trust, but that I am mad,
> Or else the Lady's mad; yet if 'twere so,
> She could not sway her house, command her followers,
> Take, and give back affairs, and their dispatch,
> With such a smooth, discreet, and stable bearing
> As I perceive she does: there's something in't
> That is deceiveable. But here the Lady comes. [4.3.1]

Here we see the capacity of a young man to love in as poetical a vein as Romeo, but without the loss of his intelligence and maturity. He juggles the glorious sensory awareness of fresh love, the wonder at the strange events, with self-awareness (his need for the counsel of his friend the pirate Antonio) and other-awareness (his assessment of the workings of Olivia's household).

Now let us return to Romeo and endow him with the same capacity to reason and to experience a heightened sensation of Juliet's beauty as a means of enhancing his self-awareness and his sensitivity to the world around him. The first place to begin is to rethink the imagery, so that it is no longer the hyperbole of new love, but rather the best metaphor for the profundity of any life-changing event. There is a reason why the metaphors take us into the heavens. The underlying comparison is to the sort of spiritual event that completely transforms one's entire worldview. Paul, who wrote the letters that form most of the second half of the New Testament, began his relationship with Christianity as Saul, a fanatical persecutor of the disciples. He was in fact on his way to Damascus to seek out and destroy the fledgling church there when he had a brief encounter that, in his view, ripped the blindfold from his eyes and transformed him into Paul, and a leader of that same church.

In our modern secular culture, we have replaced images of Paul's epiphany with other brief encounters that change individuals forever. And so I would say to the actor working on Romeo or Sebastian, "Don't draw upon an emotional memory of the first time you fell in love, but rather imagine yourself living through a real-life *Close Encounters of the Third Kind*, and let your character *know* that something otherworldly and entirely awesome has transpired. Let your character feel himself strengthened and more truly himself, as a result of this encounter, rather than falling into the trap of assuming that he is a victim of the illusion of true love."

UNDERSTANDING WHAT YOU ARE SAYING

A favorite resource of mine, because it has a handy index and chapter headings, is John Erskine Hankins's *Backgrounds of Shakespeare's Thought* (1978). This book helped me make sense, for example, of Shakespeare's references to the five senses. Unless I'd worked a bit at it, I'd have assumed that he was talking about taste, touch, smell, sight, and hearing. How "common sense" fit into that would remain a mystery. And what about the five wits, as in sonnet 141: "But my five wits, nor my five senses can / Dissuade one foolish heart from serving thee." I was forced to come to terms with the senses while working on "the most precious square of sense," to which Regan refers in her formal declaration of love for King Lear, a piece of text that has stumped me on more than one occasion. One of the actors tried valiantly to comprehend my condensed version of Hankins's excellent chapter on "The Square of Sense," until in despair this talented performer asked me simply to emphasize the words that needed to be set in antithesis with each other, so that the point could be communicated. The voice became the vessel for the meaning contained in the words, which passed through without leaving any permanent effect on the container. Another performer became fascinated with the geometric drawings I sketched on a scrap piece of paper, and found great satisfaction in the mathematical purity of the image. This allowed for great precision and pleasure in the delivery of the passage, though I suspect that the real "meaning" was equally foreign in that mind. In both cases, however, I noticed that the actors couldn't explore the moment as actors until they had some comprehension of the shape and the point of the line, those being very much the same thing.

BRIDGES

And when good will is showed
Though't come too short
The Actor may plead pardon.

Cleopatra [*A&C* 2.5.8]

The last thing I would ever want to see would be productions that made every choice based upon historical research. If I had to choose between a passionate and naive performance given by someone who had barely looked at the notes at the bottom of the cheapest edition of the play, and one by a studious group of scholarly performers dedicated to presenting the play "as Shakespeare intended," I would choose the passionately naive over the dryly correct.

But I would be much happier by far not having to make that choice. I must confess to having very little patience with an actor who has not taken the time to find out what she is actually saying when she gives voice to the words she has memorized off the page. That is just as likely to be bad theatre as any production that privileges history over the theatrical.

Even with what I would consider the ideal rehearsal process, a theatrical production might not succeed. Ours is a risky business, and it always puzzles me why critics and audience members don't seem to realize that no one involved in a flawed production wanted anything other than for the show to be successful. True, there are lazy and self-indulgent people working in the theatre, just as in any other profession, and sometimes, by trying to ensure success by sticking to something safe rather than risking dangerous failure, we produce only dullness. But if there is anything I have learned over the years of working in the theatre, it is that there is no possible surefire recipe for success. All there can ever be is hard work, constant experimentation, intelligent guesses, intuition, common sense, and the smiles and frowns of fortune herself.

What attributes make for an actor best able to tackle the plays of Shakespeare? Let us place a well-trained, flexible, and connected vocal and physical instrument at the top of our wish list. These plays are marathons, even if severely edited, and require the ability to speak the speech trippingly on the tongue. But even these attributes are hollow and dull without an emotional and intellectual capacity and flexibility to match. How does one develop a capacious and flexible intellect and emotions? The easy answer is by performing the plays of Shakespeare.

❧ 2 ❧

The Conditions of Rehearsal and Performance

> If the tag-rag people did not clap him, and hiss him, according as he pleased and displeased them, as they use to do the Players in the Theatre, I am no true man.
>
> Casca [*JC* 1.2.258]

Several of the logistics of Shakespeare's theatre contributed to the unique collision of strategies and conventions. First of all, he was himself a writer and actor. Moreover, he wrote for actors whose work he knew well. There is a great deal of evidence that suggests that the playscripts were shaped specifically to meet the needs of the acting company.

Although some of the conventions of theatrical presentation were well established and so shared by actors, writers, and audience members, the profession of actor was relatively new and as the troupes solidified and gained social status, the means by which their excellence was verified shifted. Formerly, the improvised antics of the fairground vagabonds and the high-sounding oratory of the university amateurs were well-established standards; the new breed of master-actor absorbed the raw energy of the rogues in order to vitalize the intellectuals, while excelling in the oratorical brilliance of the educated in order to elevate and expand the range of the entertainers.

We know that the fireworks roles in Shakespeare's plays were written by master-actors, primarily Richard Burbage but also others of remarkable skill and capacity; their excellence shaped his plays just as his excellence both demanded and supported their mastery of the craft.

Modern actors are almost immediately aware of something that both audiences and experts often forget: that Shakespeare was an actor himself and wrote for actors, and that these plays are filled with all of the things that actors most appreciate, most require, and also that bring out the best in any and all. This is why even the most naive actor, in the sense of lacking any scholarly assistance in her encounter with the plays, can cut to the heart of the matter and deliver a performance that works for a modern audience.

I would argue that such performances succeed because the connection between the actor and the play bypasses the inevitable tensions between acting strategy and convention. How much better, then, is a performance that benefits not only from the actor/play connection, but also from a productive alliance of strategy and convention?

For this to occur, modern actors must build a bridge for two-way traffic between Shakespeare's theatre and ours. Some of what worked back then can be translated into something that will work now, allowing the actor/play connection to catch fire even more richly. Some of what works now can be adapted to be of use with the four-hundred-year-old script, with the same positive result.

REHEARSING IN SHAKESPEARE'S GLOBE

> Our Revels now are ended: These our actors,
> (As I foretold you) were all Spirits, and
> Are melted into Air, into thin Air,
> And like the baseless fabric of this vision
> The Cloud-capped Towers, the gorgeous Palaces,
> The solemn Temples, the great Globe itself,
> Yea, all which it inherit, shall dissolve,
> And like this insubstantial Pageant faded
> Leave not a rack behind.
>
> Prospero [*Tempest* 4.1.148]

We know the rate at which the companies introduced new plays, and the repertory system that saw them performing a different play each afternoon. Actors today are familiar with the sort of brush-up rehearsals needed to bring a play back into the company's repertoire, and they also know the amount of memorization required to "upload" one major or several minor roles into the forebrain, where it can be drawn upon for that day's performance. Our school system does not utilize rote learning, so we can only envy Shakespeare and his actors the mental "muscle" acquired in an Elizabethan school, which assisted them in the memorization process. Even so, the task was daunting, and it didn't stop there. It was not enough simply to memorize the words. The staging had to be sorted out, and that included not just who entered from which door, and the sword fights, but also how the actors would adjust their relative positions on stage to suggest the emotional journey of the scene, and also to keep everyone in the audience interested and able to see as well as hear the best bits. Why not assume that Shakespeare, who was after all an actor and shareholder, would do everything in his power to assist his actors in the speedy memorization and sorting out of staging?

Let's go one step further. Acting was, after all, a new profession. There were no schools, textbooks, or coaches. If we imagine Burbage, William Kempe, Edward Alleyn, and Shakespeare making it all up as they went along, experimenting with the medium of the theatre and the medium of the human psyche to see just what extremes of passion they could capture, then let's assume that Shakespeare the playwright also sought to do everything in his power to assist in the presentation of character and the evocation of emotion, inventing as he went along.

But we must be careful not to assume that words like "character" and "emotion" represent the same theatrical shorthand then as they do now. Modern actors come at these words burdened with the twentieth century's assumptions and superstitions, better known as psychological theories. While it is tempting to sneer at "the humours" or "guardian angels," we would do better to reconsider our own attitudes so that they do not direct our choices without our deliberate consideration.

Training Actors in Shakespeare's Company

As best we can tell, there was no systematic acting training in place in Shakespeare's theatre. It appears as if the apprentices were assigned to a single actor and perhaps were trained to take over that individual's "line" or type of role when a special skill or aptitude was required (e.g., clown roles). As resident playwright, Shakespeare could tailor the role to the double-edged reality of his casting: write only what the actor could reasonably be expected to achieve, while at the same time setting a challenge that would ensure the actor's growth and continued enthusiasm.

Remember, first of all, that Shakespeare was a shareholder in a company of players that was in the flux of transition from roaming entertainers just above the level of vagabonds into a guild-like profession. They had only recently started a system of formal apprenticeships, journeymen, and shareholders, and by modelling themselves on the flourishing urban guilds of London they made a commitment to the development of skilled actors that continues to this day. As the resident shaper of plays and senior actor, Shakespeare would have shared the company's interest in nurturing and expanding the skills of the junior members of the company, for where else was the next Burbage to come from? We don't know enough about how plays were rehearsed to conclude what, if any, coaching the less experienced actors received from the more experienced, but we can see, in the supporting roles of the plays, an effort being made to offer the junior members of the company opportunities to try their hands at creating characters. Even today, the actors entrusted with such minor gems as *Hamlet's* Osric marvel at the number of details Shakespeare manages to cram into their short appearance on stage, each of them opportunities to practice the art of creating and playing a role.

We do not know the exact sequence in which the plays were written, though we can chart the general pattern and set dates within a year to two, so that we can speculate about the inner workings of the company. It is tempting, for example, to imagine a young actor with considerable talent and physically and emotionally suited to playing women's roles, first assaying Julia in *The Two Gentlemen of Verona*, then growing into Juliet, and then anchoring the company's success with *As You Like It, All's Well That Ends Well, Measure for Measure*, and *Twelfth Night*. These are the roles that modern actresses grow into: Rosalind, Helena, Isabella, and Viola. There were a pair of these young actors, in fact, given equal chances in *A Midsummer Night's Dream* as Helena and Hermia, one taller than the other, one dark and one fair. The shorter one played Celia to the taller's Rosalind, Olivia to the other's Viola.

But then what happened? We get to *Hamlet*, and we find dear sweet Ophelia who scarcely drives the play. Desdemona, though important, is not a set of acting challenges that a Rosalind could master. Cordelia is also a relatively uninteresting role. Did the apprentices grow too big and masculine? Did they die, as did so many, whether from the plague or another of the common killers of Shakespeare's England? The only thing we know for certain is that none of them was really a woman in disguise, no matter what fiction writers might have imagined in everything from *Cue for Treason* to *Shakespeare in Love*.

These speculations serve to remind us of two things: that we will never know, and that Shakespeare's was a working theatre company, dedicated to the creation not only of popular, and hence lucrative entertainments, but also to the perpetuation of the professional actor through the creation of a guild-like system of apprentices, journeymen, and shareholders.

From the number of plays produced per season, and the time required to set even the most rudimentary staging—entrances and exits, dances and sword fights, props and scenic pieces, musical interludes, and costume changes—it is quite clear that the actors would have had little time for the contemplation of their craft, much less the systematic transmission of the techniques of the stage. The apprentices could pick it up as they labored in the most menial roles, learning by failing or succeeding in the small roles just as a tinsmith would learn by pumping the billows for the master and making the smallest and least visible of joints.

I like to think of Shakespeare taking pity on these actors-in-training, and injecting into even the most humble of roles the sort of challenge that teaches and supports the fledgling efforts of the novice. Today, many a young member of a Shakespearean acting company has had reason to be thankful for just such a role as the terrified servant in *Macbeth*.

Macbeth enters with the doctor and other attendants, one of whom is Seyton, a servant with a slightly larger role.

Macbeth: Bring me no more reports, let them fly all:
                    Till Birnam wood remove to Dunsinane,
                    I cannot taint with Fear. What's the Boy Malcolm?
                    Was he not born of woman? The Spirits that know
                    All mortal Consequences, have pronounced me thus:
                    Fear not Macbeth, no man that's born of woman
                    Shall e'er have power upon thee. Then fly false Thanes,
                    And mingle with the English Epicures,
                    The mind I sway by, and the heart I bear,
                    Shall never sag with doubt, nor shake with fear. [5.3.1]

Now, a servant enters. Imagine a young apprentice in his first speaking role.

Macbeth: The devil damn thee black, thou cream-faced Loon:
                    Where got'st thou that Goose-look.
Servant: There is ten thousand.
Macbeth: Geese Villain?
Servant: Soldiers Sir.
Macbeth: Go prick thy face, and over-red thy fear
                    Thou Lily-livered Boy. What Soldiers, Patch?
                    Death of thy Soul, those Linen cheeks of thine
                    Are Counsellors to fear. What Soldiers Whey-face?
Servant: The English Force, so please you.
Macbeth: Take thy face hence.

And that is his cue to run off stage. Notice how Shakespeare does all of his directing from within the scene. The actor is told how to look: like a goose, in other words, scared out of his wits. Most likely not much acting would be required by the poor lad, facing a fiery Burbage in full rant. If the apprentice succeeded in picking up the tricks of the trade, he could offer the audience the temporary relief of a laugh or two before the final horrible Armageddon. If, however, he proved a disaster, Burbage/Macbeth could cover for him, virtually saying his lines, and literally boot him off the stage.

   Actors have often noticed the riches available even to the supporting cast of one of Shakespeare's star vehicles. Take, for example, this gem of a moment from earlier in the same Scottish play. The actor playing the role very likely quickly changed his costume and reappeared as all sorts of characters in the remainder of the show. It might have been that this role was given to the man who takes on Macduff, in which case he would be well suited to the style and demands of the role: fierce, strong emotions, short bursts of striking language. However, this might have been entrusted to a junior member of the company, as it often is today. If he does well, then better things await him in the next round of casting. If he sinks under the emotional and linguistic challenge, then there are plenty of spear-carriers and messengers for him to play.

This is the second scene of the play, immediately following the short, eerie chanting of the witches. We can imagine the entrance of as large a contingent of supporting players as Shakespeare's company can manage, one of whom has been entrusted with a nameless role, usually labelled the "bleeding sergeant." Notice how other supporting players paint the scene and inform the audience just how to "read" the character our junior company member is assaying, just in case he's not doing such a good job of presenting the physical and emotional state of the war-wounded soldier. The scene begins:

Duncan: What bloody man is that? He can report,
            As seemeth by his plight, of the Revolt
            The newest state.

Malcolm: This is the Sergeant,
            Who like a good and hardy Soldier fought
            'Gainst my Captivity: Hail brave friend,
            Say to the King, the knowledge of the Broil,
            As thou didst leave it.

Sergeant: Doubtful it stood,
            As two spent Swimmers, that do cling together,
            And choke their Art: The merciless Macdonwald
            (Worthy to be a rebel, for to that
            The multiplying Villanies of Nature
            Do swarm upon him) from the Western Isles
            Of Kerns and Gallowglasses is supplied,
            And Fortune on his damned quarrel smiling,
            Showed like a Rebels Whore: but all's too weak:
            For brave Macbeth (well he deserves that Name)
            Disdaining Fortune, with his brandished Steel,
            Which smoked with bloody execution
            (Like Valours Minion) carved out his passage,
            Till he faced the Slave:
            Which ne'er shook hands, nor bade farewell to him,
            Till he unseamed him from the Nave to th'Chops,
            And fixed his Head upon our Battlements.

Duncan: O valiant Cousin, worthy Gentleman.

Sergeant: As whence the Sun 'gins his reflection,
            Shipwrecking Storms, and direful Thunders:
            So from that Spring, whence comfort seemed to come,
            Discomfort swells: Mark King of Scotland, mark,
            No sooner Justice had, with Valour armed,
            Compelled these skipping Kerns to trust their heels,
            But the Norweyan Lord, surveying vantage,
            With furbished Arms, and new supplies of men,
            Began a fresh assault.

Duncan: Dismayed not this our captains, Macbeth and Banquo?

Sergeant: Yes, as Sparrows, Eagles;
          Or the Hare, the Lion:
          If I say sooth, I must report they were
          As Cannons over-charged with double Cracks,
          So they doubly redoubled strokes upon the Foe:
          Except they meant to bathe in reeking Wounds,
          Or memorise another Golgotha,
          I cannot tell: but I am faint,
          My gashes cry for help.

Duncan: So well thy words become thee, as thy wounds,
          They smack of Honour both: Go get him Surgeons. [1.2.1]

At this point, the character seems to have been taken from the stage, presumably to change and prepare for another appearance as a supporting player.

Notice that this actor is being challenged with some difficult language. He has to negotiate his way around the parenthetical comments, pitching his voice so that the audience can easily make the connection between the merciless Macdonwald, with his multiplying villainies, who is supplied with foot soldiers from the western islands, and the slave who is also the "him" whom Macbeth unseamed and whose head now adorns the battlements. Notice too the imagery, not just a simple comparison but a complex set of interconnected allusions to storms coming out of the east, justice personified, the hierarchies of nature, and the place of the cross, where Christ died. And then, Shakespeare offers the young actor an opportunity for some physical acting, whatever will justify the broken line and the explanation, "my gashes cry for help." Duncan's response can be praise for the actor as well as the character, a relatively senior member of the company, perhaps Shakespeare himself, complimenting the junior member who has pulled off this challenging little bit.

There are also some wonderfully gem-like roles for the young apprentices being trained to play women's roles. If they began with servant girls and advanced to supporting roles, they might assay first something like Virgilia in *Coriolanus*, whose presence in a scene is shaped by what others say, who is given a few lines here and there, and about whom Coriolanus says, when he returns victorious from Coriolii,

     My gracious silence, hail:
     Wouldst thou have laughed, had I come Coffined home,
     That weep'st to see me triumph? Ay my dear,
     Such eyes the Widows in Corioli wear,
     And Mothers that lack Sons. [2.1.175]

If the young apprentice can enact weeping, then the moment is well served, but even if he has to hide his head and shakes his shoulders in the worse sort of mimicry, then the acting of Burbage in the leading role will fill the moment and nothing will be lost.

Shakespeare's plays are not ensemble pieces. There are leading roles requiring immense stamina, striking supporting roles that offer a less experienced
actor a few great scenes, the bread-and-butter roles that keep the plots moving
forward by delivering dry, informative speeches with some regularity, and a
kaleidoscope of minor characters, many of whom appear in only one scene
and so can be grouped for ease of playing by a troupe of fourteen to sixteen
men and boys. It was through working his way up the hierarchy, from non-
speaking to minor to supporting to significant, that an apprentice received his
training in the profession.

There were a few basic skills, however, that an apprentice would be required
to demonstrate before being taken on by an acting company. We can imagine,
then as now, shareholders scrutinizing perspective apprentices, looking for a
certain aptitude for appearing in public, a certain pleasantness, flexibility, and
strength in the voice and body, an attractiveness in the face and physique, and
the empathetic imagination required to mimic a weeping wife or wounded
soldier, or the lively sense of the ridiculous to clown and ape. Dancing, singing,
sword fighting, and the capacity to memorize large amounts of dramatic text
might be tested. And for the last of these, the would-be actor would of necessity
be literate.

This simple fact hides from our view one of the single most significant
elements of an actor's training in Shakespeare's theatre, the acquisition of the
classical art of the spoken word: rhetoric. Any young man who could read
was most likely the product of the public education system established by the
Tudors, from which Shakespeare himself benefited. The primary activity in
any given school day was the learning by rote, guaranteed to strengthen an
actor's capacity for memorization. Once the schoolboys had acquired basic
numeracy and literacy (addition tables, the alphabet), they would begin their
studies in the art of language through the memorization of Latin and English
models of rhetorical excellence.

We can imagine, then, a young actor in Shakespeare's company, aged anywhere from fourteen to twenty-eight, reading at about the grade-three level,
always aloud, familiar with the basics of rhetoric and so always alive to the
power of language. Such a young man would be able to appreciate and make
use of the language-based manipulations of the company's resident playwright,
as these were based in large part on the shared conventions of rhetoric. As an
apprentice, he spent the long hours of his working week receiving his sides,
learning his lines, using his onstage time to acquire a mastery of the techniques
of the trade, and always hoping that the next new play might include an
especially wonderful part just for him.

I would argue that much of the reason why the plays are accessible today
is the result of the careful, actor-friendly guideposts and safety nets inserted
into the texts for the apprentice members of the company, which provide even
today the support and suggestion most needed by the otherwise bewildered
performer. I would also argue that much of the reason why even experienced

actors are lost in Shakespeare's plays today is that we have mislaid the simple and effective map that the apprentices brought to their first day on the job. However, an introduction to the basics of rhetoric will provide just such a map, and a modern actor's passion, training, intuition, and common sense will do the rest.

Rehearsing with Sides

As an unperfect actor on the stage,
Who with his fear is put besides his part.

Sonnet XXIII

I don't think we'll ever know for sure what went on at the performances in the Globe, how the actors communicated emotions, how they moved and spoke, or how they suggested character and relationships, even with all of the evidence buried in the plays. It is even less likely that we'll ever be able to do more than speculate about how rehearsals were run in Shakespeare's company. I have found, though, that a certain set of assumptions turns the focus of the modern actor towards the riches of the text in a rewarding way.

Contemporary rehearsal practices allow modern actors a great deal of time to sort out characterization and emotions while seeking solutions to staging. Something quite wonderful happens, however, when they are denied that time and in fact experience something akin to the conditions in Shakespeare's theatre.

For example, let us take the issue of "parts." We know that these consisted of the lines the actor was responsible for memorizing, and a cue line for which to listen. When working on a new play, the actor would know nothing else. What happens when modern actors work through a scene using parts?

There are several Shakespeare companies that do this. They gather together a group of skilled and experienced Shakespearean actors, have them memorize their sides, and bring them together for the first time in front of an audience. This can be great fun for actors and the audience, provided everyone gets into the spirit of improvisation and accident that such events invite. However, today it is very difficult to find anyone who does *not* know the plot and the relationships of the plays; the actors naturally have access to the entire play and may even have played their role before in a well-rehearsed production. I'm not sure an audience would want to sit through a rough rehearsal when the actors did not know the play, the characters, or the scene.

When I use sides in the training of actors, I demand that we work on a play that none of the actors know. Even with experienced actors this is quite easily accomplished if the scene is selected from one of the plays by Shakespeare's contemporaries. Remember that Shakespeare's company also performed these plays using the same rehearsal techniques and the writers used the same theatrical conventions as Shakespeare did.

What is immediately apparent, when an actor has been given just a side, is how differently the actor reads the part. When you have the entire play, you read quite naturally from a perspective from which you'd receive the entire play, that of the audience. You might zoom in on your character, maybe stepping up onto the stage for "your" scenes, but you eagerly read all of the other scenes to understand the plot and the context within which your character will function. Your lines leap out at you, because you will be responsible for memorizing them, but they are no more or less important than the lines of other characters during this important first encounter.

Now, imagine that you encounter the play first entirely and only through the words your character will speak. Imagine also that you read slowly, because reading is not the familiar and easy task it is for modern actors after our lengthy stay in our book-based education system. In fact, it will probably take you all of the available time between receiving your side and the first rehearsal just to get through the lines once. So you must make the reading count!

Paper is very expensive, which is why you have only your part and not the entire play. The lines have been copied by hand, and you must be alert to errors while at the same time knowing it was copied directly from Shakespeare's original. You know Shakespeare wrote the role for you, and wanted to give you an opportunity to do what you do best. You know he will be there on stage with you, playing one or more of the important supporting roles. But you also know that there is no time to waste, and that you must leap to the heart of the role effectively during the first performance, or the play will fail, and the company will lose its investment.

I encourage the actors to read the side line by line, slowly and carefully, and reading *always* out loud. I have them hold a blank piece of paper so that it covers all that follows, so that the eye cannot dart down before the mouth and the mind have digested the ten syllables, more or less, that sit before them in the line they are currently saying.

The next stage of the exploration works well if the actors have just been given the sides. This denies them the contemplative time to puzzle through character, and so I am cutting them off from the acting techniques they've mastered for modern rehearsal practices. I sit the two actors, each with the side of her character only, and each using the white paper to cut off everything but the first line.

Whoever speaks first reads the first line. It is impossible to give the line a "correct" reading, because the actor has no idea who the character is and what is coming next. Even so, the actors are required to engage in the speech act invited by those words. The words alone hang there in space. They attract meaning, just by being said and heard. If the speaker is careful not to cadence down at the end of the line, unless there is a period, the thought hangs waiting for whatever will follow, open-ended and full of potential. The meaning of the words, their intellectual content, in combination with their texture and shape, invite the actor to color the words with vivid emotions, even before he is sure he knows why his character might be feeling that way.

The other actor listens. If the first line that has just been spoken ends with the words that form the cue, then the responsibility for speaking has just passed over to the listener. If not, how much longer will the speech go on? What in the speech is going to prompt the response? There's nothing to do but listen, carefully, absorbing every word as it is spoken, open to any and every emotion. You know *what* your response is going to be, but without knowing exactly *when* the character is going to respond, you discover a fresh variation of that thing we all strive for in our lengthy rehearsals: the spontaneous enactment of planned events.

One of the things I like best about working from sides is how it invites the actor to remain open to all possibilities far longer than we are able to if we can read the entire play. Lines are spoken and heard at face value on first encounter, because you don't yet know the "true" situation. So maybe that "true" situation isn't entirely true!

Let us take for example the great manipulator, Iago. Until a run-through, no other character in the play could know the content of his soliloquies, because only he would have received the side containing them. Because we know the play so well, it is almost impossible to recapture the discovery awaiting the actor playing Cassio as he works his way through his side, slowly reading aloud his lines, having learned that Iago is someone he trusts, who offers him comfort and good counsel, and who calls him brother, only to reach the final section of his side, the second-last speech, reporting Rodrigo's final words, and finally it is clear: Iago is a villain.

I don't think we should underestimate the impact of the first encounter an actor has with a character represented by words on the written page. Knowing that Iago is a villain, the modern actor reading Cassio cannot escape seeing Cassio as duped, a bit thick, a victim. But the actor who has been given only the side sees Cassio as flawed (his drinking, his relationship with Bianca) but fortunate in his friends, particularly that honest and reliable comrade Iago.

What other unique tensions are revealed if we examine Cassio through his side? Let's have a look. I'll reproduce the folio's punctuation and capitalizations, to see what clues they might provide, and I'll assume that this young actor missed the plot summary, if there was one when the parts were distributed. All he'll know is that he enters and exits and listens for cues and speaks.

[*Othello*: What is the News?]
The Duke does greet you (General)
And he requires your haste, Post-haste appearance,
Even on the instant.

Clearly, I'm a messenger, some sort of servant? Of the Duke? Of the General? Is Othello the general, or is he just the one who first addresses me?

[*Othello*: What is the matter, think you?]
Something from Cyprus, as I may divine:
It is a business of some heat. The Galleys
Have sent a dozen sequent Messengers
This very night, at one anothers heels:
And many of the Consuls, raised and met,
Are at the Dukes already. You have been hotly called for,
When being not at your Lodging to be found,
The Senate hath sent about three several Quests,
To search you out.

Well, I seem to know a fair amount, and could I be laughing a bit at the image of all these messages being sent out, from the Galleys, the Senate, the Duke. Interesting, he wasn't at his lodgings. I'm going to assume that the General is Othello, and that I've been the one to find him, wherever he is.

[*Othello*: I will but spend a word here in the house,
And go with you.]
Ancient, what makes he here?

Oh, hurray, I'm going to get an answer to the question! I'll have no problem remembering that line—I'm dying to know where we are, what house, and who he has to talk to inside. Whoever this is I'm addressing, I'd better find out if I'm higher or lower than him in rank. And look, my line completes Othello's verse line. Should I jump right in or wait until he's gone? He might have more to say, and need me to pick up my cues so he can get out and back.

[*Iago*: If it prove lawful prize, he's made for ever.]
I do not understand.

Another easy line. I don't understand. Sounds sneaky, and also something to do with a fortune. He can't be perfectly well set in life now, if this prize will make him.

[*Iago*: He's married.]
To who?

Good question. I'm going to find this easy to memorize.

[*Othello*: Have with you.]
Here comes another Troop to seek for you.

OK, I won't know until we I get to the theatre how much Iago has time to tell me before Othello comes back in, or how long Othello talks before he turns to me, but there will be some action here, as people arrive before we can leave. This is my first scene.

[*Gentleman*: For every Minute is expectancy
Of more Arrivance.]
Thanks you, the valiant of this warlike Isle,
That so approve the Moor: Oh let the Heavens

Give him defence against the Elements,
For I have lost us him on a dangerous Sea.

Is the war-like isle the same or a different location? Could it be Cyprus, that's an island? The gentleman must be a native, and if I've lost Othello in a storm at sea, it's probably some scene of arriving. So I must be attached to Othello, not just a messenger for the Senate.

[*Montano*: Is he well shipped?]
His Bark is stoutly Timbered, and his Pilot
Of very expert, and approved Allowance;
Therefore my hopes (not surfeited to death)
Stand in bold Cure.

Some suspense here: but not likely we're going to lose the title character so early in my side. And I'd better be careful. There are several people on stage and I can't assume that there aren't more speeches between these. I'm going to have to listen careful, watch for those who might be preparing to speak, but be ready to dash through this section if these comments follow on tightly.

[(*Within*): A Sail, a Sail, a Sail.]
What noise?

OK, we must be within sight of the sea, where there's a lookout waiting for Othello, because they like him here.

[*Gentleman*: The Town is empty; on the brow o' the Sea
Stand ranks of People and they cry a Sail.]
My hopes do shape him for the Governor.

I can just imagine everyone looking and waiting and hoping. I've seen it myself, down on the docks when there's been a bad storm and the ships come limping home, and a crowd gathers to watch for the stragglers. Some never return, of course. Now, is Othello the Governor? That would make sense. No wonder the people are concerned.

[*Gentleman*: They do discharge their Shot of Courtesy,
Our Friends, at least.]
I pray you Sir, go forth,
And give us truth who 'tis that is arrived.

OK, now I understand war-like. They don't do this unless they're afraid of attack. And if they're under threat of attack, they must be desperate to have the Governor safely back. Hey, I'm as eager to know who it is as anyone.

[*Montano*: But good Lieutenant, is your General wived?]
Most fortunately: he hath achieved a Maid
That paragons description, and wild Fame:
One that excels the quirks of Blazoning pens,

And in th'essential Vesture of Creation,
Does tire the Ingenuer.

Thanks, Bill. I'm a lieutenant of Othello's. Nice of you to let me know. And I know the answer to my question: Othello got his good fortune. But sounds like she's worth something because she's beautiful, not because she's wealthy. Also sounds like I'm in love with her myself. Or that I've been practicing writing poetry to flatter her and please my general. Is this business of her fame literal—is she well known—or metaphorical—she's outstanding and worthy of great fame?

[*Gentleman*: 'Tis one Iago, Ancient to the General.]
Ha's had most favourable, and happy speed:
Tempests themselves, high Seas, and howling winds,
The guttered-Rocks, and Congregated Sands,
Traitors ensteeped, to enclog the guiltless Keel,
As having sense of Beauty, do omit
Their mortal Natures letting go safely by
The Divine Desdemona.

What on earth was all that about? Does Iago enter? Or is it his ship? Why aren't I unhappy it's not Othello? Then a terrifying list of all the things that can sink a ship, but Nature lets this ship go by because it carries the beautiful . . . what do you want to bet this is the name of the woman I went on about a few moments ago.

[*Montano*: What is she?]
She that I spake of:
Our great Captains Captain,
Left in the conduct of the bold Iago,
Whose footing here anticipates our thoughts,
A Senights speed. Great Jove, Othello guard,
And swell his Sail with thine own powerful breath,
That he may bless this Bay with his tall Ship,
Make loves quick pants in Desdemona's Arms,
Give renewed fire to our extincted Spirits.
Oh behold,
The Riches of the Ship is come on shore:
You men of Cyprus, let her have your knees.
Hail to thee Lady: and the grace of Heaven,
Before, behind thee, and on every hand,
Enwheel thee round.

This explains a lot. For some reason, Othello's sent his wife to a war zone. They've arrived a week before they were expected, and meanwhile Othello's overdue. A prayer for the man, and then what? Clearly this is a passionate love match, because I'm inviting everyone to envision them making love. And then, there she is. Talk about renewed fire! I'm probably the one panting. Has to be some reason for all those capital letters. Look at the images of grace as well as beauty—grace of heaven, that is. I call her Lady, like I was praying to the Virgin Mary (though of course we don't do that out loud any more) and earlier I called her our Captain's Captain—that's something people call Jesus. Whatever's going on, this lady has got to be the center of attention when she enters.

> [*Desdemona*: What tidings can you tell me of my Lord?]
> He is not yet arrived, nor know I aught
> But that he's well, and will be shortly here.

Oh boy, the great lady speaks to me. I'm probably overwhelmed with my renewed fire, but it gets worse. She asks about Othello. So I have to be the one to tell her he's missing in the big storm at sea. How can I know he's well and will be here soon? I'm treading that narrow line between lying and wishful thinking.

> [*Desdemona*: How lost you company?]
> The great Contention of the Sea, and Skies
> Parted our fellowship. But hark, a Sail.

Why do I feel like this is my fault? I'm going to feel terrible if I live and he dies. It must be pretty tempting to comfort her, she's so terrified.

> [*Gentleman*: This likewise is a Friend.]
> See for the news:
> Good Ancient, you are welcome. Welcome Mistress:
> Let it not gall your patience (good Iago)
> That I extend my Manners. 'Tis my breeding,
> That gives me this bold show of Courtesy.

I have to read this carefully to get what's going on. I'm not addressing Desdemona as "Mistress," because I call her "my Lady." So there's another woman here, and my guess is it's Iago's wife, and I give her a kiss or something, to justify calling it a "bold show." So with Desdemona I'm all poetical, kneeling at her feet, and with this other woman I'm a bit of a flirt. Unless we already know each other well and this is the way we kid around?

> [*Desdemona*: How say you (Cassio) is he not a most profane, and liberal
> Counsellor?]
> He speaks home (Madam) you may relish him more in the Soldier, than
> in the Scholar.

I'm not sure how this connects with what I say the speech before. I'll have to wait and find out. Oh joy, Desdemona is talking to me, I'll enjoy that. What's this about profane? Doesn't fit with my images of heavenly grace, but I don't seem to take offense; seems like I'm commenting on a soldiers blunt truth learned not from books but in battle. Wonder what it was that the counsellor said, and who the counsellor is. Must be one of the military unit.

> [*Iago*: The Moor I know his Trumpet.]
> 'Tis truly so.

Now that's good news.

[*Desdemona*: Let's meet him, and receive him.]
Lo, where he comes.

Great, I get to announce his entrance. Get ready to pull back and give him center stage. Big reunion scene? Will we get to see Desdemona in Othello's arms? I'll have to wait and see. And that's the end of my second scene.

[*Othello*: Let's teach ourselves that honourable stop,
Not to out-sport discretion.]
Iago, hath direction what to do.
But notwithstanding with my personal eye
Will I look to't.

My next bit is with Othello. Iago's got the orders, but I'm going to supervise. Whatever it is, this answers my questions about how the lieutenant and the ancient work out the division of the duties of attending the general. What that has to do with discretion, I'll have to wait and see.

[*Othello*: Goodnight.]
Welcome Iago: we must to the Watch.

OK, our instructions have to do with the Watch.

[*Iago*: and she is sport for Jove.]
She's a most exquisite Lady.

Sounds like some guy talk to me.

[*Iago*: And I'll warrant her, full of Game.]
Indeed she's a most fresh, and delicate creature.

Seems like Iago's working on his own enraged fires, while I'm back in poetical mode. He's doing how sexy she is, I'm thinking she's like a fresh young girl.

[*Iago*: Methinks it sounds a parley to provocation.]
An inviting eye:
And yet methinks right modest.

Now I know it's not my imagination. Iago is painting her as a flirt and maybe worse, but I'm only temporarily swayed. Yes, her eye's inviting, but I'm sure she's truly modest. Soldiers' metaphors, like love's a game of war.

[*Iago*: Is it not an alarum to Love?]
She is indeed perfection.

I don't come through with much after his great image of the call to a love battle in her voice. All I can fall back on is some dumb poetical generalization. How old am I, anyway?

[*Iago*: to the health of black Othello.]
Not to-night, good Iago, I have very poor, and unhappy Brains for
drinking. I could well wish
Courtesy would invent some other Custom of entertainment.

OK, why is he "black Othello"? Is he evil or does he have dark hair? And here's my answer to that business about discretion. Othello must have been warning me not to drink. I can't be too young, if I've figured out that I shouldn't drink. And hey, we're in prose-land. With all those short lines before it sometimes wasn't clear if I was doing poetry or not, but here it's clear. We've stepped down, somehow, into the more relaxed, easy-going energy so that poetry no long suits.

[*Iago*: Oh, they are our Friends: but one Cup, I'll drink for you.]
I have drunk but one Cup to-night, and that was craftily qualified too:
and behold what innovation it makes here. I am unfortunate in the
infirmity, and dare not task my weakness with any more.

Maybe I'm not so old. Having just said I didn't want to drink, I did.

[*Iago*: 'Tis a night of Revels, the Gallants desire it.]
Where are they?

Must be some big party, but we're supposed to be taking care of something. Iago has the directions and I said I'd supervise.

[*Iago*: I pray you call them in.]
I'll do't; but it dislikes me.

This is really bad. I must be pretty drunk already, and too young to stand up to someone yelling, "Let's party!" What about the Watch?

[*Iago*: My Boat sails freely, both with wind and Stream.]
'Fore heaven, they have given me a rouse already.

I don't know what Iago's doing, but I have a very bad feeling about this situation. I have to go out and come back on again, but this is clearly a continuation of the previous party.

[*Iago*: Some Wine boys.]
'Fore Heaven: an excellent Song.

It's a real party now. Music, probably more drinking.

[*Iago*: your swag-bellied Hollander, (drink hoa) are nothing to your
English.]
Is your Englishman so exquisite in his drinking?

OK, I'll get to do great "drunk acting" here, slurring my words, and crafty Bill to give me something like "exquisite"—same word I used of Desdemona. Shows how far I've sunk.

[*Iago*: he gives your Hollander a vomit, ere the next Pottle can be filled.]
To the health of our General!

There's probably some jokes in here that'll get the audience roaring. Then, when everyone's falling around, drunk and laughing, I'll stand up and salute in a military fashion, but maybe miss or something ridiculous that will get another laugh. This scene is going to be fun. Iago must be really drunk too, to carry on like this.

[*Iago*: Some Wine hoa.]
Why this is a more exquisite Song than the other.

I'll slur this one even more. I'm really hooked on the word "exquisite."

[*Iago*: Will you hear't again?]
No: for I hold him to be unworthy of his Place, that does those things.
Well: heaven's above all: and there be souls must be saved, and there
be souls must not be saved.

Now I must be so drunk I'm rambling on, thinking I'm making perfect sense, but I'm not. And what's so funny is that this is all true. I'm not sure what I mean by the first bit: it will depend on what's gone before. Is "those things" something in the song, or just hearing it again?

[*Iago*: It's true, good Lieutenant.]
For mine own part, no offence to the General, nor any man of
quality: I hope to be saved.

Whenever someone says, "no offence," you just know they're going to come out with something offensive. And towards Othello, "the General"? Not clear what I'm saying, but that may be because I'm blotto.

[*Iago*: And so do I too Lieutenant.]
Ay: (but by your leave) not before me. The Lieutenant is to be saved
before the Ancient. Let's have no more of this: let's to our Affairs.
Forgive us our sins: Gentlemen let's look to our business. Do not think
Gentlemen, I am drunk: this is my Ancient, this is my right hand, and
this is my left. I am not drunk now: I can stand well enough, and I
speak well enough.

Amazing how modern this all feels. "I'm not drunk," says the drunk just before keeling over into his beer. Look at how I'm pulling rank on Iago (Lieutenant v. Ancient) plus maybe some class tension, given how often I say "Gentlemen," which Iago isn't. And since when did he become "my" Ancient?

[*All*: Excellent well.]
Why very well then: you must not think then, that I am drunk.

I'm probably falling down about now, and stagger off for some reason.

[*Iago*: But hark what noise?]
You Rogue: you Rascal.

I've got to make an entrance with this bit, so I'm probably the noise he was hearing. What's been going on? Why the capitals? These guys are the essence of rogueness and rascaldom?

[*Montano*: What's the matter Lieutenant?]
A Knave teach me my duty? I'll beat the Knave into a Twiggen-Bottle.

Oh, oh, looks like I'm getting into it with somebody. Either I'm too drunk to do any harm, or I'm a mean drunk, and things are getting dangerous. What's Montano doing here? He was with us when we welcomed Othello, asking about Desdemona.

[*Roderigo*: Beat me?]
Dost thou prate, Rogue?

Nose-to-nose time. Who is this guy? First encounter with him.

[*Montano*: I pray you Sir, hold your hand.]
Let me go (Sir)
Or I'll knock you o'er the Mazzard.

Looks like Montano is trying to hold me up or back before I hurt myself or someone else.

[*Montano*: Come, come: you're drunk.]
Drunk?

No kidding. I bet part of me, no matter how drunk, still knows this guy is right. So I have to shout down that inner voice as well as this outer voice.

[*Othello*: How comes it (Michael) you are thus forgot?]
I pray you, pardon me, I cannot speak.

My blood runs cold when I read this. Othello is here. He calls me Michael. I can't believe I'd be doing this in front of the General. Am I throwing up in the bushes? Did I take on someone and get beat up good?

[*Iago*: What are you hurt Lieutenant?]
Ay, past all surgery.

Hey, am I going to be killed off this soon?

[*Iago*: Marry Heaven forbid.]
Reputation, Reputation, Reputation: Oh I have lost my Reputation. I

have lost the immortal part of myself, and what remains is bestial. My
Reputation, Iago, my Reputation.

*Guess not. It's not a physical wound. I must be sobering up. I'm realizing just what a fool I made
of myself. Not yet clear just what I did that was so terrible, but given how many times I say
"reputation," and the fact that Othello was there, well, can't be good.*

[*Iago*: Sue to him again, and he's yours.]
I will rather sue to be despised, than to deceive so good a Commander,
with so slight, so drunken, and so indiscreet an Officer. Drunk? And
speak Parrot? And squabble? Swagger? Swear? And discourse Fustian
with one's own shadow? Oh thou invisible spirit of Wine, if thou hast
no name to be known by, let us call thee Devil.

Looks like I'm in terrible trouble as an officer. And in front of someone I respect so much.

[*Iago*: What had he done to you?]
I know not.

*Now some of what really happened is coming clear. I chased some guy with my sword, and I don't
even know why I was so mad at him! Perhaps that Roderigo fellow?*

[*Iago*: Is't possible?]
I remember a mass of things, but nothing distinctly; a Quarrel, but
nothing wherefore. O God, that men should put an Enemy in their
mouths, to steal away their Brains? that we should with joy, pleasance,
revel and applause, transform our selves into Beasts.

*Hey, but I knew this before I started drinking. I said I couldn't handle booze, but I accepted a drink
anyway. I must be pretty young, not to have figured out how to take responsibility for my own stupidity,
or stay away from alcohol.*

[*Iago*: how came you thus recovered?]
It hath pleased the devil drunkenness, to give place to the devil wrath,
one unperfectness, shows me another to make me frankly despise my
self.

*Am I the sort of person who does this regularly, in other words a weak, self-indulgent, deluded and
self-excusing alcoholic, or am I truly capable of reforming as a result of this sort of horribly embarrassing
incident?*

[*Iago*: but, since it is as it is, mend it for your own good.]
I will ask him for my Place again, he shall tell me, I am a drunkard:
had I as many mouths as Hydra, such an answer would stop them all.
To be now a sensible man, by and by a Fool, and presently a Beast. Oh
strange! Every inordinate cup is unblessed, and the Ingredient is a devil.

Oh, no. I've lost my place. What does that mean for me? I'm over here in Cyprus, or wherever, and I've been fired, or whatever they do to lieutenants when they lose their place, and if I ask to be reinstated, the commander (Othello) will just say what's true, that I'm not reliable because I'm an alcoholic.

[*Iago*: And good Lieutenant, I think, you think I love you.]
I have well approved it, Sir. I drunk?

Hard to say what's really going on here, between me and Iago. On the one hand, he's saying nice things to me, must be the only friend I have left after tonight, but it also seems sort of formal with "good Lieutenant" and "Sir" rather than personal names, like with Othello.

[*Iago*: this crack of your Love, shall grow stronger, than it was before.]
You advise me well.

Sounds like Iago is older and wiser, somehow. Or am I surprised to get such good advice from this guy?

[*Iago*: I protest in the sincerity of Love, and honest kindness.]
I think it freely: and betimes in the morning, I will beseech the virtuous
Desdemona to undertake for me: I am desperate of my Fortunes if they
check me.

I must be recovering. The whining has stopped, and I seem to be able to think straighter. This is a good plan. Thanks, friend, for talking me round. Something special must have happened when I connected with Desdemona, because I feel OK about asking her to speak to Othello for me, so I'm not ashamed to let her know what a mess I've made of things. And as his new bride, well, she'll be able to talk him round.

[*Iago*: Good night, lieutenant; I must to the watch.]
Good night, honest Iago.

Looks like Iago has proved himself a real friend after my embarrassment. I leave now, going somewhere to stew in my hung-over shame, while he goes to work.

[*Iago*: Dull not Device, by coldness, and delay.]
Masters, play here, I will content your pains,
Something that's brief: and bid, good morrow General.

OK, this is clearly the next morning. I enter on Iago's lines that close the previous scene.

[*Clown*: Go, vanish into air, away.]
Dost thou hear me, my honest Friend?

OK, who is this fellow, and what is my attitude towards him? I'll have to wait to figure out what's going on.

[*Clown*: No, I hear not your honest Friend; I hear you.]
Prithee keep up thy Quillets, there's a poor piece of Gold for thee: if the
Gentlewoman that attends the General be stirring, tell her, there's one
Cassio entreats her a little favour of Speech. Wilt thou do this?

*OK, enough with the joking, Clown, and take a message for me. Who's this gentlewoman? Guess I
can't ask for Desdemona directly, but it looks like I'm carrying through on my plan from last night.*

[*Clown*: I shall seem to notify unto her.]
Do, good my friend.
In happy time, Iago.

OK, Iago must arrive. Looks like everything's working out for me.

[*Iago*: You have not been a-bed then?]
Why no? the day had broke before we parted.
I have made bold (Iago) to send in to your wife:
My suit to her is, that she will to virtuous Desdemona
Procure me some access.

*OK, now I've figured something else. Iago's wife is Desdemona's waiting gentlewoman. This is the
same lady I kissed while we were all waiting for Othello. I wonder how Iago feels about me being
so "bold" with his wife? I don't seem to have anything to hide. I'm back in poetry land, which figures,
if I'm on a roll with my plan to get back in Othello's good books.*

[*Iago*: that your converse and business
May be more free.]
I humbly thank you for't. I never knew
A Florentine more kind, and honest.

*Iago is a Florentine. That probably meant something pretty specific to Shakespeare's first audience. I'll
have to find out. Am I surprised he's so decent? Notice the "humble" business. Quite a switch from
my drunken "the Lieutenant before the Ancient!"*

[*Emilia*: To bring you in again.]
Yet I beseech you,
If you think fit, or that it may be done,
Give me advantage of some brief Discourse
With Desdemona alone.

Looks like Emilia answered the message I sent. Why do I want to see Desdemona alone?

[*Emilia*: I will bestow you where you shall have time
To speak your bosom freely.]
I am much bound to you.

Looks like Emilia is on my side. She really understands my situation and is really going to help me. I leave after this, probably in a lot better mood than my last exit!

[*Desdemona*: As friendly as you were.]
Bounteous Madam,
What ever shall become of Michael Cassio,
He's never any thing but your true Servant.

Hurray! Looks like Desdemona's also on my side. I must just worship this woman, by this point!

[*Desdemona*: He shall in strangeness stand no further off,
Than in a polite distance.]
Ay, but Lady,
That policy may either last so long,
Or feed upon such nice and waterish diet,
Or breed it self so out of Circumstance,
That I being absent, and my place supplied,
My General will forget my Love, and Service.

Oh oh, looks like things aren't going as smoothly as I'd hoped. She's explaining Othello to me, and I'm worried that he's going to like his new lieutenant better than me.

[*Emilia*: Madam, here comes my Lord.]
Madam, I'll take my leave.

Someone enters so I have to go. Iago? I thought he was in on the whole plan.

[*Desdemona*: Why stay, and hear me speak.]
Madam, not now: I am very ill at ease,
Unfit for mine own purposes.

Maybe "my Lord" from Emilia means Othello? Looks like Desdemona is about to speak to him for me right now. No way I can stay and listen. And that's the end of that scene.

[*Desdemona*: How now (good Cassio) what's the news with you?]
Madam, my former suit. I do beseech you,
That by your virtuous means, I may again
Exist, and be a member of his love,
Whom I, with all the Office of my heart
Entirely honour, I would not be delayed.
If my offence, be of such mortal kind,
That nor my Service past, nor present Sorrows,
Nor purposed merit in futurity,
Can ransom me into his love again,
But to know so, must be my benefit:
So shall I clothe me in a forced content,

And shut my self up in some other course
To Fortune's Alms.

I'm still waiting, still asking Desdemona to speak for me. How long has it been since the last scene? Look at all those extra commas. It's like I'm running out of breath, and yet the speech feels memorized. Perhaps I'm getting desperate?

[*Desdemona*: If I do find him fit, I'll move your suit,
And seek to effect it to my uttermost.]
I humbly thank your Ladyship.

Seems very polite.

[*Bianca*: Save you (friend Cassio)]
What make you from home?
How is't with you, my most fair Bianca?
I' faith (sweet Love) I was coming to your house.

Hey, hey, hey. Who is this? How do I know her? She lives locally. Are we still in Cyprus? How well do I know her, to call her "sweet love"? I really hope that Desdemona and Emilia have left the stage before Bianca enters.

[*Bianca*: O weary reckoning.]
Pardon me, Bianca:
I have this while with leaden thoughts been pressed,
But I shall in a more continuate time
Strike off this score of absence. Sweet Bianca
Take me this work out.

Looks like I haven't visited her for a while, because I've been depressed. So it seems like some time has passed with me still out of work and waiting for Desdemona to speak for me to Othello. But I don't have an exit, so I'll have to wait to find out how all of this fits together.

[*Bianca*: Is't come to this? Well, well.]
Go to, woman:
Throw your vile guesses in the Devils teeth,
From whence you have them. You are jealous now,
That this is from some Mistress, some remembrance;
No, in good troth Bianca.

Looks like Bianca is jealous, suspecting me of getting gifts from a mistress. I'm pretty sure that no one else is listening to all of this. At least, I hope not!

[*Bianca*: Why, whose is it?]
I know not neither:
I found it in my Chamber,
I like the work well; Ere it be demanded

(As like enough it will) I would have it copied:
Take it, and do't, and leave me for this time.

Whatever it is, I found it, and I'm asking Bianca to copy it for me and otherwise leave me alone. Who is this woman and what is our relationship, that I treat her this way?

[*Bianca*: Leave you? Wherefore?]
I do attend here on the General,
And think it no addition nor my wish
To have him see me womaned.

Whoever she is, I don't want Othello to see me with her. Something else I'm ashamed of?

[*Bianca*: Why, I pray you?]
Not that I love you not.

Hmmm. I'm starting to think that she's my mistress, perhaps lower class than me, and it's hard to say from this if I really do care for her or if I'm just saying whatever to get her out of here.

[*Bianca*: And say, if I shall see you soon at night?]
'Tis but a little way that I can bring you,
For I attend here: But I'll see you soon.

Not sure who won that one, but looks like I have a relationship with someone, on top of all of my other problems. I leave now, to take her home? So much for waiting to see Othello.

[*Iago*: How now, Cassio?]
What's the matter?

I just love entrance lines like this. Doesn't give me a clue what's going on.

[*Iago*: This is his second Fit: he had one yesterday.]
Rub him about the Temples.

Who are we talking about? Is this what I walked in on? Some guy having a fit? Whatever is going on, I leave right away.

[*Iago*: How do you Lieutenant?]
The worser, that you give me the addition,
Whose want even kills me.

As I figure this, I'm saying that he's still calling me "Lieutenant," but I'm not one any more, and I miss it terribly, like it's killing me. How much time has passed since the last scene? How come I don't ask about the guy having fits?

[*Iago*: How quickly should you speed?]
Alas poor Caitiff.

Who am I talking about?

[*Iago*: I never knew woman love man so.]
Alas poor Rogue, I think i' faith she loves me.

Some woman is in love with me. Is this the caitiff?

[*Iago*: Do you intend it?]
Ha, ha, ha.

What is going on here? I don't sound like someone so depressed I feel like I'm dying!

[*Othello*: Do you triumph, Roman? do you triumph?]
I marry. What? a customer, prithee bear
Some Charity to my wit, do not think it
So unwholesome. Ha, ha, ha.

*Is Othello here too? What is going on? I'm laughing about the idea of marrying some woman. Bianca,
probably, unless there's still another woman I'm connected with.*

[*Iago*: Why the cry goes, that you marry her.]
Prithee say true.

So people are talking about me marrying this woman.

[*Othello*: Have you scored me? Well.]
This is the Monkeys own giving out:
She is persuaded I will marry her
Out of her own love and flattery, not out of my promise.

*Is this true, or have I said I'll marry her to sleep with her, and now I'm changing my tune? This
really sounds like guy talk to me.*

[*Othello*: Iago beckons me: now he begins the story.]
She was here even now: she haunts me in every place. I was the other
day talking on the Sea-bank with certain Venetians, and thither comes
the Bauble, and falls me thus about my neck.

*Oh, I get it. Othello is listening in, and so I'm probably not supposed to hear what he says. Looks
like I'm really enjoying this guy talk, complaining (boasting) about Bianca (assuming it's her we're
talking about).*

[*Othello*: Crying oh dear Cassio, as it were: his gesture imports it.]
So hangs, and lolls, and weeps upon me:
So shakes, and pulls me. Ha, ha, ha.

So I don't hear that cue. I'll have to find something to do to create a space for Othello to speak into. Maybe some quieter laughter? I'm doing a lot of "ha, ha, ha."

[*Othello*: but not that dog, I shall throw it to.]
Well, I must leave her company.

Another pause so that Othello can get his line in. More laughter? Some rude gestures?

[*Iago*: Before me: look where she comes.]
'Tis such another Fitchew: marry a perfumed one?
What do you mean by this haunting of me?

Looks like the women are after me everywhere. How irritated am I? Or am I glad to show off in front of Iago?

[*Bianca*: I'll take out no work on't.]
How now, my sweet Bianca?
How now? How now?

This must have something to do with what I asked her to do with whatever it was I found in my chamber. Same words: "taking work out."

[*Iago*: After her: after her.]
'Faith, I must, she'll rail in the street else.

Looks like Bianca's a bit of a wild one. Can't have that!

[*Iago*: Will you sup there?]
'Faith, I intend so.

Where is "there"? Bianca's? Or some other place?

[*Iago*: for I would very fain speak with you.]
Prithee come: will you?

This is my exit line. Not clear if Iago comes with me or not.

[*Roderigo*: know his gait, 'tis he: Villain thou diest.]
That thrust had been mine enemy indeed,
But that my Coat is better than thou know'st:
I will make proof of thine.

OK, now I walk in and get attacked by the guy I attacked while drunk. If I hadn't been wearing this good coat, I'd be dead.

> [*Roderigo*: Oh, I am slain.]
> I am maimed for ever:
> Help hoa: Murther, murther.

Nasty. Looks like we both go down. Big stage fight? Hope so.

> [*Othello*: It is even so.]
> Oh help hoa: Light, a Surgeon.

Othello is here. Am I going to die in his arms? Hope he forgives me before I go. Hope I get a great death speech.

> [*Othello*: Thy Bed lust-stained, shall with lusts blood be spotted.]
> What hoa? no Watch? No passage?
> Murder, Murder.

This does not sound good. I'm still calling for help, and he's talking about lust and blood.

> [*Gratiano*: 'Tis some mischance, the voice is very direful.]
> Oh help.

Who is Gratiano? I don't really care, as long as he helps me!

> [*Iago*: Did not you hear a cry?]
> Here, here: for heaven sake help me.

Oh, good, someone I can count on. If Iago's here, he'll be able to handle things.

> [*Iago*: What are you here, that cry so grievously?]
> Iago? Oh I am spoiled, undone by Villains:
> Give me some help.

I bet I'm glad to recognize him.

> [*Iago*: What villains have done this?]
> I think that one of them is hereabout,
> And cannot make away.

Good. I'll be revenged on the assassin!

> [*Roderigo*: O help me there.]
> That's one of them.

That's the one who attacked me when I walked on. But I attacked him when drunk, so maybe he's not a complete villain.

[*Iago*: How is't Brother!]
My Leg is cut in two.

OK, now I know what part of me to clutch all this while! Interesting that Iago finally stops calling me lieutenant. He truly is a brother, a fellow soldier, a trusted friend.

[*Iago*: Cassio, may you suspect
Who they should be, that have thus mangled you?]
No.

I knew he'd get to the bottom of things. Looks like I don't remember the drunken fight.

[*Iago*: What malice was between you?]
None in the world: nor do I know the man?

Is Iago saying that Roderigo was his dear friend? Oh, no. What a terrible thing, to have killed the friend of my friend. At this point I'm off, probably carried, feeling like dying physically and morally.

[*Lodovico*: Did you and he consent in Cassio's death.
Othello: Ay.]
Dear General, I never gave you cause.

Everything has changed. Who is Lodovico? Seems like he's sorting out the truth, and what a terrible thing for me to hear. Othello was involved in the plan to kill me. Why? What have I done to justify that? All I did was get drunk, and I was punished for that. I've only ever loved and respected the man, and tried to get him to forgive me.

[*Othello*: O Villain!]
Most Heathenish, and most gross!

Who are we talking about? At least Othello and I seem to feel the same way, given how I echo him.

[*Othello*: How came you (Cassio) by that Handkerchief
That was my wifes?]
I found it in my Chamber:
And he himself confessed but even now,
That there he dropped it for a special purpose,
Which wrought to his desire.

Now I'm getting answers. That thing I gave Bianca, that she thought was a gift from a mistress, turns out to be Desdemona's handkerchief, which someone, probably that heathenish villain we're talking about, has just confessed he dropped in my chamber. Who is this devious person?

[*Othello*: O Fool, fool, fool!]
There is besides, in Roderigos Letter,
How he upbraids Iago, that he made him
Brave me upon the Watch: whereon it came
That I was cast: and even but now he spake
(After long seeming dead) Iago hurt him,
Iago set him on.

Oh. It's Iago. Roderigo who tried to kill me was also duped. We were all duped, by the sound of it. Maybe me most of all. I really believed he was my friend.

[*Othello*: Killing myself, to die upon a kiss.]
This did I fear, but thought he had no weapon:
For he was great of heart.

My last lines. I don't like them at all. I have a terrible feeling that Othello kills himself in front of me. That I never get to apologize for being drunk. That somehow I was involved, even though I didn't know it, somehow with that handkerchief. Iago used me to get at Othello, the same way he used Roderigo to get at me. And at this last moment, even though I knew it was coming, I made another stupid mistake. I assumed he was unarmed. So it's all my fault. The greatest general, the man who called me Michael, is dead and I'm still alive. God, I hate it when Bill writes tragedies.

ᕰᖇ 3 ᕰᖇ

Theatrical Conventions

Actions that a man might play.

Hamlet [*Hamlet* 1.2.84]

How can individual actors contribute to the creation of "lively, entertaining, and faithful to the text" productions? How can they endow long-lost theatrical conventions with contemporary energy? How can they combat the forces of tradition that place greater restrictions on the production of these plays than were ever placed when they were first performed?

By considering just how conventions work, we realize that our theatre is as conventional as Shakespeare's, and four hundred years from now actors will find what was normal for us to be as laughable as we find Shakespeare's handling of, for example, the staging of death scenes.

ENACTING DEATH

In this borrowed likeness of shrunk death.

Friar [*R&J* 4.1.104]

An interesting example of shifting conventions is found in the final scene of *Othello*, which contains that most horrific of murders:

Desdemona: O banish me, my Lord, but kill me not.

Othello: Down Strumpet.

Desdemona: Kill me to-morrow, let me live to-night.

Othello: Nay, if you strive.

Desdemona: But half an hour.

Othello: Being done, there is no pause.

Desdemona: But while I say one prayer.

Othello: It is too late.   *Smothers her.*

          Emilia at the door.

Emilia: My Lord, my Lord? What hoa?
          My Lord, my Lord.

Othello: What noise is this? Not dead? not yet quite dead?
          I that am cruel, am yet merciful,
          I would not have thee linger in thy pain?
          So, so.

Emilia: *within.* What, hoa? my Lord, my Lord?

Othello: Who's there?

Emilia: Oh good my Lord, I would speak a word with you.

Othello: Yes: 'tis Emilia: by and by. She's dead.
          'Tis like she comes to speak of Cassio's death:
          The noise was high. Hah, no more moving?
          Still as the Grave. Shall she come in? Were't good?
          I think she stirs again. No, what's best to do?
          If she come in, she'll sure speak to my wife:
          My wife, my wife: what wife? I have no wife.
          Oh insupportable! Oh heavy hour!
          Me thinks, it should be now a huge Eclipse
          Of Sun, and Moon; and that th'affrighted Globe
          Did yawn at Alteration.

Emilia: I do beseech you
          That I may speak with you. Oh good my Lord.

Othello: I had forgot thee: oh come in Emilia.
          Soft, by and by, let me the Curtains draw.
          Where art thou? What's the matter with thee now?

          Enter Emilia

Emilia: Oh my good Lord, yonders foul Murders done.

Othello: What? now?

Emilia: But now, my Lord.

Othello: It is the very error of the Moon,
          She comes more nearer Earth than she was wont,
          And makes men mad.

Emilia: Cassio, my lord, hath killed
          A young Venetian, called Roderigo.

Othello: Roderigo killed? and Cassio killed?

Emilia:	No. Cassio is not killed.
Othello:	Not Cassio killed? Then Murders out of tune,
	And sweet Revenge grows harsh.
Desdemona:	O falsely, falsely murdered.
Emilia:	Alas! what cry is that?
Othello:	That? What?
Emilia:	Out, and alas, that was my Ladys voice.
	Help, help hoa, help. Oh Lady speak again,
	Sweet Desdemona, oh sweet Mistress, speak.
Desdemona:	A guiltless death, I die.
Emilia:	Oh who hath done this deed?
Desdemona:	No body: I my self, farewell:
	Commend me to my kind Lord: oh farewell.
Othello:	Why, how should she be murd'red?
Emilia:	Alas: who knows?
Othello:	You hear her say her self, it was not I.
Emilia:	She said so: I must needs report the truth.
Othello:	She's like a Liar gone to burning hell,
	'Twas I that killed her.
Emilia:	Oh the more Angel she, and you the blacker Devil! [5.2.78]

Modern audiences, accustomed to conventions of murder as enacted on film and television, find two things very strange, almost laughable, in this scene. First, it seems to take the powerful warrior Othello a considerable length of time not only to kill his wife, but also to be sure she is dead. And he's wrong, for she pops up a few minutes later. In fact, it's not at all clear exactly when she dies. Some editors add a stage direction, indicating that she does in fact die after bidding Emilia "farewell," but there is no such direction in the folio, and since she's popped up once before, perhaps the audience is intended to spend the rest of the play hoping that she is in fact only unconscious, and that someone will revive her and reunite her to her reformed Othello? Shakespeare pulls off just such a return from the dead in *The Winter's Tale*, but here there is no further sound from Desdemona, and both Othello and Emilia will die before the final words are spoken.

"A guiltless death, I die," is not the same sort of pronouncement as Emilia's final words, "So speaking as I think, alas, I die," which baldly state, so there will be no doubt, that the prone actor is to be taken for a dead body. Modern audiences find such statements ludicrous. I have not personally been present at a sufficient number of murders (in fact, none at all) so I don't know which version, Shakespeare's or ours, is more "realistic." In a scene like the end of *Othello*, it doesn't seem to matter. Desdemona's final words are important as much for the plot as for the theme and for the emotional impact on Emilia and on Othello. Emilia has to be prompted to tell Othello the truth right now, and she can't if Othello is able to hide the murder because it took place in his private chamber and he has hidden the body out of sight. Emilia's final words are important so that we know that, unlike Desdemona, there is no chance that she will revive unexpectedly to accuse her villainous husband, Iago. There's no need to tell anyone what happened, because the murder took place in front of several witnesses.

Some actors, in playing Desdemona and/or Othello, need to have medical assurances that the events of the scene are credible. And yes, if Othello "stiffles" his wife, as the folio stage direction suggests, suffocating her perhaps with a pillow, then she could lose consciousness temporarily and revive to speak. It's not quite clear why she would then die. It's very unlikely she would be able to speak if he has crushed her windpipe or broken her neck. If he follows the suffocating with a stab wound, during the lines when he's trying to make sure she is in fact dead, then we can imagine her recovering consciousness but then bleeding to death.

But I suspect it is modern films and television that have aroused in us a fascination with the graphic details of murder and death. The real drama of the moment is emotional and spiritual, not physical. Will Desdemona risk her very soul to save her husband, even though he murdered her?

When Desdemona speaks after being thoroughly killed by Othello, she does so in order to cry "murder," the essential accusation of the victim against evil. If the mouth cannot speak, the very wounds cry out by bleeding afresh, when the murder is present, as we see in *Richard III*.

> Oh Gentlemen, see, see dead Henrys wounds,
> Open their congealed mouths, and bleed afresh.
> Blush, blush, thou lump of foul Deformity:
> For 'tis thy presence that exhales this blood
> From cold and empty Veins where no blood dwells.
> Thy Deeds inhuman and unnatural,
> Provokes this Deluge most unnatural.
> O God! which this Blood mad'st, revenge his death:
> O Earth! which this Blood drink'st, revenge his death.
> Either Heaven with Lightning strike the murderer dead:
> Or Earth gape open wide, and eat him quick,
> As thou dost swallow up this good Kings blood
> Which his Hell-governed arm hath butchered. [1.2.55]

But then, instead of using her dying breath to speak against Othello, she defends herself. Imagine the impact on Othello, a member of a society that believed that it was impossible to lie when you are poised, one foot in this world, one in the next. This belief is voiced by John of Gaunt, on his deathbed, as he waits to offer his nephew Richard II some final words of advice:

Oh but (they say) the tongues of dying men
Enforce attention like deep harmony,
Where words are scarce, they are seldom spent in vain,
For they breathe truth, that breathe their words in pain.
He that no more must say, is listened more,
Than they whom youth and ease have taught to glose,
More are mens ends marked, than their lives before,
The setting Sun, and Music at the close
As the last taste of sweets, is sweetest last,
Writ in remembrance, more than things long past;
Though Richard my lifes counsel would not hear,
My deaths sad tale, may yet undeaf his ear. [2.1.5]

Is it possible that Othello might be convinced of his error, entirely on the strength of Desdemona's pain-filled words, "A guiltless death, I die"? We'll never know, because Emilia does what anyone would do, who comes upon a murder victim still able to speak; she asks the victim to name the killer.

And Desdemona lies. Not only does she protect her husband, she also accuses herself of the most heinous sin of suicide, condemning herself to the treatment received by poor Ophelia, maimed rites. As the priest explains to her brother,

Her Obsequies have been as far enlarged,
As we have warrantise, her death was doubtful,
And, but that great Command, o'ersways the order,
She should in ground unsanctified have lodged,
Till the last Trumpet. For charitable prayers,
Shards, Flints, and Pebbles, should be thrown on her:
Yet here she is allowed her Virgin Rites,
Her Maiden strewments, and the bringing home
Of Bell and Burial. [5.1.226]

A police officer at the scene of a modern incident of domestic violence would have no trouble putting two and two together, and would realize that the wife was lying. But Emilia simply cannot be sure. It is, at this moment, inconceivable that Desdemona's words, while *in extremis*, could be false. It is Othello who points out the terrible irony: Desdemona, by lying as she died, has condemned herself to hell. The implication for him: if she can lie at a moment like this, then there's no reason why she couldn't have been lying all along. She is, in fact, "Liar," the embodiment of the essence of falsehood. The word is capitalized in the folio.

But Emilia sees another implication: if she would sacrifice her very soul in love of her husband, to protect him, then she is a saint indeed, and the last person to betray her marriage vows. It is Emilia's interpretation that survives the rest of the scene. Othello asks that he be remembered as "one whose hand /

(Like the base Judean) threw a pearl away / Richer than all his tribe." By comparing Desdemona to Jesus, the promised messiah rejected by the Jewish leaders and condemned to die, Othello simultaneously affirms his return to a Christian ethos even as he pronounces himself outside the bounds of Christian forgiveness.

Did Desdemona's sacrifice save her husband? He kills himself in truth, while she was lying when she said she committed suicide. However, he sees the world clearly and tells the truth as he dies, while she damned herself by lying. Her lie saved him from dying while still believing her an unfaithful liar.

Given this amount of spiritual irony, coupled with the raging emotional roller coaster of the final moments of the play, I don't think the medical reality of Desdemona's death is at all important. It gives shape to the struggle for Othello's soul. It connects reality with truth the same way a metaphor does: love is like a red, red rose, but it isn't really a red, red rose. The death of this relationship is like the death we watch Desdemona experience. That makes it a true death, which is much more important than that it be a real death.

When I have seen this scene work best, it seems to be because the production team solves the medical reality sufficiently so that the actors can play and the audience can focus on the emotional and spiritual reality. The scene is not about how Othello kills Desdemona, and when exactly she dies, and why, but on how this tragic sequence of events culminates in the tossing away of a pearl beyond value.

Inopportune Laughter

The shifting conventions of death are disturbing because anything that triggers an audience's sense of the ridiculous or incredible at moments sabotage all of the actor's work in pursuit of such extreme feeling. And Shakespeare gives modern actors some real challenges in that regard.

Here is the death scene written for Harry Percy, called Hotspur, who is so vivid a character as to almost steal the first part of *Henry IV* from young prince Hal.

> Oh Harry, thou hast robbed me of my youth:
> I better brook the loss of brittle life,
> Than those proud Titles thou hast won of me,
> They wound my thoughts worse, than sword my flesh:
> But thought's the slave of Life, and Life, Times fool;
> And Time, that takes survey of all the world,
> Must have a stop. O, I could Prophesy,
> But that the Earth, and the cold hand of death,
> Lies on my Tongue: No Percy, thou art dust
> And food for– [5.4.77]

At this point there is a long dash in the folio, and Hal finishes the line, "For Worms, brave Percy. Farewell great heart." Clearly, at the beginning of this speech Hotspur must be dying, and a modern actor thinks that it is his job in this moment to enact all of the agony of a death-wound or three and the inevitable loss of lucidity that should follow. We are all familiar with the sequence from whichever is our favorite medical series or dramatic film version of death in full color and extreme closeup. But if we look at what Shakespeare has created here, we discover quite a different tone. This is no death agony, but a speech of prophecy, as Hotspur foresees the loss of reputation and the wounding of thoughts rather than the loss of life and sword cuts in flesh. There is even a glimpse of his sense of humor in the reference to time's fool, and self-disparagement in his final address to himself as being food for worms.

Any temptation to become too clinical and self-indulgently tragic is offset by the context within which the death occurs. The folio stage direction just before this speech reads, "Enter Douglas, he fights with Falstaff, who falls down as if he were dead. The Prince killeth Percy." This means that when Hotspur dies he is in fact the second body on stage. Hal eulogizes over both of them and then leaves, at which point Falstaff rises up to comment on the eulogy, and to drag off the body of the actor playing Hotspur.

Now, we know that neither actor is dead. And perhaps, given the stage direction in the folio, Falstaff falls down in such a way that we never doubted he was playing possum. Or perhaps not. Perhaps, we think Falstaff is dead, and we solemnly listen to Hal's final words over the body of his beloved friend, sad to see the end of the great tub of guts that had so amused us earlier in the play. What joy, then, when he rises. But if he can rise, why can't Hotspur? Well, of course he does, to bow at the end of the play, as do Desdemona, Emilia, and Othello at the end of their play. When Shakespeare writes a formal processional to carry away the dead bodies, the rising will take place out of sight. Was that the custom, even when nothing is so indicated by the closing lines of the play? Or did the actors ever rise right there in front of the audience, in the full light of the open-air Globe theatre, with no curtain or trap to hide the transition from corpse to acknowledger of applause?

And how did they bow? Were they still "in character?" Did William Kempe bow as Falstaff? Did the apprentices curtsey as young ladies if receiving applause for Juliet or Desdemona? Is that any more peculiar than playing someone dead, come to life? If we look at the epilogues written for Prospero, Puck, or Rosalind, we see Shakespeare negotiating the collision of fiction and fact: these are actors, playing characters, acknowledging that they are characters as the character would. Prospero addresses the audience with:

> Let me not,
> Since I have my dukedom got,
> And pardoned the deceiver, dwell
> In this bare Island, by your Spell,

> But release me from my bands
> With the help of your good hands. [*Tempest* Epilogue, 5]

Puck's call for applause is a similar collision of character and actor: "Give me your hands, if we be friends, / And Robin shall restore amends" [*Dream* 5.1.437]. Rosalind is both a boy and a girl, the actor and the character, and her "conjuring" of the audience's good will includes: "If I were a Woman, I would kiss as many of you as had beards that pleased me, complexions that liked me, and breaths that I defied not: And I am sure, as many as have good beards, or good faces, or sweet breaths, will, for my kind offer, when I make curtsy, bid me farewell" [*AYLI* Epilogue, 17]. Can we imagine then an Othello and Desdemona bowing, actor and character, alive and dead, representing a timeless reality beyond the events of the play, when divisions no longer divide but find unity in the dream-like Globe?

SOLILOQUY AND ASIDE

> Then York unloose thy long-imprisoned thoughts,
> And let thy tongue be equal with thy heart.
>
> York [*2HVI* 5.1.88]

Many modern playwrights break the fourth wall of naturalistic illusion to have a character address the audience directly, and so it is more than likely that this particular convention is the least alien to a modern actor. We are also accustomed to voice-over commentary in films, when we hear the protagonist's voice narrating events or sharing thoughts hidden from the other characters. We are accustomed to the form such musing customarily take: not the racing, flowing jumble of thoughts that mirrors the manner in which our minds actually work, but a coherent, comprehensive, and sometimes quite strikingly beautiful monologue. Little wonder that some of the best-known and often recited speeches are the product of Shakespeare's exploration of this convention of his theatre. Every actor who has played Hamlet will report the sensation of having a significant portion of the audience recite "To be or not be" along with him.

One of the markers of the centrality of a Shakespearean character is the allocation of a speech that does not seem to be heard by anyone else on stage. If other characters are still present, these might appear in the text with the stage direction "Aside," though this term does not appear in any of the first editions of the plays. When the speech contains a lengthy display of emotional fireworks and private musings, it is inevitably one of the showcase soliloquies so frequently used in auditions.

Actors can choose from among several performance strategies for delivering a soliloquy or an aside. The most common, under modern lighting, is to deliver the lines straight out, as if directly to the audience, but without actually making contact or responding to anything that a single audience member might give back, hidden as they are in the dark. So customary is this approach that it is quite difficult to get some actors to deliver such speeches, even in the rehearsal hall, to those who are listening, much less to do so actually wanting a response and building upon whatever response occurs. And the listeners, being conditioned to polite silence, are not likely to provide a lively response. If it can be arranged, an audience more akin to patrons of a comedy club can breath new life into a tired soliloquy, if the actor is very brave and the "audience" knowledgeable about the play. This might seem an obvious choice for the sort of comic story-telling as presented by Launce in *The Two Gentlemen of Verona*, when he amuses us with a description of leaving home, complete with props and dog:

Nay, I'll show you the manner of it. This shoe is my father: no, this left shoe is my father; no, no, this left shoe is my mother: nay, that cannot be so neither: yes; it is so, it is so: it hath the worser sole: this shoe with the hole in it, is my mother: and this my father: a veng'ance on't, there 'tis: Now sir, this staff is my sister: for, look you, she is as white as a lily, and as small as a wand: this hat is Nan our maid: I am the dog: no, the dog is himself, and I am the dog: oh, the dog is me, and I am my self: I; so, so: now come I to my Father; Father, your blessing: now should not the shoe speak a word for weeping: now should I kiss my Father; well, he weeps on: Now come I to my Mother: Oh that she could speak now, like a would-woman: well, I kiss her: why there 'tis; here's my mothers breath up and down: Now come I to my sister; mark the moan she makes: now the dog all this while sheds not a tear: nor speaks a word: but see how I lay the dust with my tears. [2.3.13]

It is more startling to imagine a heckling, laughing, questioning group of listeners responding to a much more serious offering, such as that spoken by poor Julia, disguised as a page, in service to her unfaithful lover Proteus. Having agreed to his request to fetch a picture of his new girlfriend, Julia is left alone to ask, "How many women would do such a message?" [*Two Gents* 4.4.90]. An uninhibited audience member might, in response, call out, "None, and don't you do it either!" prompting Julia to continue, and the scene might proceed something like this:

Julia:	Alas poor Protheus, thou hast entertained A Fox, to be the Shepherd of thy Lambs;
Heckler:	Time to skin that fox, honey. Kill him dead and get on with your life.
Another Heckler:	Check out those lambs.
Still Another Heckler:	You're the lamb, Julia. Don't let that fox get you down.
Julia:	Alas, poor fool, why do I pity him That with his very heart despiseth me?

Heckler:	Good question.
Another Heckler:	So stop, already, you idiot. He's a jerk. Dump him.
Julia:	Because he loves her, he despiseth me,
Heckler:	You don't need him, baby.
Another Heckler:	You're too stupid to live, no wonder he dumped you.
Julia:	Because I love him, I must pity him.
Heckler:	Don't do it, Julia.
Another Heckler:	You just want to get him back in your bed.
Still Another Heckler:	Dump him.

Because we have all seen movies containing scenes where well-scripted hecklers are put down by brilliant speakers, we can imagine just such a series of challenging and supporting voices, and interject them into a monologue like Julia's as a part of our exploration of the speech. Better still, we might be able to recruit some fellow actors to heckle as we rehearse the scene, to bring alive the soliloquy's potential to initiate a true interaction with an engaged and enthusiastic audience.

Some directors rediscover the living heart of a soliloquy by defying convention and providing the actor with another on-stage character available to receive, silently and empathetically, all that pours out in such a moment. At the other end of the scale, some productions have pre-recorded the soliloquies to run, like cinematic voice-overs, as the character silently emotes. It is easy to imagine more of Julia's soliloquy in just such a production. Immediately after the lines quoted above, she takes out a significant object, and her words could just as easily be silent thoughts: "This Ring I gave him, when he parted from me, / To bind him to remember my good will," could be broadcast over the sound system as she silently looks at the ring. This would be even more effective in a film, when the camera could move in close to show us the intimate detail of her touching the ring and remembering. What follows could be clarified and sharpened if she could say it to someone else, someone listening with complete empathy and perhaps even responding with supportive gestures and sounds:

> And now am I (unhappy Messenger)
> To plead for that, which I would not obtain;
> To carry that, which I would have refused;
> To praise his faith, which I would have dispraised.

Who might this on-stage listener be? Lucetta, Julia's waiting-woman, is back in Verona. That need not stop us from bringing her on stage in rehearsal, to shake her head, to snort in ironic appreciation, perhaps even to say aloud, "I told you so," or "This is what I tried to warn you about, before you left home. Don't you remember me saying that oaths and tears are servants to deceitful men?" [2.7.71]. It is actually quite likely that Julia imagines Lucetta's reaction to what she is now experiencing, and bringing the character into the rehearsal hall might further illuminate Julia's way of expressing her state of mind in this particular soliloquy.

If, however, the director wanted the audience to see someone listening to Julia, might he bring back the observant Host, who brought his young guest to find Proteus, arriving just in time to witness a most romantic scene, complete with songs under Silvia's window and fervent vows of love? How much did this individual guess, when he asks, "How now? are you sadder than you were before; / How do you, man?" [4.2.54]. It would, I think, be entirely credible to have Julia share her deepest feelings with such a person in a later scene; the audience would assume either that the Host has figured it all out, or that Julia blurted out the truth and now has someone in whom to confide, "I am my Masters true confirmed Love, / But cannot be true servant to my Master, / Unless I prove false traitor to my self" [4.4.103].

Alternatively, we might imagine Julia in conversation with Launce. Once she has been employed by Proteus, in her disguise as a Sebastian the page, there is every reason to think that the two servants, each so busy assisting Proteus in wooing Silvia, might talk about their contrasting exploits, in which case the next two lines of her soliloquy might elicit a knowing laugh: "Yet will I woo for him, but yet so coldly, / As (heaven it knows) I would not have him speed." Fortunately, and actor's imagination knows no limits and, even if a director is not interested in anything so untraditional, the performer can imagine such responses and even ask colleagues to listen and respond in character to her soliloquies. She could even deliver the entire speech to the actor playing Proteus.

In exploring the nature of a character's soliloquy, some teachers have suggested that the actor address the words to "the one who has all the answers," perhaps God or the gods or the great prompter in the sky. This brings a significance to the utterances and furthermore frames the overarching experience as one of questioning, which suits the language patterns of many of the soliloquies. When Proteus first meets Silvia and falls in love, he has a soliloquy in which he asks, "Is it mine, or Valentines praise? / Her true perfection, or my false transgression? / That makes me reasonless, to reason thus?" [2.4.196]. There's a way of asking these questions rhetorically, not expecting an answer, in fact suggesting with your tone of voice that, as there are no answers, there is no need to struggle too long and hard with philosophizing. Better to move on and do what you have every intention of doing, regardless of any moral issues like the fact that this particular woman loves and is loved by your best friend. There is also a way of asking someone who might conceivably have the answer, in other words, truly asking the question in hope of an answer. It is important to avoid the trap of assuming that all questions in a soliloquy are rhetorical, simply because there is no other mortal on stage with you.

Imagining that you are speaking in the presence of the divine also illuminates another aspect of the soliloquy: that these are never duplicitous. What would be the point of lying to such an audience? And so when Proteus in his third soliloquy confirms prior as well as intended self-indulgence, why mince words? His speech tells us not only what we already know to be true, his various betrayals of friends and acquaintances, but also some embarrassing details that one would hesitate to confide in a friend:

> When I protest true loyalty to her,
> She twits me with my falsehood to my friend;
> When to her beauty I commend my vows,
> She bids me think how I have bin forsworn
> In breaking faith with Julia, whom I loved;
> And notwithstanding all her sudden quips,
> The least whereof would quell a lovers hope:
> Yet (Spaniel-like) the more she spurns my love,
> The more it grows, and fawneth on her still. [4.2.7]

As a variation on speaking to an auditor who already knows the truth and cannot be lied to, you can imagine speaking to a gathering of people very much like your character, who see the world his way, share his values, and are entirely supportive of every choice your character is making. Villains speak to a convention of villains, procrastinating heroes to a convention of tortured and delaying sons-who-must-avenge-a-father's-murder. Proteus would share with friend-betraying, multi-girl-friended comrades thoughts like,

> She is fair: and so is Julia that I love,
> (That I did love, for now my love is thawed,
> Which like a waxen Image 'gainst a fire
> Bears no impression of the thing it was.)
> Me thinks my zeal to Valentine is cold,
> And that I love him not as I was wont:
> O, but I love his Lady too-too much,
> And that's the reason I love him so little, [2.4.199]

receiving back waves of affirmation, "I know just what you mean," or "Isn't that always the way!" Such an audience can be set up in a rehearsal or imagined in private exploration, and in delivering the speech you can invite the sort of sharing that can only take place in group therapy, when like reflects back to like all the joys and sorrows of a shared affliction.

Another common strategy for exploring the conventions of a soliloquy is to find the argument, in fact to discern the internal debate and shape the speech into a statement of the problem, an exploration of the opposing sides, and a resolution. We can see this at work as Proteus comes to terms with his sudden passion for his best friend's girl. He begins with the observation, "Even as one heat, another heat expels, / Or as one nail, by strength drives out another: /

So the remembrance of my former Love / Is by a newer object quite forgotten"
[2.4.192]. He ends with the resolution, "If I can check my erring love, I will, /
If not, to compass her I'll use my skill" [2.4.213]. In between, he gives little
stage time to that voice which might assist him in checking his passion, except
to acknowledge that he is acting without advice, his reason dazzled by her
perfections. Even so, it would be possible to rewrite and stage this scene as a
debate, with a good and bad angel, like Gobbo's Conscience and Devil [*Merchant* 2.2.1], counselling loyalty and subterfuge, respectively. The debate ends
in a draw, but as the contestants leave, the Devil (who has had all the best
lines) would give the judge a secret greeting, his eventual victory assured.

That the Devil is not afforded too easy a victory is suggested by Proteus'
next appearance, alone and deep in his second soliloquy. He begins with a
statement of the essential conflict: "To leave my Julia; shall I be forsworn? /
To love fair Silvia; shall I be forsworn? / To wrong my friend, I shall be much
forsworn" [2.7.1]. The voice speaking on behalf of the affirmative next weighs
in with the realization, "And ev'n that Power which gave me first my oath /
Provokes me to this three-fold perjury. / Love bad me swear, and Love bids
me forswear"; then the case for self-indulgence is presented through compelling
images and a cynical aphorism:

> O sweet-suggesting Love, if thou hast sinned,
> Teach me (thy tempted subject) to excuse it,
> At first I did adore a twinkling Starr,
> But now I worship a celestial Sun:
> Un-heedful vows may heedfully be broken,
> And he wants wit, that wants resolved will,
> To learn his wit, t'exchange the bad for better;

until another voice intervenes with, "Fie, fie, unreverend tongue, to call her
bad, / Whose sovereignty so oft thou hast preferred, / With twenty thousand
soul-confirming oaths." There is nothing for Proteus to do but restate the
problem, exploring its complexity:

> I cannot leave to love; and yet I do:
> But there I leave to love, where I should love.
> Julia I loose, and Valentine I loose,
> If I keep them, I needs must loose my self:
> If I loose them, thus find I by their loss,
> For Valentine, my self: for Julia, Silvia.

Having come to this realization, Proteus' choice is clear (for him), and easily
rationalized:

> I to my self am dearer then a friend,
> For Love is still most precious in it self,

And Silvia (witness heaven that made her fair)
Shows Julia but a swarthy Ethiope.
I will forget that Julia is alive,
Rememb'ring that my Love to her is dead.
And Valentine I'll hold an Enemy,
Aiming at Silvia as a sweeter friend.
I cannot now prove constant to my self,
Without some treachery used to Valentine.

At this point, Proteus launches into a description of his plot to have Valentine exiled.

We find an even more compelling portrait of internal torment in the soliloquy that sits at the exact center of *Hamlet*, and it is one given, not to the title character, but to his great adversary. Whatever we might think about Claudius until that moment, he is transformed before our eyes by his capacity to express his guilt "like a man to double business bound" [3.3.41]. Claudius is torn in half by two forces, one represented by words such as "inclination" and "will" and the fruits of his crime, "My Crown, mine own Ambition, and my Queen" [3.3.55], the other by words such as "prayer" and "guilt" and the promise implicit in his question, "What if this cursed hand / Were thicker than it self with Brothers blood, / Is there not Rain enough in the sweet Heavens / to wash it white as Snow?" [3.3.43]. If we were to stage this particular debate, or enact the agony of his tormented soul, on one side we would place Gertrude, to represent the prize and the sin, while on the other we might place Ophelia, whose goodness held out a promise to Hamlet that prompted him to greet her with the request, "Nymph, in thy Orisons / Be all my sins rememb'red" [3.1.88]. Such a configuration is reflected in, and illuminates, two other scenes in the play. When Ophelia in her madness sang of sexual relations and promises made and betrayed, does she deliver to the King the flowers of rosemary for remembrance and pansies for thoughts, as well as the fennel of flattery and the columbine of ingratitude [4.5.175]? There are many reasons for Claudius to take personal responsibility for Ophelia's madness, and drawing a direct line between the torment of his soliloquy and the torment of her poor lost soul enhances the exploration of both scenes. There are even fewer opportunities for Gertrude and Claudius to build and explore their relationship, but Claudius confides in Laertes, responding to the younger man's question why he didn't move against Hamlet when Polonius was killed:

O for two special Reasons,
Which may to you (perhaps) seem much unsinewed,
And yet to me they are strong. The Queen his Mother,
Lives almost by his looks: and for my self,
My Virtue or my Plague, be it either which,
She's so conjunctive to my life, and soul;

That as the Starr moves not but in his Sphere,
I could not but by her. [4.7.9]

Gertrude's participation in his soliloquy, suggested by his confession to Laertes, will benefit both performers. It might be that each woman takes him by the hand, drawing first to one side, then to another, creating a dance that expresses the complexity of the relationship between Claudius and Gertrude, and the reflection that Ophelia the innocent girl casts upon the soul of Claudius.

Not every soliloquy is as clearly an invitation for a debate, alone or assisted by other characters in the play. Many appear to be arias of pure feeling, where time stops and the passion felt in an instant is given shape and substance by a sustained evocation of a single, multi-faceted sensation. For example, returning to *The Two Gentlemen of Verona*, here is a speech given to Valentine immediately following his banishment under threat of death:

And why not death, rather then living torment?
To die, is to be banished from my self,
And Silvia is my self: banished from her
Is self from self. A deadly banishment:
What light, is light, if Silvia be not seen?
What joy is joy, if Silvia be not by?
Unless it be to think that she is by
And feed upon the shadow of perfection.
Except I be by Silvia in the night,
There is no music in the Nightingale.
Unless I look on Silvia in the day,
There is no day for me to look upon.
She is my essence, and I leave to be;
If I be not by her fair influence
Fostered, illumined, cherished, kept alive.
I fly not death, to fly his deadly doom,
Tarry I here, I but attend on death,
But fly I hence, I fly away from life. [3.1.170]

We can imagine these thoughts flooding Valentine's brain, far faster than it takes for these lines to be said, on the instant that he hears his banishment pronounced by the Duke. Much as we enjoy receiving this insight into what is going on in our character's brain, what is problematical in this aspect of the convention of soliloquies is that this significant chunk of text contains no forward movement; there is no conflict, there is no evolution or even much of a build to the feelings being expressed. It is possible to bring conflict, discovery, change, and a build to such a speech, but such components do not seem to be a requirement of such soliloquies, which start intensely and remain intense throughout.

Even more problematical are those speeches which provide an insight into the mental state of a character who is not engaged in any particularly intense activity. Shakespeare's audience might have appreciated philosophical musings such as Valentine's later soliloquy:

> How use doth breed a habit in a man?
> This shadowy desert, unfrequented woods
> I better brook then flourishing peopled Towns:
> Here can I sit alone, un-seen of any,
> And to the Nightingales complaining Notes
> Tune my distresses, and record my woes.
> O thou that dost inhabit in my breast,
> Leave not the Mansion so long Tenant-less,
> Lest growing ruinous, the building fall,
> And leave no memory of what it was,
> Repair me, with thy presence, Silvia:
> Thou gentle Nymph, cherish thy for-lorn swain. [5.4.1]

Fortunately, Valentine is interrupted at this moment with offstage noises, followed by the arrival of Silvia, Proteus, and Julia, and the speedy resolution of the plot. Modern sympathies, however, quickly fade if these musings go on too long.

I suspect that Hamlet's most famous monologue has long been misperceived as a tortured contemplation of suicide simply because audiences have lost touch with the convention of the philosophical soliloquy. If we look at the sequence of events in the play, we will notice that the most painful doubt and self-loathing has already been endured, way back in the second scene of the play, when Hamlet wishes that "the Everlasting had not fixed / His Canon 'gainst Self-slaughter" [1.2.131]. By the time we reach "To be, or not to be," Hamlet has met the ghost, put on his antic disposition, tormented his friends and family, and laid his plans to use the play to trap the conscience of the king. Why then would he revert to a suicidal depression? Far more credible is an interpretation of his words as a direct response to what he is reading, an extended musing on the philosophical question of the essence of one's being. That his meandering thoughts take him round about to a discovery that has some implications for his own situation is interesting, but not particularly momentous. After all, if it might have been said that his revenge against Claudius had come to lose the name of action, prior to the arrival of the Players, that cannot be the case at this moment, as he awaits the performance this very evening of *The Murder of Gonzago*.

Let us consider more carefully what it might actually mean to have a theatrical convention that stops the action of the plot in order to reveal to the audience the workings of the mind of the protagonist. Of course it is exciting to gain access to such workings at moments of intense feeling or the plotting of future villainies. How fascinating, in contrast, to gain insight into how this particular mind works when it is entirely rational, contemplative, and fully engaged in thought for its own sake. It is like getting to know someone quite well through a long and fascinating discussion, wherein that individual's breadth of reading, range of life experiences, calibre of intellect, and world view are made manifest. Sometimes it might be necessary for a modern actor to put aside every strategy designed to transform a soliloquy into dramatic action, in order to allow the speech to work as an exchange of ideas, no more, and no less.

One aspect of a soliloquy, like its cousin the aside, is that time often seems to stop for the delivery of the lines. Sometimes productions will draw our attention to this through anti-naturalist staging: freezing everyone on stage, for example, while a spotlight picks up the speaker, restoring natural light and movement when the direct address to the audience is completed. This might be effective early in *The Two Gentlemen of Verona*, when Proteus, still at this point passionately in love with Julia, is abruptly sent to the court at Milan. Modern editors add a stage direction removing all but Proteus so that he can bemoan his fate with, among other observations, the quatrain:

> Oh, how this spring of love resembleth
> The uncertain glory of an April day,
> Which now shows all the beauty of the Sun,
> And by and by a cloud takes all away. [1.3.84]

The editors then add an entrance for Panthino, calling Proteus to attend his father. There are no such stage directions in the folio, and it makes just as much sense to have the other characters withdraw a distance and continue about their business, or even freeze in a characteristic attitude as Proteus shares with us his private reaction to his father's announcement.

I have always felt that this is exactly what happens when Polonius instructs Ophelia how to walk around just where Hamlet is most likely to run into her, with a prayerbook in her hands, and observes, "We are oft to blame in this, / 'Tis too much proved, that with Devotions visage, / And pious Action, we do surge o're / The devil himself" [*Hamlet* 3.1.45]. Claudius has the next speech, which begins with a response that seems to indicate that Polonius hears what he has to say next:

> Oh 'tis true:
> How smart a lash that speech doth give my Conscience?
> The Harlots Cheek beautied with plast'ring Art
> Is not more ugly to the thing that helps it,
> Than is my deed, to my most painted word.
> Oh heavy burden!

Unless Polonius is privy to Claudius's terrible secret, these references to a lashed conscience and a heavy burden must be heard by no one else on stage. Has Polonius withdrawn with Ophelia, returning only to warn the King that someone is coming? Or does Claudius in effect move out of the time frame in order to give voice to the split second agony of his guilt, which is over before it can register to any witness in the world of the play? If so, Polonius would experience no pause between his pious observation and the arrival of Hamlet.

Whatever staging strategy is employed at such moments, it is clear that others on stage are not intended to hear certain comments simply because they do not remark upon what has just been said. Often this is used for great comic effect, as when Julia comments on the duping of Thurio, another of Silvia's suitors, by the duplicitous Proteus. Thurio, who has foolishly employed Proteus as a go-between, asks, "How likes she my discourse?" Proteus responds, "Ill, when you talk of war." Thurio then concludes, "But well, when I discourse of love and peace." Julia has the next line, "But better indeed, when you hold your peace" [5.2.15]. Modern editors usually label this as an aside, but it might be that she says this so that Proteus hears perfectly well, though Thurio does not as his next line refers only to his obsession with Silvia: "What says she to my valour?" However, if only the audience hears, it might be because Julia is sitting and observing the exchange between the two men, and her comments are more in the form of heckling or audience chit-chat. In the last scene of the play she is a witness to Proteus's final assault on Silvia's virtue, and comments on Silvia's "By thy approach thou mak'st me must unhappy," with "And me, when he approacheth to your presence" [5.4.32]. However, this scene has another witness, Valentine, who earlier commented on the scene with another unheard statement, "How like a dream is this? I see, and hear: / Love, lend me patience to forbear a while" [5.4.26]. And so we have an audience watching Valentine watching Julia watch Proteus woo Silvia.

In *Troilus and Cressida* Shakespeare tops this, creating a scene in which Thersites watches Ullyses and Troilus watch Cressida with Diomedes, all watched by us. In his passion, Troilus finds it very difficult to remain a silent observer, and Ullyses must repeatedly warm him to remain quiet, while Thersites mocks them all with snide remarks like "How the devil Luxury with his fat rump and potato finger, tickles these together: fry lechery, fry" [5.2.55], and Cressida and Diomedes remain entirely unaware that they are not alone. When Diomedes asks for a token of her love and she offers him something once given her by Troilus, Troilus cries out, "O beauty! Where is thy Faith?" and Ullyses cautions him with, "My Lord," to which he replies, "I will be patient, outwardly I will" [5.2.67]. Shortly after, Cressida takes back the token and breaks with Diomedes, saying:

> O all you gods! O pretty, pretty, pledge;
> Thy Master now lies thinking in his bed

Of thee and me, and sighs, and takes my Glove,
And gives memorial dainty kisses to it;
As I kiss thee. [5.2.77]

Except for Diomedes, all who watch her, including Ullyses and Thersites, are struck with the bitter irony: her beloved is not safe in his bed thinking of her and kissing her glove, but here, hidden deep in the enemy camp, spying on her and listening to her thoughts, along with us.

Cressida's last lines in the play occur after Diomedes has left, with the pledge and her promise of sexual favors, leaving Cressida alone, except for her audience. She says:

Troilus farewell; one eye yet looks on thee;
But with my heart, the other eye doth see.
Ah poor our sex; this fault in us I find:
The error of our eye, directs our mind.
What error leads, must err: O then conclude,
Minds swayed by eyes, are full of turpitude. [5.2.107]

Is this a soliloquy? It has many of the familiar attributes: we are hearing her thoughts and she is not speaking to another character, but can others on stage hear her? Thersites is the next to speak, saying, "A proof of strength she could not publish more; / Unless she say, my mind is now turned whore." A few lines later, Troilus announces that he intends to "make a recordation to my soul / Of every syllable that here was spoke" [5.2.116] but continues to discuss Cressida's interaction with Diomedes. I have always suspected that somehow Thersites, in his position as cynical commentator, joins the audience and so can hear those final words of Cressida, but that Troilus, caught has he is in the evidence of his eyes and ears, cannot read her mind within the conventions of the soliloquy. I'm not sure about Ullyses, that wily Greek. He has an astute understanding of human nature, but I have never been able to fathom exactly why he brings Troilus here to witness this betrayal.

There is one more approach to the soliloquy that suggests a similarity between the convention of the spoken thoughts of a silent observer of the action, in what might be called an aside, with the lengthy musings of a central character who, following an intense scene, is left alone to share his thoughts with the audience, in other words a soliloquy. This strategy invites direct connections between sections of the monologue and events in the preceding scene. *Hamlet* provides us with two such examples, one relatively self-evident, the other subtle and thought-provoking. Let us begin with the easier example.

The first time we see Hamlet again, after his meeting with the ghost of his father, he enters reading a book, torments his step-father's chief counsellor (and the father of his beloved Ophelia) with a demonstration of his antic disposition, and then enjoys a reunion with his old school-fellows turned kings' spies, Rosencrantz and Guildenstern. So far, so good. Hamlet provides the engine of the scene, up to and including the arrival of the players and his invitation to the leading performer to demonstrate his talents with a passionate speech. And then he gives over center stage to another speaker. Once the showcase performance grinds to a halt, Hamlet again welcomes all these visitors to Elsinore and dismisses them, so that he can announce, "Now I am alone," and launch his soliloquy with, "Oh what a Rogue and Peasant slave am I?" [2.2.549]. However, after more than thirty lines of berating himself for being a dull rascal, a coward, and an ass, he instructs himself, "About, my brain" [2.2.588] and changes the direction of his thinking with the following:

> I have heard, that guilty Creatures sitting at a Play,
> Have by the very cunning of the Scene,
> Been struck so to the soul, that presently
> They have proclaim'd their Malefactions.
> For Murther, though it have no tongue, will speak
> With most miraculous Organ. I'll have these Players,
> Play something like the murder of my Father,
> Before mine Uncle. I'll observe his looks,
> I'll tent him to the quick: If he but blench
> I know my course. The Spirit that I have seen
> May be the Devil, and the Devil hath power
> T'assume a pleasing shape, yea and perhaps
> Out of my Weakness, and my Melancholy,
> As he is very potent with such Spirits,
> Abuses me to damn me. I'll have grounds
> More Relative then this: The Play's the thing,
> Wherein I'll catch the Conscience of the King. [2.2.588]

He then exits, and it is tempting to conclude that he has just thought of this brilliant plan and is off to put it into action. However, he is in fact informing us of a plan that he has already put into action. When he dismissed Polonius and the actors and the following exchange took place:

Hamlet: Follow him Friends: we'll hear a play to morrow. Dost thou hear me old Friend, can you play the murther of *Gonzago*?

Player: Ay my Lord.

Hamlet: We'll ha't to morrow night. You could for a need study a speech of some dozen or sixteen lines, which I would set down, and insert in't? Could ye not?

Player: Ay my Lord.

Hamlet: Very well.

In a very real sense, the famous rogue and peasant slave soliloquy does not follow the scene, but occurs in parallel time to the First Player's performance. As Hamlet is watching and listening, one part of his mind is saying, "What

would he do, / Had he the Motive and the Cue for passion / That I have?"
We know just about exactly the moment when Hamlet's brain began to move
in this direction. He is completely engrossed in the first part of the Players'
performance, and it is only after Polonius' ill-mannered interruption, "This is
too long" [2.2.498] that Hamlet begins to see this well-known and specially
requested section in quite a new light, and asks himself the questions with
which he begins his soliloquy:

> Is it not monstrous that this Player here,
> But in a Fiction, in a dream of Passion,
> Could force his soul so to his whole conceit,
> That from her workings, all his visage warmed;
> Tears in he eyes, distraction in's Aspect,
> A broken voice, and his whole Function suiting
> With Forms, to his Conceit? [2.2.551]

This corresponds with Polonius' report, "Look where he has not turned his
colour, and has tears in's eyes" [2.2.519].

Once we open ourselves to a backward shift in time frame for a soliloquy,
we can reject the linear progression of naturalism, within which Hamlet must
be seen having certain experiences, and then be overheard thinking about those
experiences. Instead, we can view the convention of the soliloquy as, in effect,
a break in the play during which a central character comes to us and says, "I
bet you were wondering what on earth has been going on in my brain for the
sequence of events you've just seen, right? Well, here's a taste. Remember
when I was quietly watching the First Player performing and he started to
weep? This is what was going on in my head. And when I'm done, you'll
have a clue as to why I asked the First Player about *The Murder of Gonzago*!"

Let us now take this idea and apply it to a more compelling example. In
the second scene of the play Hamlet is silent for the first sixty-five lines. After
a brief exchange with his mother and new stepfather, Hamlet has his first
soliloquy. Therefore, the first appearance of the title character is as a silent
auditor of the combined eulogy and marriage announcement made by Claudius:

> Though yet of *Hamlet* our dear Brothers death
> The memory be green: and that it us befitted
> To bear our hearts in grief, and our whole Kingdom
> To be contracted in one brow of woe:
> Yet so farr hath Discretion fought with Nature,
> That we with wisest sorrow think on him,
> Together with remembrance of our selves.
> Therefore our sometimes Sister, now our Queen,
> Th'Imperiall Jointress of this warlike State,
> Have we, as 'twere, with a defeated joy,

With one Auspicious, and one Dropping eye,
With mirth in Funeral, and with Dirge in Marriage,
In equal Scale weighing Delight and Dole
Taken to Wife; nor have we herein barred
Your better Wisdoms, which have freely gone
With this affair along, for all our Thanks. [1.2.1]

Now let us consider how Hamlet's soliloquy. As he silently listens to Claudius's opening lines, might he be thinking:

That it should come to this:
But two months dead: Nay, not so much; not two,
So excellent a King, that was to this
Hyperion to a Satyr: so loving to my Mother,
That he might not beteem the winds of heaven
Visit her face too roughly. Heaven and Earth
Must I remember: why she would hang on him,
As if increase of Appetite had grown
By what it fed on; and yet within a month?
Let me not think on't: Frailty, thy name is woman.
A little Month, or ere those shoes were old,
With which she followed my poor Fathers body
Like *Niobe*, all tears. Why she, even she.
(O Heaven! A beast that wants discourse of Reason
Would have mourned longer) married with mine Uncle,
My Fathers Brother: but no more like my Father,
Then I to *Hercules*. Within a Month?
Ere yet the salt of most unrighteous Tears
Had left the flushing of her galled eyes,
She married. O most wicked speed, to post
With such dexterity to Incestuous sheets:
It is not, nor it cannot come to good.
But break my heart, for I must hold my tongue. [1.2.137]

There is of course no reason why, in his soliloquy, Hamlet might not be putting into words at last a large number of barely-formed observations and reactions, so that they are fresh and new at the moment when he is finally alone to say them. However, something quite remarkable happens when we overlay the two speeches and imagine the public oration of Claudius balanced by the silent thoughts of Hamlet in italics:

That it should come to this:
Though yet of *Hamlet* our dear Brothers death
But two months dead:
The memory be green: *Nay, not so much; not two,*

and that it us befitted
So excellent a King,
To bear our hearts in grief,   *that was to this*
Hyperion to a Satyr:
and our whole Kingdom
To be contracted in one brow of woe: *so loving to my Mother,*
That he might not beteen the winds of heaven
Visit her face too roughly.
Yet so far hath Discretion fought with Nature,   *Heaven and Earth*
That we with wisest sorrow think on him,
Must I remember:
Together with remembrance of our selves.   *why she would hang on him,*
As if increase of Appetite had grown
By what it fed on;
Therefore our sometimes Sister,   *and yet within a month?*
now our Queen,
Let me not think on't:
Th'Imperiall Jointress of this warlike State,   *Frailty, thy name is woman.*
Have we, as 'twere, with a defeated joy,
A little Month, or ere those shoes were old,
With which she followed my poor Fathers body
With one Auspicious, and one Dropping eye,
Like Niobe, all tears.
With mirth in Funeral,   *Why she, even she.*
(O Heaven! A beast that wants discourse of
Reason
Would have mourned longer)
and with Dirge in Marriage,   *married with mine Uncle,*
My Fathers Brother: but no more like my
Father,
Then I to Hercules. Within a Month?
In equal Scale weighing Delight and Dole
Ere yet the salt of most unrighteous Tears
Had left the flushing of her galled eyes,
Taken to Wife;   *She married.*
nor have we herein barred
Your better Wisdoms,   *O most wicked speed, to post*
With such dexterity to Incestuous sheets:
which have freely gone
With this affair along,   *It is not, nor it cannot come to good.*
for all our Thanks.
But break my heart, for I must hold my tongue.

Not every soliloquy lends itself to this sort of overlapping, but those that do, if rescripted and rehearsed once or twice in counterpoint, are revealed to serve a double function, not only of giving shape to the silent presence of the protagonist in the earlier scene, but also of sharpening the unspoken relationships he has with those who can read his mind through his facial expressions, his posture, and in his eyes.

RELATIONSHIPS

> Since my dear Soul was Mistress of my choice,
> And could of men distinguish, her election
> Hath sealed thee for her self.
>
> Hamlet [*Hamlet* 3.2.63]

Another area for negotiation by the modern actor is the relationships between the characters. Contemporary acting training and play writing conspire to lock a modern actor's eyes firmly upon this aspect of human experience; in the plays of Shakespeare, we can find ourselves struggling to make sense of the action of a play if the relationships therein are our primary focus.

A reorientation is required in the reading of the plays of Shakespeare, because the contribution of relationship to the overall impact of the play is quite different. Furthermore, the way relationships are expressed follows a different set of theatrical conventions.

Let me make this point by comparing Sam Shepherd's *Fool for Love* with Shakespeare's *Romeo and Juliet* and *Hamlet*, or, more specifically, the relationships between Romeo and Juliet and Hamlet and Ophelia. Shepherd's examination of the complex relationship between a man and a woman shows us the two interacting in two sixty-minute acts. During the interaction, the context within which the relationship exists is clarified for us, by factual information that emerges in the dialogue that clarifies why they interact the way they do. This is a tour de force for modern actors, who develop and then present to an audience a relationship that draws out of the characters, and the actors, varied and strong emotions. Not much happens that could be called a plot, but a great deal happens that involves striking actions and compelling acting.

In contrast, Romeo and Juliet have one brief moment together at the party, the wonderful balcony scene, the brief exchange before the marriage, the rushed farewell after their wedding night, and the horrific near-miss as each embraces the other's body in the Capulet's family vault. Total number of lines of dialogue between them, in which we cannot count the finale: 121. Actors who have played the roles will tell you that it is not easy to develop a relationship of great complexity in such short encounters. Instead, the images of the two young lovers are established vividly and then the story moves on to other interactions. Romeo spends more time on stage in the company of his male companions than with Juliet, and his relationship with Benvolio, Mercutio, and the Friar are as complex and detailed as with Juliet, as is hers with her Nurse.

Hamlet and Ophelia have an even smaller canvas upon which to paint the nature of the relationship. She discusses things with her brother and father; she reports a nasty incident when Hamlet scared her with his "antic disposition" and then finally we see them together in what we call the "nunnery scene," where he berates her and she weeps for the destruction of the wonderful man she used to know. They have a few embarrassing exchanges before the play begins wherein Hamlet hopes to catch the conscience of the king, and then he kills her father and is banished, she goes mad, and Hamlet returns just in time to fight with her brother in her grave, shouting, "I loved Ophelia." Well, we just have to take his word for it, because the actors have not been given a love scene to play.

Actors who have been trained to find the core of a character in the relationships that dominate the play are very much at a loss to find the enduring truth of these lovers without love scenes or, in the case of Romeo and Juliet, of these characters with just love scenes. However, if we transfigure our modern concern with relationships into an Elizabethan mold, we might be able to find a way for these vivid portraits of individuals connected by ties of passion and tenderness to work on the modern stage for and with modern actors.

Several interrelated concepts will help us here. First, we will see how the complexity of the patterns of relationships, rather than the complexity of any given relationship, fuels the dramatic engine of these plays. Next, we will see how conventions of staging require an actor's focus to shift from subtle, intimate interactions to larger-scale invasions, retreats, sieges, and other military-style engagements. Finally, we will consider the potential of Jungian archetypes and contemporary nonrealist acting styles to assist an actor in developing and presenting Shakespeare's characters.

Shakespeare's England was a place of elaborate public rituals used in part to reinforce the strict sense of hierarchy that kept every member of society clearly located. The physical relationship between any given individual and another was an overt manifestation of the relative status of each. Status could be established by several means: position in line, as in a procession or the order in which one entered or left a room; distance, as in relative proximity or distance from the head table or the baptismal font; comfort, as in who was able to sit and who was allowed to keep the head covered and warm in the presence of a dignitary; and silence, as in who was allowed to speak, in what order and at what length, during a formal occasion.

The enactment of fictional events on the platform stage of the Globe quite naturally made use of the indicators of status that would be familiar to everyone in the audience. When every member of the acting company appeared on stage in one of the court scenes, you didn't need a program to figure out who was playing the ruling monarch, who represented the various levels of the nobility, and who were the more humble courtiers in the room. The presence of an outsider, like Joan of Arc, called La Pucelle by Shakespeare in the first part of *Henry VI*, or the Bastard in *King John*, would be strikingly felt by the violation of the expected staging of hierarchy. Joan addressed her monarch intimately and directly, and so challenges the emotional distance expected between a crown prince and a shepherdess. The Bastard hangs around making rude comments while the kings of France and England negotiate a piece: again, an appropriate gap between the powerful and the disenfranchised is bridged.

This concept of patterns of relative proximity, comfort, and silence are available for the presentation of relationships that exist outside the political sphere. Let us have a look at what we might call the hierarchy of feeling charting the relative relationships between central and supporting characters in a few tragedies and comedies. In order to do this, we need to position the characters in a physical space in a manner that reflects the relative emotional distance or intimacy they have with the central character. In plays where there might arguably be two central characters, we may find that we need two different diagrams.

Working on the metaphor of the court, we will position our protagonist on the throne. Close by might be counsellors and favorites who do not have a high social status but have achieved proximity because of some other service they offer the one on the throne. Then, there are the equivalent of the nobles of the land, who are accorded proximity because of inherited land and title, with whom the monarch may have an alliance, a rapport, a trust, or not. Ranged round the perimeter are those many individuals who ensure that the business of the court continues; for our purposes, these are the carriers of the plot. There is room also for a court jester, for a representative of the church, for foreign ambassadors, and for the outsider who challenges the hierarchy briefly. And of course these relationships are not static. There is an initial configuration, and then as the play progresses different courtiers are invited closer or pushed further away by the protagonist/monarch.

Let us begin with Hamlet. As the play begins, he sits on the throne with his mother and uncle holding the accepted positions of the hereditary nobles. They have a right to be intimate with him, by nature of their bond of kinship. Similarly privileged are longtime friends Rosencrantz and Guildenstern, though they have yet to arrive in the play. They have every right to assume intimacy. Horatio does not so assume. When he greets Hamlet in the second scene of the play, he does so quite formally; it is Hamlet who initiates deeper sharing. So we can imagine Horatio as counsellor or familiar, chosen from the lower ranks and brought ahead of the hereditary nobility to stand behind the monarch's throne.

Where is Ophelia? Her father and brother make it clear that she has no right to expect a relationship with the crown prince. At some time before the play began, she was drawn much closer to the throne, but she is pushed away by other concerns and pulled away by the men in her family. And yet she does not recede into the lesser courtiers surrounding the central players. She hovers and shifts, first closer, then thrust back, then closer again, then pushed away. No wonder the poor girl goes mad.

Polonius is a character who presumes upon proximity far in excess of what the protagonist intends or desires. He is like the courtier who appears to be very connected and "in the know" who is in fact quite outside the real sphere of influence and so repeatedly breaks the rules, by moving in too close, until pushed back, by talking when he should be silent, and by being relaxed and comfortable when his life is in danger. He dies a most ignoble death, totally unprepared for the role he is to play in Hamlet's court of personal relationships. His primary function, after his death, is to be an exiled agitator of Laertes and Ophelia, who retain their place in Hamlet's life after his death.

Hamlet in fact makes use of several characters who think they have a relationship of relative intimacy; this is one of the less pleasing aspects of his character. In order to isolate and destroy Claudius, he must push everyone but Horatio away. He draws Ophelia to him for their one intimate exchange, and then expels her from any proximity. He invites his mother into a closeness of interaction greater than any other character, but for one scene only, and then she must return to the more distant relationship of her kinship. There is also a brief encounter with Laertes, who otherwise holds a position of some distance from Hamlet. It is almost like a sudden, intimate encounter with a foreign dignitary, possible only because they are about to be separated permanently, by death.

Where does the Ghost fit in Hamlet's imaginary internal throne room? The contrast between the vast distance that separates them in death, and the extreme intimacy of the exchange, combined with the natural ties of blood, could be physically represented by a noble courtier who visits court rarely, but when he does he alone of all the nobles gains immediate private access to the monarch.

Now, let us have a look at the central characters in a different setting but involved in a similar pattern of relationships. On our throne we will put Rosalind, and surround her with the other characters from *As You Like It*.

At the beginning of the play, the person closest to the throne, relaxed and talkative and even sitting down beside the queen, is Celia. By the end of the play, she is almost completely silent, though still close enough to receive regular bulletins that are for her ear only. Orlando, who arrives in Rosalind's imagined internal throne room early in the play, takes his natural position as love interest close to the throne, receiving many opportunities to interact with the monarch, but we never feel him achieve the equality of status accorded Celia at the beginning of the play. He is never awarded as intimate a glimpse of Rosalind's real feelings, he is never her equal in amount spoken, and in her presence his own needs are always secondary to hers.

ENTRANCES AND EXITS

They have their Exits and their Entrances.

Jaques [*AYLI* 2.7.141]

If we remove act and scene demarcations, which were added after Shake-speare's death when the publisher of the first folio decided to bring his plays into line with the five-act structure of classical drama, then very much in fash-ion, and instead revert to what in the theatre are called "french scenes," a new scene beginning with the entrance and/or exit of every character, we discover the true shape of the plays in performance. Modern theatre practice demands at least one interval during which patrons can visit rest rooms and the bar, thus increasing their viewing pleasure if diminishing the forward movement of the dramatic action. The location of the interval(s) is arbitrary, and each pro-duction solves the conundrum to suit the taste of that director and producer. Some opt for the cliff-hanger commercial break style and cut off the action on the brink of some momentous event. Leaving the auditorium is a more sig-nificant reaction to a break than simply changing the channel or turning off the television, and these cliff-hanger intervals can prove trying for the actors who must maintain energy and focus during the break.

In Shakespeare's open-air theatre, it appears that patrons simply stepped outside to relieve themselves against the wall of the theatre, and solicited re-freshments from the merchants circulating among the audience throughout the performance. A different shaping of dramatic event would be required to keep the attention of a crowd that was not conditioned to sit quietly in the dark until cued for laughter or applause.

Even when performing at court the players could count on the commentary of the wiseacres in the crowd, if the performance scenes in *A Midsummer Night's Dream* and *Love's Labour's Lost* are any indication. Claudius's interruption of "The Murder of Gonzago" in *Hamlet* bears a remarkable resemblance to a reported incident when Elizabeth interrupted a performance by calling for lights and leaving the hall. That's what I call a bad review.

We can feel the untheatricality of the act and scene divisions if we look at the transition at the end of the closet scene in *Hamlet*. Gertrude has just endured the interview with her son, which included the murder of Polonius, whom Hamlet took to be the king himself, and the appearance of the ghost, which only Hamlet could see. Hamlet leaves dragging the body of Polonius, saying, "Good night Mother." The next speaker is the King, who says, "There's matter in these sights. / These profound heaves / You must translate; 'Tis fit we understand them. / Where is your son?" The 1604 quarto has Gertrude say, "Bestow this place on us a little while" before saying "Ah mine own Lord, what have I seen tonight." Her speech begins, "Ah my good Lord, what have I seen tonight," in the First Folio.

If there is anything in the stage setting at this point to indicate the queen's private chamber, it must either be removed before the king can address her, or he and two others, usually Rosencrantz and Guildenstern, must enter the queen's closet. If, however, there is just the bare stage, then the location merely shifts in and out of focus; when it needs to be the queen's room, it is, but now it is some other place where people like Rosencrantz and Guildenstern might be expected to be present.

The next question is: Does Gertrude exit along with Hamlet, only to wait a moment for Claudius and the others to enter and establish themselves before running in, or do the others enter directly to her? The first quarto has the stage direction, "Exit Hamlet with the dead body. Enter the King and Lordes." The second quarto has an "Exit" immediately after Hamlet's last line, then, "Enter King, and Queene, with Rosencraus and Guyldensterne." The folio has "Exit Hamlet tugging in Polonius," followed by "Enter King," but the very large Act Four demarcation intervenes.

The *Riverside* takes this combined evidence and concludes the last scene of the third act with, "Exeunt [severally, Hamlet tugging in Polonius]." The first scene of the next act begins with the stage direction, "Enter King and Queen with Rosencrantz and Guildenstern."

Is the action continuous from 3.4 and 4.1, or does Gertrude leave her private room by another door and then enter into wherever Claudius is, sighing and heaving profoundly? If the latter, then her entrance bears a remarkable similarity to the one made by Ophelia in 2.1, hard on the exit of Reynaldo, in order to tell her father, "O my lord, my lord, I have been so affrighted." But Polonius's long discussion with Reynaldo created a scene into which Ophelia could enter. To adhere to the transition suggested in the *Riverside*, Gertrude would leave only to appear again immediately. If she entered with Claudius, we could imagine one offstage sequence; if he entered through one door and she another, we could imagine a slightly different story. The effect seems to be similar to a jump cut in in a film: we see Hamlet pulling out the body, then we cut to Gertrude bursting in on Claudius with his lords.

Modern directors solve such transitions with a variety of strategies, and actors will report on the immensity of the difference it makes to the playing of what is called 4.1 if (a) only Hamlet leaves and Gertrude remains, so that the king comes in to her asking why she is sighing and heaving, or (b) Gertrude also leaves only to return again after the shortest of pauses, perhaps only to give time for a change of setting and the entrance of Claudius and his lords so that she can arrive to interrupt them. Both options work to drive forward the dramatic action of the play; what does not work is placing an act division at this point in the play. Imagine, if you will, that you have been assigned by a teacher the reading of the play act by act. The first act takes you through to the charging of Hamlet by the ghost, and of Hamlet's companions by Hamlet. There is a natural break in the action there, and all goes well. The reading of the second act takes you to the planning of the mousetrap, and that excellent cliff-hanger, "The play's the thing wherein I'll catch the conscience of the king!" However, breaking there and taking fifteen minutes or a week off from the play severely undercuts the power of the beginning of the next scene, wherein Gertrude and Claudius pump their two spies Rosencrantz and Guildenstern to see what they've learned about Hamlet. However, the play sets it up so that the last scene of the second act is clearly the day before the scenes of the third act, so a division there has some logic. Taking a break between acts three and four, however, would be disastrous. The natural break occurs after the lords have chased Hamlet around the castle, brought him to Claudius, and the two enemies have faced off against each other. Act four, scene four, which gives us a glimpse of Fortinbras and contains still another of Hamlet's famous soliloquies, "How all occasions do inform against me," only appears in the second quarto. In the fifth scene included in this act we launch into the terrible portrait of Ophelia's madness. Surely, this is the logical place to insert an act division, if one is needed? The announcement of her death is a logical place to end this act, as in the folio.

Sometimes an entrance establishes a clear shift in location: when we move from the palace to the graveyard at the beginning of Act Five of *Hamlet*, we know where we are because that two characters are clearly not courtiers and are talking about making graves. Sometimes an entrance establishes a clear shift in time: when Polonius sends Reynaldo with money for Laertes in Paris we know some time must have passed since Laertes left Denmark in the third scene of the play.

Sometimes, however, the entrance of a new character may or may not indicate a shift in location or the passage of time. If such information matters to the telling of the story, it is usually, but not always, included in the dialogue; every actor knows that the geography and the time schemes of these plays simply do not add up. How much time has passed since your last appearance on stage? Is this location one in which you are comfortable or ill at ease? Are we in a public or private space? Have you had time to think about things, or are you caught up in the heat of action?

The company of actors can usually agree upon a time scheme and a geography of locales that is workable and credible, though sometimes they have to resort to the assumption that a specific time reference is inaccurate. So when Hamlet says to Ophelia, "What should a man do, but be merry. For look you how cheerfully my Mother looks, and my Father died within these two hours," and Ophelia replies, "Nay, 'tis twice two months, my Lord," how long is it since the first scene of the play? In his first soliloquy, Hamlet says that Gertrude married Claudius within a month of the funeral. It is not clear, however, what sort of a gap might have existed between the death of the old king and his formal entombment. It is also possible that Hamlet is exaggerating his case slightly, thinking not of thirty days but rather a short time, "a little month," which becomes "two hours" when talking to Ophelia. What is clear is that time has passed between the instructions of the Ghost and the mousetrap, and the actors who need to make some specific choices about exactly how long and just what they have been doing in the interim have some latitude within which to set the time frame.

Here is another example. *Othello* has a rather strange set of signals about time, but it is possible to play the entire action in Cyprus as taking place within twenty-four hours. If we imagine that Othello and Desdemona are denied their wedding night by the arrival of Brabantio and his armed men, and if we imagine that Othello sails immediately to Cyprus on his command ship while Desdemona journeys on another, then when they are reunited in Cyprus in the first scene of the second act they have yet to consummate their relationship. Again, their time together is interrupted by a brawl, and Othello discharges Cassio; it is during their first day together as a married couple that Desdemona resolves to plead for Cassio and Iago plants the seeds of jealousy. It is late in that first day as husband and wife when he strikes her in front of the embassy from Venice, and he murders her just twenty-four hours after consummating their marriage.

It is also possible to mark the transition from loving newlyweds to jealousy and murder over a longer period of time. So many scenes could mark another day, or a change of season, so that the request from Othello that Desdemona put her wedding sheets on her bed could arouse in her a hope that their happiness together might be restored after a long break.

The positioning of an interval or two serves to elongate the actors' and audiences' experience of the duration of the action and, if well placed, can allow for everyone to return to the world of the play refreshed and even transformed by the break, as Hamlet is by his time away from the play (he does not appear in 4.4, 4.5, and 4.6). Something quite wonderful happens, however, if everyone can endure the flow of action without a break.

An interesting facet of the language becomes apparent when running the plays without any breaks between scenes. The ending of the previous scene often informs the scene that follows in interesting ways. Therefore, I always suggest to an actor making an entrance that he listen carefully to the words leading up to his cue, to find the emotional energy compelling his entrance.

Sometimes the absence of a scene break serves to confuse the modern actor, because the conventions of naturalism are freely violated in the fast-paced forward movement of the dramatic action. In the first scene of the second act of *Richard II* a great deal occurs. Old John of Gaunt dies, having in his final words pronounced many wise and wonderful things. Richard promptly confiscates his estates that should rightfully go to Bolingbroke, and announces his intention of leaving immediately for the Irish wars. Everyone leaves the stage except a few lords, who discuss what has just occurred, and then announce that Bolingbroke is coming to England to reclaim his confiscated lands.

Either Bolingbroke sailed for England before his father died, making his self-justification a lie, or we have just jumped an indefinite period of time: the duration of a message travelling to Bolingbroke, the soliciting of eight tall ships and three thousand soldiers from his French supporters, and the return sea voyage of the messenger who brings word of their embarkation and imminent arrival.

Clearly, within the conventions of Shakespeare's theatre, such shifts in time and even space are possible. A modern actor's realist predisposition will actively work against the demands of the play.

As an alternative to a clear and credible answer to the question of how much time has elapsed, where have I been since last I appeared on stage, and where are we now, the modern actor can substitute an alternative cue to action. This comes from the conventions of Shakespeare's theatre that were built around exits and entrances.

SHIFTING TIME AND PLACE

> Antres vast, and Deserts idle,
> Rough Quarries, Rocks, Hills whose heads touch heaven.
> Othello [Othello 1.3.140]

If you go to the computerized library catalogue and seek books on Shakespeare and "time," you will find a good number of dusty discussions of how Shakespeare shapes our perception of time in these plays. These are interesting studies, but most come to the conclusion, if they consider the plays in the theatre at all, that the rush of events as experienced in performance is such that the audience members simply do not notice the vague or even conflicting references to the passage of time.

Even if such a conclusion were valid, it is of little help to an actor exploring the plays as she were on the inside. It's important to know how long it has been since you were last on stage, particularly if your best acting is unlocked by close attention to the given circumstances of the situation. Can a modern actor find a realistic equivalent to build a bridge to the way time is framed in Shakespeare's theatre?

First, we have to clarify just how time "works" in Shakespeare's plays. Scholars have dissected the plays and charted the references to time, but probably the most significant insight comes from Shakespeare himself, out of the mouth of Rosalind in *As You Like It*, "Time travels in divers paces with divers persons." This gives Rosalind an excuse to demonstrate her quick thinking as Orlando puts her through her paces: Who does time amble with, trot with, gallop with, and stand still with? If time is a horse, anyone who has ridden can tell you that the sensation of a walk, a trot, and a lope are hugely different than what it feels like to sit on a horse's back when it is standing still.

The psychological truth of Rosalind's commonplace is immediately recognizable to us all. We've all had situations of looking up at the clock and saying, "Oh, no, it can't be that late already! Where's the time gone!" And we've all looked at a clock and said, "Only five minutes gone! This is taking forever!"

Suddenly, vague or contradictory references to time become metaphors for how time is felt. The events that take place in the forest during *A Midsummer Night's Dream* are clearly contained in a single night. The title tells us that. The marking of dusk with the arrival of the fairies and of dawn with their departure, all according to folk legend, tell us that. However, the characters emerge in the morning light so changed, so transformed, that it is as if they had slept away days, weeks, years. And somehow, the four days marked to pass between the first scene and the marriage have slipped by. Scholars can tell us how Shakespeare creates this contradiction, but actors can make this slippage real, by focussing on the difference between dreamtime and awake time.

Have you ever had a very high fever, filled with strange dreams and fleeting moments of awareness? Then, as you heal, you realize that many more days have passed than you realized. I once was rushed into hospital in the fall, and walked out again into winter. Ten days and a change of season had passed me by; I was able to mark consciously the passing of only a few days.

A similar slippage occurs for me in jet travel. I get on the plane and it is clearly a specific time of day, even if I don't look at a clock. The sky is light or dark. People are just starting up or slowing down. I'm fresh or tired. Then there is a strange passage of time in an enclosed space. I'm aware of getting more and more tired, but if I doze, it's the sort of sleep I have during the day. Food is brought at intervals that connect neither with my stomach nor my sense of time passing. This passage ends, and I arrive in a new place, at a new time, where the sky is light or dark, and people are just starting up or slowing down. If someone told me that three months had passed, I'd find it no more or less bizarre than being told that it is 6 A.M. local time the day before I left.

It often happens that characters travel long distances and we pick them up again once they've arrived. The actors in these roles are curious: How long was I on the road? A little bit of research reveals that, travelling by foot, by horse, by boat from place to place would take four days, three months, six hours, whatever. But the minute you start imagining long waits and all of the tedious exhaustion of travel between scenes, the forward-moving energy of the play collapses. However, if a journey were not important, why mention it at all? Clearly, the psychological experience of travelling, of exhaustion and stress, of dislocation and disorientation, is important. But the focus of the actor can zoom in on exactly the aspect of the experience that interests Shakespeare, and fuse the other "real" aspects into the equally real "slippage" that is the inevitable result of the exhaustion, stress, dislocation, and disorientation.

If Shakespeare shows us characters midjourney, then the midjourney "feel" is what is important. For example, in *The Winter's Tale*, we encounter Cleomenes and Dion on their journey home from the Oracle at Delphi to Leontes's court in Sicilia. The last speech immediately preceding established that they have landed and are hurrying to court, and that they have been gone twenty-three days, which is judged to be a good speed.

Cleomenes: The Climate's delicate, the Air most sweet,
          Fertile the Isle, the Temple much surpassing
          The common praise it bears.

Dion: I shall report,
          For most it caught me, the Celestial Habits,
          (Methinks I so should term them) and the reverence
          Of the grave Wearers. O, the Sacrifice,
          How ceremonious, solemn, and unearthly
          It was i' th' Offering!

Cleomenes: But of all, the burst
          And the ear-deafening Voice o' th' Oracle,
          Kin to Joves Thunder, so surprised my Sense,
          That I was nothing.

Dion: If th' event o' th' Journey
          Prove as successful to the Queen (O be't so)
          As it hath been to us, rare, pleasant, speedy,
          The time is worth the use on't.

Cleomenes: Great Apollo
          Turn all to the best: these Proclamations,
          So forcing faults upon Hermione,
          I little like.

Dion: The violent carriage of it
          Will clear, or end the Business, when the Oracle
          (Thus by Apollo's great Divine sealed up)
          Shall the Contents discover: something rare
          Even then will rush to knowledge. Go: fresh Horses,
          And gracious be the issue. [3.1.1]

We think we know exactly where we are when the messengers enter, because
we've just been presented with an image of them hurrying to court. So when
Cleomenes talks about the delicate climate and sweet air of the fertile island,
it sounds like a travelogue about Sicilia, until he mentions the temple. Delphi
is not on an island, but even if it were, these two men are not there now, are
they?

Dion's response seems to explain why Cleomenes is using the present tense:
they are planning how to describe the events they observed at Delphi. Dion
is going to describe his most vivid memory, of the clothing and ceremonial
actions of the ritual sacrifice. As we've already heard, Cleomenes liked the
area around the temple, but now he talks about the horrendous sound of the
oracle.

Now we know where we are in the reality of the moment. These are two
tourists, sharing favorite memories of the trip in the final moments of the
journey home. They even discuss the journey itself and no complaints are
there: an exotic trip, minimal stress, and "speedy."

Do they mean that it has taken less time than they'd expected? That matches

Leontes's comment. Do they also mean that they have not had the sensation of time ambling or standing still, the boring waiting and sheer endurance required of the traveller? It will have been time well spent, they conclude, so there is a sense of having given up time, a precious commodity, in exchange for something of worth, they hope. However it turns out, there will be a sensation of rushing, of speeding up to the point of surprised senses.

A quick look at a map and some speculation about land and sea travel suggests that the call for horses at the end of the scene is not particularly "real" for Delphi as it actually is: the temple is a steep climb up a mountainside from a port, and Leontes's capital is presented to us as a coastal town as well. The messengers would have no need for "fresh horses" in that reality. But the call for fresh horses summons up another reality, that of travel across the English countryside, in stages, with an exchange of horses at each post. These sites also featured taverns and inns so that travellers could relieve themselves, take refreshment, and rest overnight.

Why have they paused, if they are in such a rush? They are only an hour from the court, and yet they needed fresh horses? Why would they need horses anyway? Couldn't they walk from the port to the castle?

But Shakespeare wasn't concerned about those aspects of travel. He wanted to capture the very special sensation that occurs when there is a break in the tedium of travel, which feels timeless because the body's senses are so consumed by the physical experience of moving from one place to another, and because of the break the traveller has a moment to remember backward and think forward. Such breaks don't happen just outside the door of the palace. Shakespeare has suggested a scene with one last rushing horse ride from their destination. If a modern actor draws upon personal travel experiences, squeezed through a sieve of historical information and aided by imagination, it is possible to set aside concerns of "real" time just as one does when experiencing "travel time" in reality.

DOUBLING

> One face, one voice, one habit, and two persons,
> A natural Perspective, that is, and is not.
>
> Orsino [*12th Night* 5.1.216]

There are many theories about the doubling Shakespeare and his contemporary playwrights would have expected and facilitated in the staging of their plays. Modern companies also undertake doubling and for similar reasons: it seems foolish to pay the salaries of a very large company so that some actors can appear in just one scene.

Some doublings are particularly evocative. Cordelia disappears before the fool's first entrance; she returns to the action after the Fool disappears. Shakespearean scholars feel very strongly that these two roles could not have been doubled, as the members of Shakespeare's company who specialized in playing the women or the fools did not cross over to other lines of business. But when Lear says, over the dead body of Cordelia, "And my poor fool is hanged!" it is difficult not to imagine the pay off of that double casting in a modern production.

Theseus and Oberon are never on stage together; nor are Hippolyta and Titania. Comparisons between these two sets of monarchs are inevitable, and many a modern production has double cast the roles and enjoyed playing with images of Theseus/Oberon and Hippolyta/Titania as inverted images or two halves of human experience. Scholars don't much like this doubling either, and in fact very few of the doublings that scholars suggest pay off in acting terms, except for the smooth running of the logistics of mounting a big-cast play with a small company.

Quite often, a doubled character has the privilege of discussing the other role. Oberon and Titania have a few gossipy comments to make about Oberon and Titania, and it is gleefully delicious watching the hyperrational Theseus expound on the stories of the lovers in the woods, if the actor has just finished playing the extraordinary Oberon.

Doubling will always make sense to theatre people because they understand that if you have two people in the company who can really *do* king and queen well, you don't ask them to sit around for the middle section of the play, but rather put them in front of the audience to carry as much of the story as possible. Similarly, if you have a strong supporting actor, you don't write him out midway through the play unless you plan to bring him back in a crucial role. The absence of certain characters in key scenes is thus explained. In *Romeo and Juliet*, Benvolio does not appear after the death of Mercutio because he is needed to play other characters; he could play almost any of the supporting characters in the second half of the play. Mercutio is more problematical: on the one hand, he is such a striking character that he'd have to be completely transformed to remain firmly dead in the minds of the audience; on the other hand, the role would have been undertaken by a leading player and it seems foolish to waste that talent for the first, fourth, and fifth acts of the play. Some scholars have suggested that Mercutio was doubled with the Prince, thereby making powerful the point that the Prince himself loses a close relative when Mercutio is killed. You will notice that Mercutio manages to get off stage before dying while Tybalt's body is still on stage when the Prince enters: in just such a fashion is a doubling challenge solved.

These doublings suggest something of a strategy for use by modern actors. Rather than expending all one's energy in disguising oneself so that the two characters are never confused, explore the possibility that the similarity is in fact intentional. Gratiano is a minor character who appears at the end of *Othello*. Among other things, he announces the death of Brabantio, Desdemona's disapproving father. It turns out that he is in fact Brabantio's brother. Perhaps the two characters are very much the same age because they are played by the same actor? Is Gratiano's comment on the terrible events in the final scene all the more significant because his voice and manner recall Brabantio for us? By and large, his function is relatively neutral: he clarifies what is happening on and off stage, with such lines as "He's gone, but his wife's killed," and "Torments will ope your lips." His one big speech would be enhanced massively if he had also played Brabantio:

> Poor Desdemona:
> I am glad thy Father's dead,
> Thy Match was mortal to him: and pure grief
> Shore his old thread in twain. Did he live now,
> This sight would make him do a desperate turn:
> Yea, curse his better Angel from his side,
> And fall to Reprobation. [5.2.204]

If the actor playing Gratiano in a modern production was not also cast as Brabantio, there is no reason for him not to take advantage of the very special resonance that these lines might have, by imagining the closest possible personal relationship to the other character. For example, they might be close associates, very similar in education and class, intimate friends, or, if Gratiano is to be played by a far younger man, Brabantio might have been his mentor or guardian. Any imaginary "backstory" is possible. At this moment in the play, Gratiano stands in Brabantio's place, and everyone on stage will benefit from seeing the one character strongly reflected in the other.

The Theatrical Traditions of Personification

O, good my Lord, you have lost a friend indeed:
And I dare swear, you borrow not that face
Of seeming sorrow, it is sure your own.

Gloucester [2HIV 5.2.27]

In this manner does one brother comfort another on the loss of the king their father in the final moments of the second part of *Henry IV*. A moment's thought will clarify the meaning of what is said: this is real, not fake, sorrow. But what has been said, precisely? What is the face of seeming sorrow, and how can anyone borrow a face?

The answer to these questions rests in the theatrical conventions that dominated the theatre of the generation immediately preceding Shakespeare's. In the popular morality plays of the late medieval period, actors played characters with names like Good Deeds, Knowledge, Friendship, Gluttony, and Repentance. These plays were known as psychomachia, and they told the story of the life's journey of the central character, Everyman or Mankind, and dramatized philosophical concepts and psychological experiences through the conventions of personification.

A quick look at medieval morality plays will demonstrate the theatricality of the older tradition that saw actors playing attributes. In *The Castle of Perseverance*, for example, which dramatizes the metaphorical battle between good and evil for the soul of man, one of the attacking troupes is captained by Flesh and boasts the ferocious warriors Gluttony, Lechery, and Sloth. Gluttony has set aside his customary flagon of wine to wave a firebrand, Lechery carries the coals she uses to make a fire in the posterior of the castle, and Sloth sets to work diverting the grace-giving water from around the castle. These three are defeated by Abstinence, Chastity, and Industry, the last distracting Sloth from a job that bears too close a resemblance to hard labor to hold his attention. Not surprisingly, the most interesting characters are the vices; the virtues win the day but don't have much theatrical appeal.

In *Mankynde*, the most memorable roles are, once again, a quartet of personifications of worldly temptation: Nought, New-Guise, Nowadays, and Mischief. Nought is a fool who knows nothing and cares for nothing and creates great comedy in the process. New-Guise and Nowadays are concerned solely with the latest fashions in dress, behavior, and attitude, and allow for delicious satire of the gallants of the day. Mischief is, as his name suggests, an energetic troublemaker ideally suited to driving the engine of the plot as Mankynde is tempted, falls, and narrowly avoids losing his soul to eternal damnation.

We can see an overt example of theatrical personification, wherein a concept or an experience is given human form, in the first moments of the same play. The second part of *Henry IV* is introduced by a lone actor on stage, who announces:

> Open your Ears: For which of you will stop
> The vent of Hearing, when loud Rumour speaks?
> I, from the Orient, to the drooping West
> (Making the wind my Post-horse) still unfold
> The Acts commenced on this Ball of Earth.
> Upon my Tongue, continual Slanders ride,
> The which, in every Language I pronounce,
> Stuffing the Ears of men with false Reports:
> I speak of Peace, while covert Enmity
> (Under the smile of Safety) wounds the World:
> And who but Rumour, who but only I
> Make fearful Musters, and prepared Defence,
> Whiles the big year, swoln with some other griefs,
> Is thought with child, by the stern Tyrant, War,
> And no such matter? Rumour is a Pipe
> Blown by Surmises, Jealousies, Conjectures;
> And of so easy, and so plain a stop,
> That the blunt Monster, with uncounted heads,
> The still discordant, wavering Multitude,
> Can play upon it. But what need I thus
> My well-known Body to Anatomize
> Among my household? Why is Rumour here?
> I run before King Harrys victory,
> Who in a bloody field by Shrewsbury
> Hath beaten down young Hotspur, and his Troops,
> Quenching the flame of bold Rebellion,
> Even with the Rebels blood. But what mean I
> To speak so true at first? My office is

To noise abroad, that Harry Monmouth fell
Under the Wrath of Noble Hotspur's Sword:
And that the King, before the Douglas Rage
Stooped his Anointed head, as low as death.
This have I rumoured through the peasant-Towns,
Between that Royal Field of Shrewsbury,
And this Worm-eaten-Hole of ragged Stone,
Where Hotspurs Father, old Northumberland,
Lies crafty sick. The posts come tiring on,
And not a man of them brings other news
Than they have learned of Me. From Rumours Tongues,
They bring smooth-Comforts-false, worse than True-wrongs.

The history of the theatre provides us with many examples of overlapping theatrical conventions, something that we can witness in our own theatre even today. A cursory examination of new plays performed in the last year will reveal some "traditional," perhaps even "old-fashioned" offerings alongside those that are "innovative," "cutting edge," or "bizarre." Actors today must be equally comfortable performing retro-realism and mind-bending trendsetters.

We can imagine that Shakespeare's actors were equally flexible. They could proclaim themselves with, "Open your ears; for which of you will stop the vent of hearing when loud Rumour speaks?" or with "This is I, Hamlet the Dane" [5.1.257].

The cross-fertilization that occurs when theatre professionals work with a variety of theatrical conventions provides the rich soil in which a playwright like Shakespeare can flourish. Modern actors do not have access to this richness of tradition and variety of performance strategies. Instead, we must fashion some mixture of modern acting strategies that seems to suit best the challenges of playing characters like Rumour and Hamlet the Dane. However, an understanding of the elemental concepts of personification can become an invaluable tool for creating a modern actor's approach to Shakespearean characterization.

Let us return to Rumour's wonderful monologue. What we find is an entire company of characters. Notice the invitation to the listener to provide a human face to Continual Slanders, who ride Rumour's tongues. Picture impish ugly shrunken creatures saddling up the impatient, constantly moving arch of a horse-like tongue, preparing to ride fast and furious in every direction. Next we meet Covert Emnity and Smiling Safety. The first has a drawn sword with which to strike deep into Earth herself. Perhaps he hides behind a large cape, slinking along in the shadows, while Safety steps forward into the light to distract us with a warm embrace. The next character to walk onto the Rumour's imaginary stage is hugely pregnant. No one knows the father of Year's child, but Rumour is busy telling everyone that War himself, that stern tyrant, is the father. Will the father be like the son? Is she about to give birth to a monster? No, it is another, unnamed grief that will soon appear, perhaps the dread Famine. The next scene is a musical interlude, with four musicians playing a simple, single-stopped pipe. Three of the musicians are fairly normal looking: they are Surmises, Jealousies, and Conjectures. But the fourth is a strange creature with many heads, yet even this monster can play the simple pipe that Rumour provides.

The remainder of the speech describes the common aftermath of a medieval battle: the outcome is not known in fact for many days, even by those most directly involved in the conflict. As a result, the common populace is in a dangerous state of uncertainty, and the nobility is equally exposed to danger if decisions are made upon false information. In this section of the speech, Rumour uses his own name as a verb, to describe that familiar activity of gossip and word-of-mouth spreading, in this case, the exact opposite of what really transpired at the end of the previous play.

Let us look at another example, to see how the habitual use of personification is not, in fact, a literary device, but rather an invocation of a slightly old-fashioned theatrical convention.

In *All's Well That Ends Well*, the Countess discovers that Helena is in love with her son, Count Bertram. Helena's face reveals the truth, which the Countess observes as if it were a dumb show performed by actors:

> My fear hath catched your fondness! now I see
> The mystery of your loneliness, and find
> Your salt tears head, now to all sense 'tis gross:
> You love my son, invention is ashamed
> Against the proclamation of thy passion
> To say thou dost not: therefore tell me true,
> But tell me then, 'tis so, for look, thy cheeks
> Confess it th' one to th' other, and thine eyes
> See it so grossly shown in thy behaviors,
> That in their kind they speak it, only sin
> And hellish obstinacy tie thy tongue
> That truth should be suspected, speak, is't so? [1.3.170]

Who is in the cast of this production? We have two Cheeks who carry on a dialogue with each other. They are dressed in blushing red. The Eyes have a big speech. The Tongue is there as well, but two bad characters, called Sin and Obstinacy, dressed very much like devils, have tied her up so that Truth remains hidden, probably in a deep and secret place: the heart?

But other characters might have a role to play in this little drama or mystery play. There is Loneliness, who is the title character; this is her story. There is Invention, which earlier in the play had a prominent part but now, at the climactic moment when all is revealed, is hanging her head in shame. Across from her, with an accusatory declamation, stands Passion. All in all, a veritable crowd scene, suitable for such a revelation.

In fact, the gathering of characters, each with a distinct attitude and function, reminds me of the closing scene of many a play. For example, in the closing moments of *Measure for Measure* the Duke has gathered around him at the city gate not only the chief protagonists—Mariana, Isabella and Angelo—and secondary characters with a vested interest—the Provost, Escalus, and Lucio—but also a variety of others more recently introduced, for no clear reason, such as Friar Peter and Varrius, and one can presume whichever players the company could muster, representing citizens, lords, and perhaps even the whores of Mistress Overdone.

When Isabella kneels to cry out for justice, she addresses the Duke. He in turn offers Angelo as the embodiment of Justice; Isabella and the Duke know, as does the audience, that Angelo wears the face of seeming justice, hiding his true character.

PLAYING PERSONIFICATIONS

> I did never know so full a voice issue from so empty a heart: but the saying is true, The empty vessel makes the greatest sound, Bardolph and Nym had ten times more valour, than this roaring devil i'th'old play.
>
> Boy [*HV* 4.4.67]

How can a modern actor borrow the face of true justice, or sorrow, or rumor? When we rely entirely upon the strategies of psychological realism, we deny ourselves access to the richest possible mixture of theatrical conventions, a basic requirement when exploring the complexities of Shakespeare's theatrical creations. A better understanding of borrowing the face of a concept will prove invaluable on those many occasions when Shakespeare's stagecraft sets acting challenges that psychological realism does not meet well.

Take, for example, the strategies of characterization used in the formation of Isabella in *Measure for Measure*. We first meet her as a novitiate eager to bind herself with the strictest rules of the religious order. She is summoned to debate Angelo in two intense confrontations. Then she confronts her brother in the cell where he awaits his death. This brings her to the midway point in the play. Her personality is made apparent to us in the many impassioned speeches she is given to speak, and modern actresses can build many bridges between their lives and what she feels and experiences. And then, abruptly, she becomes a secondary character, existing only to be manipulated by the Duke and propelled into the final confrontation to serve her function there.

Two events set immense obstacles for a modern actress. Isabella, when offered the opportunity to sleep with Angelo in order to save her brother's life, is able to say, "More than our Brother, is our Chastity" [2.4.185]. Even when Claudio pleads with her for his life, she sticks to her resolve, "Then Isabel live chaste, and brother die" [2.4.184]. No matter how much weight we might give to her calling to the sisterhood, the absence of any equivocation on this point makes Isabella's psychology an unpleasant one. The second obstacle occurs at the very end of the play when the Duke has revealed the extent of his manipulations of Isabella.

If we view Isabella as a hybrid creation, nurtured in a blend of theatrical conventions, then those events that are so problematical for a psychologically based characterization become less puzzling. We can continue to make use of all of the acting strategies for the creation of three-dimensional, complex characters, in keeping with Shakespeare's experimentations with multifaceted character portraits; and we can mix in alternative acting strategies to address those aspects of Shakespeare's stagecraft that partake of an alternative set of theatrical conventions.

Playing a concept like Chastity is not so very different from playing a stereotype like Jock or Bimbo, which modern actors are often expected to do in comedies, commercials, and secondary roles. What is unexpected is to play a hybrid character that functions at one moment as a stereotype and the next as an individual reacting to a unique situation. This is different from a well-developed character who shares some characteristics of the expected stereotype but is revealed in greater depth, a characterization strategy often employed in modern realistic narratives. In the case of Isabella and, I would suggest, every Shakespearean character, what we have is an acting challenge: to blend the requirements of two different characterization strategies, so that first one, then the other predominates.

Just as a the stereotype of Jock or Bimbo is a shared convention of costume, vocabulary, habitual actions, and expected attitudes, so too the personifications upon which Shakespeare's actors drew their strategies were a shared set of images. We can see the visual representations and read descriptions of the central cast of personified characters, known as emblems. But it is only when they are brought alive on an imaginary stage that they help us develop acting strategies.

The habit of personification floods Shakespeare's plays with snapshots of the enacting of an idea. In *Measure for Measure*, wherein an examination of the nature of justice and mercy is at work, the face of seeming Mercy is passed from person to person. The Duke, who inherited the task of juggling the masks of Justice and Mercy when he inherited his dukedom, attempts to recast the role in the first scene of the play, when he instructs Angelo, "Mortality and Mercy in Vienna / Live in thy tongue, and heart" [1.1.44], during his pretended absence. Escalus observes Angelo's success when he notes, "Mercy is not it self, that oft looks so, / Pardon is still the nurse of second woe" [2.1.283].

Isabella continues the personification when she pleads with Angelo, hoping that her most powerful arguments will so affect Angelo that "mercy then will breathe within your lips / Like man new made" [2.2.78]. When Angelo offers his foul bargain, Isabella responds, "lawful mercy / Is nothing kin to foul redemption" [2.4.112]. She explains the situation to her brother with, "There is a devilish mercy in the Judge, / If you'll implore it, that will free your life,

/ But fetter you till death" [3.1.64]. When her brother begs her to accept Angelo's offer, she offers the least flattering of descriptions: "Mercy to thee would prove it self a Bawd" [3.1.149].

While observing a comic subplot incident, Escalus summarizes the portrait of Mercy to this point in the play: "This would make mercy swear and play the Tyrant" [3.2.194]. Angelo, who was asked to play the role of Mercy by the Duke, has resisted the opportunity to make himself into a new person and truly become Lawful Mercy. Instead, he has become Foul Redemption or Devilish Mercy, which seeks to play the role of a bawd or jailer.

At this point in the story, the Duke steps in to set up a bed trick so that Angelo, wearing the mask of the Tyrant Mercy, can be revealed. But the Duke has made a false assumption about the character behind the mask. He assumes that Angelo, now as guilty as Claudio of fornication, will pardon Claudio as he promised Isabella. Therefore, Angelo is in truth the character Vice (here specifically the deadly sin of Lust) hiding first behind the mask of Seeming Virtue, then behind the mask of Devilish Mercy. The Duke concludes, "When Vice makes Mercy, Mercy's so extended, / That for the faults love, is th'offender friended" [4.2.112]. In other words, when Monsieur Vice enacts the role of Mercy, he constructs the events of the scene so that Mercy befriends Master Offender because it secretly loves Mistress Fault.

However, the situation is not so simple. Angelo's true face is not simply that of Lust, but a darker character. He betrays his own terrible bargain, and orders Claudio executed. The Duke now must scramble to save Claudio and bring Angelo to some sort of public unmasking. He pulls it off using Isabella as his chief accuser.

When Isabella kneels before the Duke in front of the assembled cast in the last scene of the play, she seems to be cast now in the role of Avenging Retribution, as she cries out for, and to, Justice. But later the Duke will cast her in a different role, when he says, "The very mercy of the Law cries out / Most audible, even from his proper tongue. / An Angelo for Claudio, death for death" [5.1.407]. Since we have just seen Isabella crying out most audibly, it seems an appropriate bit of casting. She didn't in fact ask for any specific sentence when she accused Angelo. More puzzling, however, is the association of Mercy with the strict, Old Testament justice embodied in the aphorisms, "An eye for an eye" and "measure for measure." We are more likely to associate Mercy with a different "proper tongue" or appropriate dialogue, perhaps such as delivered by Portia, representing New Testament values, to the Old Testament Shylock:

> The quality of mercy is not strained,
> It droppeth as the gentle rain from heaven
> Upon the place beneath. It is twice blest,
> It blesseth him that gives, and him that takes,
> 'Tis mightiest in the mightiest, it becomes

The throned Monarch better than his Crown.
His Sceptre shows the force of temporal power,
The attribute to awe and Majesty,
Wherein doth sit the dread and fear of Kings:
But mercy is above this sceptred sway,
It is enthroned in the hearts of Kings,
It is an attribute to God himself;
And earthly power doth then show likest Gods
When mercy seasons Justice. [*Merchant* 4.1.184]

Even so, it is true that sometimes Mercy has a less gentle function, as Claudius suggests when he contemplates his particular sins: "Whereto serves mercy, / But to confront the visage of Offence?" [*Hamlet* 3.3.46]

Isabella has made many of the same arguments to Angelo when trying to save her brother as Portia makes to Shylock. Now, Angelo no longer wears the mask of Mercy and it is time for Isabella herself to step into the role and see if it will be a face that she borrows, or one that she reveals beneath the mask of Chastity.

At different times in the play, Isabella has received acting coaching from supporting characters. Lucio, her brother's friend, urged her to be more passionate in her pleading for mercy from Angelo. The Duke coached her on how to trick Angelo and then reveal his duplicity. Now Mariana, who perhaps foolishly loves Angelo and pleads now for his life, urges Isabella into the pose and action of Mercy: "Isabel: / sweet Isabel, do yet but kneel by me, / Hold up your hands, say nothing: I'll speak all" [5.1.436]. But as it turns out, Isabella is able to speak, and in so doing does she discover that hers is not the face of seeming Mercy, borrowed (or thrust upon her) by the occasion, but her own true face?

I would argue that the habits of mind that Shakespeare demonstrated, whereby "the forms of things / Unknown; the Poets pen turns them to shapes, / And gives to airy nothing, a local habitation, / And a name" [5.1.15], as Theseus puts it in *A Midsummer Night's Dream,* can be easily accessed by actors today through a theatrical "triple-blessing" of historical artifact, textual exploration, and some theatrical acting games.

The historical artifacts are the emblem books and any other repository of the Renaissance visual imagery of personifications. Simply paging through a book of reproductions of the paintings of the European masters will reveal examples of the human face of Time, Love, Revenge, Justice, and Fortune. Look also for the correspondences between the classical gods and goddesses who were associated with certain concepts: a portrait of Venus the Goddess of Love lying beside Mars the God of War is also a portrait of Love and War. Certain biblical subjects also acquired such iconographic significance: a painting of Samson and Delilah could just as easily have been given a label like Subjugated Strength in the lap of Wanton Luxury.

The morality plays that flourished immediately before the emergence of the professional playwrights in London are also available, though they can prove heavy going. Large amounts of rather tedious moralizing must be endured to glean the nuggets of theatrical gold. Here is one of my favorite exchanges, which occurs in a play entitled *Wit and Science* and features a comic dialogue between Ignorancy and Idleness:

Idle: Lo, sir! yet ye lack another toy!
    Where is my whistle to call my boy?

Ign: I come! I come!

Idle: Come on, ye fool!
    All this day or ye can come to school?

Ign: My mother will not let me come.

Idle: I would thy mother had kissed thy bum!
    She will never let thee thrive, I trow!
    Come one, goose! Now, lo! men shall know
    That Idleness can do somewhat, yea!
    And play the scoolmistress, too if need be.
    Mark what doctrine by Idleness comes!
    Say thy lesson, fool!

Ign: Upon my thumbs?

Idle: Yea, upon thy thumbs: is not there thy name?

Ign: Yeas.

Idle: Go too, then; spell me that same!
    Where was thou born?

Ign: Chwas i-bore in England, mother said.

Idle: In England?

Ign: Yea!

Idle: And what's half Ingland?
    Here's Ing; and here's land. What's tis?

Ign: What's tis?

Idle: What's tis? whoreson! what's tis?
    Here's Ing; and here's land. What's tis?

Ign: Tis my thumb.

Idle: Thy thumb? Ing, whoreson! Ing, Ing!

Ign: Ing, Ing, Ing, Ing!

Idle: Forth! Shall I beat thy narse, now?

Ign: Um-m-m–

Idle: Shall I not beat thy narse, now?

Ign: Um-um-um–

Idle: Say no, fool! say no.

Ing: Noo, noo, noo, noo, noo!

Idle: Go to, put together! Ing!

Ing: Ing.

Idle: No!

Ing: Noo.

Idle: Forth now! What saith the dog?

Ing: Dog bark.

Idle: Dog bark? Dog ran, whoreson! dog ran!

Ing: Dog ran, whoreson! dog ran, dog ran!

Idle: Put together: Ing!

Ing: Ing.

Idle: No!

Ing: Noo.

Idle: Ran!

Ing: Ran.

Idle: Forth now; what saith the goose?

Ing: Lag! Lag!

Idle: His, whoreson! his!

Ing: His, his-s-s-s-s!

Idle: Go to, put together: Ing.

Ing: Ing.

Idle: No.

Ing: Noo.

Idle: Ran.

Ing: Ran.

Idle: Hys.

Ing: His-s-s-s-s-s.

Idle: Now, who is a good boy?

Ing: I, I, I! I, I, I!

Idle: Go to, put together: Ing.

Ing: Ing.

Idle: No.

Ing: Noo.

Idle: Ran.

Ing: Ran.

Idle: His.

Ing: His-s-s-s-s.

Idle: I.

Ing: I.

Idle: Ing-no-ran-his-I.

Ing: Ing-no-ran-his-s-s-s.

Idle: I.

Ing: I.

Idle: Ing.

Ing: Ing.

Idle: Foorth!

Ing: His-s-s.

Idle: Yea, no, whoreson, no!

Ing: Noo, noo, noo, noo.

Idle: Ing-no.

Ing: Ing-no.

Idle: Forth now!

Ing: His-s-s-s.

Idle: Yet again: ran, whoreson! ran, ran!

Ing: Ran, whoreson, ran, ran.

Idle: Ran, say!

Ing: Ran-say.

Idle: Ran, whoreson!

Ing: Ran, whoreson.

Idle: Ran.

Ing: Ran.

Idle: Ing-no-ran.

Ing: Ing-no-ran.

Idle: Forth, now! What said the goose?

Ing: Dog bark.

Idle: Dog bark? His, whoreson! his-s-s-s.

Ing: His-s-s-s-s.

Idle: I. Ing-no-ran-his-I.

Ing: Ing-no-ran-his-I-s-s-s.

Idle: I.

Ing: I.

Idle: How sayest, now, fool? Is not there thy name?

Ing: Yea.

Idle: Well then; can me that same!
            What hast thou learned?

Ing: Ich cannot tell. (214)

This reads like a transcript of a vaudeville sketch, where the fool is tricked into calling himself silly names by the tormenting, mocking, pretended friend.

The ridiculous or naughty characters are the most vividly portrayed in the morality plays. The language they are given to speak need not pronounce upon any weighty moral theme, and therefore all manner of experimentation in the creation of striking theatrical effect can be undertaken. In particular, the entrance of these characters, that moment when they announce who they are and provide the audience with a vivid snapshot of their personality, are often memorable. The following is the entrance of a character named Mischief in the play called *Mankynde*:

> I beseech you heartily leave your calculation!
> Leave your chaff! leave your corn! leave your dalliation!
> Your wit is little; your head is mickle; ye are full of predication!
> But, sir! I pray you this question to clarify:
> Driff, draff! mish, mash!
> Some was corn, and some was chaff;
> My dame said my name was Raff. (45)

Don't you just love this character's language? And how about the clothing that Pride describes for himself, when he first appears in the play called *Nature*, after introducing himself with, "Know ye not how great a lord I am?"

> How say ye, sirs, by mine array?
> Doth is please you, yea or nay?
> In the best wise, I dare well say!
> By that ye know me awhile
> And one thing I put you out of doubt;
> I have werewith to bear it out
> As well as any man hereabout
> Within these hundred mile.
>   Behold . . .
> A staring colour of scarlet red:
> I promise you a fine thread
> And a soft wool.
> It cost me a noble at one pitch—
> The scald capper swore sithich
> That is cost him even as much—
> But there Pride had a pull.
>   I love it well to have side hair
> Half a wote beneath mine ear;
> For, evermore, I stand in fear
> That mine neck should take cold.
> I knit it up all the night;

And the daytime comb it down right;
And then it crispeth and shineth as bright
As any purled gold.
    My doublet is on-laced before—
A stomacher of satin and no more;
Rain it, snow it never so sore,
Methinketh I am too hot.
Then have I such a short gown,
With wide sleeves that hang a-down—
They would make some lad in this town
A doublet and a coat.

Here we see that clothes make the man, indeed.

What is so fascinating, in having a look at the medieval traditions that Shakespeare's first actors inherited, is the close connection between the interactions between personifications and those of Shakespeare's characters. One of Shakespeare's most original and memorable creations is that fat old knight Falstaff, and the enduring popularity of the *Henry IV* plays rests in part on the marvellous exchanges between Falstaff and his young friend the crown prince, Hal. Here is a scene from a play called *Youth*, in which we meet the title character and his companion Riot.

Riot: Huffa! Huffa! who calleth after me?
I am Riot, full of jollity.
My heart is light as the wind,
And all on riot is my mind
Wheresoever I go.
But know ye what I do here?
To seek Youth my compeer:
Fain of him I would have a sight,
But my lips hang in my light.
God speed, master Youth, by my fay.

Youth: Welcome, Riot, in the devil way!
Who brought thee hither to-day?

Riot: That did my legs, I tell thee:
Me thought thou didst call me,
And I am come now here
To make royal cheer
And tell thee how I have done.

Youth: What! I weened thou hadst been hanged,
But I see thou art escaped,
For it was told me here
You took a man on the ear,
That his purse in your bosom did fly,
And so in Newgate you did lie.

Riot   So it was, I beshrew your pate:
          I'm come lately from Newgate,
          But I am as ready to make good cheer
          As he that never came there;
          For and I have spending,
          I will make as merry as a king,
          And care not what I do;
          For I will not lie long in prison,
          But will get forth soon,
          For I have learned policy
          That will loose me lightly,
          And soon let me go.

Youth: I love well they discretion,
          For thou art all of one condition;
          Thou are stable and steadfast of mind,
          And not changeable as the wind.
          But, sir, I pray you at the least,
          Tell me more of that jest,
          That thou told me right now.

Riot: Moreover, I shall tell thee,
          The Mayor of London sent for me
          Forth of Newgate for to come,
          For to preach at Tyburn.

Youth: By our Lady! he did promote thee,
          To make thee preach at the gallow-tree!
          But, sir, how didst thou 'scape?

Riot   Verily, sir, the rope brake,
          And so I feel to the ground,
          And ran away, safe and sound:
          By the way I met with a courtier's lad,
          And twenty nobles of gold in his purse he had:
          I took the lad on the ear,
          Beside his horse I felled him there:
          I took his purse in my hand,
          And twenty nobles therein I found.
          Lord, how I was merry! (149)

What is so remarkable, in reading this scene from the old morality play, is how closely it prefigures Shakespeare's treatment of his youthful hero and the riotous old Falstaff. In their first encounter, they also have jokes to make about hangmen. Because Hal will someday be king, Falstaff enjoys imagining England under the rule of Riot:

Falstaff: But I prithee sweet Wag, shall there be Gallows standing in England when thou art King? and resolution thus fobbed as it is, with the rusty curb of old Father Antic the Law? Do not thou when thou art a King, hang a Thief.

Hal: No, thou shalt.

Falstaff: Shall I? O rare! By the Lord I'll be a brave Judge.

Hal: Thou judgest false already. I mean, thou shalt have the hanging of the Thieves, and so become a rare Hangman.

Falstaff: Well Hal, well: and in some sort it jumps with my humour, as well as waiting in the Court, I can tell you.

Hal: For obtaining of suits?

Falstaff: Yea, for obtaining of suits, whereof the Hangman hath no lean Wardrobe. [1.2.58]

Like Riot, Falstaff loves to describe his interactions with the high and mighty, whose conventions he challenges and whose morality he mocks, almost as much as he loves his reputation as a breaker of laws.

Falstaff: An old Lord of the Council rated me the other day in the street about you sir, but I marked him not, and yet he talked very wisely, but I regarded him not, and yet he talked wisely, and in the street too.

Hal: Thou didst well: for wisdom cries out in the streets and no man regards it.

Falstaff: O, thou hast damnable iteration, and art indeed able to corrupt a Saint. Thou hast done much harm upon me Hal, God forgive thee for it. Before I knew thee Hal I knew nothing: and now am I (if a man should speak truly) little better than one of the wicked. I must give over this life, and I will give it over: by the Lord and I do not, I am a Villain. I'll be damned for never a Kings son in Christendom.

Hal: Where shall we take a purse tomorrow, Jack?

Falstaff: Zounds where thou wilt Lad, I'll make one: and I do not, call me Villain, and baffle me.

Hal: I see a good amendment of life in thee: From Praying, to Purse taking.

Falstaff: Why, Hal, 'tis my Vocation Hal: 'Tis no sin for a man to labour in his Vocation. [1.2.83]

Like Riot, Falstaff will meet and escape shame and punishment, and rise as from the dead to steal again.

PERSONIFICATION IN IMAGERY

Textual exploration takes the modern actor into the heart of the imagery that makes Shakespeare's language so vital and vivid. It is imperative, however, that the actor avoid settling simply upon what the image means, and instead dedicates a healthy amount of energy to the imagining of a company of actors presenting the scene, as captured in the imagery of the personifications.

Immediately following Hamlet's famous "To be, or not to be" soliloquy, he encounters Ophelia and accepts from her the love tokens he sent her before the play began. The following exchange then takes place.

Hamlet: Ha, ha: Are you honest?

Ophelia: My lord.

Hamlet: Are you fair?

Ophelia: What means your Lordship?

Hamlet: That if you be honest and fair, your Honesty should admit no discourse to your Beauty.

Ophelia: Could Beauty my Lord, have better Commerce than with Honesty?

Hamlet: Ay truly: for the power of Beauty, will sooner transform Honesty from what it is, to a Bawd, than the force of Honesty can translate Beauty into his likeness. This was sometime a Paradox, but now the time gives it proof. I did love you once.

Ophelia: Indeed my Lord, you made me believe so.

Hamlet: You should not have believed me. For virtue cannot so inoculate our old stock, but we shall relish of it. I loved you not.

Ophelia: I was the more deceived. [3.1.102]

For a modern actor and actress, the enduring human truth of this exchange is carried by "I did love you once," "You made me believe so," "I loved you not," and "I was the more deceived." But when playing the scene, they must also make sense of, and make use of, the rest of the text.

Hamlet's questioning of Ophelia's honesty and fairness plays with the multiple connotations these words had for Shakespeare's audience. "Honesty" meant not only "not given to lying" as it means today, but also "not given to laying, that is, chaste." "Fair" meant, as it does today, blonde, beautiful, and avoiding injustice.

So far, so good. We are on firm ground with Hamlet's unexpected questions and Ophelia's uncertain answers. But what on earth does Hamlet mean when he suggests that Honesty should admit no discourse with Beauty, of Ophelia when she responds that Beauty could have no better commerce than with Honesty?

The emotional thrust of the scene suggests that this sequence has something to do with Hamlet's conviction that sexual chastity in particular and trustworthiness in general is something that cannot be found in beautiful women, like his mother and Ophelia.

But why do those words mean exactly that, and why did Hamlet choose this convoluted way to begin an attack on Ophelia? Can the *form* of the dialogue give us any clues to the emotional *content* and so help to explain why Hamlet is attacking her, and why she responds as she does?

At the heart of this exchange is a simple device much favored by Elizabethan writers and orators: the personification. By capitalizing "Honesty" and

"Beauty," and imagining them as people engaged in a relationship, we can understand the intellectual and emotional content of the exchange.

The energy of every personification is located in the verbs used to bring intellectual concepts to life. Here we have Honesty and Beauty "admitting no discourse" and "having commerce." What do these verbs mean, and who in Hamlet's world performs these actions?

To have discourse with someone is talk to them, to be involved in an exchange of ideas, observations, feelings, thoughts, and the variety of nonverbal communication such as looks, sighs, touches, embraces, and so forth. Some time ago, in the third scene of the play, Ophelia's father instructed her: "I would not, in plain terms, from this time forth, / Have you so slander any moment leisure, / As to give words or talk with the Lord Hamlet" [1.3.132]. And then, after he entered her private rooms in such a startling fashion, her father asked Ophelia, "Have you given him any hard words of late?" to which she replied, "No my good Lord: but as you did command, / I did repel his Letters, and denied / His access to me" [2.1.104]. This is a precise description of "admitting no discourse." What about having commerce?

Commerce was already at this time a word associated with economic exchanges, although it was still used in a general sense for any sort of exchange, including social, intellectual, spiritual, or emotional. If we return to the scene where Ophelia is forbidden to admit any further discourse with Prince Hamlet, we find her father using the language of the market place repeatedly, including, "Set your entreatments at a higher rate, / Than a command to parley" and "Do not believe his vows, for they are Brokers, / Not of that dye, which their Investments show."

Now let us return to Honesty and Beauty admitting no discourse and having commerce. Ophelia has told Hamlet she can admit no further discourse with him. In a similar fashion, Honesty should admit no discourse to Beauty, should cut Beauty off without any explanation, and should not, as Polonius instructed, "so slander any moment leisure / As to give words or talk" with Beauty. Just as Ophelia needed to be protected from Hamlet and the political skullduggery of the court, so her honesty, honor, and virginity need to be protected from the corrupt power of the power and corruption that goes along with being so very beautiful.

Now, we can easily imagine the very personalized emotional impact of the personification, spoken by the rejected and dejected Hamlet, placing onto the personified Beauty his own isolation from Ophelia's goodness, and admitting that she does need to be protected from the corruption that surrounds her and in which he is drowning.

What of Ophelia's response? Surely she would recognize the reference to her own treatment of him in the personification of Honesty's rejection of Beauty. She responds by making Beauty the active agent, asking is there is any better economic exchange than when Hamlet "made many tenders of his affection" to her. Even though her father insists on framing what Ophelia called "all the holy vows of heaven" as cheating, flashy salesmen's chatter, they are still held up as the best commercial transaction available. This reinforces her intellectual rebuttal: that a beautiful woman is in very great need of personal honesty and physical chastity.

So we see how the personification in this exchange allows each of the actors to remember earlier events shown or reported, and bring the emotions associated with the language of earlier scenes into the subtext of this scene.

Let us move on to the third interaction between Honesty and Beauty, wherein Beauty is accorded the power to transform Honesty into someone who trades in prostitutes, a power far greater than the force Honesty might use to translate Beauty.

Although "transform" and "translate" were synonyms, there were special applications for each. "Transform" was used in reference to a change in the character or essential condition as well as the external appearance, while "translate" was used to describe a move from one place to another, or from one shape or appearance to another. It was also used to describe the transition from living on the earth to a life in heaven or any other nontemporal condition without death. "Translate" was also used as a synonym for enrapture. So when Beauty transforms Honesty into a Bawd, Honesty is changed in appearance and essential character. But when Honesty translates Beauty, Beauty is changed in shape and location, perhaps even from something mortal to something eternal, or changed the way one is when one falls in love.

One final question: What does "into his likeness" mean? This is what Beauty would be translated into, if only Honesty's force were greater. Whose likeness? Whenever Shakespeare constructs a sentence that allows two or more interpretations, each of the interpretations is added to the subtext of the sentence. On one level, the corrupt and corrupting Beauty could be changed into something honest and chaste. On another level, Hamlet, who has been translated into something terrible in this "antic disposition" he has put on to the point where we cannot tell what is just acted and what is the release of real torment and despair, might be transformed back into the man he was, when Ophelia's goodness still had power over his soul.

The male pronoun "his" is our clue here. Hamlet is, after all, discussing Ophelia's attributes, and female Beauty and Chastity were female when personified in Elizabethan popular culture. That Hamlet might be talking of his own special circumstances is borne out by what follows. Ophelia's goodness might have cured his madness and indeed the disease the infects all of Denmark, had not the "old stock" of the royal family been so corrupted that the smell of the infection will always linger, no matter what new plant is grafted on, in marriage.

Emblems

We are all familiar with Death personified as the cloaked and hooded carrier of the reaper's scythe. We are also familiar with the Cupid-like child with quiver of arrows, and so are not particularly surprised when Love has wings or giggles at lovers' sighs. A blend of textual exploration and emblem hunting can bring other roles alive.

In *Twelfth Night*, Viola makes reference to one such emblem when she tells the story of her imaginary sister who suffered her unrequited love with ennobling patience:

> She never told her love,
> But let concealment like a worm i'th' bud
> Feed on her damask cheek: she pined in thought,
> And with a green and yellow melancholy,
> She sat like Patience on a Monument,
> Smiling at grief. Was not this love indeed? [2.4.110]

Now we know that Viola is describing what it is like loving Orsino but not being able to express that love because she is disguised as a boy. But in doing so, she paints a picture of a well-known emblem, that of Constant Faith or Patience.

The University of South Carolina Press has issued an attractive modern edition of the George Wither's *A Collection of Emblemes*, originally published in 1635, in which we find one version of the very monument Viola describes. At the top of the page is the message, "They, after suffering, shall be crowned, / In whom, a Constant Faith is found."

The drawing shows a woman standing on a monument. She is crowned and holds a cross in her right arm and a cup in her left hand. Behind her in the distance we can see the three crosses of Golgotha as well as two other small groupings. One shows a man being escorted to prison, the other a man being slain in battle. In the distance there can be seen a castle and a medieval town.

Here is the explanation provided by Withers:

> Mark well this Emblem, and observe you thence
> The nature of true Christian confidence.
> Her Foot is fixed on a squared stone,
> Which, whether side foe're you turn it on,
> Stands fast; and is that Cornerstone, which propose
> And firmly knits the structure of our hopes.
>   She, always, bears a cross, to signify
> That there was never any Constancy
> Without her trials: and, that her perfection
> Shall never be attain'ed, without Affliction.
>   A Cup she hath, moreover, in her hand;
> And, by that Figure, thou mayst understand,
> That she hath draughts of Comfort, always near her,
> (At ev'ry brunt) to strengthen, and to cheer her.
> And, lo, her head is crowned, that we may see
> How great her Glories, and Rewards will be.

Hereby, this Virtue's nature may be known:
Now, practise, how to make the fame thine own.
Discouraged be not, though thou art pursued
With many wrongs, which cannot be eschewed;
Nor yield thou to Despairing, though thou hast
A Cross (which threatens death) to be embraced;
Or, though thou be compelled to swallow up
The very dregs of Sorrow's bigger cup:
For, whensoever griefs or torments pain thee,
Thou has the same foundation to sustain thee:
The self same cup of comfort is prepared
To give thee strength, when fainting fits are feared:
   And, when thy time of trial is expired,
   Thou shalt obtain the Crown, thou hast desired. (28)

We learn from this emblem that Patience was more than simply waiting one's turn in the grocery store line. It embodied for Shakespeare's audience a primary Christian virtue, one that was a requirement for the endurance of life's hardships without succumbing to the deadly sin of despair.

There was another emblem of Patience, mentioned by Petruchio in his bombastic praise of the shrewish Kate: "For patience she will prove a second Grissel," referring to the folk legend of Patient Griselda. And other characters, along with Viola, present themselves as a possible emblem, or pattern, of Patience. Troilus, watching his beloved Cressida in the arms of another man, says, "I will not be my self, nor have cognition / Of what I feel: I am all patience" [T&C 5.2.63]. King Lear, faced with the duplicity of his elder daughters, announces, "No, I will be the pattern of all patience, / I will say nothing" [3.2.37].

Does Patience have any other characteristics than the capacity to stand on a square block and endure almost unbearable trials? If not, she won't be much use for theatrical presentation, unless we're staging the final scene of *The Winter's Tale* when the statue of the falsely accused Hermione magically comes to life and embraces her repentant father and long-lost daughter.

A survey of the various personifications of Patience in Shakespeare's plays reveals a wider range of acting possibilities encompassed in this particular role. Although she is usually silent ("do not press / My tongue tied patience with too much disdain: / Lest sorrow lend me words" [Sonnet 140]), she speaks when the situation calls for it ("Her very silence, and her patience, / Speak to the people, and they pity her" [*AYLI* 1.3.78]).

Patience's most familiar companion is Sorrow, also mentioned in Wither's emblem book. Here is a gentleman of the court describing Cordelia's reunion with her now mad father:

Patience and sorrow strove
Who should express her goodliest: you have seen

Sun shine and rain at once, her smiles and tears,
Were like a better way: those happy smilets,
That played on her ripe lip seemed not to know,
What guests were in her eyes, which parted thence,
As pearls from diamonds dropped: in brief,
Sorrow would be a rarity most beloved,
If all could so become it. [*Lear* 4.3.16]

What a beautiful evocation of the traditional feminine qualities associated with Patience. How boring she would be if that were her only function: to stand around, mostly silent, but weeping very prettily.

Fortunately for the actor playing the role of Patience, she is given a bit more to do in the imaginary stage play of the internal conflict in a character's mind. She is also given a specific function in the world of this imaginary play, which is configured like a court with the central character, representing the essential humanity in any individual, sits as ruling monarch. In this imaginary court, Patience is a member of the inner circle of advisers.

Kent asks King Lear, "Sir, where is the patience now, that thou so oft have boasted to retain?" [3.6.58]. Malcolm, in *Macbeth*, provides a list of the counsellors that a king should gather round him: "the King-becoming Graces, / As Justice, Verity, Temperance, Stableness, / Bounty, Perseverance, Mercy, Lowliness, / Devotion, Patience, Courage, Fortitude" [4.3.92]. If we imagine Patience as such a companion to the monarch, many common phrases take on a heightened, theatrical energy. "Hear me with patience, but to speak a word" [*R&J* 3.5.159], conjures a picture of a courtier addressing not only the king but asking specifically that the counsellor Patience attend and listen.

Positioned so close to the throne, Patience would have many significant responsibilities. "There is between my will, and all offences / a guard of patience" [*T&C* 5.2.53], boasts Troilus. "Quite besides / The government of patience" [*Cymbeline* 2.4.149], is an exclamation that reminds us even Patience can be pushed too far. "Yet surely Cassio I believe received / From him that fled, some strange Indignity, / Which patience could not pass" [*Othello* 2.3.244], is the only explanation of Cassio's rash behavior while on guard duty. When she receives Phebe's letter, Rosalind jokes, "Patience her self would startle at this letter / And play the swaggerer, bear this, bear all" [*AYLI* 4.3.13].

The most dramatic activity in which Patience is involved is during the extreme trials of the monarch. "Patience, be near me still, and set me lower, / I have not long to trouble thee" [4.2.76], begs Queen Katharine in *Henry VIII*. Later in the same play, her husband advises the Archbishop of Canterbury, "Till further Trial, in those Charges / Which will require your Answer, you must take / Your patience to you, and be well contented / To make your house our Tower" [5.1.103]. Only Patience will be allowed to accompany the Archbishop to the Tower. In the next scene, this same man invites us to imagine his close companion Patience enduring the torture of pressing, when he avows that he will clear himself, "Lay all the weight ye can upon my patience."

"Patience perforce, with wilful choler meeting, / Makes my flesh tremble in their different greeting" [1.5.89], says Tybalt of his forced endurance of Romeo's presence at the Capulet's feast. This is the collision of mighty opposites, reminding us that endurance is a strength, and patience is not a passive weakness.

PSYCHOMACHIA REVISITED

> My Brain, I'll prove the Female to my Soul,
> My Soul, the Father: and these two beget
> A generation of still breeding Thoughts;
> And these same Thoughts, people this Little World.
>
> Richard [*RII* 5.5.6]

The following is an enjoyable theatre game that brings alive the potential of the staging of a complex personality using a group of actors. The game works best with a group; if you are working alone there is nothing to stop you from imagining the outcome of just such a game, making use of actors with whom you have worked or studied, or a cast of favorite stars; alternatively, you can write the parts and imagine it coming to life on the movie screen of the mind.

To begin with, the group works together to create the cast of characters. When working in a training situation, I ask them to prepare a psychomachia of a student actor. The protagonist, standing in for every young actor, we call Everyactor. Quite quickly, the supporting roles emerge:

Lazy Bones: This role is played for comic relief as a lethargic, sloppily dressed, self-indulgent sleepyhead. This one is very adept at talking Everyactor out of personal warm-ups, waking in time for a good breakfast, and extra research in the library.

Body Image: This fast-talking, mirror gazing hypochondriac is forever announcing weight-gain, facial blemishes, unwanted hair and odor, and unfavourable comparisons with photographs in the movie magazines offered for Everyactor's perusal.

Envy: This quieter, nasty individual tends to slink around and whisper in Everyactor's ear. Whenever a negative comment can be made about someone else's work, Envy is sure to be the one to make it.

Gossip: This chatterbox walks the talk, and often pairs up with Envy to do as much damage as possible to the reputation of other actors.

Lust: In some versions of the game, this character has a prominent role, getting Everyactor into a great deal of trouble when a rehearsed love scene gets a little too realistic.

Audition Anxiety: A terrifying and hilarious cameo appearance of a jittering, stuttering, humiliated survivor of one too many auditions.

Shakespeare Shock: This character sports an exaggerated British accent and swoons around the stage spouting Shakespeare, alternatively encouraging Everyactor to indulge in Bardolatry and despair of ever mastering the Iambic Code.

Performance Rush: This character bursts onto the scene with an explosion of movement and emotion, just in time to keep Everyactor from despairing.

Theatre: Sometimes this is a youthful, attractive character, the obvious love interest for Everyactor, and the story follows a romance pattern of meeting, separation, and reconciliation. Sometimes, however, this is a very old magical creature who sets Everyactor on the journey or offers guidance and inspiration.

These are just some of the characters developed by one group of student actors. Any group can create their own cast, simply by thinking about the types of behavior that are typical for a student actor, and then developing a character that embodies, literally, each type of behavior, attributes, and worldview in a bold and striking manner.

Because Everyactor is representative of every member of the group, any member of the group could play Everyactor and should contribute to Everyactor's dialogue. In many ways, Everyactor is an empty vessel into which the entire group will contribute ideas, situations, experiences, attitudes, reactions, and so on. Everyactor is like the ventriloquist's manikin manipulated by the group.

Once everyone has an interesting character to develop, and someone has been designated to perform the role of Everyactor, the group can begin to shape the journey that Everyactor will experience. The archetypal journey from naivety to wisdom provides an obvious and workable framework for the sequence of events experienced by Everyactor. At this point in the exercise, the group may discover that some additional characters are required to present the narrative. It may seem that these are extraneous to Everyactor if they are identified as Famous Director or Voice Teacher, but the problem is in the label, not the characterization. The group needs to ask: What aspect of Everyactor is reflected in the Famous Director and the Voice Teacher? What concepts or values are at work that Everyactor has encountered and so absorbed, if only as negative attitudes to avoid? Famous Director can then be relabelled something like Theatrical Fame and Voice Teacher can become Beautiful Voice. They can in other ways be portrayed as the stereotypical Famous Director and Voice Teacher or present a satirical or flattering portrait of someone the group knows, but the label clarifies their function in the psychomachia.

The member of the group who has been delegated to portray Everyactor misses out on the possibility of playing a variety of roles, with contrasting costume, demeanor, attitude, and even gender and age. The supporting cast has the most fun developing the perfect presentation of the essence of their assigned attribute.

Although the group can polish up their psychomachia for performance, it is really the planning that serves the purpose of this exercise when considering the plays of Shakespeare. The laughter of recognition that comes from a community of student actors, and the subtle or overt discussion of serious considerations that is possible in this style of theatre serves to remind us all that

Shakespeare did not take a silly, boring playwriting style and transform it. Rather, he joined an already vibrant and exciting theatre scene and participated in the natural evolution that is only possible if the actors and audience share a belief in the capacity of theatre to entertain and speak to important issues.

And One Man in His Time Plays Many Parts

Having explored the excitement of a group-created psychomachia, we can turn our attention to another application of this theatrical personification that brings us one step closer to Shakespeare's plays. In this exercise, we play a form of charades or "Who Am I?" that dissects famous people into a cast of characters that are then enacted in tableau.

Working in small groups, we first select a well-known individual to be the subject of our charade. Then we consider aspects of this person's life experiences that make up the composite reputation or image we have when we say that name. Each member of the group will embody the famous person and, at the same time, one particular aspect of the individual. Here are three examples that demonstrate how different actors have solved the puzzle.

The first group presented four images. The first was an upright stance, with one arm upraised, mouth open as if addressing a large group of people. The second was an image of pain, with the body twisted and one hand on the small of the back. The third was created by a pair, one male and one female. The female was in a stereotypical cheesecake pose with pouty kissing lips, and hands on half-bent knees. The male was crouched with a clenched fist to represent sexual desire, clearly in response to the female. The fourth figure was across the room from the other three, and was in the stance of someone shooting a gun. At first the images were separated, but then they moved together so that the phallic fist of the third image was visible through the legs of the first image, and then the sound of a gun shot was heard and the first figure transformed into the same pose as the second, while the sexy woman transformed into an upright, sombre pose. The sexy man also transformed, and stood beside the woman and placed his right hand flat, as if on a Bible while the left hand was raised as if swearing an oath. The actor who created the second image of the original twisted body also transformed into a photographer snapping pictures of the twisted man on the ground and the new male/female grouping.

This group was working on John F. Kennedy. They were interested in the contrast between his power and authority as president in contrast to his private life in which he not only endured almost crippling pain from a war injury, but also in which he formed a relationship with Marilyn Monroe. The man with the gun was Oswald, and the final image was intended to be a recreation of the picture of Jackie Kennedy standing beside Lyndon B. Johnson as he was sworn in as president.

The actors also represented aspects of this complex man's personality: his great capacity for Leadership, his endurance of debilitating Pain, his personal weakness of Lust, and his Death, here in a very modern form so that the assassin with the gun has replaced the hooded cloaked figure with the scythe. The double female role of sexual object and public widow was the embodiment of his experience of Love, and the photographer was his experience of Fame.

Another group chose Stephen Hawking. Their picture did not transform; instead, they created the image and then continued until we succeeded in reading it. One actor knelt on a chair after tucking his arms into his sweater. He tilted his head into an unnatural position, opened his mouth, and appeared to stare vacantly into space. The second actor stood behind the first and held a lightbulb above his head, for a quick laugh but also a clear indication of his role. The third simply walked in a set pattern around the other two. After a time, we realized that the pattern created the symbol for infinity.

The third group presented their creation in a line, one behind the other. The line first formed so that we could see each of the characters, because the first was on the ground, the second kneeling, and the last were taller than the others. This allowed us to see the beginning and the end before we realized what they were. Then the line began to move towards us, as each figure came to life.

The first figure sitting on the ground began to stroke gently some small creature on her lap, and then suddenly raised her head as if hearing someone call. She looked around, startled and afraid, and then ran away, leaving the kneeling figure at the front of the line. This figure was clearly in prayer. Then she raised her head, then mimed cutting off her long hair, then arose and mimed putting on heavy upper garments and taking up a sword. This figure then strode toward us at the head of the rest of the line, as if leading them, before turning and joining the end of the line.

This revealed the next figure, who enacted the exhausted defeat, the dropping of arms, and the kneeling in subjugation. This kneeling revealed the final character fully, at which point he raised his arms as if making a pronouncement over the kneeling figure. At this point the second actor, who had first knelt in prayer and then put on armor, came forward as if to escort the defeated warrior away. All three moved aside to reveal the first actor, who had been sitting on the ground, standing with arms behind as if pinioned, and the two warriors mimed stacking wood at her feet and lighting the flames while the tallest and last actor prayed.

This was Joan of Arc, taken from her life as a simple country girl hearing voices, through her decision to fight as a man, her victories and her defeat, and her final martyrdom.

The benefit of this exercise is that it reminds us that supporting characters in a play can be simultaneous reflections of the central character and individuals in their own right. These two functions support and enhance each other, and are of equal importance when addressing the acting challenges presented in Shakespeare's plays.

PERSONIFICATIONS AND ARCHETYPES

Thou know'st no less, but all: I have unclasped
To thee the book even of my secret soul.

Orsino [*12th Night* 1.4.13]

Let us have a look at two examples, Rosalind and Hamlet, and tease out the implications of psychomachia for the actors playing the central and the periphery characters. This exercise, then, is for everyone in the cast of the play, not just the one entrusted with the protagonist's role.

Make a chart listing every character in the play except the central character. These will be in the first column of your chart. The second column will be your notes on what aspect of yourself this character represents. Because this is a private exercise, you can include here *any* association you can make with your life experiences, you attitudes, habits, fantasies, values, secrets, *or* any element of society's codified presence in your life. The third column will be your psychomachia casting. Rather than feeling, you must settle on the perfect label and record anything that might be worth exploring. A few entries in the Rosalind chart might look like Table 4.1. Table 4.2 is a sample chart for some characters in *Hamlet.*

Playing an Archetypal Relationship

Let us take it for granted that the traditions of psychomachia were similarly just below the surface for Shakespeare's actors and audience. People were used to plays in which the central character was called Everyman or Mankind, and all of the other characters had names like Good Deeds, Knowledge, Friendship, Cowardice, and so forth. These supporting characters appeared in order to demonstrate one of the internal or external pressures that are at work upon the protagonist, sometimes functioning antagonistically to the hero, and some- times suffering on behalf of the hero. Because they were at the same time a reflection of some aspect of the central psyche, they allowed for the creation of a complex character, as every relationship was in essence a mirror.

This habit of mind would serve to reinforce the function of secondary char- acters to Hamlet or Rosalind. It doesn't take much of a leap to imagine Horatio as the Friendship character of the piece. Ophelia shows back to Hamlet the face of that part of himself that he must abuse, then exile, and finally destroy in order to enact the task set upon him by the Ghost. In turn, the Ghost provides Hamlet with an opportunity to look into his own soul and discover there a capacity for horror and disgust that existed before the beginning of the play. One of the reasons Hamlet can so effectively cleft Gertrude's heart in twain is because it is simultaneously his own heart and the manifestation of an internal pressure that rips Mankind apart. He shares this sensation with

Table 4.1
Psychomachia for Rosalind

Touchstone	The part of me that loves to get off a good one, playing the class clown as a kid, talking on and on when I've had a drink or two, even if no one is listening.	Fast Talker; Quick Wit The part of Rosalind that hides what she's feeling behind the witting exchanges. Also her capacity to see what's really important.
Silvius	The part of me that has, in the past, made a total fool of myself over someone long after I knew perfectly well he wasn't interested.	Lovestruck; Love's Fool The part of Rosalind that just loves Orlando even if she's not supposed to.
Olivier	The part of me that just can't get over sibling rivalry, that's always prickly around my sister especially. "Mom always liked you best"— I can relate to that! That part of me that might get angry at being put down and take that anger out on someone weaker.	Sibling Rival; Cat Kicker The part of Rosalind that is jealous of Celia? That part of Rosalind that has been badly hurt and can turn on someone like Phebe?
Audrey	The secret part of me that would love to be rude and crude and do it with anyone, anywhere. The part of me that laughs at fart jokes in stupid movies.	Let's Boogie; Down & Dirty The part of Rosalind that jumps into men's clothes and hangs out with the guys, with all the physical freedom, and saying whatever she feels like.
Hymen	The part of me that likes romantic movies and books that always end in a wedding, wedding fantasies when I was a kid, crying at weddings, being shown an elaborate wedding photo album, film versions of typical weddings.	The Wedding Singer; Mr. Marriage; Happy Ending The part of Rosalind that really does want to get married, that doesn't care if it means getting back into women's clothing and the restrictions of women's social roles.

the mirror image he likes least, that of Claudius, who compares himself to "a man with double business bound."

Let us expand our metaphor of the court by imagining that at a few significant moments in the play a portrait is painted of the protagonist surrounded by all of the characters of the play, a snapshot as it were of the relative intimacy of every character in connection with the central character. Such a portrait would feature the protagonist in the center, with every other character ranged around. But some characters would be suggested by simply a face or perhaps a part of the body visible beyond a more developed character.

One aspect of the genius of painters, and of Shakespeare with some regu-

Table 4.2
Psychomachia of Hamlet

Horatio	The part of me that sticks by my friends, that likes being one the people come to when they've got a problem. Also, I could really see myself being a hanger-on of a movie/rock star.	True Friend; Study Buddy The part of Hamlet that is a loyal friend, that loved being at the university and studying things.
Osric	The part of me that just can't stop worrying about what the big cheeses think about me. I don't quite suck up as much as he does, but I know I could/would under different conditions.	Ass Kiss; Get Ahead The part of Hamlet that keeps his eye on the main chance, that is very aware of where he stands in relation to the throne.
Ophelia	The part of me that gets hurt very easily, that doesn't seem able to fight for what I need sometimes, that cops out rather than hanging in there and putting up with painful things.	Frailty; Drowning Tears The part of Hamlet that has been deeply hurt by Gertrude, that feels the most grief for his father, that cries over Polonius even as he's hiding the body under the stairs. The part that loved Ophelia.
Laertes	The part of me that does the right thing for my family. Also my temper and show-off tendencies.	Revenge; Proper Son/Brother The part of Hamlet that wants to avenge his father's death, that knows what he needs to do to Claudius. Also the part that thinks of Ophelia as a sister, now that he's caught up in catching Claudius.

larity, is the ability to suggest, with a small technical detail, that the small visible part is connected to an entire human being, otherwise out of sight. Moreover, if the freeze frame were to unfreeze, every person in the picture would move and some would, in fact, go into other rooms containing thrones upon which they would sit as the central character. But we must acknowledge that this is an optical illusion. A character like Ophelia or Orlando has no reality except as a means by which Hamlet or Rosalind is presented to us.

For the actor playing Ophelia or Orlando, it is disconcerting to discover that the shape of the play is designed to present a pattern of relationships charting your relative intimacy with or distance from the central character, and to present only those aspects of what we might call a personality that are required for the composite portrait of the variety of human attributes that surround and reflect the experience of one individual.

When enacting such roles, one learns to be thankful for the details that trick the audience into seeing a real character, because these become the pegs that anchor your other relationship duties into the bedrock of real human experience. By all means, anchor your thinking of your character in the creation of a full-fledged, naturalistic character, but do not expect that the playing of such a character will contribute to the success of the play. Instead, take the anchor and tie to it a harness that will sustain you and rescue you as you venture into a much less secure, but more suitable approach to character.

We must now weave in the third element of our discussion of relationships: the acting of archetypes. We can find many examples of archetypal acting today, but never in realistic plays or films. They were quite common on the nineteenth-century stage and so we can find them in the great romantic operas. When the grandeur of the music is matched up perfectly with a scale of acting compelled by emotions of that impressive scale, we might well find ourselves looking at a fictional representation that suggests simultaneously a specific person in a time and place to specific things and, in addition, a resonating sense of something greater, something that links every artistic attempt to capture the great mystery of human experience with a clarity that suggests the complexity without getting bogged down in mundane details.

Let us consider just two of Carl Jung's archetypes: the anima and the shadow, and return to Hamlet. We can see that Ophelia provides the energy of the anima, or soul, while Claudius represents the shadow, the dark side. But other than offering an intellectual point of interest, how can this provide guidance to the actors in the roles?

For Ophelia, it means that building a relationship with Hamlet isn't as important as finding ways of expressing the attributes that Hamlet cherishes and that he is destroying inside himself as the play progresses. Fortunately, Shakespeare provides you with a list:

> O what a Noble mind is here o'erthrown?
> The Courtiers, Soldiers, Scholars: Eye, tongue, sword,
> Th' expectancy and Rose of the fair State,
> The glass of Fashion, and the mould of Form,
> Th' observed of all Observers, quite, quite down.
> And I of Ladies most deject and wretched,
> That sucked the Honey of his Music Vows:
> Now see that Noble, and most Sovereign Reason,
> Like sweet Bells jangled out of tune, and harsh,
> That unmatched Form and Feature of blown youth,
> Blasted with ecstasy. Oh woe is me,
> T' have seen what I have seen: see what I see. [3.1.150]

Where in the play is Ophelia given an opportunity to demonstrate the nobility of mind that she reflects? Where does she embody expectancy, where the attributes of a rose? We might relegate to other characters the function of reflecting as courtiers, soldiers, and scholars, because characters like Rosencrantz and Guildenstern, Marcellus and Bernardo, and Horatio are offered to play those roles.

I think we can find these attributes in the simple and effective strokes that

Shakespeare uses as he presents her to us, and therefore in the actions that the actor is given to perform. And in so doing, the actor is given all that is needed to hook into the immense power of the archetype. Ophelia does not need a great deal of stage time alone with Hamlet to be the embodiment of his very soul, in his eyes and her own.

Presenting Ophelia as the essence of rose-like expectancy and nobility of mind need not get in the way of finding the familiar human relationships between brother and sister in her first scene. But if you think your job is to create a fully formed individual, you will be frustrated by the very few lines with which you must accomplish this, and the lack of any complexity in your opinions, ideas, and reactions. But if you reposition your focus onto archetypal acting, you will discover that your few speeches, which are entirely in reaction to your brother and father, are opportunities to demonstrate the qualities of Hamlet's anima, not Ophelia's personality. That is why so often a relatively superficial actor who looks the part and can create a few simple and striking images succeeds better in this scene than a skilled performer seeking a naturalistic solution to this role.

Because she represents an aspect of Hamlet's experience, the second part of her description must also come into play well before this scene. She represents that part of Hamlet that is the sweet bells now jangled. Those honeyed vows have turned harsh, and so has she. She is lying to him. She knows perfectly well where her father is, and he is not at home. Though not yet blasted with madness, she has sacrificed the nobility that might be associated with reason and kingship, to be a participant in this illicit observing. There is just enough of the youthful stature to make her acquiescence disturbing. When Polonius sets up the plot, announcing that he and Claudius will eavesdrop on the young lovers to confirm whether Hamlet's strange behavior can be attributed to unrequited love, Ophelia is silent, save for one line, "Madam, I wish it may," in response to Gertrude's speech to her,

> And for your part Ophelia, I do wish
> That your good Beauties be the happy cause
> Of Hamlets wildness: so shall I hope your Virtues
> Will bring him to his wonted way again,
> To both your Honours. [3.1.37]

The words correspond to the values Ophelia reflects in Hamlet, but they are presented obliquely, and in the context of being "loosed" to Hamlet, as a mare is to a stallion, Ophelia cannot possibly mistake the dissonance.

The madness of Ophelia provides an actor with a pair of showcase scenes, first with Gertrude and Claudius and then with her brother. Even though Hamlet is not present, Ophelia is enacting the profound psychic damage that occurs when the soul is expelled, when the rational, noble mind is destroyed, leaving only a budding flower blasted by the heat of sexuality and mental illness. If in her first scenes Ophelia must embody the attributes of a perfect rose, here she must find her character in the image of that rose now opened to the point of decadence, infested with insects, brown and breaking apart after days in the hot sun.

As soon as an actor realizes that the job at hand is to create archetypal images, to create reflections of an attribute, to create a single note or brief melody to be woven into the larger pattern that is the play, then the important clues in the play emerge with greater clarity, and the frustrations can be set aside. Yes, you are playing a stereotype. Yes, in many ways it is just like in a melodrama. Played badly, archetypal acting can be hokey, overblown, predictable, stagey, in a word, terrible. Played well, it is Shakespeare.

AN ACTOR WRITING FOR OTHER ACTORS

> The lines are very quaintly writ.
>
> Silvia [*Two Gents* 2.1.122]

One of the aspects of the genius of Shakespeare that receives too little attention is his acting experience. It is clear, from the images taken from the theatre that Shakespeare has put into his plays, that there were certain shared assumptions about what an actor does in the theatre. His first responsibility is to play the assigned role, defined by generic type: "I hold the world but as the world Gratiano; / A stage, where every man must play a part, / And mine a sad one" [*Merchant* 1.1.77]. In addition to whatever lines one might be given to say, and which might be forgotten in a moment of panic: "As an unperfect actor on the stage / Who with his fear is put besides his part" [Sonnet 23], "Like a dull Actor now, I have forgot my part; / And I am out, even to a full Disgrace" [*Coriolanus* 5.3.40], the actor's job is to come on and go off as instructed by the plot: "All the world's a stage, / And all the men and women, merely Players: / They have their Exits and their Entrances" [*AYLI* 2.7.139]. Sometimes those entrances are made with great effect: "As in a Theatre, the eyes of men / After a well-graced Actor leaves the Stage / Are idly bent on him that enters next, / Thinking his prattle to be tedious" [*RII* 5.224]. Above all, the actor must provide the onlookers with whatever they require to believe in the character and the role. Staging and significant objects can be used to great effect; so too can anything that conforms to audience expectations with regard to age, status, gender, or social function:

> And look you get a Prayer-Book in your hand,
> And stand betwixt two Church-men, good my Lord,
> For on that ground I'll make a holy Descant:
> And be not easily won to our requests,
> Play the Maids part, still answer nay, and take it. [*RIII* 3.7.47]

This last example, wherein Buckingham is coaching Richard on just how to appear in order to trick the mayor and chief citizens of London, is a continuation of a play-acting motif in *Richard III*, demonstrating that the craft of the actor can be used by crafty politicians. Here is Richard soliciting Buckingham's acting credentials:

Richard: Come Cousin,
              Canst thou quake, and change thy colour,
              Murder thy breath in the middle of a word,
              And then begin again, and stop again,
              As if thou wert distraught, and mad with terror?

Buckingham: Tut, I can counterfeit the deep Tragedian,
              Speak, and look back, and pry on every side,
              Tremble and start at wagging of a Straw:
              Intending deep suspicion, ghastly Looks
              Are at my service, like enforced Smiles;
              And both are ready in their Offices,
              At any time to grace my Stratagems. [3.5.1]

Here, we have a list of some of the actor's repertoire in facial expressions, perhaps the same ones that Hamlet refers to when he instructs the actor playing Lucianus, "Begin, murderer. pox, leave thy damnable Faces, and begin" [3.2.2 52].

The similarity between an actor's playing of a role and a politician's role-playing is also demonstrated in *Coriolanus*, both in the title character's use of a theatrical metaphor, quoted earlier, and in the theatrical nature of the instruction he receives on the political act he needs to perform to become consul:

    Go to them, with this Bonnet in thy hand,
    And thus far having stretched it (here be with them)
    Thy Knee bussing the stones: for in such business
    Action is eloquence, and the eyes of th'ignorant
    More learned than the ears, waving thy head,
    Which often thus correcting thy stout heart,
    Now humble as the ripest Mulberry,
    That will not hold the handling. [3.2.73]

In this instance, the man cannot bring himself to play the role convincingly, and so is destroyed politically.

In the induction to *The Taming of the Shrew*, the Lord decides to play a trick on the beggar Christopher Sly, who has fallen into a drunken stupor; he instructs his servants to dress Sly like a nobleman, dress the page as Sly's Lady, and convince Sly he is recovering from a seven-year delusion of being nothing more than a beggar. The Lord pinpoints just how the page will create the character of the lady, instructing him to "bear himself with honourable action, /

Such as he hath observed in noble Ladies / unto their Lords, by them accomplished" [Ind. 1.110]. Acting, then, wasn't just manufacturing heightened facial expressions and vocal mannerisms, it was also based upon what today we call "life study," or what Hamlet describes as holding "the Mirror up to Nature; to show Virtue her Feature, Scorn her own Image, and the very Age and Body of the Time his form and pressure" [3.2.22].

Shakespeare shows us professional actors, such as those who visit Elsinor and demonstrate an actor's ability to startle his audience, as Polonius exclaims, "Look where he has not turned his colour, and has tears in's eyes. Prithee no more" [2.2.519], and Hamlet latter observes:

> Is it not monstrous that this Player here,
> But in a Fiction, in a dream of Passion,
> Could force his soul so to his own conceit,
> That from her working, all his visage warmed;
> Tears in his eyes, distraction in's Aspect,
> A broken voice, and his whole Function suiting
> With Forms, to his Conceit? and all for nothing?
> For Hecuba?
> What's Hecuba to him, or he to Hecuba,
> That he should weep for her? What would he do,
> Had he the Motive and the Cue for passion
> That I have? He would drown the Stage with tears,
> And cleave the general ear with horrid speech:
> Make mad the guilty, and appal the free,
> Confound the ignorant, and amaze indeed,
> The very faculties of Eyes and Ears. [2.2.551]

We also observe firsthand the misguided efforts of well-intentioned amateurs, including Bottom, whose confidence in his acting technique is probably not matched in performance: "That will ask some tears in the true performing of it: if I do it, let the audience look to their eyes: I will move storms, I will condole in some measure. To the rest, yet my chief humour is for a tyrant. I could play Ercles rarely, or a part to tear a Cat in, to make all split" [*Dream* 1.2.25]. Just what does the actor feel, in playing these roles? Is it possible that Polonius and Hamlet are profoundly moved, but that the actor is merely putting on vocal and facial mannerisms like Richard and Buckingham? Shakespeare gives us no insight from a professional actor, but he does draw upon an image of amateur acting, quite unlike Bottom's self-aggrandizing. This is Julia, disguised as a page, quickly inventing a reason why the boy might know exactly how tall Julia is:

> for at Pentecost,
> When all our Pageants of delight were played,
> Our youth got me to play the womans part,

> And I was trimmed in Madam Julias gown,
> Which served me as fit, by all mens judgments,
> As if the garment had been made for me:
> Therefore I know she is about my height. [*Two Gents* 4.4.158]

So far, so good. But in her fantasy, Julia goes one step further, perhaps drawing upon memories of a personal experience as an audience member at just such a theatrical event as she describes, now, from the actor's perspective:

> And at that time I made her weep a good,
> For I did play a lamentable part.
> (Madam) 'twas Ariadne, passioning
> For Theseus perjury, and unjust flight;
> Which I so lively acted with my tears:
> That my poor Mistress moved therewithal,
> Wept bitterly: and would I might be dead,
> If I in thought felt not her very sorrow. [4.4.165]

It is the sight of the audience member's tears that moves the actor to feel; the holding up of the mirror in this instance, so that the betrayed Julia sees her own story in Ariadne's passion, involves an intimate relationship between the pretense lament and the empathy with the lamenter. There is no suggestion that Richard ever feels the piety he pretends as he enacts his false role before the people of London, but there is every reason to believe that the fiction of Hecuba causes Hamlet's actor to change color and weep because he "feels her very sorrow."

Whatever Shakespeare's attitude towards his profession, it is clear that he wrote plays for a company of which he was a member, composed of actors whose capacities he knew well, and that as a shareholder he had a vested interest in creating plays that could be rehearsed easily and efficiently, that would please a large audience, and that would allow the company members to excel at what they did best.

Because Shakespeare's primary task, as playwright, was to shape the dramatic action through the medium of words, modern actors can look at the language of his plays for clues from him the "director," inserted directly into the actor's part, to guide in the creation of character. We can imagine that these clues are just what an actor might need to shape the role, given that they come from one actor to another.

ᨑ 5 ᨑ

A Character's Language

If you knew his pure hearts truth,
You would quickly learn to know him by his voice.
                                    Proteus [*Two Gents* 4.2.88]

When performing in a modern play, an actor's awareness of language as a tool for characterization can be largely intuitive. Certain questions can quite easily be answered: Is my character given a varied or repetitious vocabulary? How often and with what regularity does my character use vulgarities and expletives? Does my character use correct grammar or speak in run-on or incomplete sentences? Does my character express complex ideas using complex sentence structures and relatively uncommon words? What life experiences are suggested by the references my character makes to ideas, events, sensations, or activities?

These questions are vastly more difficult to answer when working on a Shakespearean character. To our modern eye and ear, everyone in the play seems to speak like an English professor, or worse! There are several important signifiers, however, that can be easily learned and used to gain access to the all-important language-based character clues.

EDUCATION

I would I had bestowed that time in the tongues, that I have in fencing, dancing, and bear-baiting: O, had I but followed the Arts.
                                    Sir Andrew [*12th Night* 1.3.92]

It is apparent that there is no direct connection between social status and beautiful language, when a scarcely human monster like Caliban gets to say things like:

> Be not afeard, the Isle is full of noises,
> Sounds, and sweet airs, that give delight and hurt not:
> Sometimes a thousand twangling Instruments
> Will hum about mine ears, and sometime voices,
> That if I then had waked after long sleep,
> Will make me sleep again, and then in dreaming,
> The clouds methought would open, and show riches
> Ready to drop upon me, that when I waked
> I cried to sleep again. [*Tempest* 3.2.135]

We must be equally wary of a simplistic prose/poetry division. While it is true that very many of the comic servants speak prose and the vast majority of the nobility speak poetry, Hamlet is given the following prose passage:

I have of late, but wherefore I know not, lost all my mirth, forgone all custom of exercises; and indeed, it goes so heavily with my disposition that this goodly frame the Earth, seems to me a sterile Promontory; this most excellent Canopy the Air, look you, this brave o'er-hanging, this Majestical Roof, fretted with golden fire: why, it appears no other thing to me, than a foul and pestilent congregation of vapours. What a piece of work is a man! how Noble in Reason? how infinite in faculty? in form and moving how express and admirable? in Action, how like an Angel? in apprehension, how like a God? the beauty of the world, the Paragon of Animals; and yet to me, what is this Quintessence of Dust? [2.2.295]

In terms of vocabulary, it is reasonable to assume that a nice big word like "quintessence" would signal a certain level of education, while comic misuse of fancy words would signal something quite different, as in the case of Dogberry who is given to such statements as, "You are thought here to be the most senseless [meaning sensible] and fit man for the Constable of the watch" [*Much Ado* 3.3.22]. But here too we must take some care, for there is a possibility that some apparently dull-witted peasants are, in truth, more astute and satirical than their betters comprehend. Costard is given to comments such as, "Sir the Contempts thereof are as touching to me" [*LLL* 1.1.190]. He might have meant "the contents" of the letter, but since the letter is contemptuous of Costard, perhaps his malaprop is actually an astute observation.

The surest indicator of advanced education and a corresponding sophistication of thought is in the complexity of the argument. Contrast, for example, the self-justification pronounced by Berowne with that offered by Launcelot Gobbo. Both young men are about to break vows: Berowne's made to avoid the company of women for three years, Launcelot's made in service to Shylock. In each case, the audience is invited to sympathize with the character, but the sophistication of the argument marks one as an educated gentleman and the other as a servant or apprentice.

I will not reproduce Berowne's exuberance as he does go on. Here is just a taste, from the beginning and the ending:

> Have at you then affection's men at arms,
> Consider what you first did swear unto:
> To fast, to study, and to see no woman:
> Flat treason against the Kingly state of youth.
> Say, Can you fast? your stomachs are too young:
> And abstinence engenders maladies.
> And where that you have vowed to study (Lords)
> In that each of you have forsworn his Book.
> Can you still dream and pore, and thereon look.
> For when would you my Lord, or you, or you,
> Have found the ground of studies excellence,
> Without the beauty of a woman's face?
> . . .
> Then fools you were these women to forswear:
> Or keeping what is sworn, you will prove fools,
> For Wisdoms sake, a word that all men love:
> Or for Loves sake, a word that loves all men.
> Or for Mens sake, the author of these Women:
> Or Womens sake, by whom we men are Men.
> Let's once lose our oaths to find our selves,
> Or else we lose our selves, to keep our oaths:
> It is religion to be thus forsworn.
> For Charity it self fulfills the Law:
> And who can sever love from Charity? [LLL 4.3.286]

Here is Gobbo's monologue:

Certainly, my conscience will serve me to run from this Jew my Master: the fiend is at mine elbow, and tempts me, saying to me, Gobbo, Launcelot Gobbo, good Launcelot, or good Gobbo, or good Launcelot Gobbo, use your legs, take the start, run away: my conscience says no; take heed honest Launcelot, take heed honest Gobbo, or as afore said honest Launcelot Gobbo, do not run, scorn running with thy heels; well, the most courageous fiend bids me pack, *fia* says the fiend, away says the fiend, for the heavens rouse up a brave mind says the fiend and run; well, my conscience hanging about the neck of my heart, says very wisely to me: my honest friend Launcelot, being an honest mans son, or rather an honest womans son, for indeed my Father did something smack, something grow to; he had a kind of taste; well, my conscience says Launcelot budge not, budge says the fiend, budge not says my conscience, conscience say I you counsel well, fiend say I you counsel well, to be ruled by my conscience I should stay with the Jew my Master, (who God bless the mark) is a kind of devil; and to run away from the Jew I should be ruled by the fiend, who saving your reverence is the devil himself:

certainly the Jew is the very devil incarnation, and in my conscience, my conscience is but a kind of hard conscience, to offer to counsel me to stay with the Jew, the fiend gives the more friendly counsel: I will run fiend, my heels are at your commandment, I will run. [*Merchant* 2.2.1]

In *Henry V*, Shakespeare brings together a king and a commoner to debate the morality of war in the cold hours before dawn and the battle of Agincourt. Michael Williams, the common soldier, is not denied the capacity to use language vividly to reflect his fears and his outrage. Here is his response to another soldier's glib self-justification, "If his Cause be wrong, our obedience to the King wipes the Crime of it out of us" [4.3.132]:

But if the Cause be not good, the King himself hath a heavy Reckoning to make, when all those Legs, and Arms, and Heads, chopped off in a Battle, shall join together at the latter day, and cry all, We died at such a place, some swearing, some crying for a Surgeon; some upon their Wives, left poor behind them; some upon the Debts they owe, some upon their Children rawly left: I am afeared, there are few die well, that die in a Battle: for how can they charitably dispose of any thing, when Blood is their argument? Now, if these men do not die well, it will be a black matter for the King, that led them to it; who to disobey, were against all proportion of subjection. [4.3.134]

The images and the emotion are as one; this is clearly a man speaking from his heart. King Henry, disguised as just another soldier, responds with a brilliantly reasoned argument. In order to draw attention to the complex intellectual journey on which he guides his listeners, I have separated the seven sentences which make up his prose dissertation:

1. So, if a Son that is by his Father sent about Merchandise, do sinfully miscarry upon the Sea; the imputation of his wickedness, by your rule, should be imposed upon his Father that sent him: or if a Servant, under his Masters command, transporting a sum of Money, be assailed by Robbers, and dye in many irreconciled Iniquities; you may call the business of the Master the author of the Servants damnation: but this is not so: The King is not bound to answer the particular endings of his Soldiers, the Father of his Son, nor the Master of his Servant; for they purpose not their death, when they purpose their services.

2. Besides, there is no King, be his Cause never so spotless, if it come to the arbitrement of Swords, can try it out with all unspotted Soldiers: some (peradventure) have on them the guilt of premeditated and contrived Murder; some, of beguiling Virgins with the broken Seals of Perjury; some, making the Wars their Bulwark, that have before gored the gentle Bosom of Peace with Pillage and Robbery.

3. Now, if these men have defeated the Law, and outrun Native punishment; though they can out-strip men, they have no wings to fly from God.

4. War is his Beadle, War is his Vengeance: so that here men are punished, for before breach of the Kings Laws, in now the Kings Quarrel: where they feared the death, they have borne life away; and where they would be safe, they perish.

5. Then if they die unprovided, no more is the King guilty of their damnation, then he was before guilty of those Impieties, for the which they are now visited.

6. Every Subjects Duty is the Kings, but every Subjects Soul is his own.

7. Therefore should every Soldier in the Wars do as every sick man in his Bed, wash every Mote out of his Conscience: and dying so, Death is to him advantage; or not dying, the time was blessedly lost, wherein such preparation was gained: and in him that escapes, it were not sin to think, that making God so free an offer, he let him outlive that day, to see his Greatness, and to teach others how they should prepare.

So persuasive is all of this that Williams responds, " 'Tis certain, every man that dies ill, the ill upon his own head, the King is not to answer it," despite the fact that nothing in Henry's argument has addressed the powerful emotions Williams ealier expressed. Williams is effectively silenced by the power of the language of the king, unable to challenge even the glaring illogic of closing point of the first sentence, that fathers, masters, and generals do not intend the death of their sons, servants, and soldiers. The first two examples hold true, but the third quite clearly does not.

Because Shakespeare lived at a time when occupation and family status implied specific levels of education, we need to place his witty servants and poetical monsters into the category of the remarkable; Williams is more representative of his class. We might find that these assumptions irritate our modern democratic sensibilities, as does the direct correlation made between rank and nobility of spirit. Although some of Shakespeare's most appalling villains are noble born, not a one of these is stupid. Every character who demonstrates a breadth of understanding, a questioning spirit, or complexity of feeling is a member of the gentry, and therefore a participant in the great banquet of language by right of birth and education.

EMOTIONAL INTELLIGENCE

> There is a fair behaviour in thee Captain,
> And though that nature, with a beauteous wall
> Doth oft close in pollution: yet of thee
> I will believe thou hast a mind that suits
> With this thy faire and outward character.
>
> Viola [*12th Night* 1.2.47]

As we have seen with Caliban, great sensitivity and awareness of the complexity of the human experience is never limited to a single class, race, or even religion. Shylock is given this compelling statement of his essential humanity:

Hath not a Jew eyes? hath not a Jew hands, organs, dimensions, senses, affections, passions, fed with the same food, hurt with the same weapons, subject to the same diseases, healed by the same means, warmed and cooled by the same Winter and Summer as a Christian is: if you prick us do we not bleed? if you tickle us, do we not laugh? if you poison us do we not die? and if you wrong us shall we not revenge? [*Merchant* 3.1.59]

We lose sight today of the achievement represented by this speech. The Elizabethans viewed Jews as exotic and fearsome in their unrepentant rejection of Jesus Christ. Whenever Jews appeared on the London stage, they did so in order to embody the essence of horrific and foreign villainy. Shylock is created in just such a vein, and his rantings and ravings elsewhere in the play fulfill audience expectations without challenging any of their prejudices. This speech, however, does something else. In the context of justifying his horrific revenge, Shylock builds a case for his essential humanity, including therein the privilege of enacting revenge, just as Christians do. However, the powerful elemental images of physical sensation establish his right to our empathy, thus skewing the comedy in unprecedented ways.

Today, we cannot imagine the ending of the fourth act of *The Merchant of Venice* as a redemptive comedy, because the defeat of Shylock, followed by his forced conversion to Christianity, reminds us of midcentury horrors that resulted in the death of millions of Jews in Nazi Germany. To Shakespeare's London, however, Shylock is being dragged kicking and screaming to a happiness he can barely imagine but which his passionate statement of human experience demands. This is a creature with a soul, and it could not be a comedy unless his soul was ensured redemption along with the hero at the end of the day.

Another abhorrent villain who is made almost unbearably human can be found in Shakespeare's first big hit, that seldom-read, even less often performed *Titus Andronicus*. Aaron is guilty of the worst sort of villainies, but here he addresses his infant son: "I'll make you feed on berries, and on roots, / And feed on curds and whey, and suck the Goat, / And cabin in a Cave, and bring you up / To be a warrior, and command a Camp" [4.2.177]. Later, he will agree to anything his captors wish, provided they spare his child's life.

Another puzzle that besets a modern listener or speaker of Shakespeare's language is the amount of duplicity suggested by the quality of oratory. We are accustomed, in modern contexts, to having a pretty reliable identification of empty pontificating, language that might best be described, as does Macbeth, as, "full of sound and fury / Signifying nothing" [5.5.27].

Because every character in Shakespeare partakes of the customary techniques of classical rhetoric, the natural outcome of the centrality of rhetorical exercises in the school curriculum, it is much more difficult for us to maintain a barometer for plain speaking and bombast. Shakespeare sometimes helps us by clarifying how what has just been spoken strikes the onstage listeners.

Gertrude cuts off Polonius with the crisp instruction: "More matter, with less Art." Here is what Polonius had been saying:

My Liege, and Madam, to expostulate
What Majesty should be, what Duty is,
Why day is day; night, night; and time is time,
Were nothing but to waste Night, Day and Time.
Therefore, since Brevity is the Soul of Wit,
And tediousness, the limbs and outward flourishes,
I will be brief. Your Noble Son is mad:
Mad call I it; for to define true Madness,
What is't, but to be nothing else but mad.
But let that go. [2.2.86]

Gertrude's criticism seems entirely appropriate. Polonius has yet to answer Gertrude's natural questions about Polonius's blunt observation: "your noble son is mad," and the request for more matter, that is, concrete information, and less art, that is, the artifice of beautifully constructed digressions on interesting philosophical concepts, is entirely justified. But should we therefore assume that Polonius's instructions to his son Laertes are equally empty of matter? We are so used to these precepts, as he calls them, that we neglect to give Polonius his due. True, the younger generation label him a "tedious old fool," but this particular speech demonstrates minimal artifice for its own sake and maximum matter.

        Give thy thoughts no tongue,
Nor any unproportioned thought his Act:
Be thou familiar; but by no means vulgar:
Those friends thou hast, and their adoption tried,
Grapple them to thy Soul, with hoops of Steel:
But do not dull thy palm, with entertainment
Of each new-hatched, unfledged Comrade. Beware
Of entrance to a quarrel: but being in
Bear't that th'opposed may beware of thee.
Give every man thy ear, but few thy voice:
Take each man's censure: but reserve thy judgment:
Costly thy habit as thy purse can buy;
But not expressed in fancy; rich, not gaudy
For the Apparel oft proclaims the man.
And they in France of the best rank and station,
Are of a most select and generous chief in that.
Neither a borrower, nor a lender be;
For loan oft loses both itself and friend:
And borrowing dulls the edge of Husbandry.
This above all; to thine own self be true:
And it must follow, as the Night the Day,
Thou canst not then be false to any man.
Farewell: my Blessing season this in thee. [1.3.59]

What we miss in this is how precise, helpful, and original Polonius's advice would sound to the first listeners. At a time when it was customary to instruct the junior members of the nobility in regard to their loyalty to God, to England, and to the ruling monarch, here we have a father reminding his son that, above all else, Laertes must be true to his own self.

There are occasions in Shakespeare's plays where we are not given any clues as to the relationship between rhetoric and reliability. Two modern tendencies muddy the waters still further. First, we ordinarily assume that any lengthy, ornately structured speech is inherently duplicitous, despite extensive evidence to the contrary provided by the many heartfelt and beautifully crafted speeches in the plays. The following is just one such example. Hermione is on trial for her life, and must summon every rhetorical strategy to give voice to her innocence. Nothing in the play, before or after this scene, gives us any indication that she is prone to even the slightest dishonesty, and yet her language is filled with artifice, in the form of artful presentation of ideas in order to persuade her listeners:

> Since what I am to say, must be but that
> Which contradicts my Accusation, and
> The testimony on my part, no other
> But what comes from my self, it shall scarce boot me
> To say, Not guilty: mine Integrity
> Being counted Falsehood, shall (as I express it)
> Be so received. But thus, if Powers Divine
> Behold our human Actions (as they do)
> I doubt not then, but Innocence shall make
> False Accusation blush, and Tyranny
> Tremble at Patience. You (my Lord) best know
> (Whom least will seem to do so) my past life
> Hath been as continent, as chaste, as true,
> As I am now unhappy; which is more
> Than History can pattern, though devised,
> And played, to take Spectators. For behold me,
> Fellow of the Royal Bed, which owe
> A Moiety of the Throne: a great Kings Daughter,
> The Mother to a hopeful Prince, here standing
> To prate and talk for Life, and Honour, fore
> Who please to come, and hear. For Life, I prize it
> As I weigh Grief (which I would spare) for Honour,
> 'Tis a derivative from me to mine,
> And only that I stand for. I appeal
> To your own Conscience (Sir) before Polixenes
> Came to your Court, how I was in your grace,
> How merited to be so: Since he came,
> With what encounter so uncurrent, I
> Have strained t'appear thus; if one jot beyond

The bound of Honour, or in act, or will
That way inclining, hardened be the hearts
Of all that hear me, and my near'st of Kin
Cry fie upon my Grave. [*WT* 3.2.22]

It is clear, from this example, that strong feeling and lawyer-like language are not mutually exclusive.

The other modern trick that gets in our way of assessing Shakespeare's use of bombast as an indicator of character is our excessive familiarity with the entire play before it begins. It is very difficult for us to position ourselves naively, to know only as much or as little of the story as Shakespeare's first audience knew. *Hamlet* provides us with a good example. We know that the story of the revenging prince had been presented on the London stage before Shakespeare's version, and so it is possible that some, if not all, in the audience knew the basic idea. But let us encounter the play as if for the first time, without any clear idea of who the villain of the piece might be. In the first scene of the play, we see overwhelming evidence that something rotten is at work in Denmark, what with a ghost walking and the troops on full alert expecting an invasion at any moment. If we did not know that Claudius is a murderer and a usurper, what would we assume? He is dressed like a king, and talks like a ruler dedicated to the peaceful transition from one monarch to the next. The morality of the situation remains grey. There are very good reasons why men do not marry the widows of their dead brothers, but there are also very good reasons why kings might do so, and Shakespeare's audience would remember their own King Harry doing just that, when his brother Arthur died. It is still not clear whether that was a good or bad thing politically or spiritually. The fact that this action was taken with the full consultation of the assembled nobility is a sign that it was probably a good thing, particularly if Norwegian troops are massing on the border. Claudius assesses the real reasons for Fortinbras's threat to Denmark, astutely, bluntly, and powerfully. Here is clearly a master politician and an able king. Denmark is in good hands. We can almost hear the soldiers on the battlements breathe a sigh of relief as the word goes out: Claudius has things well under control, and the transition from one king to the next will go smoothly. "Long live the king," indeed.

The soldiers were convinced that the ghost's appearance was linked to the military threat to Denmark. Someone who knows the old story of the Danish prince might smugly conclude that they are mistaken, but others are well positioned, like Hamlet, to discover the full extent of the rotten matter only when the ghost finally speaks.

Our question at hand is: Did Claudius's opening speech signal his murderous nature, so that everyone in the audience, like Hamlet, would say, "O my prophetic soul! My uncle!"? Or is Claudius's guilt successfully hidden, so that in every way he not only appears, but is an excellent ruler?

Let us have a look at the language of two characters whose duplicity is revealed from their first entrance: Iago and Don John. In the first minute of *Othello*, we learn that Iago has had money from Roderigo, and that he hates Othello. In the opening moments of *Much Ado about Nothing*, we learn something of each of Don Pedro, Claudio, and Benedick, but nothing of Don John save that he is now reconciled with Don Pedro his brother. When welcomed to Leonato's house, Don John responds, "I thank you: I am not of many words, but I thank you."

We will have to wait to gain some clue as to this man's personality. When he is alone with his close companion, he provides the necessary thumb-nail sketch:

I wonder that thou (being as thou sayest thou art, born under Saturn) goest about to apply a moral medicine, to a mortifying mischief: I cannot hide what I am: I must be sad when I have cause, and smile at no mans jests, eat when I have stomach, and wait for no mans leisure: sleep when I am drowsy, and tend on no mans business, laugh when I am merry, and claw no man in his humour. [1.3.10]

His companion then provides the history of Don John's villainy. He recently "stood out against" his brother, in other words led a rebellion against Don Pedro. It is not absolutely clear whether this was the war from which the noblemen are returning, or whether the reconciliation occurred in order that they could fight a common enemy. This, however, is how Don John describes his current situation:

I had rather be a canker in a hedge, than a rose in his grace, and it better fits my blood to be disdained of all than, to fashion a carriage to rob love from any: in this (though I cannot be said to be a flattering honest man) it must not be denied but I am a plain-dealing villain. I am trusted with a muzzle, and enfranchised with a clog, therefore have decreed, not to sing in my cage: if I had my mouth, I would bite: if I had my liberty, I would do my liking: in the meantime, let me be that I am, and seek not to alter me. [1.3.27]

One other personal attribute marks Don John: he is the illegitimate brother of the ruling prince. We know this from the cast of characters; Shakespeare's audience would have been able to read an equally clear marker of bastardy in the coat of arms worn by Don John and his followers.

But we can't assume that all bastards are evil, although Edmund the illegitimate certainly causes significant pain to the other characters in *King Lear*. The Bastard in *King John* turns out to be the most loyal of followers, and one who uses his position as a perennial outsider to critique the moral quagmire of John's court.

Nor can we assume that all who are governed by Saturn, in other words melancholics, are given to villainy. Jaques, who wanders through the forest of Arden with an equally sour disposition, wishes no one any harm, and Hamlet finds it so difficult to summon up viciousness that he fails to enact his role as a revenging son until several hours of stage events after the Ghost gives him his gruesome charge.

Iago, like Don John, makes a link between disinclination to speak and villainy, but only at the end of the play, after he has used language most effectively to seduce Othello into a murderous jealousy. When all of his cruel lies are revealed, he responds to his accusers' questions with, "Demand me nothing: what you know, you know. From this time forth I never will speak word."

There is something in this statement that is so convincing that we foresee his silence even in the face of the promised tortures. Is it any wonder that Othello calls him a demidevil and even looks towards his feet, thinking to see cloven hoofs?

It is, in fact, the words of supernatural and devilish characters that provide us with the most reliable indicator of evil duplicity, that trick of language known as equivocation. The best equivocators are the voices of prophecy that falsely comfort Macbeth with promises of invulnerability:

> Be bloody, bold, and resolute:
> Laugh to scorn
> The power of man: For none of woman born
> Shall harm Macbeth. [4.1.79]

> Be Lion mettled, proud, and take no care:
> Who chafes, who frets, or where Conspirers are:
> Macbeth shall never vanquished be, until
> Great Birnam Wood, to high Dunsinane Hill
> Shall come against him. [4.1.90]

Because Macbeth knows that every man is the result of his mother's pregnancy, and that woods are not capable of travelling, he is encouraged in his reign of terror. When, later in the play, Malcolm instructs the captains of his advancing armies, "Let every Soldier hew him down a Bough, / And bear't before him, thereby shall we shadow / The numbers of our Host, and make discovery / Err in report of us" [5.4.4], we recognize simultaneously a crafty and familiar military maneuver and the alternative meaning of the prophecy: true, the woods cannot move, but they can appear to move if soldiers carrying branches approach the castle. The messenger will tell Macbeth in the next scene, "As I did stand my watch upon the Hill / I looked toward Birnam, and anon me thought / The wood began to move" [5.5.32].

Perhaps, we are already alert to the potential for equivocation bound up in anything related to the phrase "of woman born," for caesarian deliveries date back to Julius Caesar. Something quite terrible happens to Macbeth, however, when he enters into his final battle. First, Shakespeare shows him surrounded, unable to fly the battle field, but still confident that no man lives who can kill him. He meets Young Siward and, just as he expected, easily defeats him, confirming the prophecy. Then he meets Macduff. First, Macbeth tries to avoid the fight, saying: "Of all men else I have avoided thee: / But get thee back,

my soul is too much charged / With blood of thine already" [5.8.4]. They
fight, and then Macbeth warns Macduff again:

> Thou losest labour,
> As easy mayst thou the intrenchant Air
> With thy keen Sword impress, as make me bleed:
> Let fall thy blade on vulnerable Crests,
> I bear a charmed Life, which must not yield,
> To one of woman born. [5.8.8]

To this, Macduff replies: "Despair thy Charm, / And let the Angel whom thou
still hast served / Tell thee, Macduff was from his Mothers womb / Untimely
ripped" [5.8.13]. Now we see the true significance of the prophecy: the immediate decimation of Macbeth's valor:

> Accursed be that tongue that tells me so;
> For it hath Cowed my better part of man:
> And be these juggling Fiends no more believed,
> That palter with us in a double sense,
> That keep the word of promise to our ear,
> And break it to our hope. I'll not fight with thee. [5.8.17]

Macduff then offers an alternative, that Macbeth yield and suffer the fate of
all traitors: to be exhibited to the mockery of the people. Macbeth then summons up the valor that made him a great warrior long before he received false
promises of invulnerability. In his willingness to fight, even knowing he will
die, we see the falling away of villainy's duplicity and the faint glimmer of a
spirit worthy of redemption.

> I will not yield
> To kiss the ground before young Malcolm's feet,
> And to be baited with the Rabble's curse.
> Though Birnam wood be come to Dunsinane,
> And thou opposed, being of no woman born,
> Yet I will try the last. Before my body,
> I throw my warlike Shield: Lay on, Macduff,
> And damned be him, that first cries hold, enough. [5.8.27]

Let us look at a speech of another notable villain to see if his language reveals
his misappropriation of rhetoric in service of equivocation. Edmund first appears silent alongside his father, as the shameful story of his illegitimate birth
is shared with the duke of Kent. Next, we see Edmund alone and, like Iago,
he shares with us the thoughts of his twisted mind. Only then do we hear him
go to work on his father and brother, who quickly fall completely under the
spell of his plausible and effective use of language.

The trickery of the father takes a form very similar to that used by Iago. The seeds of distrust are firmly planted, in this case by a letter rather than a handkerchief, and then Edmund argues against the suspicions, counselling patience and a rational examination of the situation:

If it shall please you to suspend your indignation against my Brother, till you can derive from him better testimony of his intent, you shall run a certain course: where, if you violently proceed against him, mistaking his purpose, it would make a great gap in your own Honour, and shake in pieces, the heart of his obedience. I dare pawn down my life for him, that he hath wrote this to feel my affection to your Honour, and to no further pretence of danger. [*Lear* 1.2.79]

All of this is well spoken and indicative of a thoughtful, reliable nature, and serves Edmund's real purpose, which is to persuade his father to spy upon his brother. We don't actually see that, because events fall even more into Edmund's plans and he stages a mock fight to prove Edgar's villainy all the more effectively. Edgar is even easier to manipulate, as no proof but Edmund's report is required of the father's anger against his legitimate son. Edmund can then play the role of friend and confident, a strategy also employed by Iago. In either exchange, Edmund's language is notable for its clarity and expressiveness. He is a skillful deliverer of whatever style of language will best persuade the listener: with his father, reasoned argument; with his brother, informal expressiveness.

Shakespeare provides us with another linguistic chameleon in Prince Hal, who seems to spend his time in the taverns of Eastcheap apprenticing to that master-manipulator of obfuscation: Falstaff. The two men trade arias of insult and mock-heroic bombast. They play with exaggeration and outright falsehood, but Hal's motivation has been clear from the end of his first scene: he is simply waiting for the perfect moment to reveal his true nobility, which he will hide behind a life of debauchery, and if he's going to play the profligate prince he'll master the part: "I'll so offend, to make offence a skill" [*1HIV* 1.2.216].

Hal can move from Falstaff's language games to the purposeful use of argument for the presentation of strong feeling, as he reveals when he hears the extent of the pain he has caused his father. He can also drop all ornamentation and speak plainly and powerfully. When Falstaff delivers a speech as expansive and bloated as his belly, "No, my good Lord, banish Peto, banish Bardolph, banish Poins: but for sweet Jack Falstaff, kind Jack Falstaff, true Jack Falstaff, valiant Jack Falstaff, and therefore more valiant, being as he is old Jack Falstaff, banish not him thy Harrys company, banish not him thy Harrys company, banish plump Jack, and banish all the World" [2.4.474]. Hal responds, "I do, I will."

It is apparent, from this cursory examination of a variety of villains and heroes, that neither rhetorical artifice nor plain-speaking, neither bombast nor rational argument, in and of themselves are clues to the character of the speaker. A skilled villain is likely to have mastered language so that he can speak the truth while manipulating the listener into incorrect assumptions, and the duplicity is seldom signalled by the form the language takes. Even the capacity to shift back and forth between different styles of speech might be a positive attribute, though it is also an appropriate tool for the manipulation of a wide variety of people.

RHYTHMIC INDICATORS

> When my heart all mad with misery,
> Beats in this hollow prison of my flesh,
> Then thus I thump it down.
>
> Titus [*Titus* 3.2.9]

The iambic pentameter of Shakespeare's blank verse is the repository of a significant number of signals as to the emotional undercurrents at work under the surface of the rhetoric. These are available for use in the formation of character as well as in ascertaining the experience the character is having while saying these words.

Generally speaking, the Iambic Code, which is in fact the variations on strict iambic pentameter that regularly occur in all of Shakespeare's dramatic poetry, marks moments when the forward flow of feeling and the capacity of language to embody that feeling are, for whatever reason, at odds. When the verse is regular, this does not signify that there is no feeling. Rather, the flood of emotion and the flow of language are perfectly aligned. The slight or profound irregularities are comparable to a river's rippled surface or rocky rapids, and hence a powerful indicator of what modern actors call the subtext of the speech.

A direct parallel can be drawn between excessive irregularities and tortured feeling. Here, for example, is Leontes, driven almost mad with paranoid jealousy:

> Inch-thick, knee-deep, o'er head and ears a forked one.
> Go play (Boy) play: thy Mother plays, and I
> Play too; but so disgraced a part, whose issue
> Will hiss me to my Grave: Contempt and Clamour
> Will be my Knell. Go play (Boy) play, there have been
> (Or I am much deceived) Cuckolds ere now,
> And many a man there is (even at this present,
> Now, while I speak this) holds his Wife by th'Arm,
> That little thinks she has been sluiced in's absence,
> And his Pond fished by his next Neighbour (by
> Sir Smile, his Neighbour) nay, there's comfort in't,

Whiles other men have Gates, and those Gates opened
(As mine) against their will. Should all despair
That have revolted Wives, the tenth of Mankind
Would hang themselves. Physic for't, there's none:
It is a bawdy Planet, that will strike
Where 'tis predominant; and 'tis powerful: think it:
From East, West, North and South, be it concluded,
No Barricado for a Belly. Know't,
It will let in and out the Enemy,
With bag and baggage: many thousand on's
Have the Disease, and feel't not. How now Boy? [*WT* 1.2.186]

This is a late play, and we can observe a growing use of verse irregularities from early to late. Even so, this is quite a remarkable blending of sounds, subject matter, and rhythm to evoke the sensation of sexual jealousy. Simply saying these words aloud provides an actor with many clues to and means by which the emotions of the character can be expressed.

The speech also contains information that can be used for characterization. Besides being a man who is consumed with jealousy, who is Leontes? In particular, what clues can we find to his attitudes and the intellectual framework within which he experiences these emotions?

Many of our insights into Leontes's character will be provided by the specific words he uses. For a king, he talks the language of the commons: pond fishing and water sluices are not concerns that we ordinarily associate with a ruling monarch. More expected are images from war: barricados letting in and out the enemy, complete with the heavy baggage carts that traditionally follow an army seems an appropriate image for a warrior king. But is he a warrior? A barricado is in fact a hastily thrown up barricade, often constructed of barrels, household furniture, and whatever stone and timber can be found, scarcely the work of a royal army.

The words "physic" and "disease" suggest a medical framework, but not a very sophisticated one, and the link to astrology suggested by the bawdy planet evokes an uneducated attitude to the spread of disease. That surely is Leontes's point in all this: everyone, from the lowliest home owner to the greatest king, can suffer from this sort of domestic betrayal. The gates that are opened are simultaneously those of a city and the frail wooden ones marking the boundary of a small plot of land. That Leontes would know of such things suggests, however, that his life at court is not entirely cosmopolitan.

Another indicator of Leontes's personality is the frequency with which he ends a line of poetry in an extra unaccented syllable, and the words or phrases that are used to create this variation on regular iambic pentameter: "a forked one," "whose issue," "contempt and clamour," "even at this present," "in's absence," "and those gates opened," "think it," and "be it concluded." These so-called feminine endings open up the line of poetry so that the idea expressed avoids the clear and strong culmination of the usual five-foot iambs, found for example in a line like, "It is a bawdy planet that will strike," where the single emphasized syllable in the final position, plus the natural rise of the iambs, results in the moving forward of the line to concluding thrust. The opening up accomplishes two things. First, it demands of the speaker a rushing on, as if the opened up, inconclusive energy must seek resolution in the next line. Second, it also demands an emotional or intellectual opening to an idea or feeling: the speaker is forced to linger momentarily, during the extra syllable, on that to which the language has given shape.

Feminine endings are sometimes called weak endings, but what they lack in thrust and resolution they make up for in their capacity for depth of perception. What is it, then, that Leontes's mind brings him to, over and over, that he cannot avoid but also cannot resolve? It is something as horrible as a snake or the devil himself, with forked tongue or cloven hoof. It has very much to do with the child his wife is carrying, and the harsh sound of those who might know of his disgrace. The immediacy of the sensation, the fact that it is going on under his very nose, at this very instant, is as much a part of what makes this so painful as the fact that the lovers take advantage of his absence to embrace, and the image of the opening of his wife's body is something that he cannot bear to think of, yet cannot stop thinking about.

That Leontes is a rational man, capable of educated logical thought, is suggested by the last of the feminine endings in the speech. "Be it concluded," follows "Think if," and the next line ends with "Know't." But this is the false logic of jealousy. The mind dwells on the image, puts together false conclusions, and then takes something as known that is merely suspected.

COMPLEXITY OF THOUGHT, COMPLEXITY OF CHARACTER

> Do not extort thy reasons from this clause,
> For that I woo, thou therefore hast no cause:
> But rather reason thus, with reason fetter;
> Love sought, is good: but given unsought, is better.
>
> Olivia [*12th Night* 3.1.153]

Love's Labour's Lost contains innumerable sentences with as complex a structure as Olivia's, and so presents a special challenge for the modern actor. Shakespeare has created a quartet of courtly couples, all of whom revel in the dance of language as they interact in the carefree world of the king of Navarre's academe. Then comes the unexpected news of the death of the king of France, ending the wooing before all can be resolved. Navarre has this to say to the Princess of France:

The extreme parts of time, extremely forms
All causes to the purpose of his speed:
And often at his very loose decides
That, which long process could not arbitrate.
And though the mourning brow of progeny
Forbid the smiling courtesy of Love:
The holy suit which fain it would convince,
Yet since love's argument was first on foot,
Let not the cloud of sorrow justle it
From what it purposed: since to wail friends lost,
Is not by much so wholesome profitable,
As to rejoice at friends but newly found. [*LLL* 5.2.740]

To which the Princess replies, "I understand you not." And so we are reminded that Shakespeare could create characters who sacrifice communication for rhetorical effect. If we have a closer look, we can discover that the thoughts all make sense, but that the tangled web reflects the tangled feeling of the speaker, who can't seem to come right out and say that he loves her. Navarre is in a difficult situation. He has fallen passionately in love with the Princess, only to have his courtly wooing of her cut short by the news of the death of her father. He is trying, delicately, to engage in a discussion of their mutual attraction, given that she is (a) filled with shocked horror and grief, (b) preparing to depart in haste, and (c) now the ruler of her country. He's caught between feeling so sad on account of her grief and yet so happy because he has found the woman he wants to marry. In fact, and this is the thought with which he begins the speech, the emergency of the situation, and her speedy departure, puts him in the position of having to rush into a statement of love, an action that would ordinarily follow a much more protracted period of wooing. But hey, love was here first, and shouldn't be elbowed aside because death has pushed his way onto the stage.

The Princess cannot understand him, more because he is dancing around the topic than because his web is too tangled to be clear, though the latter reflects and allows the former. Fortunately for Navarre, his good friend Berowne, mixing huge dollops of rhetorical artifice with whatever "matter" most interests his friends at that moment, is capable of more direct, though supremely flowery, communication.

Honest plain words, best pierce the ear of grief
And by these badges understand the King,
For your fair sakes have we neglected time,
Played foul play with our oaths: your beauty Ladies,
Hath much deformed us, fashioning our humours
Even to the opposed end of our intents.
And what in us hath seemed ridiculous:
As Love is full of unbefitting strains,

All wanton as a child, skipping and vain.
Formed by the eye, and therefore, like the eye.
Full of strange shapes, of habits, and of forms
Varying in subjects as the eye doth roll,
To every varied object in his glance:
Which parti-coated presence of loose love
Put on by us, if in your heavenly eyes,
Have misbecomed our oaths and gravities.
Those heavenly eyes that look into these faults,
Suggested us to make: therefore Ladies,
Our love being yours, the error that Love makes
Is likewise yours. We to our selves prove false,
By being once false, for ever to be true
To those that make us both, fair Ladies you.
And even that falsehood in it self a sin,
Thus purifies it self, and turns to grace. [5.2.753]

The Princess responds by naming the wooing and the speech as something less than serious:

We have received your Letters, full of Love:
Your Favours, the Ambassadors of Love.
And in our maiden council rated them,
At courtship, pleasant jest, and courtesy,
As bombast and as lining to the time:
But more devout than this in our respects
Have we not been, and therefore met your loves
In their own fashion, like a merriment. [5.2.777]

Finally, Navarre reveals his capacity for direct, plain, and heart-felt communication: "Now at the latest minute of the hour, / Grant us your loves" [5.2.787]. The answer is still no, or at least not for a year, during which Navarre and his companions must demonstrate a serious commitment to spiritual maturation, one component of which is a repositioning of language, through the silence of the hermitage and the application of Berowne's frothy wit to the near-impossible task of making the painfully sick smile.

Let's have a look at another, even more complex tangle, one that clearly is perfectly understood by other characters. The Princess has just been praised by her attending Lord Boyet. She responds,

Good Lord Boyet, my beauty though but mean,
Needs not the painted flourish of your praise:
Beauty is bought by judgment of the eye,
Not utt'red by base sale of chapmens tongues:
I am less proud to hear you tell my worth,

Then you much willing to be counted wise,
In spending you wit in the praise of mine. [2.1.13]

This sentence contains, as we have come to expect, a complete rhetorical argument. The "exordium" is compressed into the address, that praises the noble friend, preparatory to the statement of the theme of the argument, the true nature of beauty. By describing Beauty as if it were an object for sale, she uses the topoi of comparison to change Boyet by changing his perspective on flattery. The folio uses a colon to introduce these two lines and so clarifies that they arise directly out of the flow of the argument and mark the shift from one important argument to the amplification or clarification. Modern editors often put a period after "tongues," but the folio has another colon. The argument isn't over, but requires one more nail on Boyet's coffin lid. So the next step up the ladder of argument takes us to the syntactical web, laden with ethical considerations of worth, wisdom, and wit.

What is the Princess saying here? Whatever it is must work, because she then changes the subject. Boyet has been vanquished, at least in so far as she has successfully redefined beauty and flattery for him, in connection with worth, wisdom, and wit.

"I am much less" sits in an antithetical relationship to "then you much" and we see that "proud to hear you tell my worth" is brought into a collision with "willing to be counted wise" and within these contrasting phrases we see other contrast: "proud" to "wise," and "worth" to "counted." These are not opposites, but alternatives, and the imagery of Beauty for sale is reinforced by the second pair and the following line where wit is something Boyet is "spending." At the end of the thought, we are back to "praise," which echoes "proud" in its sounds and we are aware, although the Princess has not come out and said so, that "praise" often makes women "proud."

Does the Iambic Code, plus this awareness of the significance of words within the rhetorical (as opposed to grammatical) pattern assist in the delivery of the speech? Let's look at it without punctuation but with an indication of emphasized words:

GOOD Lord boyET my BEAUTy though but MEAN
needs NOT the PAINTed FLOURish of your PRAISE
BEAUTy is BOUGHT by JUDGment of the EYE
not *UTT'red* by BASE **SALE** of CHAPmen's TONGUES
I am less PROUD to HEAR you TELL my WORTH
then YOU much WILLing to be COUNTed WISE
in SPENDing **YOUR** WIT in the PRAISE of MINE.

It's immediately clear that the iambic pentameter places into the downbeat position all of the key words in the argument. In the fourth line, "by" is in the downbeat, and "base" therefore has to be topped by "sale," an effective device for the delivery of the image. In the last line, "wit" seems like an important word but it isn't in the downbeat position. "Your" must be emphasized, which balances nicely with the emphasis accorded "I" two lines earlier in one of three inverted "attacca" rhythms. I didn't put into caps the prepositions that sit in the downbeat: "though," "of" twice, and "in" plus the "to" in the second to last line. In saying the lines aloud, it is most natural to give these just the slightest of elevated stresses, in keeping with the way these words are used in ordinary speech.

What I have found, over and over, is that the saying aloud of the tangled webs, with special care to use the Iambic Code, and with an eye out for rhetorical devices, is usually sufficient to connect the speaker with the intellectual content of the convoluted syntax. What's more, the saying of the words in this particular shape illuminates powerfully the emotional significance of the moment, reflected in and expressed by the tangle.

With this sentence, Shakespeare introduces us to the quality of the Princess's mind. She is insightful. She has wisdom and an awareness of the nature of court flattery. She sees connections between things that might easily be missed by someone less wise, less alert, less admirable. She realizes that Boyet's witty flattery, disguised as wisdom, is crass, and so demonstrates her own wisdom and wit.

EMOTION AND RHETORIC

> Methinks his words do from such passion fly
> That he believes himself, so do not I.
>
> Viola [*12th Night* 3.4.373]

But students will be aware of the huge gap between their stumbling efforts, interspersed with hesitations and linguistic slips, and the articulate, flowing language of Shakespeare's great set speeches. I remember working with a young professional actor on Claudio's deeply emotional speech to his sister Isabella.

> Ay, but to die, and go we know not where,
> To lie in cold obstruction, and to rot,
> This sensible warm motion, to become
> A kneaded clod; And the delighted spirit
> To bathe in fiery floods, or to reside
> In thrilling Region of thick-ribbed Ice,
> To be imprisoned in the viewless winds
> And blown with restless violence round about
> The pendent world: or to be worse than worst
> Of those, that lawless and incertain thought,
> Imagine howling, 'tis too horrible.

> The weariest, and most loathed worldly life
> That Age, Ache, penury, and imprisonment
> Can lay on nature, is a Paradise
> To what we fear of death. [*Measure* 3.1.117]

I suggested to the actor that we explore the intensity of the terror that Claudio is feeling at this moment. The actor responded that Claudio couldn't have been too upset, given what a beautifully structured, rational speech he had at this moment. It must be something he'd prepared to say to his sister.

Now I wanted to respond to two problems arising from this actor's assumptions: if all of Shakespeare were performed as if the characters had pre-planned every speech that was well structured, then it would be just about the most boring theatre imaginable. So even if the actor were correct, we'd have to revolt against the overly rational language and superimpose the immediacy and fluidity of felt emotion whenever possible. This speech would be just such an opportunity.

But the actor was simply wrong in his assumption, because he was wrong about the attitude towards rhetorical structure held at the time the play was written. Rhetoric was there because of emotions, because of situations when the need to communicate was desperate. Claudio's brilliant speech explodes out of him despite his best efforts to play the role of gentleman, to go proudly to honorable death rather than ask his sister to sleep with Angelo to save him. The rhetoric reflects the rush of feeling, the horror and pain, the shame and desperation. The rhetoric creates, allows, and embodies the theatrical power of the moment.

And yet the young actor was correct, for our theatre. Modern audiences share his distrust of highly structured, ornately rhetorical set speeches. We associate rhetorical address with, for instance, politicians and television evangelists. We all remember Winston Churchill, John Kennedy, and Martin Luther King, but their famous orations could in no way be said to rise out the daily discourse of ordinary people. A portion of the young actor's inability to connect this powerful poetry with the sort of visceral, inarticulate pain and longing that he knew from modern playwrights came directly from his modern attitudes to the connection of language with emotion. Simply put, our modern formula is, "The greater the emotion, the less likely the sentences will be complex in structure."

The solution for the modern actor is to find a way to bridge the gap between Shakespeare's use of structured argument and our distrust of formal oration. There is a difference, even in Shakespeare's plays. Think, for example, of the carefully crafted political event stage managed by Claudius to cover the assassination attempt in the last scene of *Hamlet*:

> Set me the Stoops of wine upon that Table:
> If Hamlet give the first, or second hit,

Or quit in answer of the third exchange,
Let all the Battlements their Ordinance fire,
The King shall drink to Hamlets better breath,
And in the Cup an union shall he throw
Richer than that, which four successive Kings
In Denmarks Crown have worn.
Give me the Cups,
And let the Kettle to the Trumpets speak,
The Trumpet to the Cannoneer without,
The Cannons to the Heavens, the Heavens to Earth,
Now the King drinks to Hamlet. Come, begin,
And you the Judges bear a wary eye. [5.2.267]

Is it just because we know the plot that we distrust this man's rhetoric? And
look how Hamlet and Laertes partake of formal, preplanned oration to make
a public statement that might be the truth but is in no way the whole truth
and nothing but the truth. Hamlet speaks first, and we might want him to be
more natural and honest, but the lies are undeniable:

Give me your pardon Sir, I've done you wrong,
But pardon't as you are a Gentleman.
This presence knows,
And you must needs have heard how I am punished
With sore distraction? What I have done
That might your nature honour, and exception
Roughly awake, I here proclaim was madness:
Was't Hamlet wronged Laertes? Never Hamlet.
If Hamlet from himself be ta'en away:
And when he's not himself, does wrong Laertes,
Then Hamlet does it not, Hamlet denies it:
Who does it, then? His madness? If't be so,
Hamlet is of the Faction that is wronged,
His madness is poor Hamlets Enemy.
Sir, in this Audience,
Let my disclaiming from a purposed evil,
Free me so far in your most generous thoughts,
That I have shot mine Arrow o'er the house,
And hurt my Brother. [5.2.226]

It was not entirely madness, it did not begin as madness, and there was purposed evil, though not against Laertes and his family. Laertes responds, and
we know that he plans murder. Look at his use of the structuring strategies
of rhetoric:

I am satisfied in Nature,
Whose motive in this case should stir me most

To my Revenge. But in my terms of Honour,
I stand aloof, and will no reconcilement,
Till by some elder Masters of known Honour,
I have a voice, and precedent of peace
To keep my name ungored. But till that time,
I do receive your offered love like love,
And will not wrong it. [5.2.244]

Each of these speakers, like Claudio, use the trademark figures of speech that give structure to language. Laertes receives "your offered love like love." Hamlet has the more convoluted pattern of, "If Hamlet from himself be ta'en away: / And when he's not himself, does wrong Laertes." Claudius has the marvellous "let the Kettle to the Trumpet speak, / The Trumpet to the Cannoneer without, / The Cannons to the Heavens, the Heaven to Earth" [5.2.275]. Meanwhile, Claudio's much more emotional and spontaneous speech contains "to be worse than worst." But this last rhetorical figure is so perfectly suited to the content, that it achieves an emotional connection that the less successful, more awkward and forced devices found in the *Hamlet* examples simply cannot achieve.

So we can take from this that Shakespeare and his contemporaries had a healthy distrust of professional communicators adept at manipulating others through the art of oratory. But, unlike a modern playwright who might reinforce the contrast between honesty and manipulation by having the honest characters hesitate, stumble, and speak as seldom as possible while the manipulators' language flows unceasingly in glib verbosity, Shakespeare endows every character with a facility with language that we can only envy.

Were Elizabethans more adept at language than we are? Perhaps. Should we deliver Shakespeare's set speeches using modern speech habits of the linguistically challenged? Perhaps not.

If we grab hold of the basics of structured argument, and explore what that type of communication feels like if it is not faked, preplanned, or abnormal, then perhaps we might be able to access the theatrical power of rhetoric by setting aside our distrust and making this language truly natural and a reflection of the mind, heart, and soul of the character who speaks it, if not of the actor who says it.

Let us contrast the previous speeches with one made by a young man who spends his time modelling the language of two older men, one a father figure and the other a distant, apparently unloving father. When Hal is with Falstaff, he excels at Falstaff's prose, besting the older man in insults and wordplay. When he is with the king his father, Hal partakes of the formal rhetoric of the court and proves he can put together a set speech with the best of them. Here are two examples, the first with Falstaff, when Hal (playacting at being his own father) takes the opportunity to insult Falstaff, the second when Hal defends himself against his father's charge of degeneracy and betrayal.

There is a Devil haunts thee, in the likeness of an old fat Man; a Tun of Man is thy
Companion: Why dost thou converse with that Trunk of Humours, that Bolting-Hutch
of Beastliness, that swollen Parcel of Dropsies, that huge Bombard of Sack, that stuffed
Cloak-bag of Guts, that roasted Manning tree Ox with the Pudding in his Belly, that
reverend Vice, that grey Iniquity, that Father Ruffian, that Vanity in years? wherein is
he good, but to taste Sack and drink it? wherein neat and cleanly, but to carve a Capon
and eat it? wherein Cunning, but in Craft? wherein Crafty, but in Villany? wherein
Villanous, but in all things? wherein worthy, but in nothing? [2HIV 2.4.447]

> Do not think so, you shall not find it so:
> And God forgive them, that so much have swayed
> Your majestys good thoughts away from me:
> I will redeem all this on Percys head,
> And in the closing of some glorious day,
> Be bold to tell you, that I am your Son,
> When I will wear a Garment all of Blood,
> And stain my favours in a bloody Mask:
> Which washed away, shall scour my shame with it.
> And that shall be the day, when e'er it lights,
> That this same Child of Honour and Renown,
> This gallant Hotspur, this all-praised Knight,
> And your unthought-of Harry chance to meet:
> For every Honour sitting on his Helm,
> Would they were multitudes, and on my head
> My shames redoubled. For the time will come,
> That I shall make this Northern Youth exchange
> His glorious Deeds for my Indignities:
> Percy is but my Factor, good my Lord,
> To engross up glorious Deeds on my behalf:
> And I will call him to so strict account,
> That he shall render every Glory up,
> Yea, even the slightest worship of his time,
> Or I will tear the Reckoning from his Heart.
> This, in the name of God, I promise here:
> The which, if I perform, and do survive,
> I do beseech your Majesty, may salve
> The long-grown Wounds of my intemperance:
> If not, the end of Life cancels all Bands,
> And I will die a hundred thousand Deaths,
> Ere break the smallest parcel of this Vow. [3.2.129]

Let us use these two contrasting speeches to discuss how students of rhetoric,
like Hal, learned to structure argument.

Formal oratory recommended some sort of introduction, within which the
speaker would form the strongest possible bond with those listening. The
strength of this bond comes from an appeal to ethos, or ethics, the shared
value system that defines key words like good and bad, and all other judg-

ments. The bond might be formed by acknowledging the listeners; it might be formed by presenting the speaker in a way that validates the speaker's perspective. Only occasionally in Shakespeare's plays do characters include a formal introduction because, as in the examples we are looking at, the interaction is between people who already know each other. Marc Antony begins his famous funeral oration with striking introduction strategy. "Friends, Romans, Countrymen, lend me your ears: / I come to bury Caesar, not to praise him" [*JC* 3.2.73]. But Brutus's less often quoted oration contains a better example of an appeal to *ethos*: "Romans, Country-men, and Lovers, hear me for my cuase, and be silent, that you may hear. Believe me for mine Honour, and have respect to mine Honour, that you may believe. Censure me in your Wisdom, and awake your Senses, that you may be the better Judge" [3.2.13]. Brutus takes care to establish his ethic credential of honor and to call upon the wisdom of the listeners as he acknowledges their right to judge him. He then uses the presentation of himself and his right to speak as the means by which he moves on to the next rhetorical strategy, the presentation of the argument, if you like the point of the speech: "If there be any in this assembly, any dear friend of Caesar's, to him I say, that Brutus' love to Caesar was no less than his. If then that friend demand why Brutus rose against Caesar, this is my answer: Not that I loved Caesar less, but that I loved Rome more." You can see how Marc Antony leaps right for a simle introduction to the statement of argument, and a false one at that, for he proceeds to rouse the audience's love of Caesar and anger against the murderers. Clearly, the way the orator shapes the presentation of the argument affects everything that follows. The speaker defines the terms and sets the territory within which the battle of words will be waged. Brutus uses the key words of honor and love; Marc Antony focuses on Caesar's murder and reputation.

How does Hal handle the presentation of argument? In the first example, with Falstaff, Hal baldly states the point of the speech, that Falstaff is a bad influence on the prince, and then proceeds to explain just how bad the old man is. But in the more emotional scene with his father, when he is revealing himself more than he has ever done before in an effort to clear his name and win his father's love, there is no easy statement of purpose, just the bold, determined challenge, "Do not think so; you shall not find it so." This is of course an effective theatrical beginning to a powerful set speech. No key words have yet been used, except the personal pronoun. This is all about a son looking at a father and asking the father to see the man standing before him.

After the introduction and presentation of argument, the orator is advised by rhetoric teachers to set out the steps of the argument that will follow. This might be necessary in a lengthy presentation, but we don't find it all that often in Shakespeare's plays. This reminds us that, though characters use rhetoric, that does not mean that they know what they are going to say next.

The heart of structured argument is the mounting of detail upon detail in support of the argument. Here we see much evidence of what Shakespeare's contemporaries called *copia*, meaning more than is needed, but of such variety that the mind is pleased as well as persuaded. "Why dost thou converse with that trunk of humours, that bolting-hutch of beastliness, that swollen parcel of dropsies, that huge bombard of sack, that stuffed cloak-bag of guts, that roasted Manningtree ox with the pudding in his belly, that reverend vice, that grey iniquity, that father ruffian, that vanity in years?" says Hal, in a perfect example of a *copia* of insults directed at Falstaff. Then look at how many different ways Hal says that he will win his father's love by vanquishing Percy. Each time something subtly different is communicated, in addition to the repeated point. This is a more subtle sort of *copia*, one that reveals complexity and density as well as striking the hammer over and over on the same spot.

Arguments can also be advanced by logic. Deductive reasoning begins with a premise and builds towards an irrefutable truth by steps built around statements like, "If X is so, then Y must follow," as when Marc Antony follows his opening lines with:

> The evil that men do, lives after them,
> The good is oft interrèd with their bones,
> So let it be with Caesar. The Noble Brutus,
> Hath told you Caesar was Ambitious:
> If it were so, it was a grievous Fault,
> And grievously hath Caesar answered it. [3.2.75]

But Marc Antony's greatest rhetorical success is inductive reasoning, which has the speaker observe a wide variety of examples and conclude a general truth from them. Marc Antony blends a growing number of examples of Caesar's greatness with another aspect of oratory, the praise of those who share the same point of view and the ridiculing of those who oppose it. Marc Antony's brilliance as an orator is that he appears to be doing the opposite, but by the end of the speech his praise of his enemy Brutus has become ironic. Shakespeare endows Marc Antony with a brilliantly subversive rhetorical power demonstrated as the speech continues a few lines later:

> He hath brought many Captives home to Rome,
> Whose Ransoms, did the general Coffers fill:
> Did this in Caesar seem Ambitious?
> When that the poor have cried, Caesar hath wept:
> Ambition should be made of sterner stuff,
> Yet Brutus says, he was Ambitious:
> And Brutus is an Honourable man. [3.2.88]

Still later Marc Antony is able to call for open rebellion while seeming to do the opposite:

O Masters! If I were disposed to stir
Your hearts and minds to Mutiny and Rage,
I should do Brutus wrong, and Cassius wrong:
Who (you all know) are Honorable men.
I will not do them wrong: I rather choose
To wrong the dead, to wrong my self and you,
Than I will wrong such Honourable men. [3.2.121]

But Hal's appeal to his father is no less effective, no less rhetorical in its structuring of compelling argument within a set speech. It is also a private, honest interaction in contrast to Marc Antony's public manipulation of the plebians of Rome. Both speakers are using the power of rhetorical argument to persuade. It is not the rhetoric that is dishonest by definition, but the speaker who chooses either dishonesty or truth.

Rhetorical strategies have structured an intellectual, logical argument built upon shared value systems or ethics. But the third aspect of rhetoric is an emotional bond between speaker and listeners, and this can come in a concluding statement, or be injected anywhere, as when Marc Antony gives way to emotions that force him to stop speaking:

You all did love him once, not without cause,
What cause with-holds you then, to mourn for him?
O Judgment! thou art fled to brutish Beasts,
And Men have lost their Reason. Bear with me,
My heart is in the Coffin there with Caesar,
And I must pause, till it come back to me. [3.2.102]

To pause when overcome with feeling was a well-established oratorical strategy, so it is possible that Marc Antony is manufacturing the appearance of deep feeling here. The formal announcement of the pause suggests that it is "scripted" rather than spontaneous.

PROSE VERSUS POETRY

I was rhyming: 'tis you that have the reason.

Speed [*Two Gents* 2.1.144]

Although it is tempting to generalize Shakespeare's use of prose, concluding that poetry is for high tragedy and romance, spoken by the nobility, and prose for baser comedy and characters, we have seen that that pattern is simply not upheld by a close examination of who speaks prose and under what conditions.

For example, Shylock has two powerful speeches in which he throws back in the face his Christian tormenters the true nature of their anti-Semitism. The first, delivered to Antonio, is in poetry, the second prose speech is said to supporting characters. A comparison of the two speeches might provide us with some insight into the difference between poetry and prose. Here is Shakespeare with Antonio:

> Signior Antonio, many a time and oft
> In the Rialto you have rated me
> About my moneys and my usances:
> Still have I borne it with a patient shrug,
> (For suffrance is the badge of all our Tribe.)
> You call me misbeliever, cut-throat dog,
> And spat upon my Jewish gaberdine,
> And all for use of that which is mine own.
> Well then, it now appears you need my help:
> Go to then, you come to me, and you say,
> Shylock, we would have moneys, you say so:
> You that did void your rheum upon my beard,
> And foot me as you spurn a stranger cur
> Over your threshold, moneys is your suit.
> What should I say to you? Should I not say,
> Hath a dog money? Is it possible
> A cur should lend three thousand ducats? or
> Shall I bend low, and in a bond-mans key
> With bated breath, and whispring humbleness,
> Say this: Faire sir, you spat on me on Wednesday last;
> You spurn'd me such a day; another time
> You called me dog: and for these courtesies
> I'll lend you thus much moneys. [*Merchant* 1.3.106]

Here is the famous prose speech, which Shylock gives in answer to being asked what Antonio's forfeited pound of flesh is good for:

To bait fish withal, if it will feed nothing else, it will feed my revenge; he hath disgraced me, and hindred me half a million, laughed at my losses, mocked at my gains, scorned my Nation, thwarted my bargains, cooled my friends, heated mine enemies, and what's the reason? I am a Jew: Hath not a Jew eyes? hath not a Jew hands, organs, dimensions, senses, affections, passions, fed with the same food, hurt with the same weapons, subject to the same diseases, healed by the same means, warmed and cooled by the same Winter and Summer as a Christian is: if you prick us do we not bleed? if you tickle us, do we not laugh? if you poison us do we not die? and if you wrong us shall we not revenge? if we are like you in the rest, we will resemble you in that. If a Jew wrong a Christian, what is his humility, revenge? If a Christian wrong a Jew, what should his sufferance be by Christian example, why revenge? The villainy you teach me I will execute, and it shall go hard but I will better the instruction. [3.1.53]

In large part, the use of poetry for the first and prose for the second is the result of the scene in which it occurs, the first being entirely in poetry and the second entirely in prose. But that would not stop Shakespeare from changing gears within the scene, if that would suit his purpose. In fact, the scene in which Shylock confronts Antonio began with Shylock and Bassanio talking of the loan of money in prose; the shift to poetry came with the entrance of Antonio.

The correlation between intensity and poetry is also complex. In the earlier scene with Antonio Shylock has yet to feel the rage and pain of the loss of Jessica, stolen by a young friend of Antonio. However, in the prose speech he is not talking directly to his enemy; when Shylock confronts Antonio directly, they both speak poetry. From this we get the sense that the potential contrast between prose and poetry, although useful to Shakespeare in creating types of characters in general terms, was most useful when blended into a single scene, and in particular when an individual character shifts back and forth, as Shylock does, or when characters' contrasting rhythms result in a collision of prose and poetry until one drags the other up or down the linguistic scale.

Let us return to Hamlet and Caliban and consider the scenes in which the speeches occur. Hamlet has been engaged in a light-hearted encounter with his two schoolfellows, sandwiched between bouts of teasing Polonius with his "antic disposition." He has figured out that Rosencrantz and Guildenstern didn't drop by for a visit, but rather were sent for by his mother and stepfather/uncle in order to find out why he has been acting so strangely. Hamlet gives them the answer they might have expected: quite simply, he's suffering from a general malaise. We know that there is a great deal more going on, and are used to Hamlet sharing those thoughts with us, in blank verse soliloquies. Prose suits the task at hand: disguising his true purpose behind the mask of a false, prose self-analysis.

Caliban is a more complex beast. When he first meets Trinculo and Stephano, he has entered the scene cursing Prospero in robust, colourful, energetic verse. But with the arrival of the two drunken servants, he reverts to their prose style of language, even as he imbibes their heavenly elixir and worships them in drunken adoration. When Ariel comes upon the trio and entices them with music, Caliban's explanation absorbs the majesty of Ariel's medium, and he is elevated briefly into poetry.

It is this ascension that modern actors need to find within their mastery of Shakespeare's verse style. The following is a transition that demonstrates the heightened energy, clarity, and expressiveness that empowers the speaker when stepping from proseville into poetry land. The play is *Twelfth Night* and the scene is the first meeting between Olivia and Viola. Viola is disguised as a boy and serves Orsino, who is sending love messages to Olivia via this "boy," and Viola reluctantly obeys because she is herself in love with Orsino. It is this inner turmoil that catapults her from the prose banter she has exchanged with Olivia into the passionate outburst that expresses what she would do were she to love.

Viola: Good Madam, let me see your face.

Olivia: Have you any Commission from your Lord, to negotiate with my face: you are
           now out of your Text: but we will draw the Curtain, and show you the picture.
           Look you sir, such a one I was this present: is't not well done?

Viola: Excellently done, if God did all.

Olivia: 'Tis in grain sir; 'twill endure wind and weather.

Viola: 'Tis beauty truly blent, whose red and white,
           Natures own sweet, and cunning hand laid on:
           Lady, you are the cruell'st she alive,
           If you will lead these graces to the grave,
           And leave the world no copy.

Olivia: O sir, I will not be so hard-hearted: I will give out divers schedules of my beauty.
           It shall be Inventoried and every particle and utensil labelled to my will: As,
           Item two lips indifferent red, Item two grey eyes, with lids to them: Item, one
           neck, one chin, and so forth. Were you sent hither to praise me?

Viola: I see you what you are, you are too proud:
           But if you were the devil, you are fair:
           My Lord, and master loves you: O such love
           Could be but recompensed, though you were crowned
           The non-pareil of beauty.

Olivia: How does he love me?

Viola: With adorations, fertile tears,
           With groans that thunder love, with sighs of fire.

Olivia: Your Lord does know my mind, I cannot love him
           Yet I suppose him virtuous, know him noble,
           Of great estate, of fresh and stainless youth;
           In voices well divulged, free, learn'd and valiant,
           And in dimension, and the shape of nature,
           A gracious person; But yet I cannot love him:
           He might have took his answer long ago.

Viola: If I did love you in my masters flame,
           With such a suffering, such a deadly life:
           In your denial, I would find no sense,
           I would not understand it.

Olivia: Why, what would you?

Viola: Make me a willow Cabin at your gate,
           And call upon my soul within the house,
           Write loyal Cantons of contemned love,
           And sing them loud even in the dead of night:
           Halloo your name to the reverberate hills,
           And make the babbling Gossip of the air,
           Cry out Olivia: O you should not rest

Between the elements of air, and earth,
But you should pity me.

Olivia: You might do much:
What is your Parentage? [1.5.230]

Here we see a tug-of-war between the heightened flow of poetry and the grounded energy of prose. Olivia the countess and the young page/disguised Viola exchange witty prose, until Olivia agrees to remove her veil. Viola has five lines of poetry, shifting the scene into high gear, but Olivia draws back, insisting on the less fraught language of gentle mockery, as she inventories her beauty. Viola's passionate response cannot be denied, and she refuses to be tugged back into the world of prose. Her next speech continues the poetry, and with her naming of Olivia's pride, she draws her partner up into the world of poetry, where thoughts and feelings flow from a deeper, more significant place. Olivia now gives voice to a beautifully articulated rejection of Orsino's suit. Gone is the witty, game-playing, relaxed prose. Instead, despite Olivia's stated intentions, and Viola's best interests, this has become a passionate evocation of the power of love. We, along with Olivia, can only respond to Viola's thrilling, "Halloo your name to the reverberate hills / And make the babbling Gossip of the air, / Cry out Olivia," with the awed, understated, "You might do much."

WIT

When a mans verses cannot be understood, nor a mans good with seconded with the forward child, understanding: it strikes a man more dead than a great reckoning in a little room.

Touchstone [*AYLI* 3.3.12]

Some of the comic language in Shakespeare's plays is exceedingly easy to play in the modern theatre, because the sexually charged exchanges of battling lovers is as familiar to us today as it clearly was to the first actors who played Beatrice and Benedick, to name two of Shakespeare's witty lovers. Here they are, meeting again after some time apart, in the first scene of *Much Ado about Nothing*:

Beatrice: I wonder that you will still be talking, Signior Benedick, nobody marks you.

Benedick: What my dear Lady Disdain! are you yet living?

Beatrice: Is it possible Disdain should die, while she hath such meet food to feed it, as Signior Benedick? Courtesy itself must convert to Disdain, if you come in her presence.

Benedick: Then is courtesy a turncoat, but it is certain I am loved of all Ladies, only you excepted: and I would I could find in my heart that I had not a hard heart, for truly I love none.

Beatrice: A dear happiness to women, they would else have been troubled with a pernicious Suitor, I thank God and my cold blood, I am of your humour for that, I had rather hear my Dog bark at a Crow, than a man swear he loves me.

Benedick: God keep your ladyship still in that mind, so some Gentleman or other shall 'scape a predestinate scratched face.

Beatrice: Scratching could not make it worse, an 'twere such a face as yours were.

Benedick: Well, you are a rare Parrot teacher.

Beatrice: A bird of my tongue, is better than a beast of yours.

Benedick: I would my horse had the speed of your tongue, and so good a continuer, but keep your way, i' Gods name, I have done.

Beatrice: You always end with a jades trick, I know you of old. [1.1.116]

Although a modern actor might require the help of some scholarly footnotes to understanding exactly what these insults are, the emotional unpinning of this exchange seems entirely straightforward. What might be missed, however, is the significance of interplay of wit, that very special capacity to play with words, tossing them back and forth with speed and ingenuity. Beatrice and Benedick, two of Shakespeare's best-matched wits, play language games at every stage of their relationship. We've seen how they score off each other in their first encounter. Here is how they declare their love for each other:

Benedick: By my sword, Beatrice, thou lovest me.

Beatrice: Do not swear, and eat it.

Benedick: I will swear by it that you love me; and I will make him eat it that says I love not you.

Beatrice: Will you not eat your word?

Benedick: With no sauce that can be devised to it. I protest I love thee.

Beatrice: Why, then, God forgive me!

Benedick: What offence, sweet Beatrice?

Beatrice: You have stayed me in a happy hour: I was about to protest I loved you.

Benedick: And do it with all thy heart.

Beatrice: I love you with so much of my heart that none is left to protest. [4.1.274]

Note how the linguistic pattern holds through what follows next, as the conversation turns deadly serious:

Benedick: Come, bid me do any thing for thee.

Beatrice: Kill Claudio.

Benedick: Ha, not for the wide world.

Beatrice: You kill me to deny it, farewell.

Benedick: Tarry sweet Beatrice.

Beatrice: I am gone, though I am here, there is no love in you, may I pray you, let me go.

Benedick: Beatrice.

Beatrice: In faith I will go.

Benedick: We'll be friends first.

Beatrice: You dare easier be friends with me, than fight with mine enemy.

Benedick: Is Claudio thine enemy?

Beatrice: Is he not approved in the height a villain, that hath slandered, scorned, dishonoured my kinswoman? O that I were a man! what, bear her in hand until they come to take hands, and then with public accusation uncovered slander, unmitigated rancour? O God that I were a man! I would eat his heart in the market-place.

Benedick: Hear me Beatrice.

Beatrice: Talk with a man out at a window, a proper saying.

Benedick: Nay but Beatrice.

Beatrice: Sweet Hero, she is wronged, she is slandered, she is undone.

Benedick: Beat?

Beatrice: Princes and Counties! surely a princely testimony, a goodly Count, Count Comfect, a sweet Gallant, surely, O that I were a man for his sake! or that I had any friend would be a man for my sake! But manhood is melted into courtesies, valour into compliment, and men are only turned into tongue, and trim ones too: he is now as valiant as Hercules, that only tells a lie, and swears it: I cannot be a man with wishing, therefore I will die a woman with grieving.

Benedick: Tarry good Beatrice, by this hand I love thee.

Beatrice: Use it for my love some other way than swearing by it.

Even united now by their mutual declarations, these two cannot stop jousting:

Benedick: Sweet Beatrice wouldst thou come when I called thee?

Beatrice: Yea Signior, and depart when you bid me.

Benedick: O stay but till then.

Beatrice: Then, is spoken: fare you well now, and yet ere I go, let me go with that I came, which is, with knowing what hath passed between you and Claudio.

Benedick: Only foul words, and thereupon I will kiss thee.

Beatrice: Foul words is but foul wind, and foul wind is but foul breath, and foul breath is noisome, therefore I will depart unkissed.

Benedick: Thou hast frighted the word out of his right sense, so forcible is thy wit, but I must tell thee plainly, Claudio undergoes my challenge, and either I must shortly hear from him, or I will subscribe him a coward, and I pray thee now, tell me for which of my bad parts didst thou first fall in love with me?

Beatrice: For them all together; which maintained so politic a state of evil that they will not admit any good part to intermingle with them: but for which of my good parts did you first suffer love for me?

Benedick: Suffer love! a good epithet, I do suffer love indeed, for I love thee against my will.

Beatrice: In spite of your heart I think, alas poor heart, if you spite it for my sake, I will spite it for yours, for I will never love that which my friend hates.

Benedick: Thou and I are too wise to woo peaceably.

Beatrice: It appears not in this confession, there's not one wise man among twenty that will praise himself.

Benedick: An old, an old instance, Beatrice, that lived in the lime of good neighbours, if a man do not erect in this age his own tomb ere he dies, he shall live no longer in monument, than the Bell rings and the Widow weeps.

Beatrice: And how long is that think you?

Benedick: Question, why, an hour in clamour and a quarter in rheum, therefore is it most expedient for the wise, if Don Worm (his conscience) find no impediment to the contrary, to be the trumpet of his own virtues, as I am to my self so much for praising my self, who I myself will bear witness is praise worthy, and now tell me, how doth your cousin?

Beatrice: Very ill.

Benedick: And how do you?

Beatrice: Very ill too.

Benedick: Serve God, love me, and mend, there will I leave you too, for here comes one in haste. [5.2.42]

Wit, that capacity to shape language with ease into striking and effective rhetorical patterns, in the moment, responding immediately and directly to the rhetorical strategies of another, is not just a toy or a game, but an attribute of character, that does not come and go but is ever-present, shaping every interaction. It is not an intellectual activity, but a way of understanding the world and living in it. Rather than creating witty characters who say witty things, modern actors need to create witty characters who see the world in such a way that their language patterns reflect the way they think and feel.

Here is a scene that is almost always cut down to a snippet in performance because the jokes don't translate well. Yet the play loses something quite special when it is cut, for it demonstrates the nature of the joking relationship between Romeo and Mercutio.

Mercutio: Signior Romeo, bon jour, there's a French salutation to your French slop: you gave us the counterfeit fairly last night.

Romeo: Good morrow to you both, what counterfeit did I give you?

Mercutio: The slip sir, the slip, can you not conceive?

Romeo: Pardon Mercutio, my business was great, and in such a case as mine, a man may strain courtesy.

Mercutio: That's as much as to say, such a case as yours constrains a man to bow in the hams.

Romeo: Meaning to court'sy.

Mercutio: Thou hast most kindly hit it.

Romeo: A most courteous exposition.

Mercutio: Nay, I am the very pink of courtesy.

Romeo: Pink for flower.

Mercutio: Right.

Romeo: Why then is my Pump well flowered.

Mercutio: Well said: follow me this jest now till thou hast worn out thy Pump, that when the single sole of it is worn, the jest may remain after the wearing, sole-singular.

Romeo: O single-soled jest, solely singular for the singleness.

Mercutio: Come between us good Benvolio, my wits faints.

Romeo: Switch and spurs, switch and spurs, or I'll cry a match.

Mercutio: Nay, if thy wits run the Wild-Goose chase, I am done: For thou hast more of the Wild-Goose in one of thy wits, than I am sure I have in my whole five. Was I with you there for the Goose?

Romeo: Thou wast never with me for any thing, when thou wast not there for the Goose.

Mercutio: I will bite thee by the ear for that jest.

Romeo: Nay, good Goose bite not.

Mercutio: Thy wit is a very Bitter-sweeting; it is a most sharp sauce.

Romeo: And is it not well served in to a Sweet-Goose?

Mercutio: O here's a wit of Cheveril, that stretches from an inch narrow, to an ell broad.

Romeo: I stretch it out for that word, broad, which added to the Goose, proves thee far and wide, abroad Goose.

Mercutio: Why is not this better now than groaning for Love, now art thou sociable, now art thou Romeo: now art thou what thou art, by Art as well as by Nature, for this drivelling Love is like a great Natural, that runs lolling up and down to hide his bauble in a hole.

Benvolio: Stop there, stop there.

Mercutio: Thou desirest me to stop in my tale against the hair.

Benvolio: Thou wouldst else have made thy tale large.

Mercutio: O thou art deceived, I would have made it short, for I was come to the whole depth of my tale, and meant indeed to occupy the argument no longer.

Romeo: Here's goodly gear! [2.4.43]

The rapid-fire exchanges of wit can be played like a game of ping pong; I have had actors rehearse such scenes tossing bean-bags back and forth on the key words that set up the witty exchange. To begin with, they might need to be coached to toss on each of the words in italics:

Mercutio: Signior Romeo, bon jour, there's a *French* salutation to your *French* slop: you gave us the *counterfeit* fairly last night.

Romeo: Good morrow to you both, what *counterfeit* did I give you?

Mercutio: The *slip* sir, the *slip*, can you not *conceive*?

Romeo: Pardon Mercutio, my business was *great*, and in such a case as mine, a man may *strain courtesy*.

Mercutio: That's as much as to say, such a *case* as yours *constrains* a man to bow in the hams.

Romeo: Meaning to *court'sy*.

Mercutio: Thou hast most kindly *hit* it.

Romeo: A most *courteous* exposition.

Mercutio: Nay, I am the very *pink* of *courtesy*.

Romeo: *Pink* for *flower*.

Mercutio: Right.

Romeo: Why then is my *Pump* well *flowered*.

At this point in the "match," Mercutio has scored or set up the rally with eleven tosses, to Romeo's nine. We need handfuls of bean-bags to get through the next exchange:

Mercutio: Well said: follow me this jest now till thou hast worn out thy *Pump*, that when the *single sole* of it is *worn*, the jest may remain after the *wearing, sole-singular*.

Romeo: O *single soled* jest, *solely singular* for the *singleness*.

No wonder Mercutio begs Benvolio to come between them! At this point, I would hope that the actors have caught on to the fun of witty sparring, and can take over without prompting to toss words like "goose," "bite," "sweet," "bitter," "narrow," "broad," and of course "wit." Any exercise that can facilitate a heightened awareness of the thrust and parry of verbal games should be undertaken with all of the seriousness of exhibition fencing. Learn the rules, play by the rules, and play to win.

ᕭ 6 ᕬ

Moving Metaphors

Nay you need not to stop your nose sir: I spake but by a Metaphor.
Parolles [*All's Well* 5.2.11]

Most of us first encounter metaphors in English class, and so retain an attitude that these poetical devices are intellectual pleasures best experienced through imagination. When actors bring this preconception to their work on Shakespeare's great poetic speeches, they are cutting themselves off from a firsthand visceral experience of the imagery. Intellectual imagining is fine for the audience, but the person speaking these words needs to "own" the metaphor on a much more personal, physical plane.

Why do we use metaphors in daily life? If the desire to give and receive communication is the motivating force behind our acquisition of language, metaphors are prevalent because they accomplish that task effectively. At the heart of every metaphor is the trick of associating the known with the unknown. We might say, "You don't know anything about what I'm trying to describe, but you do know about this other thing, which is similar in this way to the thing I'm trying to describe." Instead, we probably come out with something like, "It's a jungle out there." Well, it isn't literally a jungle, but it shares many of the attributes we associate with jungles: uncertainty and the threat of danger being the two most obvious.

We also use a metaphorical leap of mind when we attribute certain verbs to certain nouns. "How time flies" we say, when of course time does not have wings or a jet engine. We might also say, "She flew across the room to greet him," meaning that her movement was so rapid and easy that it shared the speed and lightness we associate with creatures that can indeed fly.

When the metaphor is as exposed and familiar as these examples, it is relatively easy for an actor to translate them into vivid, dynamic, emotional, and physical bits of staging. The snarling viciousness of the competitors in a business setting, or the quickness and lightness of the young girl as she moves across the stage need not consciously be based upon tigers and sparrows.

However, when we encounter the dense web of metaphor that characterizes Shakespeare's language, there is a very real danger of acting entirely in the head without any connection between the imagery and the physical presence of the actor. Because so many of Shakespeare's metaphors draw a comparison between the subject at hand and some aspect of his world, we often remain oblivious to the physical implications of the metaphor. A helpful editor might define in a few words the unfamiliar word, but if more information is not readily available, the only possible engagement is entirely intellectual. For example, Buckingham has this very functional statement in an early scene in *Richard III*: "Ay Madam, he [King Edward IV] desires to make atonement / Between the Duke of Gloucester, and your Brothers, / And between them, and my Lord Chamberlain, / And sent to warn them to his Royal Presence" [1.3.36]. The word "warn" means, in this context, summon. But why? In order to understand the metaphor at work in this substitution of a simple verb, you need to know something about palaces and courtly protocol. Corridors as we know them today did not exist in the sort of palace that Shakespeare's first actors and audience would be envisioning for this scene. Instead, rooms opened into each other, and to travel from one corner of the palace to another the monarch passed through a series of rooms, in which he might find large numbers of his people waiting to approach if he should chance to stop and address them. Likewise, any member of the highest levels of the nobility would travel through the crowds of petitioners, creating a wave of noise in the distance, approaching nearer and nearer, just as the distant thunder warns of an approaching storm. To facilitate the movement of such powerful individuals through the crowds, and also to prepare the crowds for their arrival, a servant would be sent to announce their impending arrival, to "warn" them from room to room. The metaphor, then, is from a fast-moving weather system, which announces its approach with striking gusts of wind or peals of thunder, so that the ordinary folk can best prepare for its passing. Far from demeaning his brothers and brothers-in-law, Edward's sending of a servant to "warn" acknowledges the potency and nobility of his closest male relatives.

A CHARACTER'S LIFE STORY IN A WORD OR TWO

> There is a kind of Character in thy life,
> That to th'observer, doth thy history
> Fully unfold.
>
> The Duke [*Measure* 1.1.27]

In 1893, Mary Cowden Clarke published *The Girlhood of Shakespeare's Heroines*, in which she imagined what their early years would have been like for Rosalind, Juliet, Portia, among others. Although this book makes for fascinating reading, especially if you enjoy Victorian romantic evocations of the fantasy of childish perfection, it does not really suggest a fruitful avenue of creative exploration for the modern actor. However, actors are naturally inclined to imagine a time before as well as times between the scenes depicted on the stage; in fact, Shakespeare invites us to fill in the blanks by making reference to important, character-forming events that he then chooses not to describe.

One of the questions that gets the scholars sneering is, "How many children had Lady Macbeth?" The play provides us with two compelling bits of information. When Macbeth hesitates to kill Duncan, his wife urges him to the task by saying:

> I have given Suck, and know
> How tender 'tis to love the Babe that milks me,
> I would, while it was smiling in my Face,
> Have plucked my Nipple from his Boneless Gums,
> And dashed the Brains out, had I so sworn
> As you have done to this. [1.7.54]

After she has succeeded in restoring Macbeth to his murderous purpose, he says to her: "Bring forth Men-Children only: / For thy undaunted Mettle should compose / Nothing but Males" [1.7.72]. However, we also know that Macbeth has no children and will have none, because the crown he wins for himself has been promised to Banquo's issue, not his own. Macbeth addresses the irony after he's on the throne:

> Upon my Head they placed a fruitless Crown,
> And put a barren Sceptre in my Gripe,
> Thence to be wrenched with an unlineal Hand,
> No Son of mine succeeding: if't be so,
> For Banquo's issue have I filed my Mind,
> For them, the gracious Duncan have I murdered,
> Put Rancours in the Vessel of my Peace
> Only for them, and mine eternal Jewel
> Given to the common Enemy of Man,
> To make them Kings, the Seed of Banquo Kings. [3.1.60]

Macbeth says "If it be so" and so it does not necessarily have to be so; Lady Macbeth might still bear a child who will live to bear more children, and there might be several generations of kings descended from Macbeth before Banquo's line takes over. That is not the assumption Macbeth makes, however, when he speaks of his barren sceptre and fruitless crown.

Despite the absence of reliable birth control, and the direct association between marriage and childbearing, it was painfully common in Shakespeare's
England for noble lines to die out. Shakespeare himself was not survived by
any male child to carry on his name in Stratford or London.

The frequency with which young children died could easily have created a
situation of a mature couple without living children, still hoping for successful
pregnancies but having, like Capulet, endured a shared history of painful loss:
"The earth hath swallowed all my hopes but she."

A scholar is welcome to be content that, since Shakespeare never intended
to offer an answer to the question, "How many children had Lady Macbeth?"
there is no need to ask the question. An actor must ask the question, and find
an answer that constructs the life experiences suggested by the inclusion of the
reference to having given suck.

It is not surprising, given the episodic nature of Shakespeare's stagecraft,
that the actors would be responsible for imagining a wide variety of scenes
betwixt and between. Consider, for example, the two murderers interviewed
by Macbeth, to whom he says:

> Well then,
> Now have you considered of my speeches:
> Know, that it was he in the times past,
> Which held you so under fortune,
> Which you thought had been our innocent self.
> This I made good to you, in our last conference,
> Passed in probation with you:
> How you were borne in hand, how crossed:
> The instruments; who wrought with them:
> And all things else, that might
> To half a Soul, and to a Notion crazed,
> Say, Thus did Banquo. [3.1.74]

Clearly, the actors are to imagine not only a previous unshown interview, in
which Macbeth talked to the two men, but also the specifics of their shared
history. What were these times past, during which they were held under fortune? Why did they think it was Macbeth rather than Banquo? Was it in fact
Macbeth, and he's lying now? Macbeth's language suggests that the two men
were given to understand that they'd have some future with Banquo, or Macbeth, perhaps in military service as these are two of Scotland's leading generals.
But these hopes were crossed, much as Iago's expectations of lieutenancy were
crossed by Cassio:

> Three Great-ones of the City,
> (In personal suit to make me his Lieutenant)
> Off-capped to him: and by the faith of man

I know my price, I am worth no worse a place,
But he (as loving his own pride, and purposes)
Evades them, with a bombast Circumstance,
Horribly stuffed with Epithets of war,
Non-suits my Mediators. For certes, says he,
I have already chose my Officer. And what was he?
For-sooth, a great Arithmetician,
One Michael Cassio, a Florentine,
(A fellow almost damned in a fair Wife)
That never set a Squadron in the Field,
Nor the division of a Battle knows
More than a Spinster. Unless the Bookish Theoric:
Wherein the Tonged Consuls can propose
As Masterly as he. Mere prattle (without practise)
Is all his Soldiership. But he (sir) had th'election;
And I (of whom his eyes had seen the proof
At Rhodes, at Cyprus, and on other grounds
Christian, and Heathen) must be be-leed, and calmed
By Debitor, and Creditor. This Counter-caster,
He (in good time) must his Lieutenant be,
And I (God bless the mark) his Moorships Ancient. [*Othello* 1.1.8]

For Iago, and Roderigo to whom he offers this explanation for his betrayal of Othello, this is sufficient justification for intractable hatred. Perhaps, this was a tale often heard in Shakespeare's London, and so one that would need little additional explanation for actors or audience in the fast moving action of *Macbeth.*

Other invitations to imagination are even more subtle. For instance, just before Macbeth interviews the murderers, he dismisses various unnamed members of his court, presumably as many as the company can afford to put into the scene, with the following:

Let every man be master of his time,
Till seven at Night, to make society
The sweeter welcome:
We will keep our self till Supper time alone:
While then, God be with you. [3.1.40]

These same lords then appear in the banquet scene, along with Banquo's ghost. How do they spend their time?

In one sense, it doesn't really matter. Nothing more is required of them at this moment than to exit the stage in some appropriate manner. Are they concerned about Macbeth? Puzzled by his command? Is this customary? Are they happy for the vacation from the duties of attending a reigning monarch? What sort of a mood will they be in after this time off? Will they be relaxed, in a holiday mood because they've been able to engage in pleasant leisure activities, and if so what might these have been? Will they be on edge because they've spent the time without anything to do except gossip and worry? Will they have attended to the business of their personal estates? Will they have gone riding like Banquo and Fleance?

Actors deal with these questions in a manner best suited to their creative processes. What interests me is what assumptions were at work in Shakespeare's theatre when such suggestive elements were inserted into the flow of a scene. Did those first actors have lots of ideas of what courtiers might do when dismissed for a few hours by the monarch? Did they have a pretty good idea, based upon the nobility dancing attendance on the reigning monarch of their day, just what the lords might have felt when Macbeth said those words? My guess is that everyone in the theatre could fill in that particular blank with scarcely a pause, and it is only a modern actor who must actively engage a combination of historical research and imagination to bridge the gap between Macbeth's world and ours.

Metaphors can provide an anchor for the "back story" that helps an actor commit to the truth of the fictional character. We know that we don't have to have a direct experience of something in order to use it as an effective metaphor, as in "it's a jungle out there," a particularly urban cliché that assumes a shared image of jungle-ness rather than vacations in equatorial rain forests. But, since nothing makes a character come alive more readily than giving this fictional creation a life outside the confines of the play, why not use metaphors to spark such imaginings?

There is another layer of information about events before and between events of *Macbeth* that is overlooked regularly, in contrast to the preceding examples that are self-evident, if sometimes ignored. This layer is encoded in the very language of the characters, but unfortunately for actors is too often relegated to the purview of literary analysis.

When Macbeth is wracked with guilt in the immediate aftermath of killing the sleeping Duncan, he says,

> Methought I heard a voice cry, Sleep no more:
> Macbeth does murder Sleep, the innocent Sleep,
> Sleep that knits up the ravelled Sleeve of Care,
> The death of each days Life, sore Labours Bath,
> Balm of hurt Minds, great Natures second Course,
> Chief nourisher in Life's Feast. [2.2.32]

Intellectually, this is easy to comprehend. Sleep is a great refresher. An actor who has experienced firsthand the horrors of insomnia will be able to bring an immediate, sensory memory to these images. But let's have a closer look at just what these words convey.

Whenever we attempt to explain something that is unknown, we seek to create a series of comparisons between the known and the unknown. We say, "I had a wonderful new food yesterday: it was a type of casserole, with layers like lasagna, but instead of noodles they used this type of meat, I don't know what it was but it tasted a bit like chicken but with a texture that was a bit rubbery, or chewy, and the sauce was sweet and also tangy." Every detail of the recipe summons up by implication or direct reference a comparison: sweet (like sugar? like honey?) and tangy (like lemons? like chili peppers?).

It is exactly the same function taking place when Macbeth struggles to communicate to his wife the terrible price he will have to pay for committing such a heinous sin as murdering his king. However, we miss the implications of his choice of comparisons entirely if we do not take the time to think through what sort of life experiences are suggested by the images. We are invited to imagine Macbeth engaging in some labor that made his body ache, perhaps in a war scene like the one described by the Bloody Sergeant early in the play:

> For brave Macbeth (well he deserves that Name)
> Disdaining Fortune, with his brandished Steel,
> Which smoked with bloody execution
> (Like Valours Minion) carved out his passage,
> Till he faced the Slave:
> Which ne'er shook hands, nor bade farewell to him,
> Till he unseamed him from the Nave to th'Chops,
> And fixed his Head upon our Battlements. [1.2.16]

In such a battle, Macbeth might well also have sustained various injuries that would require a medicinal balm; the healing effects of such administrations in the hours following intense fighting would be well known to him, as would the individual who would undertake such personal ministrations. He would also have personal and vivid associations with feasting, and perhaps even a favorite host or master cook in mind for the chief nourisher.

But for me the most evocative image is the one most subtly suggested. What known thing is Macbeth using for his metaphor when he talks about innocent sleep that knits up the ravelled sleeve of care? A ravel is an entanglement, a loose thread, and to ravel is to become tangled, confused, or frayed. The sleeve can mean the most delicate threads of silk or, as today, the part of a garment covering the arm. It is easy to understand the concept of the cares of the day leaving one feeling confused, and today we often speak of frayed nerves. That sleep would ease this entanglement is a natural association. But as actors we must go one step further and seek the well-known experience that Macbeth is using to explain what he can scarcely bear to contemplate much less explain.

In addition to sleep being associated with nourishing food, and a warm bath when you are sore and tired followed by a rubdown with an aromatic balm, the adjective "innocent" summons up images of young children sleeping soundly. This suggests that the image at work here is Sleep like a devoted old nanny, sitting late into the night beside the sleeping little boy, who has finished his nursery supper and evening bath, whose cuts and scrapes have been kissed and soothed. As the little boy lies drowsily in his warm bed, he hears the click click of her needles as she repairs the hole in his sweater where the wool of the sleeve has come unravelled. In the morning it will be ready for him to wear again. It is this beloved individual whom he has stabbed to death along with Duncan. Is this the same person who bathed his sore muscles and smoothed balm on his cuts? Is this the same person who cooked the meals that seem in memory to be the most filling? Even Macbeth was once a little boy.

Nature's second course might have one more significance in this cluster of images. Macbeth is a member of the nobility, and his primary care giver would have been a nurse rather than his Lady Mother. She who gave him birth is, in essence, his first nature, but the humble woman who rocked him to sleep, bathed and comforted him, and nourished his body and his soul, would be nature's second provider of love and guidance.

Having created an imaginary sensory memory, of all the tastes and sights and sounds and smells and things to touch and ways of being touched, and linked all of those wonderful memories with a special person, you can make this speech about killing that person, as much as it is about bringing on insomnia. Suddenly, the number of images in the speech is necessary to express the totality of the horror. It's not as simple as, "I don't think I'm going to be able to sleep well after doing such a terrible deed." It is, "It's as if I killed my dear old nanny, and the only way you'll understand just what this means is if I give you a list of all that she meant to me, which is the list of all that I'm realizing I've sacrificed, in doing this terrible deed."

In seeking to describe the horrible crime he has committed, Macbeth reminds us that he was once a little boy, that he has lived a rich and full life in the years before the first events of the play, and that his mind is filled with memories and associations as well as fears and longings.

SHAKESPEARE'S LANGUAGE OF SENSE

> She speaks, and 'tis such sense
> That my Sense breeds with it.
>
>   Angelo [*Measure* 2.2.141]

"Sense" is such a lovely word. It sounds like what it is. It is the root of other lovely words, like sensory, sensual, common sense, horse sense, put in your five sense—well, maybe not that one.

But in this pun-y observation, Shakespeare draws our attention to two different linkages: the sense, or meaning of the word and the sensory experience of saying and hearing the word are linked, and the connection between the sense (both meanings) of the word and the arousal of feeling is direct and precise. The word impregnates the emotional body of the listener.

This insight of Shakespeare's has led me time and again to ask an actor, "Where in your body do you feel that image." Sadly, most of them respond with a blank look. They don't feel it at all. If they have given any thought to what it is that they are really saying, that is all they have done. The image remains in the mind, cut off from the senses of the body. In the mind it might make sense, but it's not going to breed anything, is it? Not where actors need to feel their inspiration, in their bellies.

Let's put this into practice with one of Macbeth's most visceral of speeches in the hours before he will kill his king (and his peace of mind).

> If it were done, when 'tis done, then 'twere well,
> It were done quickly: *if th'Assassination*
> *Could trammel up the Consequence, and catch*
> *With his surcease, Success*: that but this blow
> Might be the be all, and the end-all. Here,
> But *here, upon this Bank and Shoal of time,*
> *We'ld jump the life to come.* But in these Cases
> We still have judgment here, that *we but teach*
> *Bloody Instructions, which being taught, return*
> *To plague th'Inventor.* This *even-handed Justice*
> *Commends th'Ingredients of our poisoned Chalice*
> *To our own lips.* He's here in double trust;
> First, as I am his Kinsman, and his Subject,
> Strong both against the Deed: Then, as his Host,
> Who should against his Murderer shut the door,
> Not bear the knife my self. Besides, this Duncan
> Hath borne his Faculties so meek; hath been
> So clear in his great Office, *that his Virtues*
> *Will plead like Angels, Trumpet-tongued, against*
> *The deep damnation of his taking-off:*
> And *Pity, like a naked New-born-Babe.*
> *Striding the blast,* or *Heaven's Cherubim, horsed*
> *Upon the sightless Couriers of the Air,*
> Shall *blow the horrid deed in every eye.*
> *That tears shall drown the wind.* I have *no Spur*
> *To prick the sides of my intent, but only*
> *Vaulting Ambition, which o'er-leaps it self,*
> *And falls on the other.* [1.7.1]

Let's take the images one by one, and explore just what might be involved if we let an actor's sense breed with the sense of these words.

> If th'Assassination
> Could trammel up the Consequence, and catch
> With his surcease, Success

To understand this image, we have to do a bit of research about trammelling. A trammel, we learn, is a small net used to catch rabbits. Young boys would take their dogs and a trammel and head out towards the warren. One would hold back the dogs until the others had prepared the net, and then the dogs would be loosed. With a rush, all the rabbits would run out of the warren, and the boys would frantically try to catch as many as possible. Alternatively, the same technique could be used with small birds. Imagine the excitement, the panic, the shouts and barks and frantic flapping of wings, the desperate raising and lowering of the net as the boys tried to capture as many birds as possible. Imagine you are Macbeth, and you haven't been out trammelling for years, but you still remember doing it as a lad. You still remember the pounding heart, the exhilaration, the desperation.

The point of the image comes home at once. It simply isn't possible to catch all of the rabbits or birds with the small net, and no one expects to. The many consequences of the death of the king, swooping and darting and racing past, uncontrollable—it is impossible to foresee them all and all the directions they will head. No net is big enough, no pair of hands quick enough, to trammel them all up. But that is just the "sense" of the image. The "sense" that breeds in the body is richer, and is felt in the racing heart, the darting eyes, the flailing hands, or in the dry mouth of the waiting for the explosion of beating wings, barking dogs, and shouting boys.

> But here, upon this Bank and Shoal of time,
> We'ld jump the life to come.

Much has been written about this lovely image. Like almost everyone, I used to think this was about standing on a river bank and jumping to the sandbar without getting my feet wet, which is another image I associate with childhood. The image points to a specific split second in this memory: the moment standing, looking at the raging river, preparing, terrified, gathering the focused energy in knees and thighs.

But there is another possibility here. "Shoal" reads as "school" in the folio and "bank" was the word used for the little wooden benches upon which the schoolboys sat for lessons. That would take us directly into the next image, set in a schoolroom, filled with the memories of dusty chalk and squirming children.

> we but teach
> Bloody Instructions, which being taught, return
> To plague th'Inventor.

Suddenly, the metaphor has slipped, like things do in dreams, and we're not the children, but the teacher. We're standing in front of the classroom, and looking at a sea of faces. We'd thought these were the polite (or not) young offspring of the village, but they turn out to be something else, a horrible group of creatures, covered in blood, that we recognize from pictures (and dreams) as being representatives of something more than just monster-children. Still, the image continues, and they leave our school, and venture off to the big city. Then, the plague comes and, as was the case in Shakespeare's England, London empties as people flee to the farms and villages. Many a time someone who had moved to the big city in search of work would return to his home town to escape the plague, only to bring the infection with him, and within a few weeks every house in the community would have lost someone to the disease. This is what it means to return to plague someone.

Where would you feel that image? Would you feel the hairs on the back of your neck rise, as you looked out over those students, as you saw the young man returning from London and realize he had brought the plague to your town?

> This even-handed Justice
> Commends th'Ingredients of our poisoned Chalice
> To our own lips.

What does it mean to be evenhanded? Try the image on for size. Don't just let it sit out there and imagine looking at it, like a statue of blindfolded justice on the front of some government building. *Be* the evenhanded justice. Feel how difficult it is to be truly balanced in both your left and right hands, given that you write (and fight) with one and not the other.

Now the metaphor can shift again. You can "play the role" of justice *and* of the one who drinks the poison. What does it mean to commend the ingredients of a chalice? Think of the wine steward at a fancy restaurant. Think of the steward at a monarch's banquet. Think of the food-taster in a court who lives in fear of poison. Take a sip. Know it's poison. Then, offer it to the monarch, saying with a smile that the wine is excellent. Then be the monarch. Receive the cup to your lips. Because you are at the same time the poisoner, allow yourself to know and not know, as one does in dreams.

Where would you feel this image? In your mouth, in your nose, on your tongue? Smell the wine. Taste the poison. Feel the weight of the jewel-studded gold chalice in your hands.

> that his Virtues
> Will plead like Angels, Trumpet-tongued against
> The deep damnation of his taking-off:

Here is another image that invites you to imagine both doing and receiving the metaphoric action. If you were pleading before a judge or monarch, you'd perhaps be on your knees, you'd perhaps be trembling, almost nauseous from terror, and you're pleading not for yourself but for someone else. You have summoned up every ounce of courage in order to risk your own life to say something that the monarch does not want to hear.

And then you can be the monarch, listening to the pleading, and suddenly it's not a trembling courtier but an angel, and out of the mouth comes a sound that blasts your inner ear and rings through every bone in your body. You must fill this image with a profound faith and a belief that angels exist, and that if one were to appear and speak you would be transformed forever.

> And Pity, like a naked New-born-Babe,
> Striding the blast, or Heaven's Cherubin, horsed
> Upon the sightless Couriers of the Air,
> Shall blow the horrid deed in every eye,
> That tears shall drown the wind.

William Blake was so taken with this image that he created a marvelously surreal painting that can inspire you to allow the image to move you deeply. But you'd still be standing outside the metaphor looking at it, instead of putting it into your body.

Let us imagine when Macbeth might have held a naked newborn babe. We know that Lady Macbeth is of childbearing age. "Bring forth men-children only," says her husband in praise of her courage and determination. "I have known what it is to suck," she has said. So let us imagine that they have had at least one child together who did not survive infancy.

And so Macbeth has held a naked, newborn babe. He has felt the warm, moving, mass of flesh, his own child, in his hands. He has heard the mewling cries and smelled the gift of new life that is achieved only through blood and sweat and tears. He has probably wept over that child. But he has also watched that child die. He has held the cold, lifeless body in his hands, and exhaled a breath that contained the darkest, deepest sound of grief.

But, as in a nightmare, this image transforms, and the naked, newborn baby suddenly is astride the blast, like an expert horse rider atop a powerful and barely broken steed. The blast is linked to the sound of the angel-voice, but it's also the storm, and the horrific sound of strong winds beating against human fortifications.

This horse imagery continues, and the little baby has become the tiniest of the angels of heaven riding the wind that transports them like the monarch's high-speed letter carriers to every corner of the world. The wind blows into your eyes, making them water, and the trumpets blow, releasing the blast that is louder than any human trumpeting, and the messengers call out the news of the terrible murder. Your eyes are watering, your ears are aching, you can barely stand against the power of the wind that these tiny baby-like angels ride so effortlessly. And around you, everyone hears what you have done, and their anguish and grief is so immense that a flood of weeping rises up higher than the sky, and the wind itself is overcome by the tidal wave of outrage.

And you stand there, frozen, watching the castle-high waters rushing towards you.

> I have no Spur
> To prick the sides of my intent, but only
> Vaulting Ambition, which o'er-leaps it self,
> And falls on the other.

And now, you are astride the horse. If you've never ridden, you'll have to imagine what it feels like to be on a powerful animal, to dig your spurred heels into its sides and feel it leap forward and then up and over. But the most horrifying image is that you are leaping over *yourself*. I've always imagined going up over the fence or hedge, and as I crest the top I look down, and there, lying hidden on the far side, is a body, and a face looking up at me, and it is my face, and in my panic and horror, I begin to fall, and fall, and fall . . .

Once you have put these images into your body, once you have endowed them with the power of dreams, to transform and transport you from one sensation to another, with no need to make sense but with every sense of your body responding, tapping memories and associations, making the heart beat faster, the breathing patterns change, the skin to sweat and the stomach to twist, so that you wake with aching muscles and a dry throat, sitting bolt upright in bed out of a deep sleep, well, once you have done that maybe you are ready to have a go at enacting Macbeth's physical state as he says these words.

Visualizing Images

Some actors are blessed with a visually oriented imagination, and therefore, provided that they stop themselves from racing through the stages of association prompted by an image, can access vivid internal pictures that contain great potential for creative inspiration.

The stages of association of an image follow the trail of the similarity that has prompted the comparison. When the image is developed in a phrase or two, there is no avoiding the picture you are invited to see in your mind's eye. When Romeo first sees Juliet, he seeks ways to express the impact she has on his senses by comparing her to torches, which she teaches to burn bright like an older, successful role-model inspires lesser creatures to mimicry, and to a white dove marching with crows, if birds were ever to troop like soldiers. It is harder to put into words the logic of "It seems she hangs upon the cheek of night, / Like a rich jewel in an Ethiopes ear" [1.5.45], even with the moralizing of the next phrase, "Beauty too rich for use, for earth too dear." We can imagine the dark-skinned, exotic foreigner, and the immense earring, but it is not easy to envision night as a human face with a cheek against which

Juliet rests. However, imagery was never intended to be logical. If the sensations have been captured by the comparison, the device has served its function.

Romeo's metaphors are overt, even excessive, in keeping with his mood. But a significant portion of Shakespeare's metaphorical language is more subtle, and the comparison is encoded in a single word. Earlier in *Romeo and Juliet*, Juliet made this promise to her mother: "I'll look to like, if looking liking move. / But no more deep will I endart mine eye, / Than your consent gives strength to make it fly" [1.3.97]. Juliet's use of the words "endart" and "fly" create a metaphor of archery. The consent of her mother will strengthen the arm pulling the arrow taut in the bow, so that the dart strikes the precise depth required. In case a modern actor misses the connection, Romeo will revisit this same metaphor in the next scene, when Mercutio urges Romeo, the lover, to borrow Cupid's wings, and Romeo responds with this description of his love-sickness: "I am too sore enpierced with his shaft, / To soar with his light feathers, and so bound. / I cannot bound a pitch above dull woe, / Under loves heavy burden do I sink" [1.4.19]. The dart or arrow that Juliet describes is Cupid's, and there is no surprise in her use of such imagery to describe the way that looking can move someone into liking. Romeo, on the other hand, takes the image of flying, and links it to the soaring eagle whose pitch is the highest point of flight just before it drops down to attack its prey, usually a slow-moving and unintelligent creature, like "dull woe." Romeo's bindings, like the leather tongs or tassels on a tamed eagle's legs, will be transformed after he meets Juliet, and she will call him back to their garden rendezvous with, "Hist Romeo hist: O for a Falc'ner's voice, / To lure this Tassel gentle back again" [2.2.158], and he will respond, "It is my soul that calls my name," as he flies back to her balcony.

Envisioning Metaphor

The following is an exercise that I have often used when attempting to demonstrate to a relatively inexperienced actor how richly her inner actor's ear already hears the imagery in Shakespeare's language. This exercise works well when the actors are put in pairs, and each is working on a short speech that the partner does not know.

The first of the pair to take his turn lies on the ground with his eyes shut, in a comfortable position. His partner sits near his head, with the text of the speech in hand, and reads the words aloud, slowly, pausing after every word, making no attempt to deliver the speech or to shape the words into phrases.

The actor on the floor raises his hand whenever an image forms in his mind as a result of the word just spoken. While his hand is up, the reading partner remains silent, giving the imagining partner time to envision the image in some detail. When the interior photograph has been examined, or the minimovie run its course, the actor on the floor lowers his hand and the reading actor continues.

As soon as the reading of the speech is completed, the envisioning actor sits up and speaks the speech, with all of the images fresh in his mind. Then it is his partner's turn to be read to, and to raise her hand to stop his voice and carve out some time to go in for a close-up on the images that pop into her brain.

Some hints for this exercise: the reader must be very disciplined not to begin to give a performance of the speech. If you keep it very firmly in your mind that what you are reading is your partner's monologue, and you would be stepping on her toes if you start to enact it in any way, then you will be able to focus on your simple task, which is to assist in her exploration.

Some actors have the sort of imagination that responds profoundly and with ease to any opportunity to create imaginary pictures. Those actors whose intellect works differently will find themselves noting the images rather than experiencing the pictures they arouse. Their creative imaginations will take them in a slightly different direction. They might realize that a certain picture is suggested by the word, and then find themselves imagining a little scene in which two people interact a certain way, as prompted by that image. It doesn't really matter what you imagine, and it need not be a picture of the specific metaphor. What does matter is that you realize that your entire mental apparatus is geared towards responding viscerally and profoundly to the language of poetic imagery, which is why we as a species create and share such linguistic packages.

Let us look at a bit of text and see just where it might take different actors. Here is Romeo speaking of what he thinks is the body of the dead Juliet:

> Why art thou yet so fair? I will believe,
> Shall I believe that unsubstantial death is amorous?
> And that the lean abhorred Monster keeps
> Thee here in dark to be his Paramour?
> For fear of that, I still will stay with thee,
> And never from this Palace of dim night
> Depart again; here, here will I remain,
> With Worms that are thy Chambermaids: O here
> Will I set up my everlasting rest:
> And shake the yoke of inauspicious stars
> From this world-wearied flesh: Eyes look your last:
> Arms take your last embrace: And lips, O you
> The doors of breath, seal with a righteous kiss
> A dateless bargain to engrossing death:
> Come bitter conduct, come unsavoury guide,
> Thou desperate Pilot, now at once run on
> The dashing Rocks, thy Sea-sick weary Bark:

Here's to my Love. O true Apothecary:
Thy drugs are quick. Thus with a kiss I die. [5.3.102]

Now let's see what images have been reported by different actors exploring this speech using the exercise I have described.

Why art thou yet so fair?

If actors are being honest, they usually raise their hand following the word fair; some raise it after "thou," because a woman's face has popped into their mind. Perhaps it is an ideal image of beauty, or perhaps it is the face of someone known to them, personally or by reputation. This is not, literally speaking, a poetic image, but it reminds us that all language encodes some sort of comparison between the theoretical name and an actual experience.

Shall I believe that unsubstantial death is amorous?

Some actors' hands go up at "unsubstantial," because their mind has flipped into a picture of wisps of fog or the shimmer of light on water. Other actors realize that Shakespeare is loading up an image of death, and their mind leaps to an inner movie, perhaps a rerun of Ingmar Bergman's *The Seventh Seal* or the more recent Hollywood offering, *Meet Joe Black*. Why is it that our minds cannot resist imagining what Death would look like if it were *not* insubstantial? The final clincher in the image is the last word of the line, which is guaranteed to prompt an image of sexual activity of one sort or another, perhaps building on the images already in place or taking the actor into a completely different memory, fantasy, or surreal imagining of the love life of the insubstantial.

And that the lean

This word alone often gets the hand up, because it prompts such a strong image of emaciated flesh.

abhorred

Some actors make the imaginative leap from Shakespeare's metaphor, which he is building with this ongoing description of death, to a more personal association: What do I think of when I imagine the most repulsive thing possible, anything that I would call "abhorred"?

Monster

Lots of possibilities here. Perhaps the entire phrase culminates in a vivid mental picture of a skeletal, stinking Death-man embracing the most beautiful young girl you can imagine, or perhaps the actor's mind borrows from images of monstrosity he might have encountered in films, photographs, or the dark corners of his imagination.

> keeps
> Thee here in dark

The first part of the line often raises the hand of the listening actor, who cannot help but imagine being in the dark, either in a situation similar to that of the play, the stinking tomb, or quite removed. There's a reason why we as a species have a primal fear of the dark, and though the scene is never fully dark when performed (it would have been daylight in Shakespeare's theatre!) those simple words always work to bring forward a memory or a fantasy. If the image is building word upon word, then the idea of being kept in the dark can prompt minimovies of entrapment and terror.

> to be his Paramour?

We're back to images of Death as the lover, in the dark, and it's a rare actor who doesn't flash to something from a horror movie, or a visual image that could appear in one.

> For fear of that, I still will stay with thee,
> And never from this Palace of dim night
> Depart again;

At this point in the speech, the mind is probably working on quite a bit of momentum from previous images of darkness, horror, death, and the face of the beloved. The word "palace" leaps out of nowhere, a completely different and contrasting image of glory, wealth, worldly power, just about the opposite of what has gone before. The temptation in delivering the speech is to let the intellectual content of the speech rob you of the emotional guts of the image: yes, it's true that Romeo is saying that a tomb is Death's palace, and therefore the line remains gloomy and despairing, in keeping with Romeo's preparation for suicide, but when the image is given the time and space to expand within the imagination, and is given its full power as a vision of beauty and grandeur, only then is Shakespeare's language drawing from the actor all that he can bring to this moment in the play.

> here, here will I remain,
> With Worms

No problem acquiring images here, either of maggots feasting on dead flesh, or wiggly things on the end of fish hooks.

> that are thy Chambermaids:

A tiny bit of danger here, if the mind leaps immediately to images of the women who clean hotel rooms, in that the image in the context of Shakespeare's world referred to the wives and daughters of the peers of the realm who waited upon the queen herself in her private chamber, a singular honor for the greatest women in the land. But to be honest, I would be equally happy if an actor suddenly found the power of imagining maggots knocking on the door of his fancy hotel room with clean towels.

> O here
> Will I set up my everlasting rest:

This is where I discover if my harangues about active verbs has actually taken hold. What does it mean to "set up" something? The intellectual meaning of the line is that Romeo is preparing to kill himself. But the *metaphor* has to do with setting up what? If I ask the actor, he might say he would set up a stereo system. Another member of the class might offer the image of setting up a scaffolding, perhaps for a pageant to welcome the queen herself as she enters the city in triumphant procession. Another actor suggests that he might set up a joke or a con, like in *The Sting*, an elaborate plan that takes days to execute. I don't mind any of these images, because they are *active*. They get the actor inhabiting the verb and living the metaphor, rather than decoding it intellectually and then playing the corresponding emotion. The transformation is immediate. The actor stops playing the "I'm preparing to die" emotion and starts playing the "I'm working at something here" activity.

> And shake the yoke of inauspicious stars

Everyone gets the yoke image. Perhaps they see a picture of a heavily laden ox cart. Perhaps they imagine themselves wearing the crossbar clothing of a prisoner of war, with wrists chained to wood, head and shoulders bent and aching from the unnatural pressure. But what about inauspicious stars? Does the intellect click in, decoding the phrase into a minidiscussion of the theme of the play? Or can the actor discipline his creative imagination to, at the very least, imagine a star-filled summer night?

> From this world-wearied flesh:

Many possibilities here for exhaustion felt deeply in the body, perhaps linking up with the yoke image, or perhaps leaping in from some other experienced or imagined exhaustion.

> Eyes look your last:
> Arms take your last embrace:

We're on the home stretch here, and it is difficult to hear these words without doing these actions.

> And lips, O you
> The doors of breath,

What actual doors does your imagination summon forth, even as you are envisioning kissing someone, or the lips of someone as if in close-up? Are these the great, gold-encrusted doors of a palace? Or the swinging screen door of your family home?

> seal with a righteous kiss

The verb "seal" would, for the Elizabethans, call up images of the pressing of the crested ring into the heated wax, as well as the sealing of doors, locking them so that they cannot be reopened easily. But what is the word "righteous" going to summon forth? If linked with the word that follows, perhaps the priest kissing the chalice before serving mass? But if taken on its own, this word might summon images that are distinctly negative, such as that unpleasant Sunday school teacher who went on and on about sin, revelling in her self-righteous superiority.

> A dateless bargain to engrossing death:

Every word in this line might summon an image. Heard with modern ears, "dateless" might remind you of the Friday night blues, but if you've done your homework you'll hear another meaning, and your mind might supply a visual association for that which never ends. "Bargain" might summon up your favorite dollar store, or a deal made after a fierce debate about price. "Engrossing" meaning greedy might summon up images of gluttony, which linked with the word that follows, might create the image of an active, sexual, horror show monster, stuffing his face, perhaps with parts of human bodies.

> Come bitter conduct,

Now, the actor knows that this refers to the poison, but what does it mean? The word "bitter" should summon up a taste, perhaps an experience that left a bitter feeling, while "conduct" here means mentor, guardian, sort of like the conductor on a train.

> come unsavoury guide,

This is the same pairing of sensory experiences of taste with images of a person, like the experienced tracker who guides the hapless tourists through the northern wilds, or the museum employee who drones on about the various displays.

> Thou desperate Pilot,

Suddenly, we've changed metaphors, and the images associated with being desperate, whatever they may be, are followed by images of a pilot, in modern terms inevitably of a plane, but if you've ever been aboard an ocean liner you will know that the pilot's arrival is a requirement to guide the ship into the harbor. It's quite something to see the all-powerful captain stand aside to let the humble pilot steer the great ship in to safety.

> now at once run on

The active verb might shift you to another image, of running on and on, perhaps in terror, or perhaps with the joy of mastery and unflagging energy, such as happens only in the greatest of dreams.

> The dashing Rocks, thy Sea-sick weary Bark:

Once again, almost every word calls forth an image. The "dashing" might play upon the pun of running fast and quickly as dashing, or of the waves dashing against the rocks, while the word "rocks" might summon up hand-sized stones that are lobbed through windows or the giant residue of fallen cliffs that line unwelcoming sea shores. The word "sea" might summon a picture of a calm tropical paradise, or a heaving ocean, and the sickness that follows might be mal de mer but could just as easily be any sickness your body remembers. "Weary," likewise, might summon forth memories of physical exhaustion, and if you've done your homework, the word "bark" will have you picturing a small ship. At this point, the words might culminate into the image Shakespeare has built, as a minimovie that you witness from shore, from overhead, or from the deck of the ship itself.

Imagery As Framework

The power of imagery is not limited to pictures. Encoded in the comparison are frameworks within which actors can find relationships, activities, and a strong sensation of relative power. Let us examine how these might function by looking at an image-filled speech, that of Claudius at the midway point of *Hamlet*. So far, this man has been something of an enigma. We have the ghost's description of his seduction of Gertrude, and Hamlet's label of smiling villain. We also have multiple scenes in which Claudius seems to function like an effective ruler. We've had one glimpse of the state of the man's soul behind the mask, when he responds to Polonius's reference to hiding the devil himself with the image of devotion:

> Oh 'tis true:
> How smart a lash that speech doth give my Conscience?
> The Harlots Cheek beautied with plast'ring Art,
> Is not more ugly to the thing that helps it,
> Than is my deed, to my most painted word.
> O heavy burthen! [3.1.48]

This suggests to us that Claudius is primed and ready for the playing of "The Murder of Gonzago" to work upon him in just the manner hoped for by Hamlet:

> I have heard, that guilty Creatures sitting at a Play,
> Have by the very cunning of the Scene,
> Been strook so to the soul, that presently
> They have proclaimed their Malefactions. [2.2.588]

When the play drives Claudius from the room, we, like Hamlet and Horatio, have been studying his face intently, wondering how he'll respond to this particular mirror, and when Claudius is left alone on stage and launches into a soliloquy, we at last hear just how his conscience is managing its heavy burden:

> Oh my offence is rank, it smells to heaven,
> It hath the primal eldest curse upon't,
> A Brothers murder. Pray can I not,
> Though inclination be as sharp as will:
> My stronger guilt, defeats my strong intent,
> And like a man to double business bound,
> I stand in pause where I shall first begin,
> And both neglect; what if this cursed hand
> Were thicker than it self with Brothers blood,
> Is there not Rain enough in the sweet Heavens
> To wash it white as Snow? Whereto serves mercy,
> But to confront the visage of Offence?
> And what's in Prayer, but this two-fold force,
> To be fore-stalled ere we come to fall,
> Or pardoned being down? Then I'll look up,
> My fault is past. But oh, what form of Prayer
> Can serve my turn? Forgive me my foul Murder:
> That cannot be, since I am still possessed
> Of those effects for which I did the Murder.
> My Crown, mine own Ambition, and my Queen:

May one be pardoned, and retain th'offence?
In the corrupted currents of this world,
Offences gilded hand may shove by Justice,
And oft 'tis seen, the wicked prize it self
Buys out the Law; but 'tis not so above,
There is no shuffling, there the Action lies
In his true Nature, and we our selves compelled
Even to the teeth and forehead of our faults,
To give in evidence. What then? What rests?
Try what Repentance can. What can it not?
Yet what can it, when one cannot repent?
Oh wretched state! Oh bosom, black as death!
Oh limed soul, that struggling to be free,
Art more engaged: Help Angels, make assay:
Bow stubborn knees, and heart with strings of Steel,
Be soft as sinews of the new-born Babe,
All may be well. [3.3.36]

Let us consider this powerful language from three different perspectives, each of which, along with the capacity to create minimovies, are available for the creation of profound emotion in support of heightened language. We will begin with movement and seek verbs that figuratively or in actuality suggest the activity that Claudius's conscience initiates or to which it reacts.

Prayer, along with its physical component such as kneeling, clasping hands, raising eyes and thoughts to heaven, and bowing head and pride in humility, is the central action of the speech. But the imagery suggests a vast range of additional activity, such as washing off blood, falling or being raised up, shoving someone aside, being compelled to give evidence while trying to evade the lawyer's questions with shuffling. Perhaps the most painful image is that of a trapped bird, caught fast in sticky lime, while every movement brings more and more of its terrified body into contact with the lime.

In order to engage this source of creative energy, the actor needs to ask: What do these verbs make me want to do? More specifically: Where in my body do I feel that image? It is possible, prompted by such connections, to create the "dance of the images" to accompany the speaking of these words. In this, the actor first delivers the speech with minimal movement, just that demanded by the text with the words, "Bow, stubborn knees." Then, the actor again delivers the speech, but this time moves freely, in a sort of modern dance-style movement collage, evoking all of the powerful imagery as it resonates in different parts of his body and demands different shapes and rhythms of movement. Finally, the actor returns to the "realistic" staging, but retains the imprint of the movement, remembered in the body and breath, and lets that inform his delivery of the speech.

As an alternative source of insight and energy, the actor can focus on relationships. On the surface this is an easy task because the speech addresses directly this man's relationship with Gertrude and implies a relationship with the murdered brother in the allusion to Cain and Abel. But in order for the imagery to work as richly as possible upon the nonintellectual source of acting power, we must consider both Soul and Conscience as having the capacity for relationships, with Claudius and with each other. The central personification of the speech is of Offense, which not only stinks of filth and disease, but also is forced to look at its own face in the mirror held up by Mercy. We learn that Offense had a gilded hand to shove Justice, who must stand by and watch Pride bribe Law. There is an entire cast of characters here, tearing Claudius apart because they are all part of him, and he has significant relationships with each of them. Even as he opens himself to form a relationship with Repentance, he feels the closing off of any possibility of support from that supposed friend. Even as he knows he should destroy his deep commitment to Ambition, he cannot stop himself from clasping that devilish enemy closer to his breast.

A group of actors can get involved in the enactment of Claudius's relationship imagery. This requires "casting" the other characters into Claudius's landscape. The actor playing the role is best positioned to make these choices, but let us imagine that Gertrude appears as herself, while Ophelia represents both Prayer and Repentance. Laertes plays Ambition, Osric the Prize, and Polonius the Law. We'll cast Hamlet as Mercy, and the ghost as Offence. Now we can "stage" the speech, with Claudius engaging in a free-form interaction with first the ghost, then with Ophelia, until Hamlet shows both men their faces. Claudius again reaches towards Ophelia, but Gertrude is there along with Laertes, and together with Osric they maneuver Polonius away. However, Polonius returns and takes command, representing the higher court, and Claudius must testify, as must the ghost. Now Ophelia returns, only to turn away again, incapable of action. Now all these attributes engage with Claudius, as he struggles to free himself from them and at the same time cannot give them up, or reaches for them, only to have them turn away. Poor Claudius can only call on angels from heaven to help him. With this call, all of the personifications melt away, and Claudius at last can fall on his knees.

In contrast to minimovies, movement, or relationships, the actor can tap into images of power, and in particular that transcendent power that opens up a space beneath the feet and above the head, configured here as hell and heaven. The actor must endow Claudius with a profound faith, for otherwise there would be no struggle. When considering the immense power beyond himself, Claudius can only sink down in terror or reach up towards that which is always beyond his grasp. To balance that awe and longing, the actor can rise up to sensations of power and authority, success and influence, when considering his achievement and free will. The result will be a roller coaster of rising and falling, soaring and tumbling, climbing and retreating, as Claudius feels the power shift in and around him, reminding him of his capacity to command his own destiny and that of others, as well as the absolute power before which he is as a newborn babe. Words like, "a brother's murder"

contain both sensations: Claudius condemned his elder brother to eternal damnation, and now he is face to face with the eternal curse that rests upon his
own head for this deed. His sense of self is dwarfed by that which is beyond
his kingdom, even as his memory of the murder expands his sense of his own
potency. How weak he is to be so easily humbled and unmanned; how powerful he is to have dared damnation in pursuit of the highest honor available
to a man.

Actors need to know what types of associations spark the richest creative
associations with the images Shakespeare uses, and boldly cash in on whatever
personalizes these words. Whatever you do, you can't leave them as "just
Shakespeare being poetical!"

⤳ 7 ⤳

The Power of the Word

Oh speak to me, no more,
These words like Daggers enter in mine ears.

Gertrude [*Hamlet* 3.4.94]

In order to set aside the limitations of a psychological approach to acting, which results in setting limits to the function of language as the means by which concrete and knowable experiences are communicated, and instead to open oneself to the profound and transcendent potency of imagery, a modern actor must set aside some of our assumptions about the limitations of language, and ascribe to an attitude something more akin to that held by Shakespeare's first actors.

Remind yourself of the difficulty of trying to convey your feelings and thoughts to a bereaved friend. We invariably end by hugging and crying along with them. Think of the incredible sounds of joy and relief that emanate from us when we face a badly hurt child who has miraculously survived. No words could possibly do as much. In more frivolous circumstances, consider what might happen on a date if both parties decided to say anything and everything they felt or thought in sounds only from the first moment of greeting. The date might be over instantly. Or it might become a very intense relationship before the movie or the dinner even started. In any case, the couple would certainly know where they stood with one another in a very short period of time. (Miller 1992, 134)

Here, we see the modern attitude towards language: as the intensity of the moment rises, the ability to use language to express feeling decreases, until pure sound and action become the best indicator of deepest feeling.

And yet, this passage describes some of the most important events of *Romeo and Juliet*. Are we to believe that the feelings of the two young lovers are false, because they say everything they think and feel within a few minutes of meeting each other, in one of the most beautiful love sonnets Shakespeare ever wrote? No. We have no problem believing that they in fact form a very intense relationship, and that they know where they stand with each other in a very short period of time! Or what about the overwhelming expressions of grief on the part of those who love Juliet deeply, when they discover that she is dead. We know she is not, but they are not privy to that information. Language assists them in expressing their feelings, and they would certainly not agree that "no words could possibly do as much" as inarticulate sounds and actions.

Let us have a look at some of the most passionate speeches in *Romeo and Juliet* and see how rhetoric comes to the aid of the speaker. We have already explored the shared sonnet that marks the significance of their first interaction. Let's leap forward to the famous balcony scene to see how Shakespeare has young Juliet say everything that is on her mind.

> Thou knowest the mask of night is on my face,
> Else would a Maiden blush bepaint my cheek,
> For that which thou hast heard me speak-to-night,
> Fain would I dwell on form, fain, fain, deny
> What I have spoke, but farewell Compliment,
> Dost thou Love? I know thou wilt say Ay,
> And I will take thy word, yet if thou swear'st,
> Thou mayst prove false: at Lovers perjuries
> Then say Jove laughs, oh gentle Romeo,
> If thou dost Love, pronounce it faithfully:
> Or if thou thinkest I am too quickly won,
> I'll frown and be perverse, an say thee nay,
> So thou wilt woo: But else not for the world.
> In truth fair Montague I am too fond:
> And therefore thou mayst think my behavior light,
> But trust me Gentleman, I'll prove more true,
> Than those that have more cunning to be strange,
> I should have been more strange, I must confess,
> But that thou overheard'st ere I was ware
> My true Loves passion, therefore pardon me,
> And not impute this yielding to light Love,
> Which the dark night hath so discovered. [2.2.85]

Lest there be any doubt in our minds, Shakespeare has the character confirm that she is *not* putting on the socially acceptable "act" of a demure young woman. She is not using the power of rhetoric to disguise what she feels, as she will do later in the play when she meets up with the man her parents want her to marry.

Paris: Poor soul, thy face is much abused with tears.

Juliet: The tears have got small victory by that:
For it was bad enough before their spite.

Paris: Thou wrong'st it more than tears with that report.

Juliet: That is no slander sir, which is a truth,
And what I spake, I spake it to thy face.

Paris: Thy face is mine, and thou hast slandered it.

Juliet: It may be so, for it is not mine own. [4.1.29]

In both of these situations, language comes to Juliet's aid, in the first to help her express the rush of feelings, in the second to hide them from the well-meaning Paris, who cannot be let in on the terrible dilemma she now faces, which she will express with clarity and rhetorical power the moment she is alone with the Friar:

> Tell me not Friar that thou hearest of this,
> Unless thou tell me how I may prevent it:
> If in thy wisdom, thou canst give no help,
> Do thou but call my resolution wise,
> And with this knife, I'll help it presently.
> God joined my heart, and Romeos, thou our hands,
> And ere this hand by thee to Romeo sealed:
> Shall be the Label to another Deed,
> Or my true heart with treacherous revolt,
> Turn to another, this shall slay them both:
> Therefore out of thy long experienced time,
> Give me some present counsel, or behold
> Twixt my extremes and me, this bloody knife
> Shall play the umpire, arbitrating that,
> Which the commission of thy years and art,
> Could to no issue of true honour bring:
> Be not so long to speak, I long to die,
> If what thou speak'st, speak not of remedy. [4.1.50]

Let's move on to Allen Miller's first example of a moment when language fails: in the face of death and grief. Look at how Shakespeare's characters use language to find a pure expression of feeling:

> Howl, howl, howl: O you are men of stones,
> Had I your tongues and eyes, I'ld use them so,
> That Heavens vault should crack: she's gone for ever.
> I know when one is dead, and when one lives;
> She's dead as earth: Lend me a Looking-glass,
> If that her breath will mist or stain the stone,
> Why then she lives. [*Lear* 5.3.258]

"By the time we formulate all the words necessary to express anything deeply, the force of the feelings involved has already lessened," claims Miller (135). That may be the experience of a modern actor. Shakespeare's characters do not share that experience.

This is not to say that Shakespeare presents only an idealized view of language in his plays. There is also a notable thread to be traced from *Love's Labour's Lost* through to *Othello* and *King Lear* that demonstrates how the art of rhetoric can be used for everything *but* the expression of deeply felt feeling. Berowne, the most talkative of the young students in *Love's Labour's Lost*, and the one most likely to give lengthy flights of oratory, midway through a rhapsody to his new-found love Rosaline, proclaims, "Lend me the flourish of all gentle tongues," and then, in the next line, "Fie painted Rhetoric, O she needs it not." Just as her beauty requires none of the tricks of make-up (painting), so too the praise of her beauty requires none of the tricks of language. Of course Berowne then goes on with an additional seven lines of well-structured imagery that contains a fine collection of rhetorical figures.

> To things of sale, a seller's praise belongs:
> She passes praise, then praise too short doth blot.
> A withered Hermit, fivescore winters worn,
> Might shake off fifty, looking in her eye:
> Beauty doth varnish Age, as if new born,
> And gives the Crutch the Cradles infancy.
> O 'tis the Sun that maketh all things shine. [4.3.234]

In the later plays, we will see villains like Iago, Goneril, and Regan use all of the art of language to disguise their malevolent intentions; Shakespeare uses soliloquy and private dialogue to clarify the gap between the surface of the language and the purpose of the speaker, and invites us to watch just how skillful these evil orators can be.

Is there any specific marker that suggests oratory disconnected from the honest expression of thought and feeling? When we first meet Claudius, we do not yet have reason to suspect him as a murderer. All we know, from the first scene in the play, is that the ghost of the old king walks the battlements and that there is some possibility of threat from an old enemy, Norway. And then comes Claudius's first speech:

> Though yet of Hamlet our dear Brothers death
> The memory be green: and that it us befitted
> To bear our hearts in grief, and our whole Kingdom
> To be contracted in one brow of woe:
> Yet so far hath Discretion fought with Nature,
> That we with wisest sorrow think on him,
> Together with remembrance of our selves.
> Therefore our sometime Sister, now our Queen,

Th'imperial Jointress to this warlike State,
Have we, as 'twere, with a defeated joy,
With one Auspicious, and one Dropping eye,
With mirth in Funeral, and with Dirge in Marriage,
In equal Scale weighing Delight and Dole
Taken to Wife; nor have we herein barred
Your better Wisdoms, which have freely gone
With this affair along, for all our Thanks. [1.2.1]

Surely, it is the subject matter that makes us suspicious, rather than the quality of his rhetoric in and of itself. Here is a man talking about marrying his dead brother's wife, and even though the "better wisdoms" of Denmark have gone along freely with this affair, we can't help but suspect that there is something not quite right about the harsh juxtaposition of grief and the delights of wooing, wedding, and bedding.

When Claudius moves to the second part of his introductory statement, his subject matter shifts to something we have already heard about from the men on the battlements: the threat from Norway:

Now follows, that you know young Fortinbras,
Holding a weak supposal of our worth;
Or thinking by our late dear Brothers death,
Our State to be disjoint, and out of Frame,
Colleagued with the dream of his Advantage;
He hath not failed to pester us with Message,
Importing the surrender of those Lands
Lost by his Father: with all Bonds of Law
To our most valiant Brother. So much for him.
Now for our self, and for this time of meeting
Thus much the business is. We have here writ
To Norway, Uncle of young Fortinbras,
Who Impotent and Bedrid, scarcely hears
Of this his Nephews purpose, to suppress
His further gait herein. In that the Levies,
The Lists, and full proportions, are all made
Out of his subject: and we here dispatch
You good Cornelius, and you Voltimand,
For bearing of this greeting to old Norway,
Giving to you no further personal power
To business with the King, more than the scope
Of these delated Articles allow:
Farewell and let your haste commend your duty. [1.2.17]

This strikes us as direct, efficient, and trustworthy use of language. Claudius identifies the problem, states his strategy for defusing the situation, and dispatches his ambassadors. That job completed, he turns to the more relaxed interchanges in the personal realm.

> And now Laertes, what's the news with you?
> You told us of some suit. What is't Laertes?
> You cannot speak of Reason to the Dane,
> And loose your voice. What wouldst thou beg Laertes,
> That shall not be my Offer, not thy Asking?
> The Head is not more Native to the Heart,
> The Hand more Instrumental to the Mouth,
> Than is the Throne of Denmark to thy Father.
> What wouldst thou have Laertes? [1.2.42]

Here we are at a loss to assess the man. Is it just our modern ear that finds the repeated use of the young man's name something less than trustworthy? Or are we superimposing our knowledge of Claudius gained from his actions later in the play? Claudius has no reason to turn on the charm with Polonius's son in order to win over Polonius; the old counsellor is entirely won to Claudius's side. Is this all an act to needle Hamlet, or to persuade the observing court that he's really a very nice person, despite all evidence to the contrary, or are we to understand that Claudius has the common touch, that he is honestly friendly and interested in young Laertes, and that this great king will turn from international diplomacy to avuncular good cheer with the ease of a true man of the people?

When the ambassadors return in the second act, we learn that Claudius's strategy has been entirely successful. With a single skillful diplomatic thrust, he has defused a potential international incident. In this same scene, we see Claudius interact with young Rosencrantz and Guildenstern with the same ease and familiarity as with Laertes, but we also now have the ghost's story of just how Hamlet's uncle became his new stepfather and king.

In performance, an actor can infuse Claudius's rhetoric with anything from repugnant slime to charismatic charm. We can see from his first breath that he is a smiling villain, skilled in the arts of language for duplicity and manipulation. Or we might encounter a villain of such skill that we too are taken in, until we learn more of what is being hidden.

If there is anything specific in the language to differentiate evil uses of rhetoric from good, duplicitous from honest, it does not leap off the page at a modern reader. It takes the actor to clarify or disguise the duplicity that Shakespeare will reveal or confirm when the time is right.

THE MUSIC OF THE VOICE

> Come, your Answer in broken Music; for thy Voice is Music, and thy English broken: Therefore Queen of all, Katherine, break thy mind to me in broken English; wilt thou have me?
>
>   King Henry [*HV* 5.2.243]

An extremely musical delivery of Shakespeare's verse has quite gone out of fashion, but so too has the monotone mumble of the hypernaturalistic. Once we've gone down the dead end of trying to make all of this beautiful language sound ordinary, we find ourselves back where we started, face to face with the simple fact that Shakespeare wrote these words to be spoken by actors aloud for a live audience of people who were still part of an oral culture. While we might be embarrassed by the overt play to the emotions represented by heightened delivery, there is no denying that it is powerful and evocative.

One of the reasons why a musical delivery went out of fashion was because the surface indicators of a strong delivery of the language were easily reproduced by individuals who were too lazy to develop the internal connections that could fill the enlarged sound patterns with enlarged feelings that simultaneously demanded and were shaped by those sounds. And they did not feel it worth their while to dedicate themselves to the training of the emotional muscles required to sustain those connections between feeling and speech for the duration of even sixteen lines of verse, to say nothing of a full-length role.

Our artistic cousins in the world of dance and song could provide us with a metaphor: mastering the authentic music of the language is comparable to dancing classical ballet or singing grand opera. There are many people who can get out there and boogie on the dance floor and belt out their favorite pop tune along with the radio, just as everyone can play dramatic games, particularly if they've had a couple of drinks and are feeling uninhibited and just a little bit adventuresome. The species was designed for just such movement, sounding, mimicry, and imaginative play. Then, there are those naturally talented people who can, with minimal training, become pop or film stars, working well within their natural range and participating in a style of movement, singing, and acting that privileges the intuitive and the natural.

But the movement patterns of classical ballet are not natural. None of us go around on our toes, or jump several feet in the air in perfect time to a complex piece of music. None of us sustain notes at the top or bottom of our vocal range for lengthy periods at full volume or in the softest tones. All the same, jazz dancers and pop singers know something of the training, practice, and determination required to perform Giselle or Madama Butterfly.

I would argue that something similar is required for an actor to achieve a true mastery of Shakespeare's language. Actors are blessed and cursed by the absence of a clear training program that will take the gifted intuitive performer, like our cousins the natural dancer and singer, carefully and steadily up the ladder towards the ultimate excellence of something comparable to classical ballet or grand opera. The blessing comes from the freedom this gives every actor to have a go at Shakespeare. He is not cordoned off the way *Swan Lake* might be from all except those who can perform that particular choreography. The curse is that when someone does achieve the perfect connection between heightened emotion and heightened language, it seems more miraculous than earned, and there is no guarantee that it can ever be achieved again.

This blessing and curse combine to create generation after generation of actors who approach Shakespeare seeking a short cut. They want the sound of the music without the emotion. Or they want the emotions to a natural scale, the one they can master intuitively, and ignore or actively undercut the poetry of the language to match their emotional range.

As a profession, we have nothing comparable to the rigorous daily training of the body that every dancer accepts as the natural price of her art form. Some of us go so far as to distrust technique, under the mistaken impression that strengthening the body, the voice, the intellect, and the imagination will somehow cut the actor off from the inspiration that comes from intuition, not realizing that a strengthened instrument increases the capacity for the individual to create with that instrument.

Even so, we have nothing comparable to the set choreography or the musical notation that demands specific steps and specific musical values when performing the classical ballets and operas. We are free to find our own way into the heart of our theatrical masterpieces. In a celebration of that freedom, we all too easily lose track of the markings that do exist, in the form of the language itself, and wrongly assume that any way of speaking will do.

The source of the music of spoken language is not limited to the rhythms of the Iambic Code, and the interplay of grammatical syntax and verse line, but also to the sound patterns created by the consonants and vowels, each with its own shape and texture and capacity for duration or plosion. Because Shakespeare was himself an actor, and both spoke and heard these sounds delivered full voice in an open-air theatre, he brought to the writing an actor's sensitivity to the way that certain sounds make the actor feel. Just as a singer cannot deliver Adele's laughing aria without feeling the bursting energy of those running "ah, ah, ah's," so too an actor cannot give voice to Hotspur's explosive emotions without feeling the bite and thrust of all these sounds:

> I then, all smarting, with my wounds being cold,
> (To be so pestered with a popinjay)
> Out of my Grief, and my Impatience,
> Answered (neglectingly) I know not what,
> He should, or he should not: For he made me mad,
> To see him shine so brisk, and smell so sweet,
> And talk so like a Waiting-Gentlewoman,
> Of Guns, and Drums, and Wounds: God save the mark. [1.3.49]

Just say these words aloud, and discover how Shakespeare shapes Hotspur's feelings and our impression of his personality with this rush of consonants.

Although dancers are often telling a story, and singers delivering words, the function of music in their art forms ensures that they have a firsthand familiarity with the emotional kick of pure sound that can be described in words but does not require them to have a profound impact on the listener. Because

Shakespeare's language is so rich in meaning, we often forget that it also functions, like music, as patterns of sound. The interplay of how the words and sound and what the words mean provides an additional dimension within which emotions are communicated and experiences are evoked in the speaker and listener.

The fear of sounding artificial seems to overrule the impulse to chew up or sing out passages like Hotspur's or the following, spoken by Juliet to express her determination not to be forced into an unwanted marriage:

> Oh bid me leap, rather than marry Paris,
> From off the Battlements of any Tower,
> Or walk in thievish ways, or bid me lurk
> Where Serpents are: chain me with roaring Bears
> Or hide me nightly in a Charnel house,
> O'ercovered quite with dead mens rattling bones,
> With reeky shanks and yellow chapless skulls:
> Or bid me go into a new made grave
> And hide me with a dead man in his shroud,
> Things that to hear them told, have made me tremble,
> And I will do it without fear or doubt,
> To live an unstained wife to my sweet Love. [4.1.77]

Worse yet are the evocations of immense feeling, written to capture the ululation of the keening voice, as when those who loved Juliet and think her dead give voice to their grief:

Lady Capulet: Accursed, unhappy, wretched hateful day,
Most miserable hour, that e'er time saw
In lasting labour of his Pilgrimage.
But one, poor one, one poor and loving Child,
But one thing to rejoice and solace in,
And cruel death hath catched it from my sight.

Nurse: O woe, O woeful, woeful, woeful day,
Most lamentable day, most woeful day,
That ever, ever, I did yet behold.
O day, O day, O day, O hateful day,
Never was seen so black a day as this:
O woeful day, O woeful day.

Paris: Beguiled, divorced, wronged, spited, slain,
Most detestable death, by thee beguiled,
By cruel, cruel thee, quite overthrown:
O love, O life; not life, but love in death.

Capulet: Despised, distressed, hated, martyred, killed,
Uncomfortable time, why cam'st thou now
To murder, murder our solemnity?

> O Child, O Child; my soul, and not my Child,
> Dead art thou, alack my Child is dead,
> And with my Child, my joys are buried. [4.5.43]

All of those open "oh" sounds, repeated irregularly against the sound patterns created by repeated words, "day" and "child" and "murder" and, most beautifully and compellingly, "But one, poor one, one poor and loving child," are the score for the grief unleashed by the mourning ritual. If anyone retains a cool and distanced observer of this language, she might be tempted to giggle at the mechanical repetitions and the boring vocabulary. But if these words are given full voice with deep and supported breath, they summon up that most primal of human experiences.

Patsy Rodenberg, head of voice at Britain's National Theatre, once told me the story of a public workshop in which she coached an actress on the role of Medea, seeking just such a fully grounded and profound open vowel sound. After the workshop, one member of the audience approached her to express his anger at this demonstration of the human capacity to express such sounds. He reported that he had heard that sound once before, when his wife reacted to the news of their daughter's death, and he never wanted to hear that sound again. Patsy confessed to finding it difficult to acknowledge his pain while disguising her joy at having succeeded so clearly in achieving her goal.

All of the theories of naturalistic acting seem to imply that if you work out the character's similarities to yourself, find things that you can truly believe in, then commit yourself to experiencing the imaginary events of the play as if they were really happening to you, then you will generate a scale of emotional credibility and profundity that the language will naturally fit. Until that time, it is best simply to mark the delivery of the language, speaking in an ordinary voice, even mumbling, pausing whenever an emotional transition needs to be worked through, seeking the best motivations for the various actions your character must perform in the play, and building relationships with the other actors that mirror the relationships that dominate your personal psychic landscape.

At no point in this rehearsal process will the actor hear the music of the language, much less discover the sensations that are aroused when making that music. Sadly, the actors are cut off from one of the primary sources of inspiration available to them in this terror of the artificial.

I would be the first to agree with a dislike for the artificial in performance, but I would urge actors to give the music of the language a chance to work upon their bodies and their ears. Perhaps this can only be done in the privacy of memorization work or voice class. I would also say that you should not be surprised if your vocal instrument is simply not up to the task of making the sounds richly and vividly, if you've never used your ordinary vocal range in your acting. Just as the dancer can, with training, go up on point, so too there are notes to be sounded in the upper- and lower-speaking registers. Just as the singer can acquire the diction and breath control to deliver a patter song, so too the actor can, with dedicated practice, train the tongue, the throat, and the diaphragm to sustain the patterns of sound shaped by this language.

All of this will be a waste of effort, however, if the emotional landscape has not been cleared of barriers that arise from assumptions and laziness. The words as sounded need to resonate in some emotional center, not remain locked into the intellectual capacity of the conscious mind. It is this resonance that gives the musicality its meaning.

The fearless manipulation of a wide range of vocal colors, intonations, pitches, contrasting volume and speed, and fluidity and dynamics is a basic requirement for the shaping of complex thought. Even a natural delivery will not help an actor when delivering one of Shakespeare's long and complexly structured syntactical marathons. Here is a twenty-one line passage, the meaning of which is "This England is now leased out like a farm." However, the stakes are so high that the speaker, John of Gaunt, has to find the language to match, and so he takes nineteen lines to create layer upon layer of syntactical units, each one of which requires its own unique vocalization, in part because of its sound pattern, in part because of its emotional and intellectual association, partly to hold the listener's attention on the long climb to the twentieth line, and partly so that the listener can follow the syntactical complexity when it shifts from the straightforward linear to the interwoven interconnected.

> This royal Throne of Kings, this sceptered Isle,
> This earth of Majesty, this seat of Mars,
> This other Eden, demi-paradise,
> This Fortress built by Nature for her self,
> Against infection, and the hand of war:
> This happy breed of men, this little world,
> This precious stone, set in the silver sea,
> Which serves it in the office of a wall,
> Or as a Moat defensive to a house,
> Against the envy of less happier Lands,
> This blessed plot, this earth, this Realm, this England,
> This Nurse, this teeming womb of Royal Kings,
> Feared by their breed, and famous by their birth,
> Renowned for their deeds, as far from home,
> For Christian service, and true Chivalry,
> As is the sepulchre in stubborn Jewry,
> Of the Worlds ransom, blessed Mary's Son.
> This land of such dear souls, this dear dear Land,
> Dear for her reputation through the world,
> Is now Leased out (I die pronouncing it)
> Like to a Tenement or pelting Farm. [*RII* 2.1.40]

By finding different associations for each of the images up to and culminating in "this England," the midway point at the end of the eleventh line, almost anyone can avoid monotony. Even the untrained and entirely intuitive actor will not miss the potency of the sound and sense connection of "This precious stone, set in the silver sea." But the guts of the speech are yet to come, and the real challenge, demanding a command of vocal flexibility in order to wed sound and sense so as to clarify the pattern of thought, is just ahead. The twelfth line seems a continuation of the fairly easy pattern, but in the last word, "kings," Gaunt begins to spin a web of images rather than continue the list, because he has to tell us about these kings, who are (a) feared, (b) famous, and (c) renowned in connection to (a) breed, (b) birth, and (c) deeds. How feared/famous/renowned are they? As far from home as Jesus' tomb in Jerusalem. But before Gaunt can take us there, he must clarify something about those deeds, which are connected to Christian service and true chivalry. And rather than saying "the sepulchre of Jesus in Jerusalem," he gives the location first, but indirectly, "in stubborn Jewry," and describes Jesus with two identifying phrases, "the Worlds ransom," and "blessed Mary's Son." All of this convoluted web of imagery serves to bring to mind the Crusades, which were so important to the political landscape of medieval England. In Gaunt's opinion, the main reason that England is leased out like a farm is because the current king, his nephew, is doing a terrible job of ruling, and is altogether turning out to be very much not the man his father was. His father, the Black Prince, was one of the great lights of the Crusades, and for that reason died too soon, leaving his infant son to inherit, all in all, a terrible situation.

Quite simply, even if the actor knows what these lines mean, and why they are important to Gaunt, it is almost impossible for them to sound anything like mud unless the speaker can pitch his voice so that the listener hears the connection between the key nouns and the phrases that modify them. The actor has to find a unique vocal sound for a word like "deeds" so that, even with the phrase "as far from home" intervening, the listener immediately recognizes the "deeds" sound returning to start the phrase "for Christian service and true chivalry." And the actor needs to have a contrasting vocal color for "as far from home" to which he can return when the rest of the syntactical unit is delivered, "as is the sepulchre."

If we accept that these linguistic fireworks are the property of John of Gaunt, rather than something that the actor has to manufacture or a trick of the trade that Shakespeare is using to impress his audience, then we can set aside our fears of artificiality. If John of Gaunt isn't afraid of using a bit of high-powered oratory, why should we? If John of Gaunt has the vocal skill and the intellectual brilliance to invent such a thought and deliver it so compellingly, and on his deathbed, then in playing him we should endow him with those character attributes. His skill as a speaker is in his ability to convey the intensity of his feelings about the grandeur of what is being lost as England is transformed from the birthplace of such great kings into a leased farm. The vocal fireworks do not get in the way of caring deeply with, and for, this man. They are the means by which we feel his character, his history, his passions, as we say or hear these lines.

In addition to disciplined training of the voice so that it has maximum flexibility, control, and muscularity, the actor needs to train the breath. Our natural speaking voices require that we use only a small portion of our capacity, but there is no point in learning to say more and more on a single breath unless the *emotional* experience of a profound breath and a lengthy and controlled exhalation is explored and the capacity for profound and psychic experiences developed. Once again, naturalism is not going to be of much help to us, because we are not likely to find the scale required in our daily lives. Thank goodness for our imagination, and also for the innate connection between breathing and emotion.

The Speaking Voice

> Words of so sweet breath composed,
> As made the things more rich.
>
> Ophelia [*Hamlet* 1.3.97]

> I saw her once
> Hop forty paces through the public street;
> And having lost her breath, she spoke, and panted,
> That she did make defect perfection,
> And, breathless, power breathe forth.
>
> Enobarbus [*A&C* 2.2.228]

Thus does Enobarbus describe Cleopatra, with a sensitivity to the connection between breath and speaking that actors acquire after years in live performances. Just to say the words aloud is to discover how the pattern of sounds shapes the breath, even without the signals of the punctuation.

The punctuation in the last line, isolating "breathless" to suggest that, despite her breathlessness, she was still able to breathe forth power, is a modern editor's choice; the folio is as follows:

> I saw her once
> Hop forty Paces through the publicke streete,
> And hauing lost her breath, she spoke, and panted,
> That she did make defect, perfection,
> And breathlesse powre breath forth.

Here, "breathless" modifies power, suggesting that even silent she would personify the essence of power.

What is of even greater interest is the way that the words shape the breath of the actor who speaks them. Where do you breathe, as Enobarbus, when you are saying these words about Cleopatra's breathless power? The capacity for words to shape the voice goes even further. Certain combinations of sounds draw forth certain natural capacities within the individual's voice. If the voice is trained to be free and expressive as well as natural, in contrast to an older, highly patterned and artificially accented sound, then the great discovery of the different tonal qualities in different speeches will become a component of the rehearsal process. If, however, the actor seeks only to create the correct, aesthetically pleasing sounds of whatever accent and intonation is currently popular, then every character will end up sounding the same, beautiful but heartless.

"Hop forty paces through the public street" sits in one part of the mouth and draws out certain alterations in an uninhibited voice. In contrast, "breathless, power breathe forth" moves the mouth quite differently, and there is a noticeable shift in the "voice" that these words draw forth.

If we look at the character of Enobarbus as the sum total of the sounds that are drawn forth from the actor's voice by the words he is given to speak, then we have opened ourselves to an intimacy with the language of these plays that will take us much further into their power in live performance than an artificially constructed, contrived, "Shakespeare-speak."

Delivering lengthy speeches to an assembly is hard work that requires stamina, a strong will, and a considerable dollop of Cleopatra's ability to breathe forth power. Anyone who has had to give an important speech in a nontheatrical situation knows that the purely vocal challenges are very much part of the thrill of the event. The average civilian (i.e., nonactor) has few opportunities to test the intellect and the body against the obstacles of public speaking, but many of us have had to toast the bride or groom or, more sadly, give a eulogy at a funeral. A friend of mine, who finally married his long-time sweetheart, said it was worthwhile hosting the event, despite the expense and his own ambivalence, just to hear his formerly estranged brother's heartfelt impromptu toast to the couple.

What actors forget, in view of their efforts to master the purely technical elements of vocal production, is to endow their characters with a civilian's attitude to public speaking. When Hamlet is forced to explain his continued mourning for his father, the terror of losing his train of thought, of choosing the wrong words, of creating a grammatical mess in his effort to express a complex and barely understood sensation, are challenges to be faced bravely and overcome with exhilaration. In just the same way, the actor faces the terror of running out of breath, of choosing the wrong words to emphasize, of not being heard clearly, and can transpose to Hamlet a shared sense of challenge, effort, and incomplete success. After all, Gertrude clearly doesn't get what Hamlet is trying to communicate, just as a modern audience doesn't understand everything the actor has just said. This struggle to communicate is very much part of the comedy and tragedy of any of the plays, and we cut ourselves off from many important discoveries if we don't allow all of the characters to be like Cleopatra, making defect perfection.

One of the great paradoxes of rehearsing Shakespeare is that everyone comes to the first rehearsal burdened with a great deal that they know about the play, and as the days go by they embark on a journey of continued discovery, as if the play moves off the page and up onto its feet with them, and then dances just out of reach for the rest of the shared journey. Those things that were "known" in early days sometimes need to be thrown off quite violently, though they can also provide a shared foundation upon which the dance takes place. It's one thing to know a fact about a society, quite another to begin to see the world of the play with the attitude that the fact implies.

I feel very strongly that this miraculous dance of discovery is fuelled by the action of saying the words, of connecting breath with sound and sense, provided the actor is free and open, always seeking the richest possible delivery of the words and responding intuitively to the natural placement that she finds in the mouth, throat, chest, and body, as well as the head.

PURPLE PASSAGES

> A part to tear a Cat in.
>
> Bottom [*Dream* 1.2.29]

Modern actors have good reason to run shy of the fireworks of the most heightened of Shakespeare's poetry. Who can miss the condemnation of overdone acting in Macbeth's:

> Life's but a walking Shadow, a poor Player,
> That struts and frets his hour upon the Stage,
> And then is heard no more. It is a Tale
> Told by an Idiot, full of sound and fury
> Signifying nothing. [5.5.24]

Or in Hamlet's advice to the players:

O it offends me to the Soul, to hear a robustious Peri-wig-pated Fellow, tear a Passion to tatters, to very rags, to split the ears of the Groundlings: who (for the most part) are capable of nothing but inexplicable dumb shows, and noise: I would have such a Fellow whipped for o'er-doing Termagant: it out-Herods Herod. Pray you avoid it. [3.2.8]

Heaven forbid any of us should, like Bottom, long for a part to tear a cat in, just for the pleasure of hearing our own voices in all their glorious splendor.

If Shakespeare was so sensitive to the abuse of overblown language, why does he use it in his plays? I think we might as well assume that it was usually for theatrical effect, and a good one at that, though we must also remember that sometimes Shakespeare quite simply miscalculated.

Sometimes our confusion over the scale of the poetry, as compared to the human action being evoked, comes from a radical shift in theatrical convention. Think, for example, of all of the occasions when immensely powerful and sometimes lengthy passages are used to describe the time of day, the weather, or the locale. On the bare platform of the outdoor theatres, these served an important imaginative function. Today, it always strikes me as rather strange when a theatre has a raging sound track, wind machines, perhaps even real water falling on the poor Lear as he bellows:

> Blow winds, and crack your cheeks; Rage, blow
> You Cataracts, and Hurricanoes spout,
> Till you have drenched our Steeples, drowned the Cocks.
> You Sulph'rous and Thought-executing Fires,
> Vaunt-couriers to Oak-cleaving Thunder-bolts,
> Singe my white head. And thou all-shaking Thunder,
> Smite flat the thick Rotundity o' th'world,
> Crack Natures moulds, all germens spill at once
> That make ingrateful Man. [3.2.1]

Peter Yates's film *The Dresser* has a wonderful scene of frantic backstage thunder sheets in competition with the vocal pyrotechnics of Albert Finney in the leading role. It's funny, but in its own way terrifying. We can only imagine what it would have been like to be part of a theatre in which actors and audience conspire to *believe* in a storm created only with words like these.

A shorter but equally evocative touch of atmospherics occurs near the end of the first scene of *Hamlet*, a masterful creation of the terror of darkness, ghosts, and castle battlements. The lines are Horatio's, and the arrival of dawn in the modern theatre is usually accompanied by a striking or subtle lighting change as described by the words: "But, look, the Morn in russet mantle clad, / Walks o'er the dew of yon high Eastward Hill" [1.1.166]. What Horatio *means* is that the sun is coming up over the horizon. What he *says* is a bit of poetry that summons up a wealth of feeling, in addition to the sensory details of the terrible darkness just before dawn and our relief at the moment when the eastern sky begins to lighten and we know the cold and loneliness is almost over.

"Natural," this is not. Our customary approach to conversational language, as recreated on our stages and sets, will not serve us here. Something bigger than ordinary is happening, and the actor is required not only to help us see the dawn, but also to transport us in our imaginations to that castle wall and deep into the heart of that tragic, doomed place.

Shakespeare did not limit his poetic overkill to atmospheric touches. He also trotted out all of his best strategies when it was time to tear a few passions into tatters. One of the reasons that so many of these roles are described as an Everest for the actor is because, at the penultimate moment of the evening, after enduring several hours of exhausting work, the actor must summon up the immense amounts of energy required to deliver something like this:

> Slave, I have set my life upon a cast,
> And I will stand the hazard of the Die:
> I think there be six Richmonds in the field,
> Five have I slain to-day, instead of him.
> A Horse, a Horse, my Kingdom for a Horse. [*RIII* 5.4.9]

How tempting it must be to rip into this, as sheer bravado in the face of inevitable death; we all know Richard will die saying those words. The fact that the line is famous, quite separate from Shakespeare's play about the hunchback king, makes it difficult to go at them with anything other than full force.

One of the most famous of such opportunities for great passion and powerful language is King Henry at the walls of Harfleur:

> Once more unto the Breach,
> Dear friends, once more;
> Or close the Wall up with our English dead:
> In Peace, there's nothing so becomes a man,
> As modest stillness, and humility:
> But when the blast of War blows in our ears,
> Then imitate the action of the Tiger:
> Stiffen the sinews, commune up the blood,
> Disguise fair Nature with hard-favoured Rage:
> Then lend the Eye a terrible aspect:
> Let it pry through the portage of the Head,
> Like the Brass Cannon: let the Brow o'rewhelm it,
> As fearfully, as doth a galled Rock
> O're-hang and jutty his confounded Base,
> Swilled with the wild and wasteful Ocean.
> Now set the Teeth, and stretch the Nostril wide,
> Hold hard the Breath, and bend up every Spirit
> To his full height. On, on, you Noblest English,
> Whose blood is fet from Fathers of War-proof:
> Fathers, that like so many Alexanders,
> Have in these parts from Morn till Even fought,
> And sheathed their Swords, for lack of argument.
> Dishonour not your Mothers: now attest,
> That those whom you called Fathers, did beget you.
> Be Copy now to men of grosser blood,
> And teach them how to War. And you good Yeomen,
> Whose Limbs were made in England; show us here

The mettle of your Pasture: let us swear,
That you are worth your breeding: which I doubt not:
For there is none of you so mean and base,
That hath not Noble luster in your eyes.
I see you stand like Grey-hounds in the slips,
Straying upon the Start. The Game's afoot:
Follow your Spirit; and upon this Charge,
Cry, God for Harry, England, and Saint George. [*HV* 3.1.1]

When offered such an opportunity to out-Herod Herod [*Hamlet* 3.2.14], the modern actor cannot hold back seeking a carefully constructed and naturalistic emotional approach. There is little to be gained from solving the density of the images by imagining a resisting body of men that takes the length of this speech to be persuaded to throw themselves towards certain death. This is no time for an obsessive recreating of what it would actually have been like at Harfleur, nor even for imagining what Henry was thinking and feeling before saying these words. When confronted with this scale of language, the actor must simply get in there and deliver the words, full force and without more justification or motivation than that these words cry out to be said that way.

Another tricky emotional moment that trips up an actor deluded into creating a naturalistic emotional event is Ophelia's speech after Hamlet has left the stage at the end of the nunnery scene. Every Ophelia will testify to the roller coaster that is this short exchange, and the almost unbearable pitch of emotions that must be endured in silent reaction to Hamlet's ravings. The few short lines, "O, help him, you sweet heavens!" and "O heavenly powers, restore him!" seem to exist to give Hamlet breathing time while offering Ophelia opportunities for releasing emotion in the open vowel and the heartfelt appeal to a greater power. Her twelve lines after he has left seem at first glance, to an actress trained in psychological realism, as an invitation to convey to the audience all of the emotions that Hamlet has aroused in his onstage audience.

However, a closer examination of the actual text reveals quite a different rhetorical strategy.

O what a Noble mind is here o'er-thrown?
The Courtiers, soldiers, scholars: Eye, tongue, sword,
Th'expectancy and Rose of the fair State,
The glass of Fashion, and the mould of Form,
Th'observed of all Observers, quite, quite down.
And I of Ladies most deject and wretched,
That sucked the Honey of his Music Vows:
Now see that Noble, and most Sovereign Reason,
Like sweet Bells jangled out of tune, and harsh,
That unmatched Form and Feature of blown youth,
Blasted with ecstasy. Oh woe is me,
T'have seen what I have seen: see what I see. [3.1.150]

What we have here, as shaped the language itself, is a very specific emotional event. The opening "O" is, as always, the vehicle for a profound, heart-stopping sound, but not in order to start the flow of anguish, but instead, apparently, to clear the decks for a thoughtful, well-reasoned argument. The thesis is presented: Hamlet is insane. This is followed by an amplification of the thesis, which teases out the full significance of this insanity, given that it has affected such a noble mind. "Noble" is explored in two directions: Hamlet is the crown prince, and Hamlet is a man of unmatched form and feature. Next, Ophelia gives her evidence, presenting her qualifications as someone who had intimate contact with the quality of this man's intellectual capacity, and more recently the impact of his blasted mind. Although Ophelia describes herself as deject and wretched, this is not in fact an invitation for the actress to enact those emotions. Rather, this is Ophelia demonstrating her capacity to convey the intensity of her emotion as evidence for the validity of her conclusion: only Hamlet's madness could arouse such feeling. It is only at the phrase "Oh woe is me" that the language suggests the full release of the emotions of despair, but not to the extent that reason is lost, for the powerful closing line is a piercing, ironic summation of her status as primary witness to the events of the play.

It is not an easy task for an actor trained in the techniques of emotionally charged hypernaturalism to find the capacity for powerful thought that is no less emotional for being controlled. Ophelia has another, very similar acting challenge: the speech in which she reports to her father what happened when Hamlet visited her in her private chamber. Her entrance is marked with "O my Lord, my Lord, I have been so affrighted," a line that provides the open vowel for emotional release and a clear statement of the feeling itself. Ophelia's primary focus in this scene is telling Polonius what happened. Yes, she has strong feelings about the event, and memories of strong feelings that she felt during the event, but the scene is not about what Ophelia felt, except in that first line. The scene is about what Hamlet did, and then how those actions are interpreted by Polonius. The language has been shaped so that Ophelia's feelings are clearly and vividly presented and then become sublimated so that the character shares the focus of the scene. Put another way, it is a big mistake for Ophelia to weep and shake her way through either of these speeches, using them as vehicles for the expression of the intense emotions Ophelia is feeling. Instead, the intensity needs to be sublimated into the driving need to communicate the idea, so that the passion is tempered with the intellectual discipline of rhetoric. However, it would be equally wrong to cut out feeling altogether. If anything, the sublimation should drive the feeling inward like a pressure cooker, so that it increases in profundity even as it is given immense power through the argument.

Ophelia is not the only character whose best speeches serve to describe another character, sometimes to that person's face, creating a challenge for the modern actors of both roles. Here, for example, is the Duchess of York, con-

fronting her son who is now Richard III, following his murder of all sorts of
other family members including his two nephews, the princes in the Tower.
Richard has just suggested that, as her last-born son, he was a comfort to his
mother. She replies:

> No by the holy Rood, thou know'st it well,
> Thou camest on earth, to make the earth my Hell.
> A grievous burthen was thy Birth to me,
> Tetchy and wayward was thy Infancy.
> Thy School-days frightful, desp'rate, wild, and furious,
> Thy prime of Manhood, daring, bold, and venturous:
> Thy Age confirmed, proud, subtle, sly, and bloody,
> More mild, but yet more harmful, Kind in hatred:
> What comfortable hour canst thou name,
> That ever graced me with thy company? [*RIII* 4.4.166]

In a modern play, if the mother of the central character listed off all of the
terrible things he'd done in his youth, we'd expect an emotion-charged delivery
of the list and reaction to its delivery. What is needed here, however, is a
blending of the emotional power that comes for the psychological insights of
the modern naturalistic actor with a more Elizabethan attitude to the potency
of language.

The Duchess is *naming* Richard's attributes. By this action, she is making
them real. Once named, they have a potency that even Richard's flip response
cannot deny. Her speech is the equivalent of the pinning of an insect to the
cork board in a display case. Her deep feelings about this terrible son are not
as important as her ability to *see* him, and to *describe* him, fully.

Note the complexity of her description. The list of adjectives is not uni-
formly negative. "Daring," "bold," "venturous" "subdued," and "mild" are all
facets of this character, balancing the longer list of horrors. At this point in
the play, we might have forgotten that Richard, when still duke of Gloucester,
carved up the scenery of the third installment of the plays about Henry VI,
and that he complained in his opening soliloquy that there were no more great
battles on the go.

It is wrong, I think, to assume that the absence of a clear expression of
emotion suggests an emotional detachment from the events being described.
Rather, as with all great oration, the emotions of the speaker are very much
part of the package, but carefully controlled so that they are released powerfully in short and precisely shaped bursts, and always present to provide the
driving energy of the argument.

The following is one of the most detached speeches one could imagine,
about an event with huge emotional impact. We are back in *Hamlet*, and Gertrude is describing the death of Ophelia.

There is a Willow grows aslant a Brook,
That shows his hoar leaves in the glassy stream:
There with fantastic Garlands did she come,
Of Crow-flowers, Nettles, Daisies, and long Purples,
That liberal Shepherds give a grosser name;
But our cold Maids do Dead Mens Fingers call them:
There on the pendent boughs, her Coronet weeds
Clambering to hang; an envious sliver broke,
When down her weedy Trophies, and her self,
Fell in the weeping Brook, her clothes spread wide,
And Mermaid-like, a while they bore her up,
Which time she chanted snatches of old tunes,
As one incapable of her own distress,
Or like a creature Native, and indued
Unto that Element: but long it could not be,
Till that her garments, heavy with their drink,
Pulled the poor wretch from her melodious lay,
To muddy death. [4.4–7.166]

In this situation, Gertrude's command of the strategies of powerful communication take her entirely away from any release of emotion. Entirely absent are the open vowel soundings to signal pure release, or even a strong statement of personal feeling.

From the outside, we could talk about her function as an alternative to staging: she tells us what has happened offstage because we couldn't show such a scene in the theatre. Also, by leaving her feelings out of it, she remains ambiguous. Just how does Gertrude feel about Ophelia? How does she feel about Claudius at this point in the play? How much did she know about the murder of Hamlet's father?

But that is outside. Inside, the actress playing the role will have feelings about Ophelia, and Claudius, and will have created, for herself, a scenario for the events before and between her scenes on stage. The action of this moment, clearly, is not to convey to her onstage listeners what she is feeling, though that may come out subtly in a hundred different ways, but rather to let them know what happened, in other words to present the rhetorical argument. Laertes has just asked *where* Ophelia drowned, and Gertrude answers that question, not with a simple answer, "In the river," but rather with detail piled upon detail. It is almost impossible to imagine anyone choosing, in a realistic modern play, to inform a brother of a sister's death with this sort of language.

So how can a modern actress blend all of the things she has intuited through the techniques of psychological realism with this very specific rhetorical strategy? The strongest possible rhetoric requires the strongest possible feeling as its fuel, and the most powerful oration is offered when the stakes are the highest. What sort of debate is Gertrude engaged in, and is this an opening argument or a rebuttal? How can we transform this from storytelling poetry into dramatic dialogue?

First, let us assume that Shakespeare knew what he was doing, as a man of the theatre and an experienced shaper of dramatic event. Ophelia's drowning is a surprise, though not entirely unexpected: the link between insanity and suicide is well established. The minute it is announced, everyone onstage and off wants to know: What sort of a death was it? Gertrude needs to answer *that* question. The short answer might be, "strangely beautiful and entirely appropriate to the poor mad creature she had become, a haunting, horrible, and yet shameless death." The better answer, rhetorically, is to describe it so vividly that the listeners have no choice but to see it just that way.

To raise the stakes, it helps to know that the dominant assumption about Ophelia's death would be quite the opposite, summarized by the priest in the next scene, as "doubtful." Suicide, even without the threat of eternal damnation, summons images of bleak despair, not flowers and trees and rippling brooks.

And so Gertrude is engaged in a profound debate, and she needs every detail, every flower and every metaphor, to compel her listeners to see Ophelia's death in a very specific light. When the churlish priest of the next scene makes pointed reference to the great command that has overruled the church's condemnation of suicides to the shame of burial in unsanctified ground, our first thought is that Claudius has pulled some strings. But we can also credit this particular speech of Gertrude's with tipping the balance away from "Shards, flints and pebbles" towards "maiden strewments" and "charitable prayers."

IRONIC DISTANCE

> Therefore I have decreed, not to sing in my cage: if I had my mouth, I would bite: if I had my liberty, I would do my liking: in the mean time, let me be that I am, and seek not to alter me.
>
> Don John [*Much Ado* 1.3.34]

Ours is a cynical culture. Some of the most successful actors seem able to place an ironic twist onto every utterance, every gesture, every interaction, even those with the camera. We are surrounded by framing devices that reveal the contrast between the surface and the substance, justifying the slight sneer of disbelief, the all-pervading scepticism with which we greet passionate declarations.

Shakespeare was not unaware of the need to distrust the surface presentation of the skilled communicator and those in control of public discourse. Witness how Hamlet scores against the Claudius and Gertrude in the following exchange.

Claudius: But now my Cousin Hamlet, and my Son?

Hamlet: A little more than kin, and less than kind.

Claudius: How is it that the Clouds still hang on you?

Hamlet: Not so my Lord, I am too much i' th'Sun.

Gertrude: Good Hamlet cast thy nighted colour off,
            And let thine eye look like a Friend on Denmark.
            Do not for ever with thy vailed lids
            Seek for thy Noble Father in the dust;
            Thou know'st 'tis common, all that lives must die,
            Passing through Nature, to Eternity.

Hamlet: Ay madam, it is common.

Gertrude: If it be;
            Why seems it so particular with thee.

Hamlet: Seems Madam? Nay, it is: I know not Seems:
            'Tis not alone my Inky Cloak (good Mother)
            Nor Customary suits of solemn Black,
            Nor windy suspiration of forced breath,
            No, nor the fruitful River in the Eye,
            Nor the dejected 'havior of the Visage,
            Together with all Forms, Moods, shows of Grief,
            That can denote me truly. These indeed Seem,
            For they are actions that a man might play:
            But I have that Within, which passeth show;
            These, but the Trappings, and the Suits of woe. [1.2.64]

Hamlet makes use of the rhetorical strategies that come under the general heading of puns, which function because in English words that mean something quite different can sound very much alike. The written version of a pun always seems to miss the point, because the scribe must choose which of sun /son is written out, when both are heard, one because of the word "clouds" in the line before, the other echoing Claudius's use if the intimate address, "my son."

It is in Hamlet's response to his mother's use of the word "seems" that we have a powerful statement of the gap between those actions that might be played in a theatre and the profound experience of grief. Hamlet is probably not the only Dane to wonder just how deeply Gertrude and Claudius could have mourned the death of Hamlet's father, her husband and his brother, given that they are celebrating their marriage so soon after. Hamlet's bitter sarcasm and sardonic punning suggest an ironic distance from the events of the scene. He is able to remove himself from the blinding despair of his personal situation sufficiently to perceive the double implications of the "common" experience of death: everyone must die, and therefore death is part of our shared, common humanity, but amoral, ignoble individuals, whom we might judge as common, are the only ones who would marry their dead husbands' brothers so quickly.

Hamlet's language reflects his awareness of the irony of events, in the sense that the expected outcome of his father's death remains in his mind's eye alongside his observation of the actual outcome. His use of the rhetorical strategies of irony also serve to protect him from the intensity of his personal reaction, but only temporarily, for they burst out in a passionate soliloquy as soon as he is alone on stage.

Hamlet's ironic language has a marvellous modern feel and binds him powerfully to his audience in today's theatres. In a later soliloquy, Hamlet drives himself into a furious blood-lust, culminating in:

> Ha? Why I should take it: for it cannot be,
> But I am Pigeon-Livered, and lack Gall
> To make Oppression bitter, or ere this,
> I should have fatted all the Region Kites
> With this Slaves Offal, bloody: a Bawdy villain,
> Remorseless, Treacherous, Lecherous, kindless villain!
> O vengeance! [2.2.576]

Hamlet's next words are, "Why, what an ass am I!" His mind has suddenly caught sight of the image of himself performing these "actions that a man might play" and irony floods the gap between what he is trying to be and what he truly is.

The sensation of a double view, resulting from an awareness of the gap between the ideal and the real, between the expected and the actual, between the promise and the action, and the resulting sardonic expressions of cynicism, do not dominate Hamlet's language as they do so many of our modern cultural artifacts. In fact, any washing of Hamlet in a glaze of ironic distance will cut the heart out of the character and the engine out of the play.

Hamlet is presented to us as someone with an awareness of our capacity for seeming, and a highly skilled capacity to put on the trappings and suits of a variety of attitudes, but also as someone who has within himself something that surpasses the flimsy artifice of his manic disposition or the supercharged "O vengeance" role-play. Hamlet's attempts to use ironic distance are short-lived contrasting shades to the emotional state that characterizes him: a deep and passionate engagement of the mind, the body, and the soul in the events of the play.

A sceptical worldview, and the accompanying ironic distance, is the single greatest liability a modern actor can bring to Shakespeare's characters. Every effort must be made to put aside the cool, tempered, slightly self-depreciating tone that so easily creeps into any expression of strong feeling. Cynical undercutting of words that convey positive human values must be used sparingly, and only when signalled by the specific rhetorical strategies that set up such sarcastic shadings, as when Hamlet answers his mother's sanctimonious, "Thou know'st 'tis common, all that lives must die, / Passing through Nature, to Eternity," with the bitter, "Ay madam, it is common" [1.2.72]. Shakespeare endows many of his characters with a healthy sense of the ridiculous; he creates very few gullible innocents. His apparent cynics like Edmund, the bastard brother in *King Lear*, are presented as strongly moved more than once, and all of his central characters experience the full force of the racing energy of their emotions without a foot on the brake of ironic distance.

Let us have another look at Hamlet and the dangers represented by deciding that he is a disillusioned, ironical, modern sceptic. Here is one of his better-known speeches:

I have of late, but wherefore I know not, *lost all my mirth, forgone all custom of exercises; and indeed, it goes so heavily with my disposition* that this goodly frame the Earth, *seems to me a sterile Promontory*; this most excellent Canopy the Air, look you, this brave o'erhanging, this Majestical Roof, fretted with golden fire: why, *it appears no other thing to me, than a foul and pestilent congregation of vapours*. What a piece of work is a man! how Noble in Reason? how infinite in faculty? in form and moving how express and admirable? in Action, how like an Angel? in apprehension, how like a God? the beauty of the world, the Paragon of Animals; and yet to me, what is this *Quintessence of Dust? Man delights not me*; no, nor Woman neither, though by your smiling you seem to say so. [2.2.295]

The italicized passages, which could have been lifted from a twentieth-century philosophical treatise or beat poem, suggest to the modern actor not only the subtext for the entire speech, but also a sneering, cynical delivery for words like "goodly," "excellent," "brave," "golden," "noble," "infinite," "express," "admirable," "angel," "god," "beauty," and "paragon." This is a powerful rhetorical strategy often used in modern productions.

Shakespeare's language works quite differently. If a character is intended to feel an onslaught of a single, powerful emotional sensation, then the language will also be flooded with an overwhelming layering on of words that convey that sensation. A small number of contrasting words will serve to highlight the intensity of the dominant emotion, as shadings in a line drawing.

This speech, however, is almost equally divided between some of the most powerful words of disgust and horror and equally powerful words that, in Elizabethan terms, simply could not be spoken without opening the speaker and the listener to the spiritual significance and emotional impact they encoded. The Elizabethans did not say a word like "infinite" and sneer. Their minds could not be stopped from leaping to the most thrilling and awe-inspiring associations upon saying or hearing such a word.

The power of this speech, and the pain of Hamlet's mental state, comes not from the pervasive sense of irony, but from the repeated juxtaposition of all that elevates with all that causes despair. It is the sensation of being dropped, over and over, from the heights, that provides the burning pain of this expression of loss.

Let us have a look at a cynical character. Iago's soliloquies, wherein he shares the true nature of his bitter worldview, are filled with examples of irony, as when he quips, "The Moor (how beit that I endure him not) / Is of a constant, loving, Noble Nature, / And I dare think, he'll prove to Desdemona / A most dear husband" [2.1.288]. But what do we do with his next comment, "Now I do love her too"? The abrupt announcement that Iago loves Desdemona can be tossed off by a modern actor, and can arouse a laugh in a modern audience, with perfect credibility. It's hard to believe that it can be a statement of real feeling, particularly when Iago goes on to clarify that this is revenge "For that I do suspect the lusty Moor / Hath leaped into my Seat" [2.1.295], in other words had a liaison with Iago's wife Emilia. Is Iago lying? The convention of a soliloquy demands that the character seek the perfect expression of what he is feeling at a given moment. Iago clarifies what he means by love, not the sexual attraction he attributes to Cassio, nor the passionate and enduring commitment that he is willing to admit Desdemona might have made to her husband, but as a way of feeding his revenge. He is not saying that he is going to pretend to love Desdemona, for the ironical pleasure it would afford, though that is clearly a side effect. He is saying that she arouses in him an emotion with all of the attributes of love: obsession, longing, and passionate desire at the level of his very soul. When he talks about the poisonous jealousy eating away at his guts, he is not cooly cynical any more. Before and after these lines he is, but while saying them the modern actor must jettison the safety of ironic distance and give himself over to the fullest experience and expression of feeling.

Darker emotions prove less difficult for modern actors than positive ones, another product, I would suggest, of our cynical culture. The challenge facing modern actors asked to play one of Shakespeare's young lovers without a hint of irony reveals just how deeply ingrained ironic distance can be.

ANTIPOETRY

Do you wish then that the Gods had made me Poetical?

Audrey [*AYLI* 3.3.23]

What is it about Shakespeare's verse that sucks the heart out of young actors? Is it the deep shadow cast by the towering giants that have gone before? Is it the dead hand of bardolotry that denies the actor equal partnership in the creation of a character suggested by the shape of the language? Is it dimly remembered teachers who proclaimed the beauty and wonder of these plays while making them so tedious and interminable?

While all of these might contribute to the antipathies, acknowledged or buried, that accompany even the most enthusiastic venturing into the rehearsing of these plays, I suspect that another element is the root cause of the energy drain. Sadly, the cause is the very thing that Shakespeare created to benefit his original actors: the dramatic poetry known today as blank verse.

In the absence of the equivalent of Intrepid's code breakers, yet sensing the wealth of important emotional and character-related information contained in the poetry, the modern actor falls back on a generic acting style that might be termed "poetical," which so transgresses the conventions of contemporary acting that it allows for no transference of the actor's technique or intuition.

This "poetical" acting style is often built around an acquired accent that the actor feels is mandatory for the "correct" delivery of this, the greatest of all playwrights. It is difficult to imagine how such a historically inaccurate perception could still survive. If there was a uniform "received pronunciation" in Shakespeare's England, which is in itself highly unlikely, then it is simply impossible that the "correct" accent bore any similarity to the way the present queen of England sounds during her Christmas address.

Even if we were interested in historically accurate museum reproductions of the plays in performance, we would want to integrate a variety of accents reflecting the urban population from which the players, journeymen, and apprentices were drawn and in which we would find a wide range of regional dialects represented. We would also want to preserve the muscularity of the English language before the evolution of the eighteenth and nineteenth century that saw the loss of the growling "r" and the elongation of so many of the vibrant vowels into an open, relaxed breathiness. We would be more likely to find such a historically authentic Elizabethan accent in the outports of Newfoundland or the back hills of Appalachia than in the products of the Royal Academy of Dramatic Art or the halls of the British Broadcasting Company.

Along with a false accent comes a false sense that the heightened language of the plays represents an elevated intellectual sophistication, intelligence at the expense of feeling. We have already looked at King Henry's debate with the common soldier Michael Williams on the eve of the battle of Agincourt; let us now return to that scene and observe the effect of his words on Henry's soul. Henry delivers his final words to the other soldiers in prose and then shifts to poetry to express his most personal thoughts, a paraphrase of the powerful image earlier created by Williams:

Indeed the French may lay twenty French Crowns to one, they will beat us, for they bear them on their shoulders: but it is no English Treason to cut French Crowns, and to morrow the King himself will be a Clipper.
Upon the King, let us our Lives, our Souls,
Our Debts, our careful Wives,
Our Children, and our Sins, lay on the King:
We must bear all. [*HV* 4.1.225]

The sharp contrast between pre-battle bravado and the long-suppressed horror at the shocking accusation made by Williams is entirely credible to a modern

actor, and the contrasting rhythms and tone serve our expectations. What
follows, however, are thirty-five lines on the subject of kingly ceremony, in
which are included such ornate phrases as, "'Tis not the Balm, the Sceptre,
and the Ball, / The Sword, the Mace, the Crown Imperial, / The enter-tissued
Robe of Gold and Pearl" [4.1.261]. Sadly, all of this serves to cut a modern
actor off from the very real emotions being expressed by the king, as he continues,

> No, not all these, thrice-gorgeous Ceremony;
> Not all these, layed in Bed Majestical,
> Can sleep so soundly, as the wretched Slave:
> Who with a body filled, and vacant mind,
> Gets him to rest, crammed with distressful bread,
> Never sees horrid Night, the Child of Hell:
> But like a Lackey, from the Rise to Set,
> Sweats in the eye of Phoebus; and all Night
> Sleeps in Elysium: next day after dawn,
> Doth rise and help Hyperion to his Horse,
> And follows so the ever-running year
> With profitable labour to his Grave:
> And but for Ceremony, such a Wretch,
> Winding up Days with toil, and Nights with sleep,
> Had the fore-hand and vantage of a King.
> The Slave, a Member of the Countrys peace,
> Enjoys it; but in gross brain little wots,
> What watch the King keeps, to maintain the peace;
> Whose hours, the Peasant best advantages. [4.1.266]

An explanation of the Elizabethan attitudes towards rhetoric and human suffering cannot easily outweigh the natural reaction any modern actor would
have to the linguistic density in such a speech, and as a result he might miss
the all-important clue, the words "horrid night," thinking them a simple observation rather than an evocation of intense feeling being felt, at this very
moment, by Henry himself. Underneath this beautifully structured musing on
the proverb "Uneasy is the head that wears the crown" is a young man saying,
with Claudio, "to be worse than worst / Of those that lawless and incertain
thought, / Imagine howling, 'tis too horrible" [*Measure* 3.1.125].

Great poetry requires and invites great feeling. Modern actors quite rightly
fear contrived, overblown delivery, having too often heard hollow booming
oration, "full of sound and fury / Signifying nothing" [*Macbeth* 5.5.27]. For that
reason, when they encounter passages such as Claudio's "To be imprisoned
in the viewless winds / And blown with restless violence round about / The
pendent world" [*Measure* 3.1.123], they hesitate to sing out the howling vowels,
to punch out the ache and consonant-driven terror, to hiss the shameful sibi-

lants, even though these sounds are a primal onomatopoeia of the terror we all feel when we contemplate death.

How can modern actors use the acting muscles that they strengthen in their other work situations, from commercials to films, from Neil Simon to David Mamet, when entrusted with such complex, compelling, but ultimately alien language? How can they bring to Shakespeare the vast reserves of visceral, intuitive empathy that is the goal of so much of their training? Perhaps it is only by setting aside the habits of naturalism that we can hope to repossess the theatrical potency of these plays.

♋ 8 ♋

The Fallacy of Universality

This act, is as an ancient tale new told.

Pembroke [*John* 4.2.18]

One of the habits of character development that are brought to the rehearsal process by Method-trained actors is a desire to imagine the ordinary details that build a connection between the fictional character and the actor's sense of personal existence. I tell the story of one exchange during the preparation of *Romeo and Juliet*. The actor playing Capulet enters, stops, and asks where he has just come from. You've been at a banquet, so you should all come feeling full from good food and drink. Ah. He enters again, stops, and asks what was served at the banquet. Chicken. But I don't like chicken. Then pick something you do like. No, that's OK, it can be chicken. I just won't have any.

If planning the menu of the banquet helped this actor make Capulet come alive for the audience, then I have no problem with this residue of hypernaturalistic acting. It is for actors trained in this approach, for whom imagining the compelling details of their character's life, truly lived, is a crucial ingredient in their creative process, that I offer an approach to the metaphors in the plays that invites just such an imaginative journey.

It is without doubt possible to structure a viable character without any knowledge whatsoever of Shakespeare's England. However, there are many interesting clues about what characters think and believe, and how they see the world, that we simply cannot use unless we understand to what they are pointing. Some of these insights into character are necessary in order to make sense of the choices the characters make; if we don't understand their worldview, we might conclude that they are making these choices for quite strange reasons.

I would have to conclude that it is rather naive for an actor to assume that people in Shakespeare's time felt about things the same way we do today. So much of what his characters say fits with our attitudes that we can build a performance entirely out of the similarities between ourselves and what we assume to be the character we are playing. Anything that doesn't fit is an anomaly, an aberration, or something external to the character.

Let us take a basic example: Juliet's relationship with her parents. That she would meet and fall in love with a boy her parents do not know, that they would disapprove of her choice, and that she would sneak out to meet him: these make perfect sense. That her father would scream at her when she defies him, well, parents get a bit crazy sometimes, don't they? He's surely exaggerating in a diatribe like:

> Gods bread, it makes me mad:
> Day, night, hour, tide, time, work, play,
> Alone, in company, still my care hath been
> To have her matched: and having now provided
> A Gentleman of Noble Parentage,
> Of fair Demesnes, Youthful, and Nobly Allied,
> Stuffed as they say with honourable parts,
> Proportioned as ones thought would wish a man,
> And then to have a wretched puling fool,
> A whining mammet, in her Fortunes tender,
> To answer, I'll not wed, I cannot Love:
> I am too young, I pray you pardon me.
> But, as you will not wed, I'll pardon you.
> Graze where you will, you shall not house with me:
> Look to't, think on't, I do not use to jest.
> Thursday is near; lay hand on heart, advise,
> And you be mine, I'll give you to my Friend:
> And you be not, hang, beg, starve, die in the streets,
> For by my soul, I'll neer acknowledge thee,
> Nor what is mine shall never do thee good:
> Trust to't, bethink you, I'll not be forsworn. [3.5.176]

It's easy to hear her own father's anger, and respond appropriately. It is even possible to hear "beg, starve, die in the streets," and think of today's street kids, so many of whom have run away from abusive homes. When Juliet undertakes an elaborate stratagem: to appear dead in order to run away with Romeo, the naive actor might wonder why she doesn't just throw her favorite things into a bag and take off to Mantua. The real answer to this question, if we look to Shakespeare's time for clarification of Juliet's attitude to her parents, is one that will require a reworking of Juliet's personality.

When Juliet realizes that she has met and fallen in love with a Montague, she says: "My only Love sprung from my only hate, / Too early seen, unknown, and known too late, / Prodigious birth of Love it is to me, / That I must love a loathed Enemy" [1.5.138]. It is all too easy to forget this aspect of Juliet's character: she is the loyal and loving daughter of her family. Their enemies are hers, and she loathes them. If she had known who he was before they spoke, she would have had the same reaction as Tybalt does. If she had not been tricked into loving Romeo, she would have responded to the murder of her beloved cousin as her mother does:

> We will have vengeance for it, fear thou not.
> Then weep no more, I'll send to one in Mantua,
> Where that same banished Run-agate doth live,
> Shall give him such an unaccustomed dram,
> That he shall soon keep Tybalt company. [3.5.87]

In her first appearance on stage, Juliet says, in answer to her mother's question about Paris, "I'll look to like, if looking liking move. / But no more deep will I endart mine eye, / Than your consent gives strength to make it fly" [1.3.97]. She means this, with her whole heart, in a way that no modern women could. She is completely one with her society's attitude to the careful consideration parents take when bringing their children into matrimony, and to the complete trust that children quite naturally enjoy in their parents' loving care. The idea of talking back to her father, contradicting her mother, and worst of all lying to them about her spiritual state would be anathema to any but the most horrible and abnormal young woman, which Juliet clearly is not.

Unless a modern actor positions Juliet's prodigious love for Romeo within the context of the cataclysmic defiance of her loyalty to her family it demands of her, there will be no telling the difference between this and puppy love.

SOCIAL HISTORY

> Which is more
> Than History can pattern, though devised,
> And played, to take Spectators.
>
> Hermione [*WT* 3.2.35]

I have always liked imagining what it was really like to live in another time. Authentic details thrill me and spark rich imaginings. Because of the importance of the senses in the actor's work, I am always eager to discover details that evoke the smells, sounds, tastes, sights, and textures of Shakespeare's England.

There are so many places to look and things to know about that the onslaught of historical information can be daunting. But that cannot justify laziness, when the clarity of specific images is so important to your creativity. For example, you'll want to have a mental picture of the bridges across the Thames, the hangings at Tybourn, the laden carts coming to market, the tapster, the bear baiting, a woman at her sewing—in fact every image that ever caught Shakespeare's eye and ear has the potential to inspire yours.

You need to put specific images into a larger context, one that balances the agenda of the artist with a historian's breadth of perspective. Moreover, the idealized pictures of Elizabethan life you might have received from Hollywood need to be challenged by concrete information about poverty, unemployment, the exodus from the countryside following the enclosure of public land, the anxieties about war, famine, and political unrest, the racial prejudice, and the plagues and other diseases that swept through the cities—all of which provide the poet-playwright with the images that anchor his plays to human experience.

Many passages in Shakespeare cannot be understood without the sort of background that social historians can provide. Fortunately, the editors of the best editions of the plays include the most important facts, but a wealth of emotion-filled detail awaits the actor who is willing to dig a bit further. But how is the background information to be communicated to an audience? The theory seems to be that if the actor knows and believes, and says the lines appropriately, the audience will understand that something is at stake, even if it doesn't know what it might be. Audiences seem content to take the text at face value, provided that the words being spoken come alive in some recognizable way. "I didn't understand exactly what they were fighting about, but I had no trouble understanding what they were feeling and how much it mattered to them," is a typical comment overheard in such audiences.

Even so, we must acknowledge the puzzling or even tormenting sensation that the people on stage know something that you don't, and the irritation caused by references to objects and activities that have disappeared into the mists of time, and simply cannot be understood in a modern theatre. In practice, more and more of the most difficult passages are being cut or rewritten so that the *sense* of what is being said is as clearly presented as the emotional color or relationship issues that are conveyed around and in spite of the language.

Besides knowing something about what people ate and wore, it will be important for an actor to know what people in Shakespeare's England thought and believed and felt. The danger is falling into the trap of thinking that Shakespeare's England was made up of people who all believed the same thing. This was no more true then than today. However, just as we can speak of certain trends of thought today, we can chart similar patterns for that time, all the while acknowledging that individuals will always resist the boxes that scholars make for them.

England was in fact entering the early modern period during Shakespeare's lifetime, a time of turmoil, of uncertainty, of the obvious and undeniable crumbling of much of what we would consider traditional hierarchy in the secular political systems of the time. Therefore, balanced with the enduring fondness for the old medieval beliefs are all of the exciting new possibilities and, as a natural adjunct to change, the terrifying images of chaos, formlessness, fluidity, and upward (and downward) mobility.

What we learn from all of this is that a modern actor needs to develop strategies for learning the difference between modern and Shakespearean values, because that is the only way to be able to spot the difference between differing degrees of importance that might be attached to concepts. Actors speak of word temperature as an easy metaphor to explain difference in significance. A neutral word is functional, with no emotional charge. A "hot" word, in contrast, is highly charged. Many "hot" words are readily apparent, because they are repeated, or because they have an obvious connection with important aspects of the situations or relationships being dramatized. But some "hot" words bring that temperature directly to the play from Shakespeare's world.

Hypertext

We need a word to describe the means by which Shakespeare loads into words a huge wealth of emotional material upon which an actor can draw to fill in the complexities of thought and feeling that lie beneath the surface of any observable action. Modern actors will be familiar with the term "subtext," and perhaps also with the suggestion that there is no subtext in Shakespeare. What is meant by this observation, I believe, is that the location of the subtext is the text itself. An actor need not create the subtext, as suggested by Stanislavsky-style approaches, but rather locate the emotional engine encoded in the text that has been created to be spoken and heard.

I will call this encoding the "*hyper*text" and suggest that it coexists with the intellectual content of the words and the essential exchange being enacted at that moment in the play. Like hypertext on a computer screen, the encoded text can be tapped for entry into a network of associations and allusions, all available to the actor as a source of information about character, motivation, relationships, emotional context, and intellectual and moral significance.

HABITS OF MIND

All
That time, acquaintance, custom and condition,
Made tame, and most familiar to my nature.

Calchas [*T&C* 3.3.8]

The concept of hypertext invites us to explore how the attitudes of the characters reflected the habits of mind that permeated Shakespeare's world.

These mental and emotional norms would have provided the first actors with a set of automatic responses to individual words that a modern actor must consciously assume when undertaking the character.

Reflections

One of the habits of mind that permeates Shakespeare's England is that of analogy. This is first and foremost a rhetorical strategy, a means by which the orator develops his argument by drawing parallels between the situation under discussion and anything else, provided that the comparison persuades the listener of the orator's perspective on the issues.

Metaphor, that elemental building block of human communication, is built upon analogy. We are discussing one topic but I inject another in order to draw your mind to the analogy between two quite different things. I say "the ship of state" because we are discussing politics but our knowledge of sailing sheds light on the point I am making about the importance of a certain type of leadership and governance, like a captain, the mates, and the well-drilled crew.

One of the reasons that analogy was more deeply ingrained in Shakespeare's culture than in ours was the worldview that suggested that God's plan for every aspect of the universe could be seen in the pattern of analogies that linked every observable phenomenon with the one great event: the battle between good and evil for the soul of man. This medieval framework underwent considerable challenge during Shakespeare's lifetime, but the habit of mind that was firmly in place is as much of interest as the challenges. It doesn't matter to us as actors what Shakespeare believed, except insofar as we might be curious, but the importance of analogy to the creation of his characters is an important building block in our development of an acting style ideally suited to these plays.

Scholars have debated just how supportive or critical Shakespeare might have been of the political status quo of his time, and how he might have used his plays for subtle or overt criticism or support of the powerful. Standing outside this debate, we can observe that the plays can be gleaned equally successfully for radical or conservative agendas. For example, in a play like *As You Like It* we can find references to the forced enclosure of pastureland and the decimation of the agricultural underclass; we can also find support for the continuance of a strictly hierarchical society driven by the agenda of the ruling class.

The fact that the plays were censored, that writers who crossed the line into too obvious and pointed a satire of the powerful ended up in prison, and that Shakespeare and his company enjoyed the patronage of the nobility and often played at court would seem to point towards Shakespeare being conservative; his friend Ben Jonson was much more associated with the bitter satire that sought to correct the evils of society. Even so, it is impossible to read the histories without seeing them as conveying, in part, a series of lessons on the nature of kingship, holding a mirror up to the powerful in order to point out the relative strengths and evils that functioned in these historical models and must be embraced or avoided for the good of England itself.

It is the habit of analogy that allows for an immediate and contemporary application of every dramatized event. Henry IV is a king; he is also analogous to *our* king or queen, and as we watch him govern his unruly nobles and fret over his heir, we cannot help but see the mirror being held up to Elizabeth and her couriers.

The same analogy is at work in all of the plays. In *As You Like It*, Rosalind is in the uncomfortable position of both having a claim to the throne and not wishing to advance her cause against her uncle the current duke. When he exiles her, she denies the charge of treason by saying:

> Treason is not inherited my Lord,
> Or if we did derive it from our friends,
> What's that to me, my Father was no Traitor,
> Then good my Liege, mistake me not so much,
> To think my poverty is treacherous. [1.3.61]

Nothing else about her in any way suggests a real person in Elizabeth's court, but the analogy need not be overtly stated to register and provide this speech with contemporary significance for Shakespeare's actors and audience. There were several potential traitors against whom Elizabeth took action during her years on the throne; she herself was once very much like Rosalind and assumed to be conspiring against her sister Mary simply because of the fact she was her father's daughter.

In every case where an analogy to some powerful individual living or recently dead can be suggested by an understanding of political events in Shakespeare's England, the result for the scene is a heightened tension. As we say in acting class, the stakes are raised.

The analogy between character and some notable from Shakespeare's world is almost always going to be something that only the actors know; modern audiences will almost never be dominated by individuals who will spot the significance of dressing up Polonius to look like William Cecil. This does not mean that the analogies should not be mined for the solutions they offer the actors themselves.

Not every actor will find historical analogy useful, but for those who like to imagine that a real person inspired the fictional character, then models are readily available for the characters of the plays. I would hate, however, for the seekers of contemporary allusion to dominate our approach to interpretation. Those scholarly types who have proposed that the true author of Shakespeare's plays is the earl of Oxford are much given to pointing out the real-life figures whose reflections they find, reflections that they use as further proof of their proposition. The resulting hall of mirrors is at best an amusing, slightly ridiculous exercise in making subtle analogies concrete and reductive. The entire purpose of analogies for the modern actor is to unleash exciting rehearsal energies and performable choices, and anything that locks an actor in to playing a museum reproduction or a historical bio-pic is, in my opinion, very much a dead end.

Elizabeth

When Bassanio chooses the iron casket and discovers Portia's picture, the burden of her father's strange will is finally lifted from Portia, and she can address the man she loves and will marry with a straightforward declaration of love. Because she has no father or brother to speak for her, she must present herself by assessing her strengths and weaknesses as objectively as she can. She says,

> You see my Lord Bassanio where I stand,
> Such as I am; though for my self alone
> I would not be ambitious in my wish,
> To wish my self much better, yet for you,
> I would be trebled twenty times my self,
> A thousand times more fair, ten thousand times
> More rich, that only to stand high in your account,
> I might in virtue, beauties, livings, friends,
> Exceed account: but the full sum of me
> Is sum of nothing: which to term in gross,
> Is an unlessoned girl, unschooled, unpractised,
> Happy in this, she is not yet so old
> But she may learn: happier than this,
> She is not bred so dull but she can learn;
> Happiest of all, is that her gentle spirit
> Commits it self to yours to be directed,
> As from her Lord, her Governor, her King.
> My self, and what is mine, to you and yours
> Is now converted. But now I was the Lord
> Of this fair mansion, master of my servants,
> Queen o'er my self: and even now, but now,
> This house, these servants and this same my self
> Are yours, my Lord, I give them with this ring,
> Which when you part from, lose, or give away,
> Let it presage the ruin of your love,
> And be my vantage to exclaim on you. [3.2.149]

Portia's unhappy circumstances have a happy ending: a man is found worthy of her, and she is able to transform from the celibate queen of Belmont into a proper wife who views her husband as her lord, her governor, and her king.

To confirm the parallel between Portia and Elizabeth, here is Bassanio's response to this speech:

> Madam, you have bereft me of all words,
> Only my blood speaks to you in my veins,
> And there is such confusion in my powers,
> As after some oration fairly spoke
> By a beloved Prince, there doth appear
> Among the buzzing pleased multitude,
> Where every something being blent together,
> Turns to a wild of nothing, save of joy
> Expressed, and not expressed. [3.2.174]

Bassanio is saying he hears Portia's words exactly as the English people heard the public orations of Elizabeth, their beloved ruler, who, though she was a woman, styled herself their prince, and cast a lifelong spell over her people.

Portia is not the only Shakespearean heroine who manages a large estate in the absence of a father or brother. Olivia, the object of Orsino's intense courtship, resolves to live in isolated mourning at least until she meets Cesario and falls in love.

Shakespeare's England knew widows who administered great estates on behalf of young sons, but there was only one model for a young woman who, like Portia, was queen over herself and who, like Olivia, could "sway her house, command her followers, / Take, and give back affairs, and their dispatch, / With such a smooth, discreet, and stable bearing" [*12th Night* 4.3.17], as Sebastian notes of Olivia. That woman was Queen Elizabeth.

Like Olivia, Elizabeth lost both a father and a brother who might otherwise have ruled England. Like Portia, she was pursued by many suitors from all over Europe, none of whom proved suitable. Unlike Portia, the men she loved she could never marry; moreover, she was not prepared to offer herself to a foreign prince and say, "My self, and what is mine, to you and yours / Is now converted." England had just had an unfortunate experience with Elizabeth's sister Mary offering her love and country to Philip of Spain. When Elizabeth came to the throne, Philip tried to regain what he felt was his property by this marriage contract. Even though she defeated his armada, England, and Elizabeth, were never fully freed from Mary's marriage promises.

Elizabeth was an old woman by the time Shakespeare began to write for the theatre, and her people seem to have had a powerful ambivalence about her. On the one hand, she had ruled successfully, if with an iron hand, and England enjoyed an economic and cultural prosperity under her. On the other hand, all was not smooth sailing, and once she passed childbearing age the spectre of civil war rose to haunt the kingdom. Who would succeed her? She refused to name an heir. Would the powerful nobles line up behind the various contenders to the throne and while fighting rip England to pieces, so that the

European vultures could swoop in and scoop up the spoils? Was there some connection between failed harvests and terrible winter storms and the barren state of England's queen?

Portia and Olivia represent an alternative story pattern that could never have been Elizabeth's but that's not the purpose of romance. In Belmont and Illyria, an alternative fate awaits the Elizabeth-like Portia and Olivia. All of the things that Elizabeth so liked in a young man like Robert Dudley, later earl of Leicester, or Robert Devereux, the infamous earl of Essex, can now safely be admired in Bassanio and Cesario, as observed by Olivia: "Thy tongue, thy face, thy limbs, actions, and spirit, / Do give thee five-fold blazon" [*12th Night* 1.5.292]. All of their Elizabeth-like sensuality can be directed much more appropriately towards a husband, and Belmont and Illyria will be blessed with the heirs of these happy couples to ensure the security of all who live there.

What does it do to see Elizabeth in the reverberations of Portia and Olivia. A few important transactions suddenly come into sharp focus. It is easy to forget that Portia and Olivia manage large estates when most of their scenes involve comedic or romantic exchanges. Elizabeth said, "I know I have the body but of a weak and feeble woman; but I have the heart and stomach of a King, and of a King of England too" (Perry 1990, 286), and we can see Portia's manly stomach, a source of courage, in her confrontation with Shylock. Like Elizabeth, Portia can hold her own in the male world of intellectual discourse.

Prefigures

Historical figures were not the only source of analogies for Shakespeare's first actors and audience. A modern actor can easily miss significant aspects of character and relationships by working in ignorance of the other important sources of allusions: the classical world and the bible.

A "prefigure" is a cultural construct, widely shared and created by the artifacts of popular culture, that is readily available for cross-referencing or "quoting." Today, we would understand a comedian's satire of Dirty Harry, Rambo, or Marilyn Monroe even if we couldn't footnote the specific source of the vicious police officer, the pumped-up soldier, or the sexy blonde.

Often, the source of prefigures is the education system. Today, if every child in grade nine reads the same novel, then the characters in that novel are available for that generation as prefigures for all other cultural exchanges. The advancements in public education under the Tudor monarchs resulted in an explosion of literacy. More and more people were sending sons to school and even ensuring basic literacy and numeracy for their daughters at home. And this generation read not only their bibles, but also the popular stories of the classical gods and goddesses.

If we look at the world of the visual arts, we can trace the interplay of prefigures that were at work in the culture shared by Shakespeare's first actors. Look, for example at Sandro Botticelli's *Mars and Venus*, whose adulterous relationship cuckolded the master-smithy Vulcan. Then look at Pompeo Gi-rolano Batoni's *Samson and Delilah*, for a biblical set of prefigures that overlap sufficiently to create resonance, but are sufficiently distinct to add depth to the archetypal portrait of illicit love. Now turn to Shakespeare's *Antony and Cleo-patra*, and see how Shakespeare makes use of images of Antony the great warrior and his love of the exotic Cleopatra.

How do prefigures affect the playing of these characters? Quite simply, it propels the actor towards an alternative attitude to the individuality of the fictional creation. You are not playing one man or woman; you are playing the embodiment of a pattern of human behavior, something larger than the ordinary, whose humanity exists in striking contrast to the archetypal signifi-cance of the prefigure.

What would it be like to play the role of Venus herself? There would be no temptation to reduce her existence to the mundane. There would be no pressure to make her familiar by making her ordinary. Instead, her familiarity would arise from the juxtaposition of the recognizable forces of human expe-rience that she unleashes and embodies, with the infusion of a selected number of human traits that give her form and shape.

Let us apply that same acting strategy to Delilah. It is tempting to throw the archetypal out the window and rely entirely on the grounding of the char-acter in a lived reality. What did women wear at that time in the Middle East? How were they educated? What were their houses like? What did they eat? This characterization strategy has served our actors and audiences well for over a hundred years, and it would be foolish to ignore it in favor of a style of acting from another time and place. However, if Delilah becomes just *Any-woman* instead of remaining the prefigure of Tempting Lover, the actor in the role may find herself working at odds with the writer who was counting on the archetypal scale in the creation of the theatrical event.

This is the case with Cleopatra. She is not just a woman, though the touches of simple humanity injected into the play serve a very important function in the creation and impact of the archetype. She partakes of the heightened energy of the prefigures that informed the first actors and the first audience who encountered her in Shakespeare's play. "Age cannot wither her, nor custom stale / Her infinite variety" [2.2.234] is an apt description of Venus; it is an embarrassing hyperbole if spoken of a Delilah or Cleopatra played in an acting style that seeks only to ground the role in the ordinary.

The Famous of Athens and Rome

In *Love's Labours Lost*, the schoolmaster Holofernes announces, "For the el-egancy, facility, and golden cadence of poesy *caret*: Ovidius Naso was the man" [*LLL* 4.2.121] giving voice to a widely held opinion and practice from which Shakespeare himself benefited. When schoolboys were ready to advance to the reading of Latin texts, usually in their second or third year of study, it was to the *Metamorphoses* of Ovid that they turned.

We can find direct reference to Ovid in two other plays. Touchstone, the court fool who journeys into the forest of Arden with Rosalind and Celia in *As You Like It*, presents himself to Audrey with, "I am here with thee, and thy goats, as the most capricious Poet honest Ovid was among the Goths" [3.3.7]. The pun no longer works with modern pronunciation, "goats" and "Goths" sounding not at all alike, and modern audiences are very unlikely to understand the reference to Ovid's exile from Rome on the charge of immorality. The point of Touchstone's comparison is that Ovid, that master of the Latin language, found himself among people who could not understand a word he said, much as Audrey struggles to understand Touchstone's courtly wit. But the allusion hints at the subtext of the scene. Goats were emblems of lasciviousness, and fools also had a reputation for unbridled sexuality; Ovid's erotic writings, including the ever-popular *The Art of Love*, were well known to Elizabethan adolescents. This is the meaning of the other direct reference to Ovid, found in *The Taming of the Shrew*, when Tranio, the tricky servant of Lucentio, advises his young master not to overdo his commitment to serious philosophical study:

> Only (good master) while we do admire
> This virtue, and this moral discipline,
> Let's be no Stoics, nor no stocks I pray,
> Or so devote to Aristotles checks
> As Ovid be an outcast quite abjured. [1.1.29]

Lucentio takes Tranio's advice, and when he disguises himself as a scholar in order to woo Bianca at closer quarters, it is Ovid's *Heroides* that the lovers read together.

In his memorial poem in praise of Shakespeare, published in the first folio, Ben Jonson announced to all the world that Shakespeare had "small Latin, and less Greek." In part, Jonson wanted to contrast our Shakespeare with himself and others who could boast a university education deemed appropriate for a professional man of letters. Since we today vastly prefer Shakespeare to his better educated contemporaries, it is tempting to conclude that the overindulgence in Latin and Greek literature could do more harm than good.

On closer examination of the plays, however, it is immediately apparent to a modern actor that Shakespeare had a far greater familiarity with the classical writers than a university graduate in anything but classical studies, that shrinking academic discipline that once dominated the British curriculum. When I was in public school in Toronto, it was assumed that any child bright enough to be university-bound would enroll in five years of Latin; by the time I finished, I, too, was reading Ovid in the original. Today, I know of only one high school in the region that still offers Latin.

Thankfully, actors do not need to turn back the clock and acquire the capacity to read Ovid's amusing and artfully constructed phrases in Latin, given the availability of good translations. The *Metamorphoses* is the place to begin, followed by Virgil's *Aeneid*. These, along with the Bible, provide the modern actor with a cast of characters to serve as "prefigures" for Shakespeare's creations.

As Lorenzo and his beloved Jessica enjoy a moonlit night in *The Merchant of Venice*, they engage in a competitive who's who in the classical world:

Lorenzo: The moon shines bright. In such a night as this,
        When the sweet wind did gently kiss the trees,
        And they did make no noise, in such a night
        Troilus me thinks mounted the Trojan walls,
        And sighed his soul toward the Grecian tents
        Where Cressid lay that night.

Jessica: In such a night
        Did Thisby fearfully ore-trip the dew,
        And saw the Lions shadow ere himself,
        And ran dismayed away.

Lorenzo: In such a night
        Stood Dido with a Willow in her hand
        Upon the wilde sea banks, and waft her Love
        To come again to Carthage.

Jessica: In such a night
        Medea gathered the enchanted herbs
        That did renew old Aeson.

Lorenzo: In such a night
        Did Jessica steal from the wealthy Jew,
        And with an Unthrift Love did run from Venice,
        As far as Belmont.

Jessica: In such a night
        Did young Lorenzo swear he loved her well,
        Stealing her soul with many vows of faith,
        And ne'er a true one.

Lorenzo: In such a night
        Did pretty Jessica (like a little shrew)
        Slander her Love, and he forgave it her.

Jessica: I would out-night you did no body come:
        But hark, I hear the footing of a man. [5.1.1]

It is impossible to tell if this is love-talk or an exchange charged with all the bitter subtext of a failing love affair, given that the famous love stories mentioned all end unhappily. In addition to finding out more about Cressida, Thisby, Dido, and Medea and their lovers Troilus, Pyramus, Aeneas, and Jason, a modern pair will want to imagine just how much education Jessica and Lorenzo have received (a fair amount, to be intimately familiar with Ovid,

Virgil, and Chaucer), under what conditions (Lorenzo might have attended a
university, in keeping with the custom of young English noblemen; gently bred
young were educated at home), and, perhaps most importantly, what associations each lover might bring to these stories. Did they read them in the long
and lonely nights while they awaited an opportunity to steal away together,
thrilling at the similarities between the old stories and their current predica-
ment? Did Lorenzo copy out and send to Jessica Chaucer's description of the
forlorn Troilus wandering the streets of Troy, making his way to the walls of
the city to gaze out at the enemy camp were Cressida had been taken? Such
a school-boy exercise was often undertaken by lovers, as was the slightly more
sophisticated project of writing a fresh translation or adaptation and dedicating
such a poem to one's beloved. Did Jessica see herself in the young Medea who
helped Jason to capture the golden fleece, though it meant betraying her father,
and then fled with him to a new country and a life together? As the young
lovers stole a kiss where they could not be spied by Shylock, did they think
of themselves as a modern day Pyramus and Thisby, separated by the wall of
prejudice surrounding the Venetian ghetto?

Here is a modern adaptation of Ovid's treatment of Medea's story, not the
passage referred to by Jessica, but an earlier section, where the young princess
loves the strange visitor much as Jessica might have first loved Lorenzo:

> It makes no sense, this passion. She has never felt it before,
> doesn't even know for sure what to call this emotion.
> Is this what they mean by "love"? There are other words for it also,
> but, even while she hates herself for feeling this way,
> she cannot help herself. She is possessed, or rather
> feels that she now possesses a new, more powerful self.
> Her father, whom she has always adored, now seems a monster.
> The stranger, whose face she has never before beheld, now matters
> more to her than her life itself. She knows it's crazy,
> but that doesn't make it go away. Her desire fights
> against her reason and triumphs. Her mind itself is undon
> and can only watch from a distance and offer useless advice.
> Marriage is what she wants, and to be with this man forever,
> going wherever he goes. His noble birth and his youth
> speak for him, but his beauty alone is all he needs
> to advocate in her heart, which has melted like wax and hardened
> to bear his seal forever. (Slavitt 1994, 125)

Here, in an equally passionate passage, is a description of the desperate love
of Pyramus and Thisby:

> These two became acquaintances, friends, and, in time,
> there was love that ought to have led to marriage, but the parents
> of both, displeased, wanted something better or richer. . . . Who knows?

There were quarrels, scenes, ultimata. The boy and girl were forbidden
to see each other, but love is not so easily ordered,
and they burned, both, with a passion they tried to conceal but could
    not.
By occasional looks and nods and other signs, one could let
the other know that the fire, covered over and banked,
was still hot and alive. (65)

In passages such as these we receive from Shakespeare the inspiration to create
a very specific shared history for these minor characters.

Biblical Allusions

The Elizabethans were surrounded by the rich cultural heritage of the Christian world. Bible stories were a shared currency upon which to build a cohesive
web of allusion and direct reference. A modern actor can benefit from a familiarity with this web and use it to infuse a character and the spoken word
with not only a spiritual energy, but also resonating emotional associations.

Scholars love to debate about which subsection of the Christian faith Shakespeare might have adhered to. Was he a secret Catholic? Was he one of the
new breed of Protestants? Was he a faithful member of the Anglican church?
Scholars cite a variety of clues from the plays as to Shakespeare's personal
religious beliefs and personal stand on religious issues of his times. I'm not
sure how much it matters what Shakespeare himself believes. I think it is very
important what clues he gives the audience (and the actor playing the role)
about the beliefs of any given character. But before you consider entering into
those debates, start with acquiring some basic familiarity with the stories of
the Bible and their emotional impact.

You will find that some of the allusions are to the Book of Common Prayer
or the Marriage Service or Funeral Service or the set of homilies authorized
by the Anglican Church, such as "Against Disobedience and Wilful Rebellion."
You will also find allusions to books of the Bible that did not make it into the
King James version, which make up what modern scholars call the Apocrypha.

Some of the biblical references will be fairly obvious and self-contained.
Quickly, you will get a sense of how pervasive these allusions are in the world
of the plays. The real payoff is not just figuring out what is really meant by
something like, "Such duty as the subject owes the Prince" [Shrew 5.2.155], but
also getting a sense of the spiritual life of the character you are playing.

Shakespeare's Bible is not readily available to modern readers but the King
James Bible, though published in 1611 (after Shakespeare stopped writing for
the theatre), uses language contemporary to Shakespeare's and provides
therefore a good acclimatization for the actor's tongue. As with Shakespeare,
read aloud, savor the rhythms and the way thoughts are put together, and
much can be gained of service to your speaking of Shakespeare's plays. You
will also find a rhetorical use of punctuation similar to that found in the folio.

Exploration: The Book of the Revelation

Read the following passage out loud, slowly, enjoying the sounds of the words as much as the powerful images.

I was in the Spirit on the Lord's day, and heard behind me a great voice, as of a trumpet,

Saying, I am Alpha and Omega, the first and the last: and, What thou seest, write in a book, and send it unto the seven churches which are in Asia; unto Ephesus, and unto Smyrna, and unto Pergamos, and unto Thyatira, and unto Sardis, and unto Philadelphia, and unto Laodicea.

And I turned to see the voice that spake with me. And being turned, I saw seven golden candlesticks;

And in the midst of the seven candlesticks one like unto the Son of man, clothed with a garment down to the foot, and girt about the paps with a golden girdle.

His head and his hairs were white like wool, as white as snow; and his eyes were as a flame of fire;

And his feet like unto fine brass, as if they burned in a furnace; and his voice as the sound of many waters.

And he had in his right hand seven stars: and out of his mouth went a sharp two-edged sword: and his countenance was as the sun shineth in his strength.

And when I saw him, I fell at his feet as dead. And he laid his right hand upon me, saying unto me, Fear not; I am the first and the last:

I am he that liveth, and was dead; and, behold, I am alive for evermore,

Amen; and have the keys of hell and of death. [Genesis 1:10–18]

I'm sure that you enjoyed saying phrases like, "white like wool, as white as snow," and "flame of fire" and "his feet like unto fine brass, as if they burned" because of the alliteration. The rhythms of the prose are also appealing, as in "and have the keys of hell and of death." Just getting your mouth around these sounds, speaking slowly and carefully, following the rhythm of the words without seeking special emphasis on any given word but trusting the music and the repetition, will prepare your speaking mechanism for the words of Shakespeare, which were also crafted to be spoken and heard, and are equally memorable.

Let's look at the punctuation. These editors used colons and semicolons more frequently than modern editors, and they served a special function in the rhetoric of the language.

The lengths of pauses, from short to long:

a. Unmarked breaks were created by the combinations of sounds that demanded a small gap between them, as in "as white as snow" between "as" and "snow." Speaking clearly, so that every sound is heard and no word is slurred, will reveal these subtle breaks and minute pauses.

b. Commas suggested that the speaker take a short intake of breath. In grammar, commas have other uses, as in the separation of phrases, but in rhetoric they are used to shape how the language is phrased by the speaker so that the hearer receives arcs of sound.

c. Colons suggested that the speaker pause briefly in order to convey the importance of the connection between what has just been spoken and what is to follow. You will find that Shakespeare's contemporaries used colons quite differently than we do today, and that if you pause where they occur and convey a hint of anticipation, you will be making good rhetorical use of them.

d. Semicolons suggested a powerful and complex transition, for which the speaker paused in order to allow the listener to accompany the speaker upon the leap of thought that was about to occur. There must be no breaking of the connection between speaker and listener, nor between thought and thought. The pause must be filled with the desire to communicate.

e. Periods, and also question marks, suggested the end of one complete thought. Here, the speaker's voice can cadence downward slightly. This cadencing must be resisted on all other punctuation marks.

With these simple rules in mind, read the previous selection of Genesis aloud once again, making full use of the punctuation.

You will have to fight a modern attitude to the word "and." When it follows a period, it is quite a different speaking event than when it follows a colon, which is different than following a semicolon, and neither of those are like the use of "and" following a comma. Explore the emotional difference in these uses of punctuation to see how the ideas are linked, with different intensity, requiring a different leap of faith from the listener, depending on the punctuation used.

Now compare the biblical passage with this speech:

> In the most high and palmy state of Rome,
> A little ere the mightiest Julius fell
> The graves stood tenantless, and the sheeted dead
> Did squeak and gibber in the Roman streets
> As stars with trains of fire, and dews of blood
> Disasters in the sun; and the moist star,
> Upon whose influence Neptunes Empire stands,
> Was sick almost to doomsday with eclipse.
> And even the like precurse of fierce events
> As harbingers preceding still the fates
> And prologue to the Omen coming on
> Have heaven and earth together demonstrated
> Unto our Climatures and countrymen. [*Hamlet* 1.1.113]

We are on the battlements of Elsinore; and the ghost has appeared once and is about to appear again, interrupting Horatio's history lesson. This may seem like academic showing off by Horatio the scholar, but as he describes events in ancient Rome, he is using language that resonates strongly for his audience, on the battlements and in the theatre, and it is this emotional connection that a modern actor must seek to duplicate.

Take, for example, another passage from the King James Bible.

The first angel sounded, and there followed hail and fire mingled with blood, and they were cast upon the earth: and the third part of trees was burnt up, and all green grass was burnt up.

And the second angel sounded, and as it were a great mountain burning with fire was cast into the sea: and the third part of the sea became blood; And the third part of the creatures which were in the sea, and had life, died; and the third part of the ships were destroyed.

And the third angel sounded, and there fell a great star from heaven, burning as it were a lamp, and it fell upon the third part of the rivers, and upon the fountains of waters;

And the name of the star is called Wormwood: and the third part of the waters became wormwood; and many men died of the waters, because they were made bitter.

And the fourth angel sounded, and the third part of the sun was smitten, and the third part of the moon, and the third part of the stars; so as the third part of them was darkened, and the day shone not for a third part of it, and the night likewise.

And I beheld, and heard an angel flying through the midst of heaven, saying with a loud voice, Woe, woe, woe, to the inhabiters of the earth by reason of the other voices of the trumpet of the three angels, which are yet to sound! [Revelation 8:1–13]

Imagine you are an actor in Shakespeare's company. You have grown up hearing the words of the Bible at school, at home, and on Sundays in church. You are living in a society that considers itself modern, but cannot entirely shake off the superstitions of the past. It doesn't matter what you consciously believe about the Judgement Day. When you hear these words, the hairs stand up on the back of your neck.

Shakespeare's plays are filled with overt and subtle biblical references because his world was filled with them. Because of the political situation, Shakespeare was forbidden by the censors from including any direct reference to religious issues in his plays. But his language was what he heard around him, as well as what he invented, and so it is little wonder that the great images and stories from the Bible provide an emotional framework for his characters.

Another payoff for doing your homework about biblical allusions is the discovery of immensely powerful stories from the Bible that form a sort of emotional background to the moment of the play. You must think of this in terms of modern equivalents. If you were playing in a modern play in which your character ends a relationship with someone of the opposite sex, and this other person asks your character, "Is this your idea of a final solution?" you might not even be aware of how that question is made more powerful by the allusion to Nazi extermination camps. So too are the allusions to the stories of the Bible.

Here is an example from *Macbeth*. MacDuff, who has fled Scotland to seek asylum with Malcolm in the English court, greets his wife's cousin, Ross with questions of the troubled land all three men have left behind. He then asks after his wife and children. The audience and Ross know, because the scene immediately previous showed us, that these innocents have been butchered by Macbeth's hired assassins. Here is the dialogue:

MacDuff:	How does my Wife?
Ross: Why well.	
MacDuff:	And all my Children?
Ross:	Well too. [5.3.176]

What sense can a modern actor make of Ross's lies? Clearly, given the unusual dialogue pattern, something is going on. The scene continues:

MacDuff: The Tyrant has not battered at their peace?

Ross: No, they were well at peace, when I did leave 'em. [5.3.178]

Malcolm speaks next, clarifying the reaction we are all having to this exchange when he says in the next line, "Be not a niggard of your speech: How goes't?" and Ross launches on a general description of chaos and despair, leading up to the bitter news. Before he can give the details, Macduff says, "I guess at it." One of the reasons, besides the indications in Ross's tone of voice and demeanor, is the biblical echo at work in this scene.

To find this echo, we must revisit one of the many moving stories to be found in the Bible. Here is the King James Version:

And it fell on a day, that Elisha passed to Shunem, where was a great woman; and she constrained him to eat bread. And so it was, that as oft as he passed by, he turned in thither to eat bread.

And she said unto her husband, Behold now, I perceive that this is an holy man of God, which passeth by us continually.

Let us make a little chamber, I pray thee, on the wall; and let us set for him there a bed, and a table, and a stool, and a candlestick: and it shall be, when he cometh to us, that he shall turn in thither.

And it fell on a day, that he came thither, and he turned into the chamber, and lay there.

And he said to Gehazi his servant, Call this Shunammite. And when he had called her, she stood before him.

And he said unto him, Say now unto her, Behold, thou hast been careful for us with all this care; what is to be done for thee? wouldest thou be spoken for to the king, or to the captain of the host? And she answered, I dwell among mine own people.

And he said, What then is to be done for her? And Gehazi answered, Verily she hath no child, and her husband is old.

And he said, Call her. And when he had called her, she stood in the door.

And he said, About this season, according to the time of life, thou shalt embrace a son. And she said, Nay, my lord, thou man of God, do not lie unto thine handmaid.

And the woman conceived, and bare a son at that season that Elisha had said unto her, according to the time of life.

And when the child was grown, it fell on a day, that he went out to his father to the reapers.

And he said unto his father, My head, my head. And he said to a lad, Carry him to his mother.

And when he had taken him, and brought him to his mother, he sat on her knees till noon, and then died.

And she went up, and laid him on the bed of the man of God, and shut the door upon him, and went out.

And she called unto her husband, and said, Send me, I pray thee, one of the young men, and one of the asses, that I may run to the man of God, and come again.

And he said, Wherefore wilt thou go to him to day? it is neither new moon, nor sabbath. And she said, It shall be well.

Then she saddled an ass, and said to her servant, Drive, and go forward; slack not thy riding for me, except I bid thee.

So she went and came unto the man of God to mount Carmel. And it came to pass, when the man of God saw her afar off, that he said to Gehazi his servant, Behold, yonder is that Shunammite:

Run now, I pray thee, to meet her, and say unto her, Is it well with thee? is it well with thy husband? is it well with the child? And she answered, It is well. [2 Kings 4: 8–26]

If you read this story out loud, you cannot help but feel the terrible power of the simple human detail of, "And he said unto his father, My head, my head," and "Is it well with thee? is it well with thy husband? is it well with the child?" The great simplicity of her answer, like Ross's, contains a deep source of human suffering, suggested by what would have been, for Shakespeare's actors and audience, and hence for his characters, a familiar linguistic key embodied in "It is well."

Fortunately for those who do not yet know their way around the Bible, scholars have charted the biblical allusions and this information is often included in footnotes of scholarly editions of the plays. These citations will give you the location of the biblical allusion, but you must not stop there. It was only when I read the entire passage in which the phrase "It is well" is found that I discovered the potential of the allusion for an actor. Sometimes it is a story, and there are some great ones in the Bible, stories that mirror the experiences of the characters directly or indirectly. It might be that the differences between the Bible and the play are the source of something useful for the actor. Ross and Macduff know how the story ends for the Shunammite woman: Elisha returns to her house and raises the boy from the dead. But in Scotland there is no Elisha, only Malcolm's army and the final confrontation between Macduff and Macbeth. The precious children remain dead at the end of the play.

One layer beneath this simple story, told to illustrate the power of God's profit and the rewards awaiting the faithful, is a wealth of human detail. The woman and her son might be nameless, but we know exactly where the boy was when he became ill, what he said, and how he sat on her knees until noon, when he died.

It is such details that make the story stick in the brain, in the form of a living picture, summoned to mind with the repeated use of the word "well" to describe a child who is dead. In Macduff's story, there is no profit from God to breath life back into the child, who will then awaken with seven (count them!) sneezes. Macduff is forced to play the role of the servant Gehazi who, though armed with Elisha's staff and though following his instructions, is unable to perform the miracle.

Knowing the biblical story can help all of the actors in the scene, but most particularly Ross, who must pronounce both the simple world "well" and then the truth. I'm not sure it aids the scene to have a self-conscious little mind game going on: I don't think Ross is hoping that Macduff will catch the allusion to 2 Kings 4. I think Ross speaks from a deeply spiritual space in his grief and horror, and the allusion opens the door to a modern actor, even one without any sort of personal Christian faith, finding the very special type of emotional energy in that moment.

So when you are offered an allusion, go to the Bible and read the passages surrounding that allusion. You might find, as in the example from *Hamlet*, that huge chunks resonate profoundly for that moment in the play. I would read the entire book of the Revelation for that reason. If you put aside your intellectualism, and let the images give you goose bumps, you'll be on the track of the real benefit of biblical allusions to a modern actor.

Antithesis

> Fair is foul, and foul is fair,
> Hover through the fog and filthy air.
>
>   The Weïrd Sisters [*Macbeth* 1.1.11]

Shakespeare's plays are filled with examples of antithesis, a rhetorical strategy whereby words are placed so as to draw the listener's attention to the contrasting values encoded in each, as when the first scene of *Macbeth* ends with the presentation of a very particular topsy-turvy world in seven words: "fair is foul and foul is fair."

So prevalent is this technique that it is difficult to find a speech of longer than six lines that does not contain at least one overt and striking example of antithesis. Let us have a look at an extended example from an early play, *Richard III*, in which the speaker, the old Queen Margaret, purposefully uses an almost schoolbook rhetoric, all the better to teach the young Queen Elizabeth the lessons she must learn by imitation.

I called thee then, vain flourish of my fortune:
I called thee then, poor Shadow, painted Queen,
The presentation of but what I was;
The flattering Index of a direful Pageant;
One heaved a high, to be hurled down below:
A Mother only mocked with two fair Babes;
A dream of what thou wast, a garish Flag
To be the aim of every dangerous Shot;
A sign of Dignity, a Breath, a Bubble;
A Queen in jest, only to fill the Scene.
Where is thy Husband now? Where be thy Brothers?
Where are thy two Sons? Wherein dost thou Joy?
Who sues, and kneels, and says, God save the Queen?
Where be the bending Peers that flattered thee?
Where be the thronging Troops that followed thee?
Decline all this, and see what now thou art.
For happy Wife, a most distressed Widow:
For joyful Mother, one that wails the name:
For one being sued to, one that humbly sues:
For Queen, a very Caitiff, crowned with care:
For she that scorned at me, now scorned of me:
For she being feared of all, now fearing one:
For she commanding all, obeyed of none.
Thus hath the course of Justice whirled about,
And left thee but a very prey to time,
Having no more but Thought of what thou wast,
To Torture thee the more, being what thou art,
Thou didst usurp my place, and dost thou not
Usurp the just proportion of my Sorrow?
Now thy proud Neck, bears half my burthened yoke,
From which, even here I slip my wearied head,
And leave the burthen of it all, on thee.
Farewell, Yorks wife, and Queen of sad mischance,
These English woes, shall make me smile in France. [4.4.82]

Margaret was queen of England until her husband was deposed by Elizabeth's husband; now, Elizabeth is a widow enjoying the very special bitterness of the defeated. When Margaret says, "Decline all this," she is making use of a double set of meanings and associations. The word in this context denotes, or refers specifically to the grammatical exercise of declining Latin words, a common school exercise. But the word "decline" also connotes, or calls up our associations, with the other uses of the word, suggesting the decrease of power, authority, or moral stature, a bending down or stooping, a turning away from an allegiance or duty; the word was also used in association with the end of a day or a life.

In order to salt the wound Elizabeth feels as she mourns her dead husband, brothers, and sons, Margaret shapes each phrase in order to draw attention to the antithesis.

> For happy Wife, a most distressed Widow:
> For joyful Mother, one that wails the name:
> For one being sued to, one that humbly sues:
> For Queen, a very Caitiff, crowned with care:
> For she that scorned at me, now scorned of me:
> For she being feared of all, now fearing one:
> For she commanding all, obeyed of none.

The wife is now a widow, once happy, now most distressed; the queen has become a caitiff. The repeated sounds (wife/widow; queen/caitiff) reinforce the antithesis achieved by the choice of words.

Another set of antitheses are structured through the repetition of the key word, so that "scorned at" becomes "scorned of"; slight variations in the same word enable Margaret to contrast "being sued to" with "humbly sues," and "feared of all" becomes "fearing one." The last line of this sequence combines a pair of contrasting words with the shift from active to passive verbs, so that "commanding" sits in antithesis to "obeyed of," all against "none."

But beneath this obvious use of contrasting words, antithesis exists through implication. When Margaret makes her most horrible comparison to the younger queen, whose two young sons have just been murdered, she does not build a direct antithesis. The joyful mother now wails "the name." What name? In the scene up to this point, Elizabeth has wailed no name, although her mother-in-law has mentioned her dead son, Elizabeth's husband Edward Plantagenet. What Elizabeth has wailed is the line, "Ah my poor Princes! ah my tender babes" [4.4.9]. What is interesting about these words is that they could just have easily be said by a joyful mother, though with a different tone of voice.

The subtle antithesis at work is between the joyful mother and what she would say, in contrast with the mourning mother, and what she would say, or rather, with what tone the same words would be said by each. The absence of the antithetical word forces the listener to supply the implied opposite, in this case prompting Elizabeth towards the most painful of happy memories as well as the horror of her current situation.

Even more importantly, we do not have words for the opposites that Margaret implies. We have "widow" to contrast "wife," but what is the word for a woman whose children have died? We have wail to describe the release of grief, but what word do we have to suggest the fullest possible release of a mother's love?

Margaret's next line contains a straightforward antithesis, as we have seen, "queen" contrasted with "caitiff," as well as an implied antithesis: the caitiff is now crowned with care. The figurative use of the verb calls attention to the crown a queen would wear and evokes the emotional burden of the anxieties Elizabeth now experiences. There is a terrible irony at work here. When she was queen, she was required to wear the heavy crown, but felt only the thrills of the position; now she is freed from the heavy headpiece but is bowed down with the burden of her fragile position.

Margaret reinforces the physical nature of this experience in her final lines, "Now thy proud Neck, bears half my burthened yoke, / From which, even here I slip my wearied head, / And leave the burthen of it all, on thee." Here, the metaphor has shifted from the crown of a queen to a "yoke," which implies a beast of burden such as an ox, pulling a heavy farm cart, or the wooden bar joining two pails, used for example by milk maids. However, it also summons up the image of an ornate and heavy necklace, suitable for a queen. Buried in this metaphor, therefore, is another antithesis: you who were once queen now must accustom your neck to the burden, not of ornate jewellery, but of a peasant's daily toil.

Rhetorical strategies that shape language in order to draw attention to contrasting words demand of the actor a delivery that allows the two words to play off against each other in the minds of the listeners. But this is a trick of intonation and emphasis, easily acquired and therefore dangerously superficial, unless the contrasting words are linked to the complexity of the experience of the characters.

We should assume that Shakespeare never builds an antithesis around intellectual concepts. Rather, we should make use of the suggestion encompassed in the antithesis when constructing the three-dimensional inner lives of the characters we play and with which we interact in the play.

Two acting techniques form the foundation for our work with rhetorical strategies of antithesis: dropping in and opposites. Dropping in is a process whereby an actor connects a specific word with as many associations as possible in order to establish a depth of intellectual understanding and emotional resonance. A small proportion of this work can be purely intellectual: when speaking words from plays that are four hundred years old, you need to do a bit of research to clarify denotation and connotation. But such knowledge is not the point of the exercise. Rather, you are seeking to open yourself to the inherent power of the word as experienced by your irrational, inexplicable associations with the word. Another way of putting this: dropping in takes your understanding of what the word means and transforms it into feeling what the word means.

Let us drop in on "queen" and "caitiff" to see what might emerge. First, the intellectual preparation. Making a quick trip to the *Oxford English Dictionary*, (*OED*), we discover the expected: "queen" as wife of a king or ruler in her own right, and a few perhaps not expected—the association with Mary the mother of Jesus, with the goddesses of classical mythology, with the swan, known as the queen bird. We're also reminded of cards, chess pieces, and the rulers of bee hives and ant nests. A good priming of the pump for our dropping in.

We can add to this intellectual preparation some research on Shakespeare's models, like Queen Elizabeth, Mary Queen of Scots, or the medieval queens featured in his history plays. We could look at portraits, pictures of castles and clothing, and descriptions of palace life. All of this will anchor our dropping in experience in Shakespeare's England, but will not limit our imaginations to an exercise in history.

In order to *own* the word "queen," we must start by opening ourselves to all of the things that the word might mean to us. Say the word aloud, and set your mind free to play a grand set of variations on the idea, the images, the associations that emerge for *you*. Sometimes you might be outside observing, other times you might be inside, experiencing. You might fantasize about being a queen. You might flash to a memory of learning to play chess, or a science class film on bees. You might remember movies or imagine what it would have been like to walk to the executioner's block like Mary Queen of Scots. You might travel down a Jungian road of exploring the queen within: in your personal landscape, what aspects of your personality are most admirable, most prestigious, most powerful? Then your mind might leap to a satirical queen for a day show, where the least likely members of modern society are given a chance to experience, "Your word is my command."

Dropping in on a word is great fun. It does not have to take a great deal of time, as the mind is capable of rushing and racing and connecting and imagining richly and rapidly. However, it is easy to bypass a short, intense dropping in with a quick, glib, checklist of meanings. "Queen? Oh, yes, I know what that word means. I have an image for that."

It is important that you ground yourself in a complex and highly personal set of associations with the word before moving on to the next step in your journey towards ownership, which will help you to answer the question: What does this word mean for the speaker and listeners on stage? Three women are present when Margaret says, "For Queen, a very Caitiff, crowned with care": Margaret who was queen because she married King Henry VI, the duchess of York whose husband launched the bloody War of Roses to win the throne, and Elizabeth, who became queen when she married Edward IV. What associations might each of these women have with the word?

If playing Margaret, the actress might have a look at her character as portrayed in the three plays about Henry VI. There is much to suggest that queenship represented a bitter pill: great power, but at a terrible price. The duchess of York would probably share this ambivalence, for slightly different reasons. There is not much explanation in the history plays, so a little reading might be needed for this actress to develop this woman's attitude to the word. She is, after all, more truly a member of the royal family of England than either of the others, with all of the assurance of prerogative and moral authority that noble birth brings. But she has also lost her husband and one son to the civil war, and seen her remaining sons turn on each other in a series of betrayals, maneuvering for the ultimate power of kingship.

Elizabeth was the widow of a modest knight when she met Edward; their marriage shocked the entire kingdom. She enjoyed a fairy tale transformation from impoverished gentry to the first lady of the land, and then, just as abruptly, she slid down into a nightmare of vulnerability and horror.

The more that you know about the specific history of your character, the more you will be able to open yourself to the emotional resonances that the word touches off in your character's mind. However, the goal is to blend the results of your dropping in with your character's.

So once again, say the word "queen" to yourself several times and open yourself to whatever associations emerge, asking, "What does this word mean to me," the "me" here being defined as the character. Do not edit out any associations that pop out that are "unsuitable." For example, if you once again think of the queen bee, don't assume that your character would be oblivious to this association. If you think of a particularly modern application, assume that the core human experience would transcend time, and that your character would have a medieval equivalent of which you are not aware, and need not be aware, since you can take the essential emotional "kick" of the association and link it directly to the word, bypassing the inappropriate modern image.

An immense and complex web of links connected with the word is the intended result of dropping in. Once the word has been linked up with a conscious exercise of dropping in, you can let all of the associations sink out of your conscious mind, because the word itself will function as a repository of links quite well without any conscious effort on your part.

Now it is time to drop in on "caitiff," which will prove a different challenge. First of all, this is a word for which you are not as likely to have an immediate abundance of links until you figure out what it means. Just the sound, and the contrast suggested by "crowned with care" will set you in the right direction: a caitiff is someone who is burdened with worries.

Here are the meanings listed in the *OED*:

1. Originally: A captive, a prisoner. 2. Expressing commiseration: A wretched miserable person, a poor wretch, one in a piteous case. Expressing contempt, and often involving strong moral disapprobation: A base, mean, despicable 'wretch', a villain. In early use often not separable from sense 2 (esp. when applied by any one to himself): 'it often implies a mixture of wickedness and misery' J.: cf. wretch.

Your first dropping in on the word "caitiff" will fill you with a rich variety of associations with captivity, misery, and wickedness, in combination or separately. Sometimes you will view such examples from the outside, sometimes you will imagine the experience or remember an experience. All the time you are letting these associations into your conscious brain, keep saying the word, so that the experience of making the sound will be linked with the emotional impact of the meaning of the word.

In some ways, it will be easier to image the three medieval women's experience of "caitiff" than of "queen," because they, like you, will primarily be observers of real caitiffs; none of them has actually been a prisoner, or wretchedly poor, and though Margaret has been responsible for horrific cruelty during the civil war, it's not exactly the mixture of misery and wickedness that the word conveys. However, I'm sure the three women feel *like* caitiffs in this time of defeat and grief.

A bit of historical research will reveal some useful information about the public execution of traitors and villains, the presence of the miserable poor in places where the nobility might pass, and the inevitable association between caitiff and disease, disfigurement, terrible smells, horrible sounds, and unbearable sights. Let your imagination loose on these, as you say the word several times aloud.

It has taken me some time to write, and you to read, this description of "dropping in," but it is in fact something we do all the time and with minimal conscious effort. The extra work required for Shakespeare comes in part from the four-hundred-year gap between his world and ours, and consequently the rich associations we might be cut off from, without a bit of research. But dropping in is also necessary when the condensed language of rhetoric might trick us into racing the delivery of an antithesis instead of allowing the juxtaposition of "queen" and "caitiff" fill us with a collision of memories, associations, contrasting smells and sights, and a true complexity of emotional response to each word as well as to the two in tandem.

Antithesis is so prevalent a rhetorical strategy that it reflects a habit of mind that we must develop in order to share with Shakespeare's actors, audience, and characters. Encompassed in every evocative word is its antithesis, like the shadow cast by any object in direct and strong light. Just as shading can give us the sensation of three dimensionality in a line drawing, so too the contrasting emotional color can offset the dominant tone of a word, summoning the recognition in the listener of the complexity of human experience.

The greatest danger of performing one of Shakespeare's powerful speeches is that the actor will wash the entire speech act in a single emotional shade. Shakespeare is actually quite crafty in setting in contrasting shades. Looking back at Margaret's full speech, we can grab hold of the venom quite easily, but we should not miss the opportunities to give other colors their full due. A line like "A Mother only mocked with two fair Babes" can be delivered completely soaked in bitter aggression, so that "mother" sounds disgusted, and "two fair babes" sneering. However, the word "mother," if dropped in on, becomes filled with associations that open Margaret to a brief flash of a contrasting color: all of the complexity that any mother feels about herself, all of the complexity of feeling experienced towards ones mother. The words "fair babes" offer another color, that of love, joy, awe, and memories of the most intimate and delicate interactions between a mother and a small baby. Without a doubt, the word "mocked" is the engine of the line. It provides the key to the speech act: mock Elizabeth with her terrible grief. But unless the other colors are allowed to resonate with their words, the mockery and the grief will be suggested rather than experienced in all of their complexity. It is one thing to mock someone with someone you yourself despise; it is quite another to mock a mother mourning her two butchered children when you yourself lost your young son to the self-same murderer.

CLASS

> The heavens themselves, the Planets, and this Centre,
> Observe degree, priority, and place,
> Insisture, course, proportion, season, form,
> Office, and custom, in all line of order.
>
> Ulysses [*T&C* 1.3.85]

One of the most difficult transitions for a modern actor to make, when assuming the habits of mind appropriate to a character in one of Shakespeare's plays, is from our current understanding of status, the interplay of personal, social, economic, and physical power, and an Elizabethan model of hierarchy, loyalty, honorable service, and kingship. It simply won't do to place the relationships of a liege lord and his subjects or a princess and her waiting gentlewomen into a modern framework, even though dressing a king and his court to look like a chief executive officer and his board of directors, or putting the gentlewoman in a maid's white apron to contrast the princess's haute couture might communicate vividly other aspects of the onstage relationships to a modern audience.

Honorifics

One of the most irritating historical uncertainties for a modern actor is the meaning of all of the honorifics used in the plays. Honorifics are the way one character addresses another. These include everything from pronouns and formal titles to how one character summons or orders another character. The absence of any honorific is as significant as those that are included in the flow of dialogue.

Actors working outside the tradition-bound class system of England are even more at a loss, having no direct access to the subtly nuanced titles and rankings of the nobility. And yet the relative status of the character you are playing is of great importance in playing the role. You need to know who is above and below you in the eyes of the world in which the play takes place. You want to know when your language demonstrates respect, disrespect, equality, the natural hereditary authority of your birthright, and the power of command required by the situation.

Let us begin with the difference between thou/thee/thy/thine and you/your. If you speak a language that still retains a different pronoun for second person singular and second person plural, for example "tu" and "vous" in French, you will have some sense of the way this pronoun is used to suggest respect, authority, intimacy, and disrespect. "Tu" is reserved for close friends and children, and perhaps certain low-paid employees, though old-fashioned good manners would have a manager address almost every employee as "vous." One would never consider addressing one's boss, or teacher, or any person of advanced age as anything other than "vous." "Tu" can be something of a weapon, if used slightly sneeringly with someone who should, out of courtesy, be addressed as "vous," but it can also be offered as a signal of a hoped-for comradery, intimacy, equality.

A strict use of "thou" for intimates and inferiors and "you" for superiors and equals was in abeyance in Shakespeare's time, so we can no longer count on it as an absolute indicator of intimacy or hierarchy. However, if one character begins by addressing another in one form of the honorific, and shifts to the other, something very specific is being suggested. The following is an exchange between Duke Frederick, his daughter Celia, and his niece Rosalind. I have boldfaced key pronouns to draw your attention to the shifting back and forth on the part of the Duke. I have also placed in italics the formal honorifics that the girls use in their responses:

Duke: Mistress, dispatch **you** with your safest haste,
            And get you from our Court.

Rosalind: Me Uncle?

Duke: You Cousin,
            Within these ten days if that **thou** be'st found
            So near our public Court as twenty miles,
            Thou diest for it.

Rosalind: I do beseech *your grace*
            Let me the knowledge of my fault bear with me:
            If with myself I hold intelligence,
            Or have acquaintance with mine own desires,
            If that I do not dream, or be not frantic,
            (As I do trust I am not) then dear Uncle,
            Never so much as in a thought unborn,
            Did I offend *your highness*.

Duke: Thus do all Traitors,
            If their purgation did consist in words,
            They are as innocent as grace itself,
            Let it suffice thee that I trust **thee** not.

Rosalind: Yet your mistrust cannot make me a Traitor;
    Tell me whereon the likelihood depends?

Duke: **Thou** art thy Fathers daughter, there's enough.

Rosalind: So was I when *your highness* took his Dukedom,
    So was I when *your highness* banished him,
    Treason is not inherited *my Lord,*
    Or if we did derive it from our friends,
    What's that to me, my Father was no Traitor,
    Then *good my Liege*, mistake me not so much,
    To think my poverty is treacherous.

Celia: *Dear sovereign* hear me speak.

Duke: Ay Celia, we stayed her for **your** sake,
    Else had she with her Father ranged along.

Celia: I did not then entreat to have her stay,
    It was **your** pleasure, and your own remorse,
    I was too young that time to value her,
    But now I know her: if she be a Traitor,
    Why so am I: we still have slept together,
    Rose at an instant, learned, played, eat together,
    And wheresoever we went, like Junos Swans,
    Still we went coupled and inseparable.

Duke: She is too subtle for **thee**, and her smoothness;
    Her very silence, and her patience,
    Speak to the people, and they pity her:
    Thou art a fool, she robs thee of thy name,
    And thou wilt show more bright, and seem more virtuous
    When she is gone: then open not thy lips
    Firm, and irrevocable is my doom,
    Which I have passed upon her, she is banished.

Celia: Pronounce that sentence then on me *my Liege*,
    I cannot live out of her company.

Duke: **You** are a fool: you Niece provide your self,
    If you out-stay the time, upon mine honour,
    And in the greatness of my word you die. [1.3.66]

Whatever might be the relationship between this father and daughter, it undergoes a shift in this public scene. To begin with, both of them use "you," which is how Rosalind, in the lines preceding Celia's first speech, has addressed her uncle. The duke, however, had switched to using "thou" to Rosalind after opening with "you." The shift is made all the more notable by the duke first saying, "Thou art a fool," and then saying, "You are a fool." Parallel to the pattern of pronouns is the juxtaposition of familiar address, including names and family relations such as cousin and uncle, with the formal and respectful address of honorifics such as "good my liege and "dear sovereign."

Given the complexity of this relationship, between family members who also happen to be royalty, it is not possible to conclude simplistically that the "you" is cold and formal and the "thou" is gentle and intimate. The "you" night well be a marker of respect while the "thou" is a type of denigration, implying that the listener is a child.

If we add a third marker to this exchange we have one more clue as to what might be going on. Ruling monarchs were deemed to have two distinct bodies, the body natural and the body politic. The former is the actual, personal limbs and organs; the latter cannot be seen or harmed, because it is the role, the function, the grace and majesty. The king is spiritually and symbolically the embodiment of the country itself. This concept is expressed in *Hamlet*, first by Rosencrantz at his most sycophantic, and then by Hamlet at his most antic:

> The single
> And peculiar life is bound
> With all the strength and Armour of the mind,
> To keep it self from noyance; but much more,
> That Spirit, upon whose spirit depends and rests
> The lives of many, the cease of Majesty
> Dies not alone; but, like a Gulf doth draw
> What's near it, with it. It is a massy wheel
> Fixed on the Summit of the highest Mount,
> To whose huge Spokes, ten thousand lesser things
> Are mortised and adjoined: which when it falls,
> Each small annexment, petty consequence
> Attends the boisterous Ruin. Never alone
> Did the King sigh, but with a general groan. [3.2.11]

> The body is with the King, but the King is not with the body. [4.2.27]

Rosencrantz is describing a simple reality, when the monarch goes, so do many who followed him or her. But he is also expressing the significance of the second, symbolic body that is inevitably linked with the first, personal body that might be under threat. Hamlet, in contrast, is reminding his listeners that the man and the function can be separated; a king can be killed and neither the country nor the concept of kinship suffer.

The honor afforded a ruling monarch, and the conference of the double significance of the individual and the role, was marked by the customary use of the first person plural, as in Queen Victoria's dry dismissal, "We are not amused." Note that the duke says, "Ay, Celia, we stayed her for your sake." But the duke also says, "Let it suffice thee that I trust thee not." So there is no consistency in this regard, either.

Let us imagine that the duke enters with various of his lords, as suggested in the folio stage direction, these most likely being trusted courtiers and members of his council, who support him in the banishment of the banished duke's daughter. Therefore, this is a public scene in which a private dialogue is also conducted. When the duke first speaks, it is for all to hear, and he uses the language of a formal pronouncement. Rosalind is addressed as "Mistress," surely an insult for the daughter and niece of a duke, and Duke Frederick uses "you" and "our." Rosalind responds by making reference to their status as family, with "Me, uncle?" Frederick comes right back at her by using the same intimate tone, calling her cousin and using "thou." Somehow, the cruelty of his sentence is heightened by the shift to the less formal address. Rosalind now moves the language to the more public stage, opening with a powerful honorific, "your grace," as she launches into a formal plea. However, she keeps the personal in play with her use of "dear uncle" as well as "your Highness." Frederick rebuts with a general observation, and then states a personal, unpolitical, "I trust thee not." Rosalind's next line contains no form of address other than the pronoun "you." Frederick responds by keeping to his use of "thee," and naming her immediate relationship to his banished brother, her father. There are two uses of "your Highness" and one of "good my liege" in Rosalind's response, suggesting that she is moving the debate back into a more public context, continuing her formal plea before the monarch and his council. It is at this point that Celia speaks. She adopts Rosalind's language, addressing her father as "dear sovereign," and formally asking permission to speak in this public forum. Frederick answers by using her name and the pronoun "you." Is this a shift into the more personal? Or is he still in his public role? The use of the first person plural is the clue: "we stayed her for your sake." He did this as her king, not as her father. It is only in response to Celia's intensely personal plea, presented without an honorific and using the respectful "you," that Frederick drops into a different address, calling her "thee" and speaking of "my doom / Which I have passed upon her." It is only after Celia responds with a statement that includes the formal "my liege" that Frederick moves back to the formal "you," but he does not return to the first person plural. His final words refer to "mine honour" and "the greatness of my word," an example of a man threatening the full might of his temporal power, without adopting the formal language of a ruler.

The use of titles can be absolute or relative. Absolute titles are given to an individual as a result of that person's rank, regardless of whether the speaker is higher or lower in the hierarchy. A cardinal of the church, for example, or the Lord Chamberlain, has an absolute title and rank as a result of a job; the duke of Kent because of an inherited position. Relative use of titles are more interesting indicators of whether the speaker is below, above, or equal to the character being addressed.

One of the attributes of honorifics that modern readers find most strange is that they are used between intimates, including by wives to husbands and by children to parents, which at first glance seems to suggest a formality and lack of deep feeling quite foreign to our experience of family life. What are we to make of Ophelia's entry into the first scene of the second act, "O my Lord, my Lord, I have been so affrighted" [*Hamlet* 2.1.72]? Here is a young girl running to her father to tell him of the terrifying experience she has just endured. "O my Lord, my Lord" takes the place of "daddy, daddy" and are we to therefore conclude that, for Ophelia, her father is a distant, cold, authoritarian power? A great deal of what Polonius does to Ophelia might be described just that way, and it might be that she was raised quite separately from her father and has no intimacy or ease with him.

But what of Portia and Brutus? This is clearly a portrait of a loving couple, accustomed to the sharing of personal information; it is the withdrawal of Brutus's confiding in her that has alerted Portia to the disturbance in her husband's mind.

> It will not let you eat, nor talk, nor sleep;
> And could it work so much upon your shape,
> As it hath much prevailed on your Condition,
> I should not know you Brutus. Dear my Lord,
> Make me acquainted with your cause of grief. [*JC* 2.1.252]

Notice how in one line she addresses him by name, and by title, with no loss of intimacy.

We know from social historians that the respect accorded family members was codified in the use of honorifics as well as ritualized kneeling for blessing, something that children did with parents every morning and evening. Shakespeare's plays include so many speeches of profound love of parents for children and children for parents that we cannot assume that the formality of the respect precluded familial love and tenderness.

The concept of grace, coming as it does directly from God to humanity in the earthly realm, is an important component of the honorifics partaking of the root word "grace": your grace, my gracious lord, and so on. The inclusion of "grace" acknowledges, directly or within the broadest cultural context, that it is God's will that some people rule over other people. Any official of the church, a powerful economic and political as well as social force in these plays, is entitled by rank and by a shared belief in God's role in church appointments, to be addressed as "Your Grace." Because the ruling monarch is anointed in the coronation to signify God's grace, this becomes a title identified directly with whomever sits on the throne. But the hierarchy anchored in a relationship to that seat of power is infused with the grace of divine support that emanates downward from monarch to the lower reaches of the nobility, so that anyone with an inherited title holds that position by grace of God, and is therefore potentially "My gracious lord," if the speaker wishes to mark special reverence in the honorific.

"My liege" is an honorific that will most commonly be used when addressing one's king. It suggests a very specific and very special relationship, that between a member of the nobility, someone who can count kings in his or her own family tree, or who has sword fealty to the king and therefore acknowledges the king as his or her liege lord. Some of those who offered this commitment of service to a monarch might themselves lay claim to the throne, and from those members of the nobility who commanded vast lands and numbers of retainers, this offer of service could never be demanded. Therefore, the honorific marks not only the subservience of the speaker, but also the absolute honor and nobility of the speaker, which has been voluntarily offered in service to the ruling monarch.

A BAWDY PLANET

> Lechery by this hand; an Index, and obscure prologue to the History of Lust and foul Thoughts.
>
> Iago [*Othello* 2.1.257]

As in so much else, Shakespeare's sexuality has been shaped in the fashion of the times. When Victorian society hid the legs of a piano lest they call to mind the lower limbs of any woman in the room, special editions of Shakespeare were published with the "dirty bits" removed. How could anyone imagine the greatest of all dramatic poets making jokes about bodily functions? During the supposed sexual revolution of the 1960s, everyone climbed on quite a different band wagon, proudly exploring Shakespeare's liberal attitude toward sexual relations between consenting adults. It was still difficult to imagine him making sophomoric fart jokes, so we decided he stuck those in to please the unwashed, uneducated groundlings.

We probably don't have it right even today, despite the latest publications about Shakespeare's attitude to sexuality. In fifty years, another generation of scholars will look on our assumptions with just such a mocking attitude as the previous paragraph. There are only two constants: the language contains direct and indirect reference to a wide variety of bodily functions and sexual relationships, and the actor must find a way into the sexual energy of the plays that works equally well for the language and the actor.

It is once again time to leave our modern assumptions at the door of the rehearsal hall. We may not appreciate the attitude to women's sexuality expressed by King Lear, but a far more important questions is: For the world of the play, is this attitude normative or aberrant?

Here is what Lear has to say. At this moment in the play, he is a madman roaming the beach at Dover, in conversation with the recent blinded and suicidal Gloucester.

Behold yond simpering dame, whose face between her Forks presages Snow; that minces Virtue, and does shake the head to hear of pleasures name. The Fitchew, nor the soiled Horse goes to 't with a more riotous appetite. Down from the waist they are

Centaurs, though women all above: but to the Girdle do the Gods inherit, beneath is all the Fiends. There's hell, there's darkness, there is the sulphurous pit; burning, scalding stench, consumption: Fie, fie, fie; pah, pah; Give me an Ounce of Civet; good Apothecary sweeten my imagination: There's money for thee. [4.6.118]

To confirm this perspective, we have the devouring sexuality of Goneril and Regan; to challenge it we have the feminine purity of Cordelia. We have been given no clue as to Lear's personal history with women; Gloucester, however, had this to say about the creation of his bastard son Edmund: "Though this Knave came something saucily into the world before he was sent for: yet was his Mother fair, there was good sport at his making, and the whoreson must be acknowledged" [1.1.21]. Just as it is impossible for us to forget the long history of forced conversions of Jews when Antonio, the titular merchant of Venice, makes Shylock's conversion a condition of his moderated punishment, so too we are unable to encounter the transformation of the feisty Kate into the mouthpiece of patriarchal oppression as an entirely satisfying comic resolution to the plot.

Fifty years ago, the nature of Lear's relationship with this three daughters was discussed entirely in terms of manipulation and pretense; now the issue of incest is raised at some point in every rehearsal process. Once raised, the psychological validity of that specific type of perverted sexuality as an explanation for the division of the kingdom and all that follows resonates so completely that it is difficult to forget it in favor of a more Lear-friendly interpretation of the tragedy.

A radical shift in attitude towards homosexual relationships has brought Shakespeare and his characters out of the closet. Although there are still scholars who have concluded that Shakespeare was completely, absolutely, and undeniably heterosexual (because the scholar himself is and can't imagine Shakespeare to be anything else?), the plays demonstrate that he was able to imagine a passionate relationship between two men that has every appearance of being what today we would call homosexual. Here, for example, is the pirate Antonio speaking of the young lad Sebastian, whom he rescued from drowning and now intends to follow into enemy territory, risking capture and punishment for the sake of his love: "But come what may, I do adore thee so, / That danger shall seem sport, and I will go" [2.1.47]. At the end of the play, Sebastian is betrothed to Olivia, solving the love triangle that was created when his sister Viola disguised herself as the boy Cesario and fell in love with the duke, who was in love with Olivia, who fell in love with the boy Cesario and then mistook Sebastian for his disguised sister. A wonderful comic entanglement and resolution, except that the pirate Antonio is left unattached and silent as the couples pair off and the situation is resolved. We don't even know if the duke will pardon him for his past crimes as a pirate, for the sake of the love and service Antonio showed Viola's brother. But how happy can Antonio be to stand there and watch his beloved Sebastian embracing Olivia?

When we watch the interactions of Duke Orsino and Viola in *Twelfth Night*, we have a strange sensation of contrasting sexual relationships. We know that Viola is a girl disguised as a boy, and in an aside she has informed us of her love for the duke. We know that the duke loves Olivia but has developed an intense friendship with Viola who is, for Orsino, the boy Cesario. If we were the actors and audience who first experienced these scenes, we would also know that the actor playing Viola was in fact a young man, playing these scenes with an older man.

What then do we perceive when Orsino says to Viola/Cesario: "Boy, thou has said to me a thousand times, / Thou never shouldst love woman like to me" [5.1.267]? When the role is played by a woman, we see only Viola's truth; if the role were played by a young man, would we be invited to remember that heterosexuality is just one of many forms that human sexual contact can take?

Is there an alternative to superimposing our attitudes to human sexuality upon these plays? I would suggest not, because these attitudes will color how our actions are perceived by our audience. A production can elect to underplay or make overt these attitudes and some actors and directors enter into the rehearsal process with unshakeable interpretations as to the sexual orientation of the various characters. I would argue that there is no possible correct interpretation; that the danger lies in glib assumptions such as, "There's no way that character could be gay," or "That character must be homosexual."

From what we know of the history of human sexuality, the attitude in Shakespeare's world towards sexual relations between two men, and about male and female sexuality, were significantly different than ours. Understanding this differences becomes a critical step on the journey that a modern actor undertakes when developing a character in one of Shakespeare's plays.

Here are some of the highlights:

• In an almost complete reverse from today's assumptions, women were viewed as having rampaging sexuality and men were considered to be quite capable, for the most part, of controlling their urges. Today, there might be an attempt to exonerate a rapist when a young woman is asked what she was wearing when she was attacked, the theory being that the mere sight of bare flesh is sufficient to arouse a man's unbridled sexuality. In Shakespeare's time, married men accepted the likelihood of being made cuckolds because a woman's desire, once awakened, was all-consuming. No one man could hope to satisfy her, and so the merry wives of the community were less to be chastised than their husbands mocked.

• It was assumed that, just as men needed to reach sexual fulfilment in order to release their sperm, so too women needed to enjoy sexual pleasure in order to release an egg. Since the creation of healthy babies was so important to the community, it was important for young men and women to understand their own and each other's sexual equipment, in order that they could give each other pleasure and make healthy babies together.

- This same desire to fill the community with healthy babies influenced attitudes to the choice of marriage partners. While everyone agreed that the older generation were ideally suited to bringing together two young people who would suit each other over the long journey of married life, everyone also knew that a good match included good sexual chemistry, because that was the key to healthy babies.

- People generally married late. Young men had to wait until they came into their estates or were otherwise established, either by achieving their masters' papers in the guild into which they were apprenticed, or by rising in the service of their master to the point where the gifts they received were sufficient in size and scope to underwrite the expense of a family. Girls guarded their virginity as a part of their dowery, but almost everyone knew ways of achieving sexual pleasure without having sexual intercourse. Young men learned the map of a woman's body under the tutelage of one of the merry wives of the community while they waited for the economic wherewithal to marry.

- Young people committed themselves to a life together privately by betrothal; legally, they were bound to marry each other and could marry no other person unless released from that bond by the other or by death. When the banns were cried for three Sundays in a row in order that two young people might make public vows of marriage in a church, any prior betrothal agreements were expected to come to light; if they did, the marriage could not go forward. There is strong historical evidence that Edward of York did in fact have a prior betrothal when he married the Widow Grey, which would have made his three children by her illegitimate, as claimed by their uncle Richard of Gloucester.

- When two young people were betrothed, which they could do with a simple exchange of tokens and avowals of their intention to marry, they were then acting morally and legally if they had sexual relations with each other. The closeness of dates between church weddings and christenings of first children, which is so apparent in the records of the period, including Shakespeare's own, is as much a result of this custom as of rampant premarital sex.

- Human sexuality was viewed as natural. It became sinful when it became luxury, just as eating became a sin when it became gluttony. Luxury is the indulgence of the flesh for the sake of indulgence, and was abhorrent because of its lack of moderation.

- People's personalities were not defined by their preference in sexual partners. Some men were drawn only to other men. Some men were drawn only to women. Some men formed passionate friendships with other men that may or may not have resulted in sexual activity but that were hugely significant in the emotional and social life of the men involved. There were sexual acts that occurred between two men and between two women. The concept of someone being a homosexual was yet to come.

- Far more scandalous than sexual acts between people of the same sex, or adultery, or premarital sex, were sexual relations that broke the barriers between the classes. When a noble man formed a relationship with a woman of a lower class, he was expected to have good sport with her and acknowledge any children she bore as his own, to both their benefits. Only rarely were these liaisons formalized. John of Gaunt's mistress, Katherine Swinford, bore him many children. Late in his life, after the deaths of the two great heiresses that Gaunt had married and with whom he had produced the man who would become King Henry IV, Gaunt married his mistress and petitioned his nephew, King Richard, to retroactively legitimise that branch of his noble line. These children became the Beauford clan, that powerful group of church leaders, scholars, courtiers, and king makers. The proviso of Richard's declaration was that this line could not inherit the throne; this was conveniently forgotten when the earl of Richmond, whose only claim to the blood of English kings came from his Beauford mother, ascended the throne as Henry VII. If he had not married Elizabeth, daughter of the York branch of the family, his grand daughter Queen Elizabeth would have only the flimsiest of connections to the great King Edward III.

From these observations, we learn to look for the following aspects of sexuality in the plays:

- The relative class of the lovers is far more important than their gender. What stands in the way of Antonio and Sebastian's relationship is not the fact they are both men as much as the fact that Sebastian turns out to be a gentleman, entirely unsuitable to a close friendship with a pirate. It is that which transforms Antonio's love into dutiful service, and makes his acceptance of Sebastian's marriage to the heiress Olivia a natural reaction in the final scene.

- Even a well brought up girl like Juliet is without shame about her own sexual desire and the events that transpire in a wedding bed. There is nothing rude or untoward about the sexual jokes made by Margaret while dressing Hero for her wedding.

- When Julia and Proteus, or Miranda and Ferdinand exchange their love tokens or vow to marry each other, they are betrothed. Sexual intercourse may well follow; hence Prospero's strong charge to the young lovers to wait until a formal public ceremony that will bind them as heirs to kingdoms and rulers of their people. When Miranda sleeps with Angelo in Isabella's place, she is no more or less appropriate a bed partner than is Helena when she takes Diana's place with Bertram, even though Helena and Bertram have been married and Angelo and Miranda only betrothed.

- Proteus and Valentine, Antonio and Sebastian, Bassanio and Antonio, Brutus and Cassius, and all of the other men who avow their love to each other can do so openly and with great feeling, and be making absolutely no comment on the nature of their sexual behavior with each other or in general. If their love has taken a physical form, those actions neither validate, strengthen, nor change the nature of the love expressed, in comparison with those men who form such passionate bonds and do not express the love physically.

- Some men were widely known to prefer sexual relationships with men; the possibility of women having sexual pleasure with women was understood to exist but was thought to be a rare event. These activities and preferences did not in any way interfere with the capacity of these individuals to fulfill the ideals of masculine and feminine behavior, including the responsibility to their family lines to marry and produce healthy children.

- There was no reliable birth control. If women and men engaged in sexual relations, babies would follow. Many women died in childbirth. The connection between sex and death was not simply a metaphor.

- No one could know with certainty who his father was; everyone knew who his mother was. That a woman might have had more than one sexual partner after marriage was not as damaging to the social fabric as the tendency of certain women to violate their subservient status; adulterous women were the merry wives of a village; shrews had to be strictly contained. In marrying, every man knew he would be a cuckold; no man in his right mind would marry a shrew.

- In infancy and youth, there was little to tell apart boys from girls. But when men matured, they achieved a rational and spiritual plane of existence that uniquely positioned them to take the moral and social responsibility for the community. All women remained on the lower plane, as did children. Therefore, the governance of a man over his family was not oppression, but the source of stability and safety.

- Boys were well suited to playing the roles of girls and women because, in truth, there is little difference between them. That is why the boy actors could achieve a level of psychological realism in their own eyes and the eyes of the audience, that a modern group of actors and their audience simply wouldn't accept. The naturalism of this role-playing extended to aspects of sexuality, for the thought of older men having passionate feelings for younger boys was thinkable.

In connection with this last point, consider the situation in *As You Like It*. Rosalind disguises herself as a boy, names herself Ganymede, and then runs into her true love, Orlando, in the forest. She announces to Celia, "I will speak to him like a saucy lackey, and under that habit play the knave with him," and proceeds to ask Orlando if he is the individual who has been carving love poems to Rosalind. When Orlando admits he is this lover, the saucy lackey offers to cure him by a special process used once before, with great success:

He was to imagine me his Love, his Mistress: and I set him every day to woo me. At which time would I, being but a moonish youth, grieve, be effeminate, changeable, longing, and liking, proud, fantastical, apish, shallow, inconstant, full of tears, full of smiles; for every passion something, and for no passion truly any thing, as boys and women are for the most part, cattle of this colour: would now like him, now loathe him: then entertain him, then forswear him: now weep for him, then spit at him; that I drave my Suitor from his mad humour of love, to a living humour of madness, which was to forswear the full stream of the world, and to live in a nook merely Monastic. [3.2.407]

Here, we find a direct statement of the similarity between boys and women, reinforced by the fact that the actor who played the first Rosalind would have been just the sort of saucy lackey Rosalind pretends to be. In other words, we have a boy actor pretending to be a girl who disguises herself as a boy in order to play a game with her unsuspecting lover where she pretends to be a girl, in fact, herself, not as she really is, but as men might see her. The disguise Rosalind assumes comes with a name: Ganymede. In case you thought that the older man/younger boy sexual attraction was an invention superimposed upon Shakespeare's text, here is the story of Ganymede, taken from the tenth book of Ovid's *Metamorphoses*:

Jupiter loved the delectable Phrygian Ganymede
and turned himself into a bird for the sake of this dishy boy,
but not any bird. . . . Oh, no! It had to be one that could carry
the monstrous thunderbolts. An enormous eagle with talons
large enough to sustain the Trojan boy, which he did,
catching him up and flying back to the heights of Olympus,
where now, despite the distaste of Juno, he serves at banquets,
filling the nectar cups of his master and all the gods. (Slavitt 1994, 199)

Ganymede came to be an emblem of the catamite, and that is the name that
Rosalind chooses for herself. Like Viola, in *Twelfth Night*, who chooses to
disguise herself as an eunuch, Rosalind in her cross-dressing is summoning up
specific images of nonheterosexual relationships.

Dirty Bits

In the final scene of *A Midsummer Night's Dream*, the workmen of Athens
present their tragic masterpiece to the three pairs of newlyweds. The story of
Pyramus and Thisbe, forced to communicate through the stone way that di-
vides their two families, becomes a farcical melodrama when enacted by Bottom and company. Thisbe's first lines, addressed to the actor portraying
"Wall," seem a relatively unfunny contribution: "O wall, full often hast thou
heard my moans, / For parting my fair Pyramus, and me. / My cherry lips
have often kissed thy stones; / Thy stones with Lime and Hair knit up in thee"
[5.1.188]. Most modern editors avoid even a hint at what must have made the
groundlings roar with laughter; only the Oxford edition includes a note that
"stones" was a euphemism for testicles. Things get even more rude a few lines
later when the lovers attempt to kiss through the opening in the wall, and
Thisbe announces, "I kiss the wall's hole, not your lips at all" [5.1.201].

The final couplet of *The Merchant of Venice* contains a slightly more sophisticated double entendre. Portia and Nerissa have had a good laugh at their
new husbands, who were persuaded to give away the women's rings to a
young lawyer and his clerk, Portia and Nerissa in disguise. Now the couples
are reunited in harmony and prepare to exit for their wedding celebrations,
which had been postponed by the action of the serious plot. The closing words:
"Well, while I live, I'll fear no other thing / So sore, as keeping safe Nerissas
ring" [5.1.306]. If this husband is only worried about not losing his wife's love
token, then we'd have to wonder about the comic thrust of the couplet. However, if we learn that "ring" was a euphemism for the vagina, we suddenly
have a double entendre in keeping with the spirit of the moment.

Whenever Shakespeare's language partakes of the rich vocabulary of double
entendre, the modern actor is faced with the following:

• Who on stage should "get" the joke?

• If the rude joke is going to be lost on the modern audience, should the actors on stage accompany the joke with corresponding rude gestures?

• How is the audience going to react when they discover that the greatest dramatist who ever lived indulges regularly in the crudest and most sophomoric of bathroom humor?

• Will a modern audience accept the unabashed sexuality expressed by their favorite heroes and heroines?

Early editors of Shakespeare, who were closer to Shakespeare's language that we are by 150 years or more, were painfully aware of just how vulgar some of Shakespeare's jokes could be. The result was an editorial custom of expurgation: eliminating or replacing the most obvious "dirty bits" and carefully avoiding explaining the slightly more obscure references. We call these editions "bowdlerized" Shakespeare after the best known of such editors, Thomas Bowdler.

As a result, Shakespeare is taught by relatively naive teachers to relatively innocent school children, with no clear understanding of what is being expressed by, for example, the great poetry of dear, sweet, fourteen-year-old Juliet.

> Gallop apace, you fiery footed steeds,
> Towards Phoebus lodging, such a Wagoner
> As Phaethon would whip you to the west,
> And bring in Cloudy night immediately.
> Spread thy close Curtain Love-performing night,
> That run-aways eyes may wink, and Romeo
> Leap to these arms, untalked of and unseen,
> Lovers can see to do their Amorous rites,
> By their own beauties: or if Love be blind,
> It best agrees with night: come civil night,
> Thou sober suited Matron all in black,
> And learn me how to lose a winning match,
> Played for a pair of stainless Maidenhoods,
> Hood my unmanned blood bating in my Cheeks,
> With thy Black mantle, till strange Love grow bold,
> Think true Love acted simple modesty:
> Come night, come Romeo, come, thou day in night,
> For thou wilt lie upon the wings of night
> Whiter than new Snow on a Ravens back:
> Come gentle night, come loving, blackbrowed night.
> Give me my Romeo, and, when I shall die,
> Take him and cut him out in little stars,
> And he will make the Face of heaven so fine,
> That all the world will be in Love with night,
> And pay no worship to the Garish Sun.
> O I have bought the Mansion of a Love,

But not possessed it, and though I am sold,
Not yet enjoyed, so tedious is this day,
As is the night before some Festival,
To an impatient child that hath new robes
And may not wear them, O here comes my Nurse:
And she brings news and every tongue that speaks
But Romeos name, speaks heavenly eloquence. [3.2.1]

It is clear from the plot of the play that this is a young woman awaiting her wedding night. The horrible irony of our knowing that her beloved Romeo has just murdered her cousin and been banished from Verona might trick us into finding the imagery of death the most powerful emotional component of this opening speech.

But the actress playing Juliet needs to know that this speech is about sexual intercourse, and the death reference is to orgasm, and the stars formed at his death are the drops of sperm that will create miniature Romeos inside her body. The wings of night upon which he will lie are created by her pubic hair. When she speaks of "true Love acted," she is describing the action that will be the perfect expression of their true love, that, when viewed by the eyes of "strange Love," love that is unfamiliar, a visitor to her maiden chamber and her body, will be seen as and judged to be simple and appropriate, a sign of her shyness and humility, both of which are tokens of a maiden's modesty.

Although we are perhaps more ready now than we were in previous generations to accept that young people experience sexual desire, we are still not accustomed to thinking of sexual activities as natural, normal, and something to be discussed openly. Contemporary sexual references too often carry an additional element of anger, violence, shame, embarrassment, voyeurism, or disgust for us to feel comfortable with the blend of some of the most beautiful poetry in the play, spoken by a young and innocent girl, and the purest expression of sexual excitement and anticipation of the specific activities of heterosexual intercourse.

Here is another challenge to the actor's contribution in transcending the differences between Shakespeare's time and ours. Let us have a look at a specific example, again from *Romeo and Juliet*, and consider how to negotiate the contrast between our attitudes to sexuality and those of the characters in the play.

Everyone likes the Nurse, it seems, but it does remain a bit of a puzzle why this apparently wealthy and ambitious family, about to marry their daughter into the nobility, would keep as a close personal servant a woman who talks so openly about breast feeding and who makes rude and crude jokes about having sex and babies, as the Nurse does when she tells the story of Juliet falling and bumping her forehead and being comforted by her dear departed husband, "Yea quoth he, dost thou fall upon thy face? thou wilt fall backward when thou hast more wit, wilt thou not Jule? And by my holy-dam, the pretty wretch left crying, and said Ay" [1.3.41]. A modern reader might assume that Juliet's mother has changed the topic when she launches into her maternal advice, and says:

> This precious Book of Love, this unbound Lover,
> To Beautify him, only lacks a Cover.
> The fish lives in the Sea, and 'tis much pride
> For fair without, the fair within to hide:
> That Book in manys eyes doth share the glory,
> That in Gold clasps, Locks in the Golden story:
> So shall you share all that he doth possess,
> By having him, making your self no less. [1.3.87]

To which the Nurse responds, "No less, nay bigger: women grow by men" [1.3.95].

It may come as a surprise to discover that the two women are talking about the same thing. On one level, Lady Capulet is talking about the worldly prestige that a beautiful young wife can bring to an equally attractive and wealthy young man. But the covering of a lover, unbound by social restrictions, is of a sexual nature, and the golden story locked into their private lives is the sexual relationship that binds a husband and wife together.

The Nurse also thinks nothing of commenting on the physical attributes of Juliet's various suitors. When she concludes that Romeo's "face be better than any mans, yet his legs excels all mens, and for a hand, and a foot, and a body, though they be not to be talked on, yet they are past compare" [2.5.40], we can hardly miss the sexuality of her commentary. If we are aware that both hand and foot are euphemisms for the penis, as well as accepted visible indicators of the size and skillful dexterity of the hidden male member, we can appreciate the Nurse's highly charged reaction to Juliet's young man.

But how on earth should Juliet react to all of this? She is, after all, a virginal, well brought up young woman, protected by the wealth and guardianship of her father's house. Are we to imagine she is embarrassed by these comments? That she simply does not get the joke? Or that she understands perfectly well what is being discussed? If we select the first option, then we can imagine her losing her embarrassment in time for her wedding night. If the second, then we have to imagine someone (the Nurse?) giving her a quick offstage lesson about the facts of life.

Let's have a look at another young well brought up lady on the cusp of marriage for a comparison. In *Much Ado about Nothing*, Shakespeare includes a scene in the private room of Hero as she prepares for the ceremony that will unite her with her beloved Claudio. It is imperative for the plot that Hero be entirely chaste, as she is wrongfully accused of premarital sex at the alter. But here we see her with her maid Margaret, dressing for the wedding, acting like a typical nervous bride.

Margaret: Troth I think your other rabato were better.

Hero: No pray thee good Meg, I'll wear this.

Margaret: By my troth's not so good, and I warrant your cousin will say so.

Hero: My cousin's a fool, and thou art another, I'll wear none but this.

Margaret: I like the new tire within excellently, if the hair were a thought browner: and your gown's a most rare fashion i' faith, I saw the Duchess of Milans gown that they praise so.

Hero: O that exceeds they say.

Margaret: By my troth's but a night-gown in respect of yours, cloth a gold, and cuts, and laced with silver, set with pearls, down sleeves, side sleeves, and skirts, round underborne with a bluish tinsel, but for a fine quaint graceful and excellent fashion, yours is worth ten on 't.

Hero: God give me joy to wear it, for my heart is exceeding heavy.

Margaret: 'Twill be heavier soon, by the weight of a man.

Hero: Fie upon thee, art not ashamed?

Margaret: Of what Lady? of speaking honourably? is not marriage honourable in a beggar? is not your Lord honourable without marriage? I think you would have me say, saving your reverence a husband: and bad thinking do not wrest true speaking, I'll offend nobody, is there any harm in the heavier for a husband? none I think, and it be the right husband, and the right wife, otherwise 'tis light and not heavy, ask my Lady Beatrice else, here she comes.

Even if we do not know that the "cuts" and "sleeves" of the "quant gown" are a not-so-subtle suggestion of the sexiness of the wearer, as these words were common euphemisms for women's genitals, we cannot miss the subject matter of Margaret's thoughts on the weight that a husband places upon his wife's body during sexual intercourse. And such an action cannot be anything to be ashamed about, if it be a husband and a wife who are married to each other, for anything else would be "light," or naughty.

Can we imagine a culture wherein nice young girls would know all about the biology of sex and the emotions of sex and still be virgins? I think that is exactly what we have to do in order to play Juliet or Hero. Social historians have contributed much to our understanding of attitudes towards human sexuality in Shakespeare's England, and a strikingly different picture emerges from either our own attitudes or those of our grandparents and great-great grandparents.

Of course the church taught that sexual activity was only appropriate between husband and wife. Lust, a general term for the desire and any actions taken upon the desire, was indeed one of the seven deadly sins, but remember that it was found alongside gluttony. In other words, overindulging in sex was comparable to overindulging in food. It could harm you, it was a sign of lack of rational control, and it lowered your status towards the animal instead of towards the angels, which was where any right-thinking individual set his or her sights, but it was not the disgusting, shameful, and terrible secret that it became in later centuries.

I think we have to assume that Elizabethans were no more or less sexy on average than we are today. However, they had different restrictions upon their pleasure, and different attitudes towards sexuality, and so they conducted themselves different, but in a way that was as normal to them as our patterns of behavior are to us today.

One of the primary restrictions was the lack of reliable birth control. When a man and a woman embarked upon a sexual relationship, babies were the inevitable result. Unwed women were quickly married to someone so that the child could have a father; bastards were rare but wedding dates followed soon by baptismal dates of first-born children were common in the records of the time. Shakespeare found himself a husband and shortly after a father in just this manner.

The sexual act was considered a natural component of the relationship between men and women, because it was believed that men and women's entire biological system was geared to the bearing of children. Every community wanted strong, healthy babies, and anything that contributed to the successful conception of the next generation was clearly to the benefit of all. The last thing that anyone wanted was two young people ending up in bed together ignorant of how to make babies. Ignorance was dangerous; only later was it used as a means to safeguard morality.

The Elizabethans suspected, and the medical profession generally concurred, that a women's biology was identical to a man's but inside out, as it were, with the vagina a sort of inverted penis, a perfect fit therefore for the male member, and the uterus and ovaries like the scrotum and testes. It was only natural, then, to conclude that a woman's orgasm was as important to conception as a man's. If your wife will release an egg to match your sperm to make the children you so desire only if she enjoys herself, then you will want to ensure that your wife receives as much pleasure from the sexual act as you do.

Young men and women required pleasure maps in order to ensure that healthy babies would be the result of their couplings. We find a satirical take on the mapping of the female body in *The Comedy of Errors*, when poor Dromio of Syracuse is describing the kitchen maid Luce to his master.

Dromio: No longer from head to foot, than from hip to hip: she is spherical, like a globe: I could find out Countries in her.

Antipholus: In what part of her body stands Ireland?

Dromio: Marry Sir in her buttocks, I found it out by the bogs.

Antipholus: Where Scotland?

Dromio: I found it by the barrenness, hard in the palm of the hand.

Antipholus: Where France?

Dromio: In her forehead, armed and reverted, making war against her heir.

Antipholus: Where England?

Dromio: I looked for the chalky Cliffs, but I could find no whiteness in them. But
                I guess, it stood in her chin by the salt rheum that ran between France,
                and it.

Antipholus: Where Spain?

Dromio: Faith I saw it not: but I felt it hot in her breath.

Antipholus: Where America, the Indies?

Dromio: Oh sir, upon her nose, all o'er embellished with Rubies, Carbuncles, Sap-
                phires, declining their rich Aspect to the hot breath of Spain, who sent whole
                Armadoes of Caracks to be ballast at her nose.

Antipholus: Where stood Belgia, the Netherlands?

Dromio: Oh sir, I did not look so low.

The fact that Dromio is perfectly aware of where the "netherlands" of a woman
are to be found is the implicit context of the punch line of the exchange. It is
difficult to be offended by such a catalogue of offensive ethnic jokes; poor
Luce does not come off as being a very attractive person, but the focus of the
satire is the different national groups, including even the English.

How did the Elizabethan world view male and female sexuality? It is impossible to offer any more than generalized cultural attitudes, for every individual might have his or her own view of such matters, and woven into the
fabric of the times were many possible interpretations, theories, and of course
firsthand experiences.

Generally, though, the gender roles were almost exactly the opposite as
today. It was women who were seen to have a raging, uncontrollable sexuality,
not men. It was as if men's sexuality was seen as a natural river, perhaps
flowing more heavily in the spring time of one's life and almost drying up in
the autumn of old age, but in the mature years a calm, steady flow of desire
and fulfilment, particularly if not dammed by abstinence but allowed to run
between the solid banks of a marriage bed. And the culture was filled with
examples of men who put aside all interest in sexual matters and lived quite
happily the life monastic, even if the monasteries had been closed in England
for many years.

Women, however, were generally thought to have been given by their natural physicality a sexual energy that flowed like a simple tap with two positions: off, and full flood. The off position was experienced by girls before
puberty, but with the onset of mature sexual experience, no one man could
possibly satisfy the requirements of a woman's sexuality for breeding opportunities. Is it any wonder that even the love-sick Berowne would describe his
beloved Rosaline as "one that will do the deed, / Though Argus were her

Eunuch and her guard" [*LLL* 3.1.198], referring to the thousand-eyed god as being incapable of keeping sufficient guard of her rapacious need to "do the deed" with any man if her husband were not available or able.

There is another reason why Elizabethan culture was filled with jokes about cuckolds, that is, married men whose wives betrayed them. As best we can tell, married women did frequently have sexual relations with men other than their husbands. Whenever a younger woman was matched with an older man, whenever a woman was left behind while her husband sought fame and fortune away from home, whenever a woman's sexual needs were no longer fulfilled by her husband, she had, if she so chose, an excuse for taking a lover. Queen Margaret, married to the weak and impotent King Henry VI, takes Suffolk as her lover in a relationship that is presented as treasonous, duplicitous, and the natural result of Henry's inability to satisfy his wife's legitimate demands in the bedroom. As she explains to Suffolk, she only agreed to the marriage because, "I thought King Henry had resembled thee, / In Courage, Courtship, and Proportion: / But all his mind is bent to Holiness" [*2HVI* 1.3.53], and Henry is better suited to life as a priest.

Married women who formed relationships with unmarried young men provided another worthy cultural service. Elizabethan men tended to marry late because they had to establish themselves before taking on the economic responsibilities of a wife and family. Shakespeare's own youthful marriage is not the most common practice of men of either the nobility or the guilds. One needed to inherit the estate or be granted a portion of ones inheritance, or one needed to complete one's apprenticeship and establish oneself as a master of one's craft. But what were these young men to do with their sexual desires? And how were they to learn the map of a woman's body and the all-important secrets to bringing pleasure to a woman, the only means by which babies could be born? The presence of experienced and willing older women, and a culture that attributed these adulterous activities as the natural result of women's biology, placed these sins into a larger context that resulted in laughter at the cuckolded husband who could not accept his inevitable horns rather than disgust at the woman and the young man who took his place in the marriage bed. As Leontes says, when he assumes that his wife has indulged herself as expected,

> Should all despair
> That have revolted Wives, the tenth of Mankind
> Would hang themselves. Physic for't, there's none:
> It is a bawdy Planet, that will strike
> Where 'tis predominant; and 'tis powerful: think it:
> From East, West, North and South, be it concluded,
> No Barricado for a Belly. Know't,
> It will let in and out the Enemy,
> With bag and baggage: many thousand on's
> Have the Disease, and feel't not. [*WT* 1.2.198]

Leontes's mistake is believing that his remarkable wife Hermione is incapable of rising above the temptations that confront her sex.

Although a misogynist thread weaves its way through the plays of Shakespeare and his contemporaries, we must be careful not to attribute all negative comments made by men about women as a disgust at women's sexuality. Lear's horrified ravings at the thought of women's genitals, "There's hell, there's darkness, there is the sulphurous pit; burning scalding stench, consumption" [4.6.127], is not very likely the norm for his culture. I would argue that it is not this sort of repulsion that fuels the jealous rage of Leontes or Posthumus or Othello, but rather the sudden lack of confidence that comes with the realization that there is a very good chance that you have not succeeded in satisfying your wife, and that it is therefore inevitable that her sexuality will rise up into an irresistible flood. Posthumus, in his exile, knows that his wife's needs are not being met. Do Leontes and Othello have reason to doubt their success in bed? What is the connection between paranoid jealousy without cause and fears of sexual inadequacy?

Let us contrast the husbands of the two merry wives of Windsor, Mistress Ford and Mistress Page. Page responds to the possibility of Falstaff wooing his wife with, "If he should intend this voyage toward my wife, I would turn her loose to him; and what he gets more of her than sharp words, let it lie on my head." This is not a man who is particularly worried about wearing cuckhold's horns. But his friend Ford responds to the same possibility with, "I do not misdoubt my wife; but I would be loath to turn them together. A man may be too confident."

In order to test his wife, Ford plays what appears to have been a familiar role in Elizabethan middle-class life: he pretends to be in love with another man's wife, and as a result, confesses,

I have long loved her, and I protest to you, bestowed much on her: followed her with a doting observance: Engrossed opportunities to meet her: fee'd every slight occasion that could but niggardly give me sight of her: not only bought many presents to give her, but have given largely to many, to know what she would have given: briefly, I have pursued her, as Love hath pursued me, which hath been on the wing of all occasions. [2.2.194]

He calls this pursuit of an adulterous affair an "imperfection," one of his "follies," and hopes "that I may pass with a reproof the easier, sith you yourself know how easy it is to be such an offender."

The comedy of the play rests upon Ford pretending to be another man in love with his own wife, in order to spy upon the man he thinks is in love with his wife, in order to catch his wife with that man, while she, offended by the inappropriate wooing of the one and the unjustified jealousy of the other, demonstrates the truth of the old adage: "Wives may be merry, and yet honest too: / We do not act that often jest, and laugh, / 'Tis old, but true, Still Swine eat all the draff" [4.2.105]. In other words, the external appearance of good spirits does not suggest the inner attribute of sexual wantonness, the other meaning of "merry." The wives most likely to be betraying their husbands are the "good" wives who, like the quiet pigs of the adage manage to gobble down all the food available, fulfilling their appetite at the expense of others.

So when Rosalind makes cuckold jokes with Orlando in the forest of Arden, what tone should the actors take? Rosalind, disguised as the boy Ganymede now pretending to be the object of Orlando's passion, says that she would rather be wooed by a snail, because he already wears the mark of his destiny as a cuckold: horns. And, a few moments later, she teases him by promising to love him "Fridays and Saturdays, and all" and to have him "and twenty such," because "can one desire too much of a good thing?" [*AYLI* 4.1.124]. Then, immediately after their enactment of the marriage service, with her cousin Celia serving as the priest, Rosalind teases Orlando with the threat, "Make the doors upon a woman's wit and it will out at the casement: shut that, and 'twill out at the key-hole: stop that, 'twill fly with the smoke out at the chimney" [4.1.161]. But at the same time she reveals another reason for foreseeing adultery in any marriage: the wandering wit might be discovered in the neighbor's bed, but she will excuse herself by saying she went there to look for you! As Rosalind reminds us, men were given to straying, as well as women: "men are April when they woo, December when they wed: Maids are May when they are maids, but the sky changes when they are wives" [4.1.147].

Another couple actually enter into a debate about which of the sexes is least likely to stray from the bonds of love and marriage. Orsino thinks he is discussing love with his new young page, Cesario, but we know that this is really Viola who is not only disguised as a boy, but also very much in love with Orsino. The first part of the debate sees Orsino suggesting it is better for women to marry older men because, "Our fancies are more giddy and unfirm, / More longing, wavering, sooner lost and worn, / Than womens are" [*12th Night* 2.4.33]. But then, Viola reminds Orsino, and us, of the possibility of unrequited love, "Say that some Lady, as perhaps there is, / Hath for your love as great a pang of heart / As you have for Olivia: you cannot love her: / You tell her so: Must she not then be answered?" [2.4.89]. She is, of course, describing herself. Orsino responds with something that is, in essence the exact opposite of what he said at the beginning of the scene:

> There is no womans sides
> Can bide the beating of so strong a passion,
> As love doth give my heart: no womans heart
> So big, to hold so much, they lack retention.
> Alas, their love may be called appetite,
> No motion of the Liver, but the Palate,
> That suffer surfeit, cloyment, and revolt,

But mine is all as hungry as the Sea,
And can digest as much, make no compare
Between that love a woman can bear me,
And that I owe Olivia. [2.4.93]

Viola is perfectly positioned to offer a rebuttal to this comparison of men's capacity for love with women's. As a woman, she can speak of what she knows to be true. In her masculine disguise, she has been allowed an opportunity to experience the world of friendship and love as men do. Her conclusion: "In faith they are as true of heart, as we," because, "We men may say more, swear more: but indeed / Our shows are more than will: for still we prove / Much in our vows, but little in our love" [2.4.116].

Shakespeare shows us more faithful women than unfaithful, and more changeable men. Both Orsino and Romeo are convinced they are passionately and completely in love with another woman before they find themselves matched with the heroine of their respective plays. Berowne says he'll never fall in love with any woman, as does Benedick; this resolution is quickly dissolved. There is a lengthy list of men who doubt the chastity of their blameless wives, or generally treat the women in their lives in distinctly disrespectful and unloving ways.

The possibility of death hangs over the marriage bed because pregnancy so often took the life of the mother. But this did not stop the majority of women from entering into the passionate embrace so vividly described by Juliet. So too, with the spectre of the horns of cuckoldry, the cooling of a husband's love, or the torments of sexual jealousy a very real possibility in even the most loving of marriages, the Rosalinds and the Orlandos of Shakespeare's theatre pair up without hesitation.

The jokes simultaneously undercut and relieve the terrible tension represented by the likelihood of betrayal. We can only admire their capacity to "whistle down the wind" and laugh at the thing that most frightened them. They also carried around *momenti mori*, that is, little tokens as constant reminders of the transience of life. Escapist romances promising "happy ever after" were not as important as "happily, for now, because no one lives forever."

SILENCE

Silence is the perfectest Herald of joy.

Claudio [*Much Ado* 2.1.306]

Actors in the theatre have a greater awareness of the potency of silence than students of the written playtext, who have a tendency to forget that on stage during the scene are people listening without speaking. At times, the silent listener is actually the center of attention, as in the final moments of *Measure for Measure* when Isabella's reaction to the Duke's endgame moves is of some significance to everyone on stage.

First, the Provost reveals Claudio, who is still alive despite the express orders of Angelo. Isabella, who had knelt before the Duke and pleaded for Angelo's life, did so thinking her brother dead. How is she reacting to the Duke's explanation:

> If he be like your brother, for his sake
> Is he pardoned, and for your lovely sake
> Give me your hand, and say you will be mine,
> He is my brother too: But fitter time for that:
> By this Lord Angelo perceives he's safe,
> Methinks I see a quickening in his eye:
> Well Angelo, your evil quits you well.
> Look that you love your wife: her worth, worth yours
> I find an apt remission in my self:
> And yet here's one in place I cannot pardon.

The Duke now turns on Lucio, and the actors playing Isabella, Angelo, Mariana, Claudio, and Juliet, if she has been brought back on stage for the happy ending, must all figure out why they do not speak. Does the Duke wait for a response and receive none, or move on too quickly for anyone to say anything? Are Isabella and Claudio, and Marianna and Angelo communicating silently with physical and eye contact, embracing, gazing, laughing, weeping?

And what does the Duke mean when he says, "I find an apt remission in myself"? What unscripted response to these events is occurring before him that prompts his words? Does he remember Lucio or catch sight of him doing something, perhaps attempting to sneak away, or embracing his friend Claudio and taking some credit for his narrow escape?

The challenge of silence continues for the principal characters. After the exchange with Lucio, the Duke has a final speech:

> She Claudio that you wronged, look you restore.
> Joy to you Mariana, love her Angelo:
> I have confessed her, and I know her virtue.
> Thanks good friend, Escalus, for thy much goodness,
> There's more behind that is more gratulate.
> Thanks Provost for thy care, and secrecy,
> We shill employ thee in a worthier place.
> Forgive him Angelo, that brought you home
> The head of Ragozine for Claudio's,
> Th' offence pardons it self. Dear Isabel,
> I have a motion much imports your good,
> Whereto if you'll a willing ear incline;
> What's mine is yours, and what is yours is mine.

So bring us to our Palace, where we'll show
What's yet behind, that meet you all should know.

The Duke seems to go on a mini walkabout, making contact with Claudio
and perhaps Juliet, Angelo and Mariana, Escalus and the Provost, back to
Angelo, and then to Isabella. How does each react to what he says and to the
reactions of each of the others as the Duke works his way through the group
of central characters?

Actors grow accustomed to the responsibility they hold with regard to the
delivery of a playwright's words. They know that, with an inflection, a gesture,
a smirk or frown, they can imply a meaning quite opposite to what the words
say. The Duke's proposal of marriage can be spoken to suggest anything from
sexual desire or romantic longing to an "or else" of threatened coercion. They
also know that the silent reaction of the onstage listener can justify or compel
such alternative "readings" so that the audience is under the impression that
such a moment was exactly what the playwright scripted.

In truth, modern playwrights do sometimes resort to stage directions that
indicate a collision between literal meanings of words and the human event
that is taking place. Furthermore, a modern playwright will feel free to script
the silent reactions of the onstage listeners. Even with these promptings, however, every playtext of necessity leaves hugely significant choices unscripted.

Shakespeare's use of stage silence affords the greatest opportunities for radical revisioning for a modern actor, given the potent combination of the absence of suggestions from the playwright, and the current theatrical tradition
that privileges fresh new interpretations of characters and situations. Isabella,
Angelo, Marianna, and Claudio are unbound by the necessity of a worded
response, a window that Shakespeare himself has created.

Some of the responses have been suggested: the Duke says he sees a quickening in Angelo's eye, which seems to be directly linked to the discovery that
he is not, after all, responsible for Claudio's death, though he intended it. That
comment from the Duke shapes how the audience perceives Angelo's mental
state, for few of them are likely to be close enough to gaze into his eyes and
see the quickening. However, there is no comparable indication of Isabella's
expression.

For many years, the theatrical tradition has been that Isabella does not happily take the Duke's hand and exit with him; rather that she perceives this as
still another sexual harassment by a powerful man. The absence of any text
for Isabella following her being brought to the point where she must plead for
Angelo, the man who she believes killed her brother, gives an open space that
can be filled by any sort of gesture or facial expression, allowing for this
anticomedic interpretation.

But for Shakespeare's audience the ending would not have been as problem-
atic. Silence, traditionally as well as in a court of law, suggests consent, and it

is not really conceivable that a young woman from the gentry would be allowed by her family to turn her nose up at a marriage proposal from a Duke. Anti-Catholic sentiment had crystalized into a truism about religious orders based upon concepts of chastity, expressed by Duke Theseus in *A Midsummer Night's Dream*, when he explains to Hermia what will happen if she rejects her father's choice of husband:

> Either to die the death, or to abjure
> For ever the society of men.
> Therefore fair Hermia question your desires,
> Know of your youth, examine well your blood,
> Whether (if you yield not to your father's choice)
> You can endure the livery of a Nun,
> For aye to be in shady Cloister mewed,
> To live a barren sister all your life,
> Chanting faint hymns to the cold fruitless Moon,
> Thrice-blessed they that master so their blood,
> To undergo such maiden pilgrimage,
> But earthlier happy is the Rose distilled,
> Than that which withering on the virgin thorn,
> Grows, lives, and dies, in single blessedness. [1.1.65]

Isabella is just such a thrice-blessed young woman. She has a profound spiritual faith. She has the courage required to endure the cloistered life. She has strength of will to master her own blood. But when the Duke offers marriage, the far more natural option of happiness in a blessed union would be the expected and appropriate choice.

Shakespeare was perfectly adept at scripting his onstage company from within the text of the play, as when he dictates facial expressions:

Kate: Fie, fie, unknit that threatening unkind brow,
    And dart not scornful glances from those eyes. [*Shrew* 5.2.136]

or nonverbal vocalizings:

Claudius: There's matter in these sights.
    These profound heaves
    You must translate; 'Tis fit we understand them. [*Hamlet* 4.1.1]

and even the waterworks:

Richard: Aumere, thou weep'st (my tender-hearted Cousin). [*RII* 3.3.160]

Imogen paints an entire scene for the silent Pisano:

> What is in thy mind,
> That makes thee stare thus? Wherefore breaks that sigh
> From th'inward of thee? One, but painted thus
> Would be interpreted a thing perplexed
> Beyond self-explication. Put thy self
> Into a havior of less fear, ere wildness
> Vanquish my staider Senses. What's the matter?
> Why tender'st thou that Paper to me, with
> A look untender? If't be Summer News
> Smile to't before: if Winterly, thou need'st
> But keep that countenance still. [*Cymbeline* 3.4.4]

Given both the intrusions of Shakespeare's stage directions and the facility of the actor to convey silently these specific feelings, it is even more noteworthy when there are no clues offered for a lengthy silence of a major character at a significant moment.

The most commonly noted gesture is kneeling, an action of immense personal significance, suggested by Suffolk's vow, "No, rather let my head / Stoop to the block, than these knees bow to any, / Save to the God of heaven and to my king" [*2HVI* 4.1.124], or Bolingbroke's instructions:

> Noble Lord,
> Go to the rude Ribs of that ancient Castle,
> Through Brazen Trumpet send the breath of Parle
> Into his ruined Ears, and thus deliver:
> Henry Bolingbroke upon his knees doth kiss
> King Richard's hand, and sends allegiance
> And true faith of heart to his most Royal Person: hither come
> Even at his feet, to lay my Arms and Power,
> Provided, that my Banishment repealed
> And Lands restored again, be freely granted:
> If not, I'll use th'advantage of my Power,
> And lay the Summers dust with showers of blood,
> Rained from the wounds of slaughtered Englishmen;
> The which, how far off from the mind of Bolingbroke
> It is, such Crimson Tempest should bedrench
> The fresh green Lap of fair King Richards Land,
> My stooping duty tenderly shall show. [*RII* 3.3.31]

When Bolingbroke is finally before Richard, however, the promised kneeling does not take place, as Richard notes:

> We are amazed, and thus long have we stood
> To watch the fearful bending of thy knee,
> Because we thought our self thy lawful King:

And if we be, how dare thy joints forget
To pay their aweful duty to our presence? [3.3.72]

All of this significance is in play when Mariana says to Isabella "Lend me your knees?" [5.1.431] having sculpted Isabella's stage movement in the process with her plea, "Sweet Isabel, do yet but kneel by me, / Hold up your hands, say nothing: I'll speak all." Not even this much assistance is provided for the staging of Isabella's final silence.

In the final moments of *Measure for Measure*, Shakespeare clues the actor towards what is not being said, with such overt phrases as "but fitter time for that." Once attuned to the possibility, we can begin to sense all that the Duke could, but chooses not to say, for example when he instructs Angelo to forgive the Provost for the trick of the switched heads, and then says, "The offense pardons itself." What other words might he have used instead of "offense"? After all, it was a desperate trick undertaken by the Duke to save Claudio. The Provost was forced into it, and really it was all the Duke's doing; he can scarcely offend against his own deputy who is being stopped from committing a great offense by executing Claudio. What other word might have replaced "pardon"? Or rather, having said "pardon," how might the Duke have continued, drawing attention to the interconnectedness of the various pardons that should have been extended by Angelo, and now are being extended by the Duke?

It is in the silent reaction of the onstage listeners that the possible but unspoken words are given shape. Angelo reacts to the words and also to the silent alternatives, even if the actor playing the Duke does not signal the ironic subtext with his intonation. But what is being left unsaid by the Duke when he speaks to Isabella? In some productions, knowing that this exchange is approaching, the actors have laid in a pattern of silent communication that charts a growing attraction between the novitiate and the holy father. Such emotions would be forbidden if Isabella felt them for a priest, but might explode into consciousness when the Duke's disguise is revealed. She's already half in love with him, he turns out to have saved her brother, and then he proposes. I think her eyes alone would give him all that he needs to know in order to ask for her hand and lead her off as his publicly proclaimed bride.

In other productions, having spotted Isabella's deafening silence in response to not one, but two proposals of marriage, and knowing that manipulation tends to be more enjoyable for the manipulator than the manipulated, the actress playing Isabella might assiduously avoid any sighting of the Duke's expressed admiration prior to the last scene, creating a situation in which the first proposal is a complete surprise. How inappropriate, how untimely a comment her silence might suggest, prompting, "but time enough for that" as a crafty retreat from what is clearly an unwelcome topic. How hard is the Duke working, then, during his final maneuverings, in order to transform that response from a negative to a positive, and does he succeed? Is Isabella impressed by his care in redeeming all of the participants in the fiasco of Angelo's rule, or is she ever-mindful that the Duke himself caused the entire mess by taking off, by leaving Angelo in charge, and then by coming back in disguise to muck around with people's minds still more? Is she horrified to hear that, in his disguise as a holy father, he usurped a priest's office and heard Mariana's confession? Or does that remind her that, as her Duke, he is the spiritual father of all of her people and has only their, and her, good at heart?

The possibilities for reaction are still open; all that a careful reading of the text has accomplished is the subtle shaping of the reactions in preparation for linking them with the spoken words as demanded by text.

HUMORS

> The humour rises: it is good: humour me the angels.
>
> Nym [*Wives* 1.3.56]

Although modern psychological theory is invaluable in the work of an actor, there is a real need to supplement the approach of naturalistic acting with some consideration of the way Elizabethans viewed what we, not they, might term psychology. An exploration of humor theory opens up just such an alternative, to be blended with our intuitive or conscious use of the theories of human behavior that we use to make sense of ourselves in today's world.

Shakespeare and his contemporaries make direct reference to the humors in their plays, and present characters that illustrate the different personality types associated with each of the four humors, and so we know that this theory, which dates back to the ancient Greeks and might more truly be deemed a medieval medical practice, had not yet been eradicated from popular thought as medical historians might have us believe. This is comparable to the popularity of certain of the better known of Sigmund Freud's theories (often taken out of context and applied bluntly and superficially) even though many philosophers and psychologists largely disregard Freud these days. This does not stop the general public, however, from making use of these theories and gaining a real sense of security from them.

First, a quick introduction to the four humors.

Black bile, also known as melancholy, is not just the sort of general depression that we associate with the medical condition of *melancholia*. For the Elizabethans, the dark bile was a necessary ingredient of the rational man. It was black bile that informed the complex reasoning processes of the brain, that allowed for intellectual considerations and the careful weighing of moral complexities. Only when experienced in excess, as a result of lack of proper exercise, excessive academic activities, or lovesickness, did this bodily fluid become dangerous to the mental and physical health of the individual. This is what so worries Romeo's father, who describes the symptoms of his son's condition:

> Many a morning hath he there been seen,
> With tears augmenting the fresh morning dew,
> Adding to clouds, more clouds with his deep sighs,
> But all so soon as the all-cheering Sun,
> Should in the furthest East begin to draw
> The shady Curtains from Auroras bed,
> Away from the light steals home my heavy Son,
> And private in his Chamber pens himself,
> Shuts up his windows, locks far day-light out,
> And makes himself an artificial night:
> Black and portentous must this humour prove,
> Unless good counsel may the cause remove. [R&J 1.1.131]

Yellow bile, or choler, provided all of the impetus to action required of daily life. It fueled adventure and commerce, the quest for personal or public adoration, and the desire to complete ones allotted tasks efficiently and well. It was as admirable as the intellectual capacity of the darker bile, but most individuals had a predominance of one or the other, so England was divided into the great doers and the great thinkers, the great writers and the great actors. Only rarely did individuals excel in both.

When experienced in excess, an otherwise merely active person could become choleric: aggressive, impatient, given to great rages, and even, in extreme cases, destructive behavior. Choleric individuals like Hotspur were valiant soldiers in a king's fight, but too easily took umbrage and became implacable enemies, until their fearsome capacity for destruction ended in death. Cassius, who is being mocked by Brutus in the following quotation, is another choleric individual:

> Go show your Slaves how Choleric you are,
> And make your Bondmen tremble. Must I budge?
> Must I observe you? Must I stand and crouch
> Under your Testy Humour? By the Gods,
> You shall digest the Venom of your Spleen
> Though it do Split you. For, from this day forth,
> I'll use you for my Mirth, yea for my Laughter
> When you are Waspish. [JC 4.3.143]

Later in the scene he identifies his particular humor as something given to him by his mother, suggesting that the tendency towards excess of a particular humor could be observed as a family trait.

Phlegm is a familiar term to everyone during cold season, and this milky white substance was felt by the Elizabethans to affect personality as powerfully

as the other three humors. An individual with a tendency towards the phlegmatic would not be easily ruffled, would have a capacity for stillness and
silence, would be able to calm the choleric and temper the excesses of the
sanguine, while providing a profound and resonating spiritual element to the
most rational melancholic. However, in excess the phlegm turned the body
cold, cutting off all human interaction, resulting in extreme cases in the silence
of the insane. The potion the friar offers Juliet will result in such an excess of
phelgm that she will appear dead to her family.

> Take thou this Vial being then in bed,
> And this distilled liquor drink thou off,
> When presently through all thy veins shall run,
> A cold and drowsy humour: for no pulse
> Shall keep his native progress, but surcease:
> No warmth, no breath shall testify thou livest,
> The Roses in thy lips and cheeks shall fade
> To many ashes, thy eyes windows fall
> Like death when he shut up the day of life. [*R&J* 4.1.93]

Fortunately, in her case the natural and healthy balance of humors will be
restored.

Blood was felt by the Elizabethans to have an effect on personality just as
the two biles did, and anyone with a preponderance of blood was said to have
a sanguine temperament, a term still in use today. The warmth of blood resulted in a corresponding warmth of personality, making the sanguine person
friendly, outgoing, and pleasure-loving. In excess, blood could play havoc with
one's self-control, because the natural result was a correspondingly excessive
love of the pleasures of the flesh. Our friend Falstaff, whose humors Prince
Hal knows so well, is chastised for just such indulgences: "Thou art so fat-
witted with drinking of old Sack, and unbuttoning thee after Supper, and sleeping upon Benches in the afternoon that thou hast forgotten to demand that
truly, which thou wouldst truly know" [*1HIV* 1.2.2]. Later, when alone, Hal
says of his companion, "I know you all, and will a-while uphold / The unyoked
humour of your idleness" [*1HIV* 1.2.195].

In the Elizabethan cosmology, the four humors matched up with the four
elements. Black bile shared earth's dry cold, yellow bile shared fire's dry
warmth, blood shared the warm moisture of the air, and phlegm shared water's
cold moisture. We can find these elemental references in the imagery associated
with melancholy, choleric, sanguine, and phlegmatic characters: Hamlet is dry,
lacking in warmth, heavy, clodish; Hotspur is fiery; Falstaff is sweaty; and
"still waters run deep" is an apt description of the phlegmatic Ophelia and
Virgilia.

The concept of the four humors helped the medical profession in diagnosis
and treatment of conditions resulting from excess of one of the humors. The

standard battle plan was to reduce the humor directly or indirectly. Bloodletting would relieve the symptoms of high blood pressure; an expectorant would help the patient cough out the phlegm, but how to access the two biles? The indirect method was to give the patient such an excess of the offending humor that the body itself accomplished the purge, or the patient died in the attempt. Horrible concoctions were swallowed to induce purging: caster oil and ipecac are still used today.

The mental state of any individual mirrored the physical state. Therefore, the cure for someone excessively melancholic, choleric, phlegmatic, or sanguine in mind would be to encounter experiences of such extreme emotional impact that the excessive humor is driven out. When Hamlet returns to Denmark after his remarkable adventures at sea, we can sense that he is changed. Whatever excessive dark humor had dominated his persona in the first three acts has been replaced by a much healthier balance of the four humors. He is still capable of the great rational insights engendered by black bile, but this is nicely balanced by the phlegmatic spiritual stillness of "the readiness is all." He is better able to enjoy the warmth of friendship and physical exercise, and when threatened his choler rises and he avenges himself on his enemies.

Hotspur, the great choleric character, is not so fortunate. The repeated applications of excessive warfare, which might cause his persona to reach a saturation requiring purging, kills the patient before the body can affect the cure. Falstaff, too, shows no sign of achieving a purge when Hal administers the medicinal purge of mockery following the Gadshill robbery. Instead, Falstaff seems to absorb the laughter into his all-consuming capacity for personal pleasure. It requires Hal's rejection of Falstaff to lance this veins and release the excessive blood, but the patient shrivels and dies shortly after.

Juliet's close encounter with a phlegmatic death is avoided because the potion-induced excess is purged naturally by her body, and because she herself is not a phlegmatic character. Ophelia, however, is more easily identified as this personality type, with her gentle obedience, her spiritual aura, and the toppling into madness that results from the horrors she must endure. Fittingly, her death is by drowning, and she returns to the element to which she is most attached. As Gertrude tells us, she showed no distress but floated for a time "like a creature Native, and indued / Unto that Element" [4.7.179], and her brother Laertes tries to hold back his tears by saying, "Too much of water hast thou poor Ophelia, / And therefore I forbid my tears" [4.7.185].

One of the most striking examples of a phlegmatic character is the wife of the dynamic, choleric Coriolanus. Virgilia is greeted by her husband as "My gracious silence" [2.1.175], as she weeps at his safe return from the wars. The only other information we have about her is that she refuses all invitations to socialize while her husband is at war. She is a character only thinly sketched, but unless we understand what she is to Coriolanus, we cannot understand the title character. She is easily forgotten by scholars, who tend to write at length about her mother-in-law, the powerful and vocal Volumnia. But on stage her silent presence can have a potency that would justify Coriolanus greeting her, as the tragic action nears its climax, with a kiss "Long as my Exile, sweet as my Revenge!" [5.3.45] and a promise that his lips have touched none but hers since they parted.

Virgilia is clearly Coriolanus's still water, whe'rein he drinks deep and finds respite from the heat of his choleric temper. His mother provides the rational insights of black bile, and his dear friend Meninius the sanguine warmth of the blood. With Virgilia's phlegmatic temperament, Coriolanus can achieve balance. He must reject each of them, first Meninius, then his wife and mother. But the power of his mother's intellect, coupled with the weeping presence of his wife, puts out his fire and transforms him. He does not become more rational; he becomes more phlegmatic. He silently takes her hand, and his eyes "sweat compassion" [5.3.196], in other words, he weeps. He has finally partaken of sufficient of his beloved wife's humor to mute the fire of his choler. He might be a more well-balanced human being, but he is easy victim for his choleric mirror: Aufidius, who engineers his death.

The Elizabethans were able to use the concept of humors to create striking characterizations; at the same time, the presence of all four humors in any individual allowed for an understanding of the complexity of personality. A choleric individual like Coriolanus or Laertes could be overcome with an excess of the phlegmatic humor, momentarily stilling them to weeping and inaction. The rational, cool, articulate Berowne could be felled by a rebellion of the blood, and fall desperately into a passion for the witty, mocking Rosaline. Beatrice and Benedick are sure their blood is completely cooled, as suggested by this exchange:

Benedick: But it is certain I am loved of all Ladies, only you excepted: and I would I could find in my heart that I had not a hard heart, for truly I love none.

Beatrice: A dear happiness to women, they would else have been troubled with a pernicious Suitor, I thank God and my cold blood, I am of your humour for that, I had rather hear my Dog bark at a Crow, than a man swear he loves me. [*Much Ado* 1.1.124]

These two are most at home with in the merry war of wits that makes use of the rational black bile and the fiery yellow bile. But their blood will be warmed up by the trick played on them by their friends, as they discover in their declaration of mutual love. There is no denying the warmth of this exchange, as when Beatrice finally confesses, "I love you with so much of my heart, that none is left to protest," in response to Benedick's "I do love nothing in the world so well as you," but their wit and fire are not diminished. Benedick, in his new role as lover and beloved, now says, "Come, bid me do any thing for thee," to which Beatrice responds, "Kill Claudio" [4.1.287]. The warmth of her choleric temper equals that of her newly heated blood, though she can still weep phlegmatically for her wronged cousin and use all of her rational wit to argue her case. In this scene, we see the fully humored Beatrice in all of her complexity.

An awareness of humors need not, therefore, limit an actor's work on a role to a simplistic, stereotypical, superficial characterization. Quite the opposite: the presence of all four humors explains the apparent contradictions, the transformations, the complexity of the well-developed roles like Beatrice, and clarifies and enriches our understanding of the thinly sketched supporting roles. Virgilia might be primarily a phlegmatic character, but she need not be denied a flash of each of the other four humors. A choleric flash of anger, a sanguine element of sexuality, and sufficient black bile to be aware of the complexities of her husband's character can all be woven into the performance.

The clarity afforded by the humours can save actors from the trap of solving the puzzles of the character through application of complex twentieth-century psychological theory. In order to explain the way someone acts in the play, a dense fabrication of extraneous attitudes, events, relationships, and mental activities needs to be added to the mix, distracting the actor from what is already available in the actions and imagery embodied in the language. Ultimately, it doesn't matter if Virgilia had a cold and distant father, and so was drawn to Coriolanus as much to hurt her father as to win herself a contrasting relationship. It doesn't matter if she used to be as sexy as Valeria or as vocal as Volumnia and became so quiet and weeping only after being abused by her short-tempered husband. These stories, though they might explain her words and deeds to a psychiatrist, can seriously diminish the actor's capacity to bring to life the clarity and purity of the character written by Shakespeare.

An actor who has been trained to develop a character biography, as a means by which the character is made real for the actor and audience, might find the use of humors analysis a dissatisfying alternative. There is no reason why the two could not be combined, provided the humors were used as the sieve through which the storymaking was pressed.

The Humors Game

As an introduction to the particular attributes of the sieve that I propose, we can have some fun with the four humors as four equal components of the persona. This is a well-known theatre game for which you need eight participants; if you are working alone perhaps the following description will give you an idea of the insights to be gained.

Borrowing from psychomachia, the use of actors to embody attributes of the central character, four people will play each of the two participants in the scene. Perhaps you have seen a television commercial featuring a good angel and a tempting devil on the shoulders of the indecisive hero. With the help of technology, the same actor plays all three roles. In our bare-stage improvisation, we will have an actor for each of Melancholy (Black Bile), Choler

(Yellow Bile), Blood, and Phlegm. This represents one character in the two-person scene; the other four create the second character.

The two Phlegm actors each sit on a chair, facing each other with knees about two feet apart. The Melancholy actors for each character stand behind the two chairs, and represent the thoughts going on in the brain of the individual. The Blood actors crouch on the left side and the Choler actors on the right of the two characters.

The Phlegm actors are the only people physically present in the scene. In other words, the other team must pretend not to see or hear what the other Melancholy, Blood, or Sanguine are up to during the improvisation. The essential attribute contributed by the Phlegm actors is stillness, readiness to act, and the receiving of whatever comes to them during the scene. They read body language, mark facial expressions, and of course take in the content and tone of whatever is said. They initiate no action, however, unless prompted by one of their other internal humors.

The Melancholy actors are responsible for voicing all of the rational considerations that emerge during the improvisation. It is imperative that these two remain cool and calm, and entirely unemotional. Their job is to weigh the pros and cons, consider moral questions, speculate about the significance of new information, and propose the most rational course of action, given all of the available information and as a result of having weighed all of the considerations.

At times, it won't be easy for the Melancholy actors to remain objective, because on either side the Choler and Blood actors will be presenting their unique perspectives on the situation. Blood's point of view is simple: if something is pleasurable, then it is good; if it is painful, then it is bad. In considering a course of action, Blood will give voice to worries about the pain that might be experienced as a result, and just as eagerly anticipates the pleasure that might be in store if the action is undertaken. Choler is equally single-minded: this humor is concerned entirely with doing things and doing them now. Whatever is wanted, is wanted intensely, thanks to Choler's urging. "Do it, do it right now!" and "Stop what you're doing right now!" are Choler's favorite lines.

Here is a specific situation that always works well. In one chair we have Person A, in the other Person B, represented by the two Phlegm actors, with the three other members of each team behind and on either side. The scenario combines strong sexual attraction with some very good reasons not to act upon the attraction. Let's imagine that the given circumstances include the fact that they are in Person A's living room with parents or lover expected back in a few hours, and that Person B has a long-term relationship with someone who is temporarily out of town. Person A must decide whether to invite Person B to stay for another drink, and B must decide whether to accept the invitation. The equal balance of longing and uncertainty, desire and fear, and reasons to resist alongside reasons to proceed provide Melancholy, Blood, and Choler with plenty of raw material, and the long pauses between speaking, the desperate reading of unclear signals, and the inner turmoil gives the Phlegm actors an equal challenge.

The Humors in the Text

After everyone has had a go at all four humors, you can bring your firsthand experience of the inner balance of humors to a piece of text. Work as a team of four, with one actor anchoring the team by being the speaker of the words. You will also require a yellow, pink, and blue highlighter. Chances are that one of the other three humors will provide the obvious dominant tone to the passage. We will play with three: Kate the shrew for yellow choleric, Orsino the love-sick duke for sanguine pink, and cool blue rational Portia for black bile.

There is no correct highlighting. Whichever actor is entrusted with the responsibility for that humor tries to connect with the words using the mind-set of that humor, and intuitively highlights whatever seems to connect most strikingly as representative of the humor. This is one of those exercises that offers best results if you work quickly at this stage, having taken your time to get inside the humor in previous exercises.

Here are each of the three speeches as they might appear marked up with the dominant highlighter, indicated by the capitalized, italicized, and boldfaced text.

Kate's choler (in all caps):

> No SHAME but mine, I MUST FORSOOTH BE FORCED
> To give my hand OPPOSED AGAINST my heart
> UNTO A MAD-BRAIN RUDESBY, FULL OF SPLEEN,
> Who wooed in HASTE, and means to wed at leisure:
> I TOLD YOU I, he was a FRANTIC fool,
> Hiding his BITTER JESTS in BLUNT BEHAVIOR,
> And to be noted for a merry man;
> He'll woo a thousand, point the day of marriage,
> Make feasts, invite friends, and proclaim the banns,
> YET NEVER MEANS TO WED where he hath wooed:
> NOW MUST THE WORLD POINT AT poor Katharine,
> AND SAY, LO, THERE IS MAD PETRUCHIO'S WIFE
> If it would please him come and marry her. [*Shrew* 3.2.8]

Orsino's Sanguine humor (in italics):

> *If Music be the food of love*, play on,
> *Give me excess* of it: that surfeiting,
> The *appetite* may sicken, and so die.
> *That strain again*, it had a dying fall:

O, it came o'er my ear, like the sweet sound
That breathes upon a bank of Violets;
Stealing, and giving Odour. Enough, no more,
'Tis not so *sweet* now, as it was before.
O spirit of *Love*, how *quick and fresh* art thou,
That notwithstanding thy *capacity,*
Receiveth as the Sea. Nought enters there,
Of what validity, and pitch soe'er,
But falls into abatement, and low price
Even in a minute; *so full of shapes is fancy,*
That it alone, is *high fantastical.* [*12th Night* 1.1.1]

Portia's rational black bile (in bold):

The **quality** of mercy **is not** strained,
It droppeth as the gentle rain from heaven
Upon the place beneath: it is **twice** blest,
It blesseth **him that gives, and him that takes**,
'Tis **mightiest in the mightiest**, it becomes
The throned Monarch **better than** his Crown.
His Scepter **shows** the force of temporal power,
The attribute to awe and Majesty,
Wherein doth sit the dread and fear of Kings:
But mercy is **above** this sceptred sway,
It is enthroned in the hearts of Kings,
It is an attribute to God himself;
And earthly power **doth then shew likest Gods**
When mercy seasons **Justice. Therefore** Jew,
Though Justice be thy plea, consider this,
That in the course of Justice, none of us
Should see salvation: we do pray for mercy,
And that same prayer, doth teach us all to render
The deeds of mercy. **I have spoke thus much**
To mitigate the justice of thy plea:
Which if thou follow, this strict court of Venice
Must needs give sentence gainst the Merchant there. [*Merchant* 4.1.184]

Now it is time for the second member of the team to highlight the speech. Although it is possible to double up colors, because more than one humor can be at work in connection with a word or a phrase, in preliminary explorations of humors it is better to keep them separate. So the contrasting secondary humors need to look closely at whichever words are left. The following are the secondary colors marked on our three speeches.

   Kate's choler (in all caps) and her sanguine (in italics), plus her black bile (in bold):

No SHAME **but mine**, I MUST FORSOOTH BE FORCED
To *give my hand* OPPOSED AGAINST *my heart*
UNTO A MAD-BRAIN RUDESBY, FULL OF SPLEEN,
Who wooed in HASTE, **and means to** *wed at leisure*:
I TOLD YOU I, he was a FRANTIC **fool**,
Hiding his BITTER JESTS in BLUNT BEHAVIOR,
And to be noted for *a merry man*;
He'll *woo* a **thousand**, point the *day of marriage*,
Make feasts, invite friends, and **proclaim the banns**,
YET NEVER MEANS TO WED where *he hath wooed*:
NOW MUST THE WORLD POINT AT *poor Katharine*,
AND SAY, LO, THERE IS MAD PETRUCHIO'S WIFE
If it would *please him come and marry her*.

Orsino's sanguine humor (in italics) and his black bile (in bold), plus his choleric (in all caps):

If Music be the food of Love, PLAY ON,
Give me excess of it: **that surfeiting**,
The *appetite* **may sicken, and so die**.
That strain again, **it had a dying fall**:
O, it came o'er my ear, like the sweet sound
That breathes upon a bank of Violets;
Stealing, and giving odour. ENOUGH, NO MORE,
'Tis not so *sweet* **now, as it was before**.
O spirit of *Love*, how *quick and fresh* art thou,
That notwithstanding thy *capacity*,
Receiveth as the sea. **Nought enters there**,
OF WHAT VALIDITY, AND PITCH SOE'ER,
But falls into abatement, and low price
Even in a minute; *so full of shapes is fancy*,
That it alone, is *high fantastical*.

Portia's black bile (in bold) and her sanguine (in italics), plus her choleric (in all caps):

The **quality** of *mercy* **is not** STRAINed,
It droppeth *as the gentle rain from heaven*
Upon the place beneath. It is **twice** *blest*,
It *blesseth* **him that gives, and him that takes**,
'Tis **mightiest in the mightiest, it becomes**
The THRONED MONARCH **better than** his CROWN.
His Scepter **shows** THE FORCE OF TEMPORAL POWER,
The attribute to awe and Majesty,
Wherein doth sit THE DREAD AND FEAR OF KINGS:
But *mercy* is **above** THIS SCEPTRED SWAY,
It is enthroned in *the hearts of Kings*,

It is an attribute to God himself;
And EARTHLY POWER **doth then shew likest Gods**
When mercy *seasons* **Justice. Therefore** JEW,
Though Justice be thy plea, consider this,
That in the course of Justice, none of us
Should see salvation: we do pray for *mercy,*
And that same prayer, doth teach us all to render
The deeds of mercy. **I have spoke thus much**
To mitigate the justice of thy plea:
Which if thou follow, THIS STRICT COURT OF VENICE
Must needs give sentence 'GAINST *the Merchant there.*

If nothing else, this exercise will assist you in combatting any tendency you might have to play the speech with just one tone. Yes, Kate is very angry and a fiery, choleric personality. But she is not unaware of the nature of pleasure and pain, as she reveals in the references to wooing, wedding, feasting with friends, and what it means to give one's hand and heart. The more that the sanguine humor can be tapped in those phrases, the more striking will be her anger and pain. And of course she is still an intelligent woman, able to see the pattern at work in what she takes to be Petruchio's devilish strategy.

Although Orsino is much given to wallowing in the sensations of music and love, he is also puzzling through an intellectual concept, and giving orders to his court, so that the rational and choleric are threaded through the speech, giving the sanguine element its shape.

Portia's clear and level-headed presentation of the logic of mercy is such a striking speech because the rational argument is shot through with the warmth of the sanguine and the power of the choleric. The concept of God's grace can be an intellectual one, but her first image, comparing mercy to the gentle rain, marks all subsequent references to mercy as being potentially connected with the sanguine humor. The contrasting colors the team has found in this speech, as with the others, creates a complex emotional event suggesting a personality rather than simply a simplistic character type of dramatic function.

If you are able to work in teams of four, you can each take a turn playing the role of the phlegmatic speaker, with the other three being responsible for tracing the other three humours in the speech. When it is the phlegmatic's turn to deliver the speech, try directing the highlighted word in the direction of the team mate who selected them. If the highlighters maintain a strong physical and emotional presence indicative of each of the humors, the speaker will see and feel reflected back the tone or attitude suggested by the highlighted words.

This is not going to be a successful performance strategy, but the discoveries made in this exploration will help you to make interesting performance choices, and your understanding of the complexity of the speaker and the interweaving of emotions in the speech will serve you well in creating dynamic and original performances.

Not everyone is able to work with teams of actors, and so for those working alone, let us go together through a personal discovery of one speech, to see what can be discovered just from the words on the page. Here is Angelo, whom we discover attempting to pray as he awaits the return of the young woman he he has propositioned. We can expect that at least two of the humors are going to be in fierce contention inside his head and heart. He has been described to us as learned, and a cold fish, so we can safely assume that he is familiar with the effects of black bile. But Isabella has awakened in him a terrible passion, as if his blood is in revolt against his rational self.

We'll start by looking for words and phrases that embody the essence of the melancholy humor's rationality. Thinking, speaking, inventing, studying, reading, and the very gravity in which Angelo takes pride all leap out as being central to his rational being.

Because the logical working out of the essential problem is the function of the rational intellect, we can also highlight the most intellectual and generalized presentation of Angelo's conundrum: the question that begins, "How often dost thou."

> When I would pray and **think**, I **think**, and pray
> To several subjects: heaven hath my empty **words**,
> Whilst my **Invention**, hearing not my Tongue,
> Anchors on Isabel: heaven in my mouth,
> As if I did but only chew his name,
> And in my heart the strong and swelling evil
> Of my conception: the state whereon I **studied**
> Is like a good thing, being often **read**
> Grown feared, and tedious: yea, **my Gravity**
> Wherein (let no man hear me) I take pride,
> Could I, with boot, change for an idle plume
> Which the air beats for vain: oh place, oh form,
> **How often dost thou with thy case, thy habit**
> **Wrench awe from fools, and tie the wiser souls**
> **To thy false seeming** Blood, thou art blood,
> Let's write good Angel on the Devils horn
> 'Tis not the Devils Crest. [*Measure* 2.4.1]

At this point, we don't know quite what to do with the entire concept of prayer. On the one hand, we can imagine that it is Angelo's rational self that is at work when he prays—usually. For now, let's leave this humor and see what transpires when we zoom in on the obvious choices for the sanguine humor: anything associate with the sensual pleasures.

> When I would pray, and **think**, I **think**, and pray
> To several subjects: heaven hath my empty **words**,
> Whilst my **Invention**, hearing not my *Tongue*,

Anchors on *Isabel*: heaven in my *mouth*,
As if I did but only *chew* his name,
And in my *heart* the strong and *swelling* evil
Of my *conception*: the state whereon I **studied**
Is like a good thing, being often **read**
Grown feared, and tedious: yea, **my Gravity**
Wherein (let no man hear me) I take *pride*,
Could I, with boot, change for *an idle plume*
Which the air beats for vain: oh place, oh form,
How often dost thou with thy case, thy habit
Wrench awe from fools, and tie the wiser souls
To thy false seeming? *Blood*, thou art *blood*,
Let's write good Angel on the Devils *horn*
'Tis not the Devils Crest.

Although tongue and mouth can be words associated with the intellectual activity of the rational humor, here we can see that they can also serve the needs of the sensual humor, connected with chewing (eating) and the sexual activity that might cause the swelling of the male member and the conception of new life within the female body. The idle plume beaten in the air is another double entendre for self-indulgent sensuality; all of these images culminate in the double use of the word "blood": as he names the humor, Angelo acknowledges how it has taken over his internal emotional state.

Now let us see if we can find elements of the choleric in this man who seems never to lose his temper.

When I would pray, and **think**, I **think**, and pray
To several subjects: heaven hath my empty **words**,
Whilst my **Invention**, hearing not my *Tongue*,
Anchors on *Isabel*: heaven in my *mouth*,
As if I did but only *chew* his name,
And in my *heart* the STRONG and *swelling* EVIL
Of my *conception*: the state whereon I **studied**
Is like a good thing, being often **read**
Grown FEARed, and tedious: yea, **my Gravity**
Wherein (let no man hear me) I take *pride*,
Could I, with boot, change for *an idle plume*
Which the air beats for vain: oh place, oh form,
How often dost thou with thy case, thy habit
Wrench awe from fools, and tie the wiser souls
To thy false seeming? *Blood*, thou art *blood*,
Let's write good Angel on the DEVILS *horn*
'Tis not the DEVILS Crest.

As you can see, all I can find at this point in my analysis is the fear associated with the strong evil of the devil. These are obvious opportunities for the fiery power of the choleric to be revealed. But if we expand our consideration of this particular humor to include the intense desire to accomplish an action, we can add to the choleric highlighting all of the words that encompass Angelo's striving to achieve his contradictory goals.

> WHEN I WOULD PRAY, and **think**, I **think**, and pray
> To several subjects: heaven hath my empty **words**,
> Whilst my **Invention**, hearing not my *Tongue*,
> ANCHORS on *Isabel*: heaven in my *mouth*,
> As if I did but only *chew* his name,
> And in my *heart* the STRONG and *swelling* EVIL
> Of my *conception*: THE STATE WHEREON I **studied**
> Is like a good thing, being often **read**
> Grown FEAR Red, and tedious: yea, **my Gravity**
> Wherein (let no man hear me) I take *pride*,
> Could I, with boot, change for *an idle plume*
> *Which the air beats for vain*: oh place, oh form,
> **How often dost thou with thy case, thy habit**
> **Wrench awe from fools, and tie the wider souls**
> **To thy false seeming**? *Blood*, thou art *blood*,
> LET'S WRITE GOOD ANGEL ON THE DEVILS *horn*
> 'Tis not the DEVILS Crest.

Just a few bits of this speech now remain out of focus. What is happening during "oh place, oh form" and "let no man hear me"? What do we do with the ideas of "empty," "a good thing," and "tedious"?

Because I know that there is no correct interpretation, that any choice is better than no choice, in this exploration of the complexity of the text, I am going to elect to connect the first two with the driving force of the choleric, and the second group with the sensual and pain-avoiding blood. The result is a speech that looks like this:

> WHEN I WOULD PRAY, and **think**, I **think**, and pray
> To several subjects: heaven hath my empty **words**,
> Whilst my **Invention**, hearing not my *Tongue*,
> ANCHORS on *Isabel*: heaven in my *mouth*,
> As if I did but only *chew* his name,
> And in my *heart* the STRONG and *swelling* EVIL
> Of my *conception: THE STATE WHEREON* I **studied**
> Is like *a good thing*, being often **read**
> Grown FEARed, and *tedious*: yea, **my gravity**
> Wherein LET NO MAN HEAR ME, I take *pride*,
> COULD I, WITH BOOT, CHANGE for *an idle plume*
> *Which the air beats for vain*. OH PLACE, OH FORM,
> **How often dost thou with thy case, thy habit**
> **Wrench awe from fools, and tie the wiser souls**

> **To thy false seeming?** *Blood,* thou art *blood,*
> LET'S WRITE GOOD ANGEL ON THE DEVILS *horn*
> 'Tis not the DEVILS Crest.

Not every word is highlighted, and an argument could be made to claim much more for the rational black bile, as the speech is in large part about working out an intellectual puzzle. But I think our encounter with Angelo's torment is enhanced if we do not let him hide behind the facade of the unengaged thinker. Yes, that part of him is doing what it is accustomed to do, but the real engine of the scene comes from the other two humors, with the blood insisting on its power to deflect his purpose, sustained by his choler.

THE LIMITATIONS OF PSYCHOLOGICAL REALISM

> If this were played upon a stage now, I could condemn it as an improbable fiction.
>
>   Fabian [*12th Night* 3.4.126]

It is only natural that a modern actor would make use of the acting techniques that have served him well in his profession, even when cast in a role that was never intended to be brought to life under the dictates of psychological realism. Because the most effective connections between actors and audiences will always be achieved through the theatrical conventions that are shared by the parties on stage with the parties in the seats, modern actors must continue to develop and present credible and subtly detailed fictional creations.

This achievement, however, is just the beginning of what an actor might bring to life when acting a character in a play by Shakespeare. If she is willing to reach beyond the limitations of the observable, the believable, and the psychologically validated definitions of character into the great mysteries of the archetype, she will require acting techniques that facilitate more than the identification of given circumstances, objectives, and emotional memory. If she is interested in basing the development of her character upon an Elizabethan understanding of temperament, and configure the inner workings of this imagined person using the dynamic energy of the humors, then she will require an equally energetic and unencumbered approach to playing the character's actions and delivering the character's lines.

The best of psychology-based acting theory will be strengthened by the addition of spiritual or physical approaches; anything of your traditional method of working that falls apart when faced with the challenge is something that would be self-indulgent to cling to, simply on the grounds of familiarity.

Actors are not prolific in developing and codifying acting theory, and so most Shakespearean actors use trial and error to find their way into a new style of acting that suits modern productions of plays written so long ago. I have observed, in the variety of approaches, certain recurring attitudes and strategies. Most important is the willingness to risk a *size* of performance quite early in the rehearsal process. By launching into a heightened voice, movement, or emotional tone long before anyone is sure exactly what is going on and who these people really are, these actors jump over the tortured self-examination that fuels psychological realism. The situation and the characters come clear as the product of bold, irrational, striking, and dangerous strokes of the actors' creative intuition. In other words, these actors don't wait until things are clear before they crank up the volume. They would rather risk a big mistake in hopes of stumbling upon the sort of discovery that can only be made when they *don't* know what is going on yet.

Another recurring characteristic of this alternative approach is its inconsistency. These actors embrace paradox. They seek out contradictory attributes, extreme contrasts, and the unexplained. At all costs, they avoid settling upon any one tone, habitual gesture, or defining trait. If an effective delivery or move or attitude emerges, they almost immediately seek its opposite, or a strikingly different possibility, in the next speech or scene.

Another facet of a successful approach to Shakespeare's characters is what I would call, "keeping the door open." Because there has been so much written and said about every one of Shakespeare's major and even supporting characters, there is a real temptation to consider them "solved" or "knowable." If this dangerous inheritance from scholarship is combined with an attitude to personality that suggests that characters in plays are best understood and performed as if they were individuals pretty much like the actors who play them, then the actor approaching the role is all the more likely to conclude, after an early rehearsal or two, that she has all she needs at her fingertips to play the role effectively and truthfully. She has scholarly tradition as a guide, and her own personality as a resource. What more could there possibly be to discover in this often performed role?

It requires considerable strength of purpose to resist both of these traps. An actor must fight to keep the door to discovery open right through to the closing line of the final performance. The rich complexity of the plays, the unexpected durability of the Elizabethan theatrical conventions, and the density of possible interpretations and available strategies for character development all work together to provide a constant source of surprise, provided that the actor hasn't already decided that the character is entirely knowable.

When all of these efforts result in the effective performance of a great Shakespearean role, the rewards are self-evident. Only the actors who have risked much and tried anything and everything to tap into something more than the expected know the rewards of playing an incomplete, incredible, fragmented, unrealistic, and fictional creation that bears little resemblance to the characters of modern realism, but who thrives in Shakespeare's world of imagination and wonder.

Bibliography

Ashley, Leonard R.N. *Elizabethan Popular Culture*. Bowling Green, OH: Bowling Green State University Popular Press, 1988.

Aydelotte, Frank. *Elizabethan Rogues and Vagabonds*. New York: Barnes & Noble, 1967.

Barton, John. *Playing Shakespeare*. London: Methuen, 1984.

Berry, Cicely. *The Actor and His Text*. London: Harrap, 1987.

Berry, Ralph. *Shakespeare and Social Class*. Atlantic Highlands, NJ: Humanities Press International, 1988.

Billington, Sandra. *A Social History of the Fool*. Brighton, Sussex: Harvester Press, 1984.

Biswas, D.C. *Shakespeare in His Own Time*. Delhi: Macmillan, 1979.

Blake, N.F. *Shakespeare's Language: An Introduction*. London: Macmillan, 1983.

Booty, John E., ed. *The Book of Common Prayer, 1559: The Elizabethan Prayer Book* Charlottesville: University Press of Virginia, 1976.

Bradbrook, M.C. *Themes and Conventions of Elizabethan Tragedy*. Cambridge: Cambridge University Press, 1935.

Brine, Adrian, and Michael York. *A Shakespearean Actor Prepares*. Lyme, NH: Smith & Kraus, 2000.

Bryson, Anna. *From Courtesy to Civility: Changing Codes of Conduct in Early Modern England*. Oxford: Clarendon Press, 1998.

Burgess, Anthony. *Shakespeare*. Harmondsworth: Penguin Books, 1970.

Carroll, William C. *Fat King, Lean Beggar: Representations of Poverty in the Age of Shakespeare*. Ithaca, NY: Cornell University Press, 1996.

Cohen, Robert. *Acting in Shakespeare*. Mountain View, CA: Mayfield, 1991.

Collmann, Herbert Leonard. *Ballads & Broadsides: Chiefly of the Elizabethan Period*. New York: B. Franklin, 1971.

Cook, Ann Jennalie. *Making a Match: Courtship in Shakespeare and His Society*. Princeton, NJ: Princeton University Press, 1991.

Cressy, David. *Birth, Marriage, and Death: Ritual, Religion, and the Life-Cycle in Tudor and Stuart England*. Oxford: Oxford University Press, 1997.

Davis, Michael Justin. *The Landscape of William Shakespeare.* Exeter, Devon: Webb & Bower, 1987.

Daw, Kurt. *Acting Shakespeare and His Contemporaries.* Portsmouth, NH: Heinemann, 1998.

Evans, G. Blakemore, ed. *The Riverside Shakespeare.* Boston: Houghton Mifflin, 1974.

Fido, Martin. *Shakespeare.* Maplewood, NJ: Hammond, 1978.

Frye, Roland Mushat. *The Renaissance Hamlet: Issues and Responses in 1600.* Princeton, NJ: Princeton University Press, 1984.

Garber, Marjorie. *Coming of Age in Shakespeare.* London: Methuen, 1981.

Gurr, Andrew. *The Shakespearian Playing Companies.* Oxford: Clarendon Press, 1996.

Hankins, John Erskine. *Backgrounds of Shakespeare's Thought.* Hamden, CT: Archon Books, 1978.

Hawley, William M. *Shakespearean Tragedy and the Common Law: The Art of Punishment.* New York: Peter Lang, 1998.

Haynes, Alan. *Sex in Elizabethan England.* Stroud, Gloucestershire: Sutton, 1997.

Hibbert, Christopher. *The Court at Windsor: A Domestic History.* London: Allen Lane, 1977.

Hoeniger, F. David. *Medicine and Shakespeare in the English Renaissance.* Newark: University of Delaware Press, 1992.

Horizon Magazine, with Louis B. Wright, eds. *Shakespeare's England: A Horizon Caravel Book.* New York: American Heritage Pub. Co., 1964.

Hurstfield, Joel, and Alan G.R. Smith. *Elizabethan People: State and Society.* New York: St. Martin's Press, 1972.

Hussey, Maurice. *The World of Shakespeare and His Contemporaries: A Visual Approach.* London: Heinemann, 1971.

Hyland, Peter. *An Introduction to Shakespeare: The Dramatist in His Context.* New York: St. Martin's Press, 1996.

James I, King of England. *The English Bible, Translated out of the Original Tongues by the Commandment of King James the First, Anno 1611.* New York: AMS Press, 1967.

James, Max H. *Our House Is Hell: Shakespeare's Troubled Families.* Westport, CT: Greenwood Press, 1989.

Joseph, Sister Miriam. *Shakespeare's Use of the Arts of Language.* New York: Hafner, 1966.

Kastan, David Scott, ed. *A Companion to Shakespeare.* Oxford: Blackwell Publishers, 1999.

Kinney, Arthur F. *Elizabethan Backgrounds: Historical Documents of the Age of Elizabeth I.* Hamden, CT: Archon Books, 1975.

Komroff, Manuel, ed. *The Apocrypha; or, Non-canonical Books of the Bible: The King James Version.* New York, Tudor Publishing Company, 1936.

Laroque, François. *The Age of Shakespeare.* Translated by Alexandra Campbell. New York: Harry N. Abrams, 1993.

Laslett, Peter. *The World We Have Lost: Further Explored.* London: Methuen, 1983.

Laurence, Anne. *Women in England, 1500–1760: A Social History.* New York: St. Martin's Press, 1994.

Lester, G.A., ed. *Three Late Medieval Morality Plays.* London: A&C Black, 1990.

Linklater, Kristin. *Freeing Shakespeare's Voice: The Actor's Guide to Talking the Text.* New York: Theatre Communications Group, 1992.

MacDonald, Michael. *Mystical Bedlam: Madness, Anxiety, and Healing in Seventeenth-Century England.* Cambridge: Cambridge University Press, 1981.

McMurtry, Jo. *Understanding Shakespeare's England: A Companion for the American Reader.* Hamden, CT: Archon Books, 1989.

Miller, Allan. *A Passion for Acting: Exploring the Actor's Creative Processes.* New York: Back Stage Books, 1992.

Morrison, Malcolm. *Classical Acting.* Portsmouth, NH: Heinemann, 1996.

Moston, Doug. *The First Folio of Shakespeare* (1623). New York: Applause Books, 1995.

Norwich, John Julius. *Shakespeare's Kings.* London: Viking, 1999.

Orlin, Lena Cowen. *Elizabethan Households: An Anthology.* Washington, DC: Folger Shakespeare Library, 1995.

Papp, Joseph, and Elizabeth Kirkland. *Shakespeare Alive!* New York: Bantam, 1988.

Patterson, Annabel M. *Shakespeare and the Popular Voice.* Oxford: Basil Blackwell, 1989.

Perry, Maria. *The Word of a Prince: A Life of Elizabeth I from Contemporary Documents.* Woodbridge, England: Boydell Press, 1990.

Pinciss, Gerald M., and Roger Lockyer, eds. *Shakespeare's World.* New York: Continuum, 1989.

Prichard, R.E., ed. *Shakespeare's England: Life in Elizabethan and Jacobean Times.* Stroud, Cloucestershire: Sutton, 1999.

Rickey, Mary Ellen, and Thomas B. Stroup, eds. *Certaine Sermons or Homilies, Appointed to Be Read in Churches, in the Time of Queen Elizabeth I, 1547–1571* (1623). Gainesville: Scholars' Facsimiles & Reprints, 1968.

Ronberg, Gert. *A Way with Words: The Language of English Renaissance Literature.* London: E. Arnold, 1992.

Saccio, Peter. *Shakespeare's English Kings: History, Chronicle, and Drama.* Oxford: Oxford University Press, 1977.

Salgādo, Gāmini. *The Elizabethan Underworld.* London: J.M. Dent & Sons, 1977.

Schell, Edgar T., and J.D. Shuchter, eds. *English Morality Plays and Moral Interludes.* New York: Holt, Rinehart and Winston, 1969.

Schoenbaum, Samuel. *Shakespeare, the Globe, and the World.* New York: Oxford University Press, 1979.

Shahar, Shulamith. *Childhood in the Middle Ages.* London: Routledge, 1990.

Shaheen, Naseeb. *Biblical References in Shakespeare's Plays.* Newark: University of Delaware Press, 1999.

Sim, Alison. *Pleasures and Pastimes in Tudor England.* Stroud, Gloucestershire: Sutton, 1999.

———. *The Tudor Housewife.* Montreal: McGill-Queen's University Press, 1996.

Slater, Ann Pasternak. *Shakespeare, the Director.* Brighton, Sussex: Harvester, 1982.

Slavitt, David R. *The Metamorphoses of Ovid.* Baltimore: Johns Hopkins University Press, 1994.

Smith, Bruce R. *Homosexual Desire in Shakespeare's England: A Cultural Poetics.* Chicago: University of Chicago Press, 1991.

Smith, Lacey Baldwin. *The Horizon Book of the Elizabethan World.* New York: American Heritage Pub. Co., 1967.

Spurgeon, Caroline. *Shakespeare's Imagery and What It Tells Us.* Cambridge: Cambridge University Press, 1935.

Stern, Tiffany. *Rehearsal from Shakespeare to Sheridan.* Oxford: Clarendon Press, 2000.

Stone, Lawrence. *The Family, Sex, and Marriage in England, 1500–1800.* New York: Harper & Row, 1977.

Suzman, Janet. *Acting with Shakespeare: Three Comedies.* New York: Applause Theatre Book Publishers, 1996.

Thomas, Keith. *Religion and the Decline of Magic: Studies in Popular Beliefs in Sixteenth and Seventeenth Century England.* London: Weidenfeld and Nicolson, 1971.

Thomson, Peter. *Shakespeare's Professional Career*. Cambridge: Cambridge University Press, 1992.

Thurley, Simon. *The Royal Palaces of Tudor England: Architecture and Court Life, 1460–1547*. New Haven, CT: Yale University Press, 1993.

Trussler, Simon. *Shakespearean Concepts: A Dictionary of Terms and Conventions, Influences and Institutions, Themes, Ideas, and Genres in the Elizabethan and Jacobean Drama*. London: Methuen Drama, 1989.

Van Tassel, Wesley. *Clues to Acting Shakespeare*. New York: Allworth Press, 2000.

Vickers, Brian. *The Artistry of Shakespeare's Prose*. London: Methuen, 1968.

———. *Classical Rhetoric in English Poetry*. London: Macmillan, 1970.

Wildeblood, Joan, and Peter Brinson. *The Polite World: A Guide to English Manners and Deportment from the Thirteenth to the Nineteenth Century*. London: Oxford University Press, 1965.

Williams, Gordon. *A Glossary of Shakespeare's Sexual Language*. London: Athlone Press, 1997.

Williams, Neville. *All the Queen's Men: Elizabeth I and Her Courtiers*. London: Weidenfeld and Nicolson, 1972.

Wilson, John Dover, ed. *Life in Shakespeare's England: A Book of Elizabethan Prose*. New York: Barnes & Noble, 1969.

Wither, George. *A Collection of Emblemes, ancient and moderne* (1635). Columbia: University of South Carolina Press, 1975.

Wittkower, Rudolf. *Allegory and the Migration of Symbols*. London: Thames and London, 1987.

Wright, George T. *Shakespeare's Metrical Art*. Berkeley: University of California Press, 1988.

General Index

Index of Plays
and Characters

About the Author

LESLIE O'DELL is Associate Professor of Theatre and English at Wilfrid Laurier University and Text Consultant for the Stratford Festival in Ontario.